Computer Organization and Assembly Language Programming for the PDP-11 and VAX-11

Wen C. Lin
University of California, Davis

9163

1817

HARPER & ROW, PUBLISHERS, New York
Cambridge, Philadelphia, San Francisco,
London, Mexico City, São Paulo, Singapore, Sydney

To my Wife, Shung-Ling,
Parents, Reverend and Mrs. B. C. Lin,
and Elder Sister, Hwie-Kwang

Sponsoring Editor: *John Willig*
Project Editor: *David Nickol*
Text Art: *Fineline Illustrations, Inc.*
Production: *Delia Tedoff*
Compositor: *York Graphic Services, Inc.*
Printer and Binder: *R. R. Donnelley & Sons Company*

Computer Organization and Assembly Language Programming for the PDP-11 and VAX-11

Library of Congress Cataloging in Publication Data

Lin, Wen C.
   Computer organization and assembly language programming for the PDP-11 and VAX-11.

   Bibliography: p.
   Includes index.
   1. PDP-11 (Computer)—Programming.   2. VAX—11
(Computer)—Programming.   3. Assembler language
(Computer program language)   4. Computer architecture.
I. Title.
QA76.8.P2L56 1985   001.64′2   84-25127
ISBN 0-06-044061-9

85 86 87 88 9 8 7 6 5 4 3 2 1

Contents

Preface   ix

CHAPTER 1   Introduction   1

1.1   Basic Principle of Operation   2
Computer Organization   2
Principle of Operation   3
Software   2
1.2   A Basic Digital Computer System Structure   8
A Functional Description of Hardware Components   8
The Software Elements of the System   10
1.3   System Software and Computer Languages   12
The Hardware-Software Team   13
The Operating System   16
1.4   Man-Machine Communication   17
Exercises   19

CHAPTER 2   User Viewpoint of System Organization of the PDP-11   21

2.1   Functional Description of the System   22
2.2   System Hardware Organization   22
Central Processor Unit (CPU)   22
Main Memory   24
2.3   Operation Sequence   27
The Operation Sequence of a Simple Program   27
Exercises   29

CHAPTER 3   Representation of Information   30

3.1   Representation of Unsigned Numbers for Different Radix   31
3.2   Radix Conversion   32
   Decimal to Binary   33
   Binary to Decimal   34
   Decimal to Octal   34
   Octal to Decimal   35
   Octal to Binary to Octal   35
3.3   Negative Number Representaions   36
   Sign-Magnitude Representation   36
   Complement Representation   36
3.4   Complement Arithmetic   41
   Subtraction by Addition of Twos Complement   41
   Overflow in Complement Arithmetic   43
   Subtraction by Addition of Ones Complement   45
   Subtraction by Addition of Eights Complement   46
   Subtraction by Addition of Hexadecimals Complement   47
3.5   Floating-Point Representation   48
3.6   First Glance at the Instruction Set   48
   Instruction Format and Machine Codes   49
   Functional Classification of Instructions   50
   Program Execution   54
   A Simple Application Program   56
Exercises   59

CHAPTER 4   A Closer Look at the Instruction Set   60

4.1   Introduction   61
4.2   Addressing Modes   61
   Register (Exclusive of R7) Addressing Modes   63
   Program Counter (PC)/Memory Reference Addressing Mode   72
   Addressing of Branch Instructions   81
   Summary of Addressing Techniques   89
   Sample Programs Using Different Addressing Modes   90
4.3   Nonobvious Applications of Selected Instructions   94
4.4   Relocatable Address   99
4.5   Position-Independent Code (PIC)   100
Exercises   101

CHAPTER 5   Subroutines   103

5.1   Introduction   104
   Basic Concepts   105
   Key Instruction Pairs for Linking Host and Subprograms   106
5.2   Transmission of Parameters or Arguments   111

Parameters Next to JSR Instruction   111
Parameters in a Specific Exclusive Area   114
Transmission of Parameters Through Stack Memory   116
5.3   General Formats for Subroutine and Host-Program Documentation   119
Subroutine   121
Host Program   121
5.4   Linking or TKB Subroutines with the Host Program   122
5.5   More Examples   125
5.6   Nested Subroutines   128
5.7   Coroutines   130
5.8   Recursion   132
5.9   Bubble Sort Program   134
Exercises   140

CHAPTER 6   Macros or Macro Instructions   141

6.1   Introduction   142
6.2   Classifications of Macro Instructions   143
6.3   User-Defined Macros   144
Format   144
Automatically Created Local Symbols   145
Nesting of Macros   150
Conditional Macros   153
Exercises   162

CHAPTER 7   Input/Output Programming   163

7.1   Introduction   164
General Input/Output Devices   164
Communication Between CPU and the Input/Output Devices   165
7.2   Input/Output Programming for the PDP-11 System   166
General Structure of an I/O Interface Board   166
Input/Output Programming   168
7.3   More Detailed Examples   174
Simulation of a Security Gate Controller   176
I/O Programming for A/D and D/A Converters   176
Exercises   180

CHAPTER 8   Interrupts and Traps   181

8.1   Introduction   182
8.2   Principles of Operation   182
Hardware Structure for an Interrupt-Driven System   182
General Procedure for an Interrupt-Driven System   183
A Typical Example   184

8.3   More Examples   190
      Saving and Retrieving the Contents of Registers for the Interrupt Process   *190*
      Input/Output Data Queue Buffer Program   *195*
8.4   The Alarm Clock   200
8.5   The Stopwatch   203
8.6   Traps   211
      The Trap Handler   *213*
      A Typical Example Using Trap Instruction   *214*
      Comments on Trap Instructions   *215*
8.7   Interrupt Nesting and Priority Resolvers   215
Exercises   219

CHAPTER 9   Direct Memory Access (DMA) Operation   22

9.1   Introduction   221
9.2   Hardware Organization and Principles of Operation   222
9.3   A Typical Example   225
Exercises   227

CHAPTER 10   An Introduction to the VAX-11 System   228

10.1   Introduction   229
10.2   Machine Structure   229
       The System   *229*
       The Principle of the Virtual Memory System   *230*
       The Principle of Multiprogramming   *232*
       The Central Processing Unit (CPU)   *234*
       The Memory   *237*
       Memory Management   *244*
       The Multiprogramming Process   *247*
10.3   Instructions and Addressing Modes   248
       Data Types   *248*
       Instructions   *250*
       Addressing Modes   *251*
10.4   Macros, Subroutines, and Procedures   261
       Macros   *261*
       Subroutines   *261*
       Procedures   *262*
10.5   Interrupts and Exceptions   264
References for Further Reading   264
Exercises   264

CHAPTER 11   Laboratory Exercises   265

11.1   Introduction   265
11.2   Sample Problems for Laboratory Exercises   265

APPENDIXES

Appendix A: Codes for the ASCII Character Set   279
Appendix B: Mnemonic Instruction Index and Instruction Set   283
Appendix C: Instruction Timing   334
Appendix D: PDP-11 Numerical OP Code List   339
Appendix E: Program Development and System Software: The RSX-11M Operating System   341
Appendix F: VAX-11 Instruction Index by Mnemonic   354
Appendix G: Flowchart Symbols   364

Bibliography   365

Index   367

Preface

Since the development of the microprocessor, the requirements of assembly language programming and computer organization have become important in the undergraduate curriculum of electrical and computer engineering, and a number of texts on this subject have been published. Some focus on programming based on one minicomputer or microcomputer, and others on several different types of microcomputers. All these books present problems for the beginning student in several areas. (1) Most lack information on the elementary principles of operation of a basic computer. Most beginners do not know how a computer works. (2) Most lack a coherent description of the relationship among the system hardware, the system software, and the user's application programs. (3) They lack detailed fundamentals of developing the user's programs, such as the addressing modes of machine instructions, the format of documenting a program, and the function of pseudo-instructions. (4) There are often not sufficient explicit examples. It is my belief that explicit, even sometimes trivial, examples will quickly and efficiently build students' confidence.

Of course, one might argue that it is impossible to spell out all the details in teaching this subject. Students will eventually figure them out by themselves—if they survive until the end of the course. I have found that details and fundamentals minimize unnecessary confusion and frustration, especially at the beginning of the course. If a course in computer organization and assembly language programming should be a required core course in the electrical/computer engineering curriculum, just as in the old days a circuit course was required, then we should teach our students the fundamentals, starting with addressing modes, and complement arithmetic, just as we would teach Ohm's law and Thevenin's theory. Furthermore, our experience leads us to believe that by learning a specific machine well (preferably a popular, and a sufficiently complex and powerful one, such as the PDP-11 family), students can easily learn any other machine by reading its user manual; and that for novices, one book that covers many different types of computers would only confuse them more. For this reason I have included an introductory chapter on the VAX-11 (Chapter 10) to help students with the transition of learning about a newer computer that is gaining in popularity.

This book is structured to present fundamentals in detail and to give equal emphasis to architectural hardware, system software, and user-developed programs. The goal is not to teach students many varieties of assembly language programming techniques. In fact, there are already several texts available that deal with this topic. Rather, it is to bridge the gap between beginners who need the fundamentals and advanced students who are interested in application-oriented assembly programming techniques. The contents of this book have been used as classnotes in the computer structure and assembly language programming course. This course is supported by a laboratory equipped with RSX-11M-based PDP-11/34 LSI-11 networks, where the students obtain hands-on experience.

Chapter 1 starts from ground zero. It describes how a simple digital computer operates by means of simple example. In this example, the concept of instructions encoded by means of binary numbers is illustrated. Based on this primitive concept, Von Neumann's basic computer architecture is introduced. An overview of a computer system, complete with a disk and a terminal loaded with system software and application software, follows, along with a brief description of how they work together as a team. *Chapter 2* presents the system organization of the PDP-11 from the user's viewpoint. *Chapter 3* describes the fundamentals of representation of information on a digital computer such as the PDP-11. The information representation is subdivided into representations of numbers and instructions. Here we present the complement arithmetic for binary, octal, and hexadecimal numbers, as well as a subset of the instruction set for the PDP-11. The chapter concludes with a simple example that ties all the components together to illustrate how the basic elements work together as a team. *Chapter 4* focuses on the instruction set. We attempt to do a thorough job in describing the powerful addressing modes utilized in the PDP-11 family. The potentially confusing topics are elaborated, and examples are used to demonstrate the applications. *Chapter 5* presents the important topic in programming of subroutines. We begin with the basic concept of the subroutine and the different formats for writing subroutines. Key problems such as parameter passing, and the linkage of the host program and the subroutine, are attacked through examples. *Chapter 6* introduces the macros. Here we point out the difference between subroutines and macro instructions. We again use examples to show how system-defined macros, user-defined macros, and conditional macros can be applied to develop application software. In *Chapter 7,* the important I/O programming techniques are described. We show the harmonic operation between the hardware I/O board and the I/O program in assembly language. Examples are used to show the communication between the peripheral or the outside real world and the digital computer. *Chapters 8 and 9* deal with the interrupt and traps, and direct memory access (DMA), respectively. Again, we present them in conjunction with the hardware required for the processes. Each topic is illustrated with practical examples in which the important attributes are elaborated. *Chapter 10* is an introduction to the VAX-11 system. The final chapter, *Chapter 11,* includes laboratory exercises and sample problems.

The author is indebted to Professor H. H. Loomis, Jr., who initially introduced this interesting field to him a number of years ago and let him include the laboratory problem set he developed at the University of California, at Davis. Thanks are also due to my fellow students who were involved in teaching this course. Lief Sorenson and Simon Chiu and Miss Mei-Xing Zhao in particular have contributed to preparing the manuscript for this book. Deep appreciation is due John Willig of Harper & Row and Professor Ralph Algazi of the University of California for their encouragement. Finally, the author would like to express his thanks to the Digital Equipment Corporation for their cooperation and permission to use information from their publications on the PDP-11. Specifically, the material in Appendixes B, C, and D (information on the instruction set for the PDP-11) is reproduced in part from their microcomputer handbook series: Microcomputer Processors (1978–79), and LSI-11, PDP-11/03 Reference Card.

Wen C. Lin

Chapter 1

Introduction

This chapter introduces the elementary structure and principles of operation of a general-purpose digital computer. The objective is to describe a digital computer to students who have little knowledge of how it functions. A simple example is used to illustrate one of the many basic operations of a computer. Next, the hardware and software elements of the system are presented. Then we show how the software, the hardware, and the user work together as a team to perform a specific task.

KEY WORDS

AC	MAR
address	MDR
arithmetic and logic unit (ALU)	memory
ASCII	memory loading process
assembling process	mnemonic instruction
assembly language programming	mnemonics
BR	operating system
bus	operation code
command	PC
content	printer
control unit	program
CPU	read/write memory
CRT terminal	register
data	source operand
destination operand	stack memory
disk drive	status register
input/output unit (I/O)	system software
IR	

1.1 BASIC PRINCIPLES OF OPERATION

Computer Organization

The organization of a computer is somewhat like the physical organization of a human being. Although human beings have different personalities or skin colors, each has a brain, eyes and ears, a mouth, and so on. The cerebrum literally functions as a memory bank; the cerebellum as a controller; and the ears and mouth for communication with the outside world. A computer is normally partitioned into four major sections: the memory, the arithmetic and logic unit, the control unit, and the input/output unit. These units communicate among each other through a bus by means of electric signals, where bus is nothing but a bundle of wires used for carrying electric signals. Through the input/output unit, they communicate with the outside world, and the outside world communicates with them using peripheral equipment such as television cameras (the eye), loudspeakers (the mouth), microphones (the ear), or more commonly, a teletype, CRT (TV-like) keyboard terminal, or a card or paper tape punch/reader. Since peripheral equipment varies from system to system, depending on the nature of the application, it will not be considered here.

Figure 1.1 shows a block diagram of a basic digital computer and its four major components. The **control unit,** together with the arithmetic and logic unit, is usually called the **central processor (CPU)**; it is the heart of the system. The control unit establishes the operating sequences and the paths of data transfer within the system. The **arithmetic and logic unit (ALU)** performs the arithmetic and logic operations. The **memory unit** stores information. It functions like a set of Post Office boxes. Information is stored in a location designated by a number called the **address** of the location, and memory is normally specified by address and content. The **content** is simply a string of binary numbers, 1s and 0s, called a computer word. To store or retrieve information in or from a specified location, the CPU sends the specific address and generates a write or read

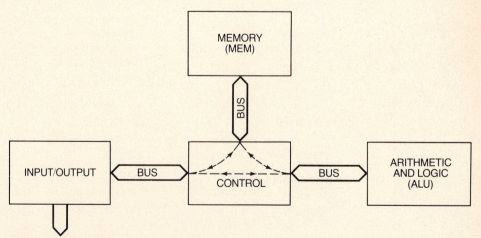

To Peripheral Equipment

Figure 1.1 Block diagram of a basic computer.

command signal, respectively, to carry out the operation. For write, the CPU provides the content; for read, the CPU receives the content. The **input/output unit** provides ports for communication with the outside world. Thanks to notable advances in solid-state technology, a basic system containing the memory, the input/output unit, and the central processor can be fabricated on just one or two electronic semiconductor chips.

Principles of Operation

Figure 1.2 is basically the same as Figure 1.1 except that the data paths and control lines are shown separately, with the dotted lines denoting the controls. Here, the ALU and the control unit are lumped together and called the CPU, as shown within the box. For convenience in describing the operation, the CPU is shown in more detail. Note that there are four **registers.** These are sets of grouped flip-flops used for storage of binary data. One might think of a register as a ''mailbox'' used for temporary storage of information. Since each register serves a specific function, it bears a specific name: PC, program counter; AC, accumulator; IR, instruction register; BR, buffer register. Most CPUs have more than six registers, but we use the minimum number of four here for simplicity.

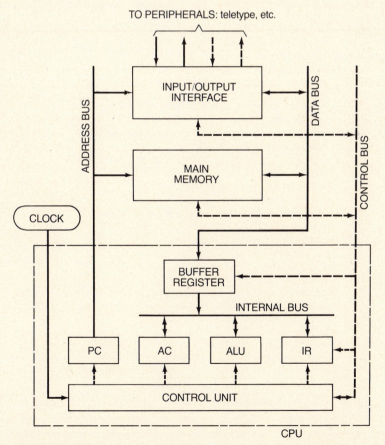

Figure 1.2 Elementary operation block diagram of a basic computer.

The control unit is a random logic network synchronized with a clock. It generates control pulses or levels for the whole system. It opens data-transferring paths with desirable sequences according to information in the IR. The basic operation a CPU performs is to obtain information from the main memory and store it in IR. Then the control unit interprets the information, generates the appropriate electric signals, and executes the instruction. The AC and BR registers are used for temporary data or information storage to support the action. A simple example will clarify the operation.

An Example

Problem   We want to design a main gate control for a building that will open the gate only to a person named John C. Smith.

Design   Let us use the computer shown in Figure 1.2, with a teletype as its only input/output peripheral. As noted above, a memory unit is like a bank of mailboxes. Each box is assigned a number as its address. Inside the box is a word called the content of the mailbox. Now, let us prestore the memory so that it contains the messages listed in Table 1.1. The visitor is instructed to type "Open the gate" on the teletype if he or she wishes to enter the building.

TABLE 1.1

Address	Contents
0	Load register AC with data in next (mail) box.
1	"Open the gate."
2	Subtract the data (message) of the register in the input/output interface from that of AC.
3	If the result is zero, fetch the content in the next box; otherwise fetch the content of the box with address 0.
4	Load register AC with the data in the next box.
5	"Type your name, please."
6	Command the peripheral teletype to type out the message stored in AC.
7	Load register AC with data in the next box.
8	John C. Smith.
9	Wait 30 seconds.
10	Subtract input data from AC.
11	If the result is zero, fetch the content in the next box, otherwise fetch the content in the box with address 0.
12	Turn on the motor that will open the gate.
13	Wait 30 seconds.
14	Turn on the motor that will close the gate.
15	Fetch the content in the box with address 0.

Let us design the hardware so that when its power switch is turned on, the computer will automatically reset or clear all the internal registers. Therefore, we can expect the register PC to be 0. The current value shown in PC is the current address of the memory box from which the computer will fetch the message. The register PC is designed so that its content will be incremented by 1 if an increment command pulse is received from the control unit (for convenience, let us call the control unit "controller" from here on). It will be reset or cleared to 0 if a reset command pulse is received. The content of PC is always the address value of the memory word (mailbox) from which the CPU will read the message or into which it will write. This is why the register is called the program counter or pointer.

Let us now follow the operation. Initially, the PC is 0. The content of the memory at address 0 will be transferred to the buffer register (BR), then to the IR. The controller interprets the message, which in this case is to fetch the message at the next address, 1, puts it into the accumulator (AC), and executes it. In other words, the controller obtains the data in address 1 and stores it in the AC. As a result the data "Open the gate" is in the AC. Meanwhile, the controller sends an increment pulse to the PC, and the PC now has a value of 2. Fetching information in 2, the controller finds that it has something to do with the input/output. The following actions are then taken. The PC is incremented to 3 and the input data "Open the gate," which was typed through the teletype by the visitor, is subtracted from what is in the AC. Recall that we have already stored "Open the gate" in the AC; the result of the subtraction will therefore be 0. This subtract operation is done by the ALU, and its result, say 0, is stored in the AC. Now the message in 3 is fetched and stored in the IR. Executing the current message in IR, the controller will check the content of AC. If it is zero, the information in 4 is fetched and stored into the IR. Otherwise, the PC is reset to 0. Note that this message causes the computer either to go on or to go back to the starting point and repeat the process—checking what is being typed by the visitor.

Assume that the result of the last subtraction is 0. The message in 4 will then be fetched and executed. Note that the messages at address locations 4 and 5 are similar to those at 0 and 1, except that the message in AC after execution is: "Type your name please." The process continues until PC = 6. Examining the message in 6, the controller finds that it again has something to do with input/output, this time outputting data that was stored in AC. It will output the data in AC, which is now "Type your name, please," by commanding the teletype to type out the message. Meanwhile, PC has been incremented to 8. The message in 8 causes the computer to load the data, John C. Smith, onto AC. The message in 9 holds the machine for 30 seconds to give the visitor time to type his or her name. Message 10 checks whether the visitor's name is John C. Smith. If so, the process continues. That is, the gate is opened for 30 seconds, then closed. Otherwise, the PC will immediately be set to 0 and the whole process will be repeated from the beginning.

Software

It is obvious that the controller does most of the work. It decodes or interprets the message in the IR and generates the proper control pulses at the proper times to transfer data from one place to the other, or to initiate operation sequences such as arthimetic and/or input/output. A hardware or logic designer would say that the controller is nothing but a sequential logic network. Although the design procedures can be tedious and somewhat complicated, its construction is quite straightforward if the problem is clearly specified. Furthermore, the controller normally is designed and fabricated in the hardware; the user is concerned only with what should be stored in the main memory.

For convenience, let us assume that the controller is designed simply to decode (interpret) the 16 messages stored in memory for the example above. Since we know that the contents of memory are either 1 or 0, the messages have to be coded in binary patterns. Fortunately there are only 16 messages, so we can use four-bit binary numbers to encode them. In other words, we only need 16 memory locations, or 16 memory words, each of which is composed of four memory cells. In computer terms, the memory is called a 16 × 4 memory unit. However, among the messages there are duplications—namely, the messages at 0, 4, and 7; 2 and 10; 3 and 11; 9 and 13. Their binary codes should therefore be identical. Let us assume that the designer of the controller encodes the messages as shown in Table 1.2.

TABLE 1.2

Memory		Comments
Address in Binary	Content in Machine Code	Content in English
0 0 0 0	0 0 0 1	Load register AC with data in the next box.
0 0 0 1	0 0 1 0	"Open the gate."
0 0 1 0	0 0 1 1	Subtract the data (message) of the register in the input/output interface from that of AC.
0 0 1 1	0 1 0 0	If the result is zero, fetch the content in the next box; otherwise fetch the content in the box with address 0.
0 1 0 0	0 0 0 1	Load register AC with the data in the next box.
0 1 0 1	0 1 0 1	"Type your name please."
0 1 1 0	0 1 1 0	Command the peripheral teletype to type out the message stored in AC.
0 1 1 1	0 0 0 1	Load register AC with the data in the next box.
1 0 0 0	0 1 1 1	"John C. Smith."
1 0 0 1	1 0 0 0	Wait 30 seconds.
1 0 1 0	0 0 1 1	Subtract input data from AC.
1 0 1 1	0 1 0 0	If the result is zero, fetch the content in the next box; otherwise fetch the content in the box with address 0.
1 1 0 0	1 0 0 1	Turn on the motor that will open the gate.
1 1 0 1	1 0 0 0	Wait 30 seconds.
1 1 1 0	1 0 1 0	Turn on the motor that will close the gate.
1 1 1 1	1 0 1 1	Fetch the content in the box with address 0.

This means that there are 16 messages, but it only requires 11 four-bit patterns to encode them. The controller then decodes the binary messages and takes the appropriate actions. Here we note the obvious conflict in preferences between humans and machines. The human would like to see the message in English as shown in Table 1.1, but the machine "understands" only the "language" in binary bits. In our example, the machine understands 11 and only 11 "words" in binary patterns; it executes only these 11 tasks.

It is clear that we must redesign the controller if actions or tasks other than those 11 are desirable. If we merely wish to change the sequence of the actions, or to implement a different set of operations using only the 11 four-bit messages or commands or instructions, we would need only to change the order of the contents of the memory listed in

Table 1.2. We cannot, however, store English contents in memory. Therefore, we must translate the English messages into four-bit binary words, and then store them in proper addresses according to the desired sequence. Fortunately, humans are not so mechanical as machines. We can understand abbreviated or even misspelled English, so the lengthy English messages we used can be considerably simplified. For instance, for the first message in Table 1.1, we may substitute as follows:

LDI Δ Load register AC with the data or content that immediately follows the current memory location

which in binary can be [0001]. (The symbol Δ means ''defined as.'') We may now define a few terms. The abbreviated notation is known as mnemonics, and [0001] or other binary words are machine codes. **Mnemonics** are for human beings, whereas the equivalent binary codes are for the machine. The contents stored in the memory are collectively called a **program.** Since we may change the sequence of operations by storing the contents in different locations or addresses without changing the electric wiring of the machine, these materials are called **software.** The contents in the memory are called **mnemonic instructions** or **data,** depending on the nature of the contents. For instance, LDI will be instruction, but John C. Smith will be data.

Since the controller is designed and built inside the CPU and is not expected to be changed by the user, a machine-recognizable instruction set should be designed to be as flexible as possible so that one can use the machine to implement many different tasks. In practice, a computer usually has many more instructions than this one. For PDP-11, there are over 70 general-purpose instructions.

Let us review the process described above. We can specify a basic software design as four steps:

1. For a given application, select the proper mnemonic instructions from a mnemonic instruction set provided by a given machine.
2. Arrange the selected instructions in a desirable order or sequence.
3. Translate the mnemonic instructions into their corresponding binary codes, as specified by the manufacturer.
4. Store the binary-code instructions in the memory.

The first two steps are known as **assembly language programming.** The third step is an **assembling process,** and the fourth step is the **memory loading process.**

Since the mnemonic instructions are normally very primitive and are closely related to machine hardware, assembly language programs are normally machine-dependent. That is, for a different machine, there will be a different set of mnemonic instructions, and a somewhat different hardware organization. A good assembly language programmer thus would need to be quite familiar with the hardware organization before he or she starts to program the machine in assembly language. Fortunately, if one can master the assembly language programming for a fairly powerful machine, one can switch to another machine with little difficulty. In the following section we will examine a general computer system and its structure in more detail. We will see that software and hardware components function as a ''team'' in a computing system.

1.2 A BASIC DIGITAL COMPUTER SYSTEM STRUCTURE

The computer described above would be merely a toy; it would be useless for any practical applications. For general applications, the memory size would never be 16 words. Due to the continuously decreasing cost of the semiconductor memory, most computer systems today would possess at least a memory of 16,000 words (or expressed as 16K words) with a width of 8 bits or 16 bits or more, instead of only 4 bits as in our example. The process of manually translating mnemonic instructions into binary codes for memory storage is impractical for a program having a hundred or more instructions. In order to be useful, a machine must have a reasonable size of memory, and should be able to accept mnemonic instruction directly from a user and translate it into binary code automatically.

Figure 1.3 depicts a system block diagram for a popular ''self-sufficient'' digital computer. Except for the three blocks labeled disk drive, CRT terminal, and printer, the system is similar to that shown in Figure 1.2. The extra three blocks are called peripherals added for the user's convenience. Note that the system has three buses through which the CPU can read or write information from or to any one of the blocks shown.

A Functional Description of the Hardware Components

Memory   Note that two registers labeled MDR (memory data register) and MAR (memory address register) are *functionally* attached to the memory block. Physically, these two registers are normally in the CPU. When the CPU wishes to read an instruction or data from the memory, it would first set the PC with the desired value of address and send it to MAR, and then to the memory unit. A READ control signal from CPU would then cause the memory to place the content of the memory word as addressed into MDR then into IR or one of the general registers in CPU, depending on whether the content is an instruction or a datum. If a WRITE signal is used instead of READ, the content of some

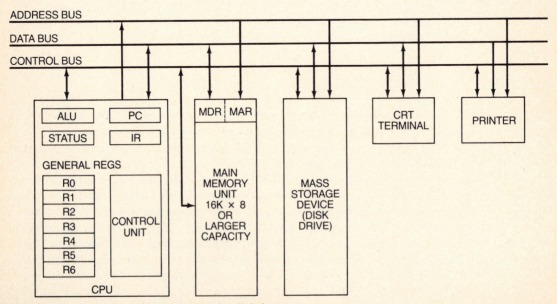

Figure 1.3 System organization of a popular digital computer.

register in CPU will be transferred to the memory at the location specified by PC via MDR and MAR, respectively. Communication between CPU and peripherals is conducted in a similar fashion. In general, each peripheral is connected to the buses through an interface board where a few specific registers are kept. The CPU then communicates with these registers in a manner similar to the way it communicates with MAR/MDR and with memory.

The Central Processing Unit   As shown in Figure 1.3, the CPU contains an arithmetic and logic unit, a group of registers, and a control unit. As the name implies, the ALU is responsible for all arithmetic and logic operations. The general purpose registers, R0, R1, . . . , R6, are used as the temporary memory that holds transient data for ALU. The PC serves as the program counter, which always points at the address of the memory whose content is to be read or written next. IR, the instruction register, holds the instruction fetched from memory so the control unit can decode it and generate proper action signals for the CPU. The **status register** is an indicator of the CPU condition or the result of the ALU action.

   For example, one of the binary bits in this register may be defined as an indicator for the result of an arithmetic operation done by the ALU. If the result is zero, the indicator bit will be 1; otherwise it will be 0. This indicator bit is generally called a *flag*. Since the status register has many binary bits, they can be used to show the current status of the CPU. This is a powerful device for implementing a decision-making process on the computer. The whole process is somewhat like a puppet show. The programmer who designs the memory contents is the master; the control unit functions as the strings, and the registers are the puppets. They perform according to the program or instructions stored in the memory, or in the brain of the master.

Bus Structure   The **bus** in a computer system is the medium for communication among the system components. It is an information highway made up of a bundle of wires. Most computers are ''bus-structured'' as shown in Figure 1.3. Here the bus is functionally divided into three groups: address bus, data bus, and control bus. Basically, the address bus conveys information about where to find instructions or data; the data bus carries what data or instruction for the CPU; and the control bus provides information about how and when the operation should be carried out.

The Peripherals   The most commonly used peripherals in a computer system are these: (1) mass-storage devices, such as the magnetic disk drives and magnetic tape transports; (2) a **CRT terminal,** which contains a typewriterlike keyboard for inputting information, and a CRT, or TV-screen device, for outputting information; and (3) a **printer** that produces readable hard copy for the user to examine and keep for future reference. As its name implies, the mass-storage device can be used to keep millions of bytes (8 bits) or words (16 bits) of information temporarily or permanently. However, it has a very slow access time in comparison with the semiconductor memory unit, so it is normally used as a secondary memory bank. When needed, the information is transferred to the memory unit first and then the CPU works with the memory, not the disk or tape. The memory unit acts as an information reservoir in which the CPU can read or write information at high speed according to the user's desire. The CRT terminal is normally the user's command and data-entering port. Through the keyboard, the user can issue commands or enter data; the CRT shows the response to the terminal user.

The Software Elements of the System

A digital computer without software would never work, no matter how sophisticated its hardware. It is just like a person who may have an expensive automobile, but without gasoline, cannot use it. Let us now look at the software elements.

Machine or Mnemonic Instructions Each machine normally has a unique set of instructions defined by the designer. The programmer then uses the instruction set to write programs that will instruct the machine to execute a task the programmer has specified. Generally speaking, an instruction tells the machine when and where to get data, what to do with them, and then where to put the result of the action. The instruction format varies in detail from one machine to another. But in general, an instruction has two essential segments: one contains the operation code, and the other contains the address information of the operand or operands involved in the operation. By *operand,* we mean the "subject" on which the CPU operates.

There are four general types of instruction formats: three-address instruction, two-address instruction, one-address instruction, and zero-address instruction. The examples that follow will clarify the concept.

EXAMPLE 1: Three-Address Instruction ────────────────────────────────

            ADD   A   B   C

This instruction tells the CPU to ADD the content at location A, and the content at location B, and store the result at location C. It has four sectional spaces known as **fields of the instruction.** The space for ADD is defined as the operation-code field; the spaces for A and B are defined as the source-operand fields; and the space for C is defined as the destination-operand field. Although the operand fields usually contain address information, they do sometimes contain data or constants. For this example, the formal format of the instruction is

            ADD   A, B, C

The operation field and operand fields are separated by a space; the address fields are separated by commas.

EXAMPLE 2: Two-Address Instruction ──────────────────────────────────

For this type, the ADD instruction format is

            ADD   A, B

It implies

            $(A) + (B) \rightarrow B$

where   (A) = the content at address A
        (B) = the content at address B

That is, the instruction tells the CPU to add the content of A to that of B and to put the result into the memory word located at B. The parentheses symbolize "the content of," and so on.

Note that if one wishes to put the result into memory C, another instruction will be needed. The following 2 two-address instructions:

Instruction	Action
ADD A, B	(A) + (B) → B
MOVE B, C	(B) → C

will do the same job as the single three-address instruction. Here, the second instruction copies (MOVE) the content of B into C.

EXAMPLE 3: One-Address Instruction _____

The ADD instruction will be

      ADD   A

It implies

      (A) + (AC) → AC

This instruction tells the CPU to add the content of A to that of the register labeled AC, and puts the result into AC. One may then ask, where is AC? Recall that in Figure 1.2, there is a register labeled AC in the CPU. That is, the machine shown in Figure 1.2 is a one-address machine and has a register in the CPU designated as the accumulator. To achieve the same operation shown in Example 1, this machine will need the following instructions:

Instruction	Action
LOAD A	(A) → AC
ADD B	(B) + (AC) → AC
STORE C	(AC) → C

Here the second operand, AC, is not explicitly shown. Since it is always the same register, AC, it is "understood" by the CPU and does not need to be shown as a part of the instruction explicitly.

EXAMPLE 4: Zero-Address Instruction _____

A machine that uses zero-address instructions is also called a stack machine. This type of machine usually has a number of AC registers residing in the CPU organized in the form of stacks. This is sometimes called stack memory. A **stack memory** is designed in such a way that it is always accessed by the rule of **last-in–first-out.** That is, a set of data can be "pushed" or "loaded" into the stack one by one from the bottom up, so that the last one pushed in would become the top layer in the stack. For retrieval, the top-layer datum will be accessed or "popped" first. So the addressing specification is not necessary. Figure 1.4 shows a numeric example for implementing the operation of Example 1. Let the contents of A, B, and C be assigned as follows:

      (A) = 2
      (B) = 3
      (C) = don't care or any number

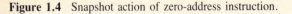

Figure 1.4 Snapshot action of zero-address instruction.

Then we will need the following set of instructions:

Instruction	Action
LOAD A	(A) → STACK 4
LOAD B	(B) → STACK 3
ADD	(STACK 3) + (STACK 4) → STACK 4
STORE C	(STACK 4) → C

A series of "snapshots" or "motion pictures" along with the instructions are shown in Figure 1.4, where xs denote "don't care" or can be any number; and N.C. denotes "no change." Note that the key instruction, ADD, has a zero address; thus this machine is called a zero-address machine.

Examining the above examples reveals that a machine having instructions for fewer operand addresses would require a larger number of instructions to implement a given operation. However, one with instructions containing more operand addresses would require wider memory word or higher number of bits to accommodate them. Since more instruction operations would require a longer time to process a task, the whole problem is a tradeoff between machine operation speed versus memory space or width.

1.3 SYSTEM SOFTWARE AND COMPUTER LANGUAGES

Earlier we pointed out the necessity of having English-like mnemonic instructions for the human beings and coded language for the machine. Of course, in theory, one could learn the binary machine language and issue commands or instructions to the machine in that language, but in practice it is not feasible to request each user to learn such a primitive language, for obvious reasons. The English language has twenty-six alphabet letters plus ten numerals. Binary machine language has only two alphabets—namely, 1 and 0. Although the binary language is simple, to human beings it is tedious and error-prone. The ideal would therefore be to have a specialist translate the mnemonics into binary language for the machine. Fortunately, however, there is one-to-one correspondence between a mnemonic instruction and a binary-coded bit pattern; the translation process is extremely mechanical. We do not really need a specialist to do it. All we need is to write a sequence of instructions at a very primitive level, in mnemonic language, for which we then have a software program to function as translator. With the software for translation installed in the machine, the user can communicate with it in English-like language. So a system, to be useful, needs software to do certain kinds of services, and the more sophisticated the software is, the more powerful or usable the system will be.

There are two kinds of software, built-in software and **application software.** The former are developed to provide convenience for the user; the latter are developed with the help of the built-in software to carry out specific tasks the user wants the computer to do. The program that controls a gate illustrated before belongs to the application software, whereas the mnemonic instruction to binary language translator belongs to the other. The built-in software is know as **system software,** and it is designed and provided by the computer manufacturer. It is a collection of program modules, each of which, like a staff member in a corporation, performs specific functions to serve the user of the system.

The Hardware-Software Team

Let us now examine a few systems with different levels of sophistication and see how the system software works with the hardware as a team. Figures 1.5(a), (b), and (c) show the hardware organization of three typical computer systems. Figure 1.5(a) depicts the most primitive one of the three. Here the user is required to communicate with the computer in binary machine language; it therefore needs no system software. Such a system is inexpensive but hard to operate. The system shown in Figure 1.5(b) is a little more advanced. Here a hexadecimal keyboard is provided. Each time the user depresses a key, a 4-bit binary code is generated and sent to the computer. Table 1.3 shows the corresponding binary code for each key of the hex keyboard. A comparison of Tables 1.3 and 1.2 shows that the hex keyboard may be used to generate and enter the address code and the instruction or message for the computer to function as a gate controller in the example used earlier. If the computer is dedicated to this application, it may still not require any system software. However, if the system is to be a little bit more flexible, some simple system software to monitor the keyboard and the display would be necessary.

TABLE 1.3   HEX-BINARY CODE

Hexadecimal Key	Binary Code
0	0 0 0 0
1	0 0 0 1
2	0 0 1 0
3	0 0 1 1
4	0 1 0 0
5	0 1 0 1
6	0 1 1 0
7	0 1 1 1
8	1 0 0 0
9	1 0 0 1
A	1 0 1 0
B	1 0 1 1
C	1 1 0 0
D	1 1 0 1
E	1 1 1 0
F	1 1 1 1

Next, let us examine Figure 1.5(c). Here, the user is given a terminal containing two independent devices, the video screen or CRT and the typewriterlike keyboard. Note that there is no direct hardware connection between the CRT and keyboard. Unlike the conventional typewriter, the CRT will not automatically show what has been typed on the keyboard unless the computer is in operation and a system program that can echo what is being depressed on the keyboard is written and installed in the computer. Just like the hex keyboard, the typewriterlike keyboard also generates a unique binary code for each key when it is depressed. There are several standard codes for the keyboard. The most popular one is known as the **American Standard Code for Information Interchange, or ASCII.** Table 1.4 highlights the ASCII (for details, see Appendix A) in binary code for

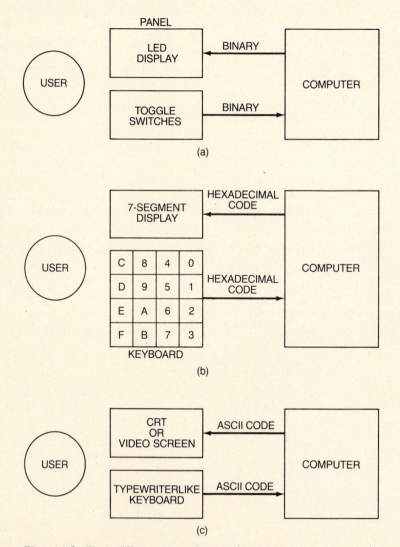

Figure 1.5 Three different types of computing systems.

each key of a standard keyboard. With this keyboard, plus a proper electronic hardware interface board, we can generate any character in ASCII and send it to the computer.

TABLE 1.4 ALPHANUMERIC ASCII BINARY CODE

Character	ASCII in Binary	Character	ASCII in Binary
0	X 0 1 1 0 0 0 0	I	X 1 0 0 1 0 0 1
1	X 0 1 1 0 0 0 1	J	X 1 0 0 1 0 1 0
2	X 0 1 1 0 0 1 0	K	X 1 0 0 1 0 1 1
3	X 0 1 1 0 0 1 1	L	X 1 0 0 1 1 0 0
4	X 0 1 1 0 1 0 0	M	X 1 0 0 1 1 0 1
5	X 0 1 1 0 1 0 1	N	X 1 0 0 1 1 1 0
6	X 0 1 1 0 1 1 0	O	X 1 0 0 1 1 1 1
7	X 0 1 1 0 1 1 1	P	X 1 0 1 0 0 0 0
8	X 0 1 1 1 0 0 0	Q	X 1 0 1 0 0 0 1
9	X 0 1 1 1 0 0 1	R	X 1 0 1 0 0 1 0
A	X 1 0 0 0 0 0 1	S	X 1 0 1 0 0 1 1
B	X 1 0 0 0 0 1 0	T	X 1 0 1 0 1 0 0
C	X 1 0 0 0 0 1 1	U	X 1 0 1 0 1 0 1
D	X 1 0 0 0 1 0 0	V	X 1 0 1 0 1 1 0
E	X 1 0 0 0 1 0 1	W	X 1 0 1 0 1 1 1
F	X 1 0 0 0 1 1 0	X	X 1 0 1 1 0 0 0
G	X 1 0 0 0 1 1 1	Y	X 1 0 1 1 0 0 1
H	X 1 0 0 1 0 0 0	Z	X 1 0 1 1 0 1 0

Note: The X in the ASCII is a binary variable that serves as the parity bit of the code for error detection purposes.

Thus, in theory one could enter English messages or commands through the keyboard to the computer and communicate with it in English. Unfortunately, being able to recognize each character entered to it does not make the computer capable of understanding an English message or command. It would have to learn English grammar, sentence structure, and the spelling or meaning of each word before it could understand our language. Therefore, we have to use what is available at present time. Although the language using mnemonic instructions is already several orders of magnitude more convenient for us to use than the binary machine language, it still is machine-dependent and harder to learn. Therefore there are a number of other so-called high-level (more English-like) languages, such as Basic, Pascal, Fortran, Algol, and Cobol, available for many computing systems. But although the high-level language is normally easier to learn and machine-independent, it is not as fast or as efficient as the assembly language.

For each language the system must possess a system program function as a specific translator for it. The translator for assembly language is called assembler, and that for high-level language is called compiler or interpreter, depending on its structure or mode of operation. All system software is normally written in assembly language or some other intermediate language.

It is now apparent that any useful or programmable computing system would at least include a terminal, system software, and the computer hardware. With it, a user can develop application software for specific requirements. Figure 1.6 shows the functional

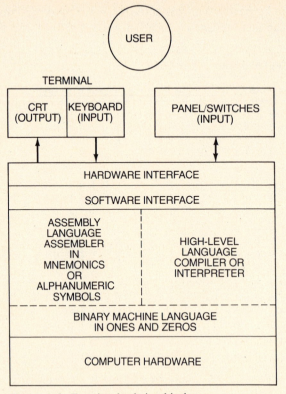

Figure 1.6 Functional relationship between user, system software, and hardware.

relationship between the user, system software, and computer hardware. Here we have highlighted some of the system programs that function as input/output routine, compiler, assembler, and so on. Actually, system software includes many more programs serving different kinds of functions.

The Operating System

The collection of system software is called the **operating system** of the computer. For convenience, in this book we will use *system software* as a collective or general term for an operating system. An operating system for a computer is somewhat like a management system for a restaurant. In a restaurant, different staff members perform different kinds of functions. The manager oversees the whole restaurant; the waiters or waitresses serve the customers. Although on the surface the customers deal only with the waiters or waitresses, the quality of the service really depends on the managing system. In the same manner, although the user appears to deal only with panel switches and terminals, the operating system that "manages" the computer is the key factor in system performance.

If we consider a user as a craftsman who wants to create a piece of art (application program), then the operating system is the toolbox in which there are different kinds of powerful tools waiting to be called on for service. Therefore, it is important that users be aware of the importance of the operating system and know how to use it as a tool. An operating system normally contains software routines for file management, utility, and debugging. It is generally stored in a mass storage device such as a disk and called a **disk operating system (DOS).** Although there are many kinds of operating systems now available for different computing systems and they are different in many aspects, a user can easily switch from one to another if he or she knows one of them well. In a later part of this book, we will study RSX-11M, which is one of the popular and powerful operating systems for the PDP-11 family.

1.3 MAN-MACHINE COMMUNICATION

Thus far, we have attempted to give an overview of the basic digital computer, from a primitive special-purpose computer to a more sophisticated, general-purpose one. We have shown how the hardware and the system software work together as a team, specifically pointed out the difference between system software and application software, and emphasized what an important role an operating system plays. In the following chapters we will examine a specific system, the PDP-11 computer system. But before ending this chapter, we need to see how a user communicates with a computer system through a terminal.

Figure 1.7(a) shows the functional communication paths between a user and a computer system. The user communicates with the computer through a terminal, which has a keyboard functioning as the input device, and a CRT or video screen as an output

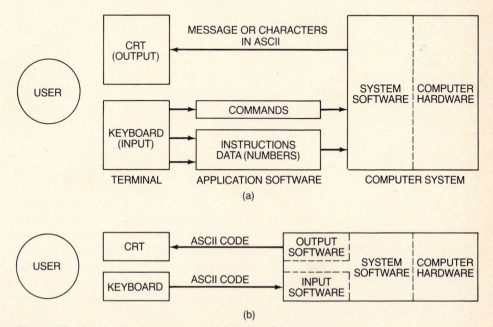

Figure 1.7 Communication between a user and a computer.

device. At the terminal, the user issues commands to the system software for services and develops application programs by inputting sequences of instructions and related data or numbers. The system software responds to the commands or echoes the instructions and data typed on the keyboard through the CRT. Two important concepts are shown in this figure:

1. Commands that normally do not belong to the application program go directly to the system software, so that the user can interact with the operating system or demand service from it. This concept might be clarified through the restaurant analogy business used before. Let us assume that a customer wants to order a ten-course dinner for a group of friends. He or she would first "command" a waitress to bring a copy of the menu. Then, using the menu, he or she might consult with the waitress, make up a "program" of a ten-course dinner, and order it. If the customer is the user or programmer of a computer, he or she issues "commands" to the system software (waitress) for assistance to develop an application program (the ten-course dinner) to be executed (cooked) by another system program (the chef). Recall that an operating system is a collection of program modules like the management system of a restaurant, which is a collection of people such as waitresses, chef, and manager. Clearly, the "commands" do not belong to the application program, and an application program contains only a sequence of instructions and data or numbers, not the commands. Unfortunately, the novice often confuses the "commands" to the system program with the instructions of an application program.

2. The output of the keyboard is a string of binary codes in ASCII. Each time a key is depressed, the keyboard will generate a unique 8-bit (including parity bit) ASCII corresponding to that key (according to Table 1.4). For example, if the instruction ADD #2, A is entered through the keyboard, the system software will "see" a sequence of ASCII as follows:

Characters	ASCII Bit Positions 7 6 5 4 3 2 1 0	Expected Action
A	0 1 0 0 0 0 0 1	2 + (A) → A
D	0 1 0 0 0 1 0 0	
D	0 1 0 0 0 1 0 0	
SPACE	1 0 1 0 0 0 0 0	
#	1 0 1 0 0 0 1 1	
2	1 0 1 1 0 0 1 0	
,	1 0 1 0 1 1 0 0	
A	0 1 0 0 0 0 0 1	

The instruction, when executed, will tell the CPU to add the number (#) two (2) to the memory located at the address A and put the result onto A. Note that the numeric character 2 is in its ASCII code, which is not a real binary number. The real binary number of 2 is 00000010. Thus, it is the responsibility of the system software to convert the inputted ASCII numbers into their corresponding "true" binary number so that the CPU can work with them. All computers, large or small, are designed to operate only with the true binary number, not ASCII. Following the same logic, if on the CRT the user wishes to see the result in A that would be a true binary number at A, the system software must convert it back into the ASCII number and display it on the CRT.

A careful consideration of the human-machine communication process depicted in Figure 1.7(a) shows that one would actually expect the system software to serve many more functions than the ASCII to binary to ASCII conversion described here. For example, the system software would have to be able to recognize whether the input is a command, an instruction, or a number in ASCII. In addition, in some stage of program development, a user may simply want to see on the CRT what has been typed at the keyboard. In this case, all the system software has to do is echo what has been keyed in through the keyboard. That is, if the A key is depressed, the output system software would have to send the ASCII of A to the CRT to "echo" the character A.

Because of the multiple functions we expect from a computer system, it is apparent that a simple standard typewriter keyboard would not be sufficient for communication. This is why the terminal keyboard has many more keys than a conventional typewriter. This elaborate keyboard often confuses beginners. Actually, no matter how complicated a keyboard is, it can be divided into three groups: alphanumeric characters and symbols, format and device controls, and special function keys. Character and symbol keys are conventional typewriter keys. Format keys, such as linefeed (LF), formfeed (FF), bell (BEL), tab (TAB), and carriage return (CR), are used for formatting the output displays at the CRT or the printer. Special function keys are those whose functions are defined by the system software. Since each key has its unique ASCII code, it can easily be identified by an input system program module that in turn "jumps" to a specific routine for a specific function. For example, one may depress the key labeled CONTROL or CONT'L concurrently with another alphabet key, say Z, to activate a special function. Unfortunately, the latter two groups of keys are mostly not yet standardized, so their definitions vary from one system to another. It is the user's responsibility to read the manual provided by the manufacturer and to learn the specific function for each key.

Note that most of the format and function keys are not printable; a special subroutine is required if it is desirable to "echo" those keys when they are depressed. For example, as the CONT'L and Z keys are depressed simultaneously, a subroutine can be written such that it will display one symbol, $\wedge$, and one character, Z, at the CRT. What or which symbol is displayed is not an essential issue; the user's awareness of what is happening after the function key is depressed is, however, important.

The next chapter contains a detailed description of a specific computer system, the PDP-11. You will need to study the principles of operation, the hardware architecture, and the operating system of the PDP-11, but you will also need to go to the laboratory to develop application programs as well as debug and execute them. Going to the lab to experiment is like going to a pool to learn swimming. No one can learn to swim without really swimming in a pool or a river or a lake. A user must be familiar with all the details of the operation of a computer system. But just studying the principles of a computer system will never make a good programmer out of anyone.

EXERCISES

1.1 Design a special purpose computer similar to the security gate controller described in this chapter. It is to function as an automatic bank teller. You may have 16 or more memory locations, and each memory word may be four-bit or more in width. Of course, the better design is a system that requires a smaller number of memory words and narrower word width. Show your design in a format like that of Table 1.2, but in both hexadecimal and binary codes, with comments in English. You may assume that your system has a terminal with a CRT and typewriterlike keyboard, and that it can input/output English messages if you, as a designer, have predefined the binary code for each message. Again, clear, short, and unambiguous messages are desirable. Your system may request the customer to present his or her full name, password, mother's maiden name, birth date, and so on. Next it would check if the customer wishes to withdraw or deposit, and the exact amount. Finally, it would respond with a message similar to this one: "The transaction is done, thank you for banking with us."

1.2 Briefly describe in your own words what an operating system is and why a computing system needs an operating system.

1.3 Briefly discuss the differences in structures and performance among the three-address, two-address, one-address, and zero-address machines.

1.4 Briefly describe the functions of the I/O software for interfacing a CRT terminal to a computer.

1.5 Briefly discuss the differences between commands and application software.

Chapter 2

User Viewpoint of System Organization of the PDP-11

This chapter introduces a typical and popular digital computer, the PDP-11. The hardware structure of the PDP-11 is examined in detail, and a simple example is used to illustrate its operation.

KEY WORDS

bit	LSB
boot	memory map
byte	MSB
flag	octal
hexadecimal	PSW register
	word

2.1 FUNCTIONAL DESCRIPTION OF THE SYSTEM

The PDP-11 computer system has a structure similar to that shown in Figure 1.3. With the aid of the operating system, a user can develop the application software at the CRT terminal. At the keyboard of the terminal, the user can enter commands or call for any specific system software to assist him or her to develop a target program to carry out the task the user would like the computer to execute. All the system programs initially reside on the disk except for the terminal or console monitor (a system program module), which is usually in the main memory after the system is activated or **booted.** The console monitor communicates with the user, interprets commands, and passes the operation to other system programs. When a specific mission is completed, the monitor will resume its responsibility to monitor the user's desires. The user is the master, whereas the monitor is the manager who has a crew (system program modules), each member of which (also a system program module) serves some specific functions. To have the computer system function properly, the master (user) must first know how to communicate with the manager (monitor) and the functions of each module under the monitor's supervision. Next comes the main course, the instruction sequence and data of the application program. Unlike high-level language programming, programming in assembly language requires the programmer to know the hardware structure well, as well as the instructions and data representation of a specific computer system.

2.2 SYSTEM HARDWARE ORGANIZATION

A typical PDP-11 system will normally consist of CPU, main memory, and peripherals such as terminals, disk drive, and printer. We have discussed the global functions of the peripherals in Chapter 1. As far as the assembly programming is concerned, all peripherals will be "seen" as a set of registers. The details will be described in Chapter 7; here we will focus our attention on the CPU and the main memory. Figure 2.1 shows a simplified system diagram of a PDP-11 which contains a CPU, a bus, and a main memory.

Central Processor Unit (CPU)

As shown in Figure 2.1, the CPU contains MAR (memory address register), MDR (memory data register), IR (instruction register), eight general-purpose registers (R0, R1, . . . , R7), PSW (processor status word), control unit, and arithmetic-logic unit (ALU). The functions of all these elements have been described in the preceding chapter except for those of the PSW and the eight general-purpose registers, which need to be elaborated on further.

Since the PDP-11 is a 16-bit machine, all registers in the CPU are 16-bits wide and conventionally defined from right to left as the **least significant bit (LSB)** to the **most significant bit (MSB)**, as follows:

$$b_{15}, b_{14}, \ldots, b_1, b_0$$

where b_i for $i = 0, 1, \ldots, 15$, is a binary variable.

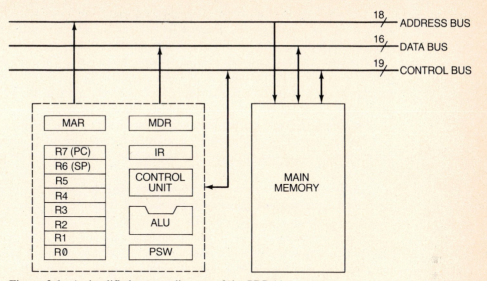

Figure 2.1 A simplified system diagram of the PDP-11.

Each register is considered to consist of a memory **word.** Here, a word is conventionally equal to two **BYTEs,** and each byte consists of eight **bits.** It is somewhat like our coin system, where a dime equals two nickels and each nickel equals five pennies. There is no mystery about it except for the sake of convenience.

For the PSW register, the values of the four LSB bits indicate TRUE (when $b_i = 1$) or FALSE (when $b_i = 0$) of the current status of the ALU or that of the result immediately following an ALU operation. They are thus known as the **FLAGs** of the ALU status. The format of PSW is defined as follows:

Bit Position	Mnemonic Symbol	Description
b_0	C	Carry
b_1	V	Overflow
b_2	Z	Zero
b_3	N	Negative
b_4	T	Trap
b_5–b_7	—	Interrupt priority
b_8–b_{15}	—	Not used

For example, if the instruction

        SUB   R0,R1

is executed, the ALU will subtract the content of R0 from the content of R1 and put the result in R1. If the result is zero, b_2 of the PSW will be set to 1 by the control unit of the CPU automatically. If the result is negative or less than zero, b_3 will be set to 1. It is important to point out that the PSW is a very important register in the CPU, since it provides information for decision making during program execution. Without the decision-making feature, a computer is almost useless.

Although the meanings of the flags for C, Z, and N are obvious, the implications of the V (overflow), T (trap), and interrupt priority bits are not. The student will learn in a later chapter that the V bit, if TRUE, indicates that the result of the latest ALU operation is not correct, and that program execution should be stopped. Unfortunately, it is often confused with the C bit, but the C bit, if TRUE, implies only that the latest ALU operation has resulted in a carry. Its result is still correct, and the execution should not stop. The implications of the T bit and interrupt priority bits will be studied in Chapter 8.

In theory, the eight general-purpose registers are at the programmer's disposal; that is, a programmer can use any one of these registers for any purpose. However, R7 and R6 are conventionally assigned as program counter (PC) and stack pointer (SP) registers, respectively.

As described in the preceding chapter, the MAR holds the current address of the instruction being executed, while the function of PC is to hold the value of the address of the next instruction to be executed. The function of SP has not yet been explored. The student at this moment may not be able to appreciate the power of SP in programming. In many cases, a programmer would like to reserve a specific area in the main memory for temporary storage called STACK-memory during program execution. If so, he or she can use SP as an address pointer like PC to point to this specific area for tentative storage of data. This specific area is like the scratch paper we often use for tentative storage of intermediate data when we want to keep a complex process systematic and clean. In the chapters on subroutines and interrupt, we will describe the use of the SP and stack-memory area in much more detail.

The rest of the six general-purpose registers, R0 through R5, are indeed general purpose. Those registers can be used by the programmer for any purpose. It is important to note that besides the ALU and control unit, there are twelve registers in the CPU. Among the twelve resisters, however, only R0, . . . , R7 and PSW are "visible" to or "reachable" by the programmer. That is, only these nine registers are accessible to the programmer.

Main Memory

The main memory unit shown in Figure 2.1 is the other important element of a computer system. In the fifties and early sixties, the majority of main memory units were made of tiny magnetic cores. As semiconductor technology has advanced, the cost of semiconductor memory has almost exponentially decreased. Presently, most main memory units are made of semiconductor devices. As described in the preceding chapter, the main memory is basically a storage area for programs and data to interact with the CPU for program preparation or execution.

Although the structure of a main memory is quite complex in the hardware sense, it is very simple to use from the programmer's viewpoint. The programmer needs to be concerned with only two things: the address and the content at that address. As shown in Figure 2.2, the structure of the main memory can be conceptually viewed as a main memory attached to two registers, MAR and MDR, the former for addressing, the latter for the addressed content. The content can be an instruction or a datum. The address is normally a numeric value (remember the analogy of the mailbox). However, a programmer can assign any one or more characters as a symbolic address to a specific address

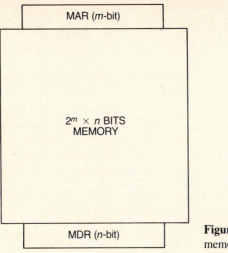

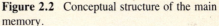

Figure 2.2 Conceptual structure of the main memory.

value and later can refer to that address by that symbolic address. For example, if there is a Holiday Inn located at 1000 Lincoln Avenue, one can refer to that hotel by the name Holiday Inn or the number 1000 in Lincoln Avenue.

For the PDP-11, the main memory is logically organized on the basis of byte and word as shown in Figure 2.3.

Symbolic Address (optional)*	8-bit Numeric Address								16-bit Contents															
									High Byte (odd)								Low Byte (even)								
	a_7	a_6	a_5	a_4	a_3	a_2	a_1	a_0	b_{15}	b_{14}	b_{13}	b_{12}	b_{11}	b_{10}	b_9	b_8	b_7	b_6	b_5	b_4	b_3	b_2	b_1	b_0
	0	0	0	0	0	0	0	0	0	0	1	0	1	1	0	0	0	1	0	0	1	0	1	1
	0	0	0	0	0	0	1	0	1	0	1	0	0	0	0	0	0	1	1	0	1	0	1	0
	0	0	0	0	0	1	0	0	0	1	0	1	0	1	0	0	0	1	1	1	1	0	0	0
	0	0	0	0	0	1	1	0	1	0	1	0	1	0	0	0	0	1	0	1	0	1	0	0
≃									≃								≃							≃
	1	1	1	1	1	0	0	0	1	0	1	0	1	0	1	1	1	1	0	0	1	0	1	0
	1	1	1	1	1	0	1	0	0	1	1	1	0	0	0	0	0	0	1	1	0	1	0	1
	1	1	1	1	1	1	0	0	0	0	0	1	1	0	0	0	0	1	1	0	1	0	1	0
	1	1	1	1	1	1	1	0	0	1	0	1	0	1	0	0	1	0	1	0	1	1	0	0

*Defined by the programmer.

Figure 2.3 Organization of main memory for the PDP-11.

Note that the memory structure shown above is called a memory map and has an 8-bit address capacity. Since the PDP-11 is a byte-addressable machine, the basic unit of the memory is thus a byte. Therefore, the memory shown has a capacity of $2^8 = 256$ words, or 512 bytes. For convenience, the contents of the memory have been filled with arbitrary binary numbers. Now, if one would like to READ a word at 100, the content 01 01 01 00 01 11 10 00 will be read into the CPU. If one would like to READ a byte at

100, the content of the low byte at 100, 01 11 10 00, will be read into the CPU instead. By a similar logic, one could WRITE a byte with a desired content, 11 11 11 11, into 101. As a result, the content of 101 (the high byte of the words at the location 100) would be 11 11 11 11.

Although the concept appears to be straightforward, the programmer may quickly find that the binary representation of data is a very inconvenient or ''uncivilized'' way to operate. Here again, we encounter the gap between human and the machine. To compromise, the programmer can use either **hexadecimal** or **octal** to represent information or data, instead of binary. Here, hexadecimal is a number representation of a group of 4-bit binary numbers (see Table 1.3), and octal, a number representation of a group of 3-bit binary numbers. The reason why the octal or hexadecimal was chosen rather than the

Numeric Address (in octal)			Contents in Octal, Byte Basis					
			High Byte			Low Byte		
a_7a_6	$a_5a_4a_3$	$a_2a_1a_0$	$b_{15}b_{14}$	$b_{13}b_{12}b_{11}$	$b_{10}b_9b_8$	b_7b_6	$b_5b_4b_3$	$b_2b_1b_0$
0	0	0	0	5	4	1	1	3
0	0	2	2	4	0	1	5	2
0	0	4	1	2	4	1	7	0
0	0	6	2	5	0	1	2	4
.	.	.	.	.	.	.	.	.
.	.	.	.	.	.	.	.	.
3	7	0	2	5	3	3	1	2
3	7	2	1	6	0	0	6	5
3	7	4	0	3	0	1	5	2
3	7	6	1	2	4	2	5	4

			Contents in Octal, Word Basis					
			b_{15}	$b_{14}b_{13}b_{12}$	$b_{11}b_{10}b_9$	$b_8b_7b_6$	$b_5b_4b_3$	$b_2b_1b_0$
0	0	0	0	2	6	1	1	3
0	0	2	1	2	0	1	5	2
0	0	4	0	5	2	1	7	0
0	0	6	1	2	4	1	2	4
.	.	.	.	.	.	.	.	.
.	.	.	.	.	.	.	.	.
3	7	0	1	2	5	7	1	2
3	7	2	0	7	0	0	6	5
3	7	4	0	1	4	1	5	2
3	7	6	0	5	2	2	5	4

Figure 2.4 PDP-11 main memory shown on byte and word basis.

decimal system is that both octal and hexadecimal systems have straightforward groupings of binary numbers. The PDP-11 has the octal representation system. As an example, we describe the memory shown in Figure 2.3 above in octal on a byte and then a word basis in Figure 2.4.

Because of the different ways of grouping the binary number for byte and word bases, the resulting representations of the same binary data on a byte basis are quite different from those on word basis. The beginner should take care to learn the distinction now, because in the PDP-11 system we mix byte and word addressing frequently in writing programs.

Once the octal representation system is defined, the programmer at the terminal can enter data in octal through the keyboard, and read the data on CRT in octal. It is the responsibility of the system software to convert the octal in ASCII to binary for input, and the binary to octal in ASCII for output.

2.3 OPERATION SEQUENCE

Assume that an application program has been developed and stored in the main memory, shown in Figure 2.1, starting at location 2000. Normally the memory spaces between location 0000 and the starting location of the application program, say 2000, are reserved for the system software. The exact starting address for executing the application program may vary from one machine to the other. We arbitrarily pick the value of 2000 for convenience.

The operation sequence of the computer can be briefly described as follows: First, the user may issue a command, 2000GO, to the operating system or system software. It starts to operate by putting 2000 into PC, which is then transferred to MAR, in the meanwhile automatically incrementing the content of PC by 2 (bytes). The content at location 2000 is then fetched through the bus, MDR, and eventually arrives at IR. The control unit interprets the content in IR and checks to see if more information is needed; if so, it will place (PC) into MAR, increment (PC) by 2, and fetch the content of the memory at the location specified or pointed by the MAR again. This fetching process repeats until all information needed for one instruction is in the CPU. Then the CPU executes the instruction and continues to fetch another instruction for execution at the next location in the memory. This fetching followed by executing process repeats until the CPU ''sees'' the HALT instruction. Then it stops execution with (PC), the content of PC, pointing at the location of the word next to where the HALT instruction resides. An example will clarify the operation.

The Operation Sequence of a Simple Program

Let us assume that a simple program has been stored in the memory starting at the location 2000. Its memory map is shown at the top of page 28.

User-Defined Symbolic Address	Numeric Address	Instructions	Comments
START	2 0 0 0	MOV #2, R0	Note 1
	2 0 0 2		
	2 0 0 4	MOV #4, R1	Note 2
	2 0 0 6		
	2 0 1 0	ADD R1, R0	Note 3
	2 0 1 2	HALT	Note 4
	2 0 1 4	? ? ? ? ?	Note 5

Note 1. The student will learn later that this instruction occupies two memory words, 2000 and 2002. The MOV instruction resides at 2000 and the number 2 resides at 2002. This instruction causes the CPU to copy 2 into R0.

Note 2. Similar to the preceding instruction except that the MOV instruction is in 2004, while 4 is in 2006. It will cause the CPU to copy 4 into R1.

Note 3. This instruction occupies one memory word. It will cause the CPU to ADD the content of R1 to the content of R0 and place the sum, which must be 6, in R0. The original content of R0 is lost.

Note 4. This instruction occupies one memory word. It will cause the CPU to stop execution.

To start the operation, the user types the 2000GO command on the keyboard. The machine will respond as follows:

1. $2000 \rightarrow$ PC.
2. $(PC) \rightarrow$ MAR; or the content of PC denoted by (PC), which must be 2000, is placed into MAR.
3. $(PC) + 2 \rightarrow$ PC; or the content of PC is incremented by 2—that is, its content becomes 2002.
4. The MOV instruction located at 2000 is fetched through MDR and placed in IR.
5. CPU interprets the instruction and discovers that more information is needed and thus places 2002 into MAR and increments (PC) by 2 again. As a result, (PC) = 2004.
6. CPU executes the instruction by placing 2 into R0.
7. CPU fetches the next instruction by placing (PC) into MAR, which must be 2004, and updates the PC to 2006.
8. The MOV instruction gets into CPU. The CPU fetches again. As a result, 4 is in R1, and the (PC) = 2010.
9. CPU fetches the next instruction by placing 2010 into MAR, updates (PC) to 2012, and the ADD instruction is fetched and placed into IR.
10. CPU executes the ADD instruction and places the SUM, 6, into R0.
11. CPU places (PC), which is now 2012, into MAR; increments PC to 2014; and fetches the HALT instruction into IR.
12. CPU interprets and executes the HALT instruction, and the machine stops operation.

The (PC) is left pointing at 2014, and the machine stops operation due to the HALT instruction. Since we never did store anything at location 2014, the content of 2014 is "undefined," which can be considered nothing but garbage.

EXERCISES

2.1 Briefly describe in your own words the functions of the ALU, the control unit, and the main memory in the PDP-11 computer system.

2.2 Briefly describe the function of the following elements in the CPU of the PDP-11 computer: MAR, MDR, R0, R1, R2, R3, R4, R5, R6, R7, IR, PSW.

2.3 The functions of the general-purpose registers R0, R1, . . . , R5, appear similar to those of the memory words in the main memory; why do you need them in the CPU?

2.4 Discuss the difference in application between symbolic address and numeric address.

2.5 Using Appendix A, translate the following into binary numbers and store them in the memory of the PDP-11 in an ascending order, but starting at the address 0: HELLO, PDP 11.
  a. Show your memory contents with respect to its own address, in binary numbers.
  b. Translate the same memory contents in octal numbers on the byte basis.
  c. Translate the same memory contents in octal numbers on the word (16-bit) basis.

Chapter 3

Representation of Information

This chapter describes the representation of information which is being stored, manipulated within the machine, and transferred between human and machine. We first present the different types of representation of numbers being used by humans and machines, and the conversion of number representations from one type to the other. Next, we introduce the complementary arithmetic used within the machine. Finally, we examine a partial set of the mnemonic instruction for the PDP-11 to illustrate the processing of information between user and machine. Again, we use a simple example to demonstrate the basic principle of operation.

KEY WORDS

base	object program
BCD	ones complement
comment	overflow
complement	pseudoinstruction
complement arithmetic	radix
debugging	sevens complement
directive	sign magnitude
eights complement	sixteens complement
fifteens complement	source program
floating-point representation	symbolic address
instruction format	tens complement
nines complement	twos complement

We have shown that the contents stored in the memory are information. The information can be a sequence of instructions or a set of data or numbers. The instructions tell the CPU what to do and with what data to do it. Before we learn how to program, we need to learn how the instructions and data or numbers are represented and how the numbers are manipulated in the CPU. In the following sections, we will examine first the representation of number and how the CPU deals with negative numbers, or how addition and subtraction are implemented in the CPU. Since the programmer uses octal numbers, we will study octal number manipulation along with binary number manipulation. Next we will briefly examine some of the simple but essential instructions. (A detailed study of the instruction set is postponed to a later chapter.)

3.1 REPRESENTATION OF UNSIGNED NUMBERS FOR DIFFERENT RADIX

Human beings have been using the decimal system for centuries. For a three-digit representation of a decimal number, say, 789_{10}, we really mean that the number represents a value

$$V_{10} = 7 \times 10^2 + 8 \times 10^1 + 9 \times 10^0$$

Similarly, the binary number representation 1011_2 has a value

$$V_2 = 1 \times 2^3 + 0 \times 2^2 + 1 \times 2^1 + 1 \times 2^0$$

The octal number 761_8 has a value

$$V_8 = 7 \times 8^2 + 6 \times 8^1 + 1 \times 8^0$$

and the hexadecimal number $A1C_{16}$ has a value

$$V_{16} = 10 \times 16^2 + 1 \times 16^1 + 12 \times 16^0$$

where the subscript indicates the **base** or the **radix** of the number. In general, for an n-digit number, its value is

$$V_b = (x_{n-1}, x_{n-2}, \ldots x_1, x_0)_b = x_{n-1} \, b^{n-1} + x_{n-2} \, b^{n-2} \ldots + x_1 \, b^1 + x_0 \, b^0 \quad (3.1)$$

where b is the base of the number

x_i is the ith digit, for $i = 0, 1, \ldots, n - 1$, and $0 \le x_i \le b - 1$

However, since the world outside the computer system uses decimal representation, it is necessary to have a standard way of coding a decimal number in binary format for input and output processing to a machine. This code is called the **binary coded decimal (BCD)** representation. It is defined as:

Decimal	BCD Equivalent
0	0 0 0 0
1	0 0 0 1
2	0 0 1 0
3	0 0 1 1
4	0 1 0 0
5	0 1 0 1
6	0 1 1 0
7	0 1 1 1
8	1 0 0 0
9	1 0 0 1

It is important not to confuse the BCD with the binary value of a decimal number. For example, the decimal number 17_{10} has an equivalent binary value 10001_2; in other words:

$$17_{10} = 10001_2$$

However, the decimal number in BCD will be

0001   0111

Here, 0111 is the code for the first digit, 7, while 0001 is the code for the next digit, 1. It has nothing to do with the real values of the number. Note that the former requires five bits, whereas the latter requires eight bits.

In the PDP-11 computing system, because the octal representation is the standard notation, the subscript for the octal number is normally omitted. In contrast, the decimal number is always followed by a period instead of a subscript 10. For example:

$$\text{Decimal: } 17. = 1 \times 10 + 7 \times 10^0$$
$$\text{Octal:} \quad 17 = 1 \times 8 + 7 \times 8^0$$

Table 3.1 illustrates the number representations for different systems with values from zero to 15_{10}.

TABLE 3.1

Decimal	Octal	Hexadecimal	Binary	BCD		
0 0	0 0	0	0 0 0 0	0 0 0 0	0 0 0 0	
0 1	0 1	1	0 0 0 1	0 0 0 0	0 0 0 1	
0 2	0 2	2	0 0 1 0	0 0 0 0	0 0 1 0	
0 3	0 3	3	0 0 1 1	0 0 0 0	0 0 1 1	
0 4	0 4	4	0 1 0 0	0 0 0 0	0 1 0 0	
0 5	0 5	5	0 1 0 1	0 0 0 0	0 1 0 1	
0 6	0 6	6	0 1 1 0	0 0 0 0	0 1 1 0	
0 7	0 7	7	0 1 1 1	0 0 0 0	0 1 1 1	
0 8	1 0	8	1 0 0 0	0 0 0 0	1 0 0 0	
0 9	1 1	9	1 0 0 1	0 0 0 0	1 0 0 1	
1 0	1 2	A	1 0 1 0	0 0 0 1	0 0 0 0	
1 1	1 3	B	1 0 1 1	0 0 0 1	0 0 0 1	
1 2	1 4	C	1 1 0 0	0 0 0 1	0 0 1 0	
1 3	1 5	D	1 1 0 1	0 0 0 1	0 0 1 1	
1 4	1 6	E	1 1 1 0	0 0 0 1	0 1 0 0	
1 5	1 7	F	1 1 1 1	0 0 0 1	0 1 0 1	

3.2 RADIX CONVERSION

Since all the number representations on different bases are used in assembly programming, conversion from one system to the other is often needed. The following set of numeric examples illustrates the conversion process. Basically, in these examples we use longhand division to achieve the conversion. For convenience, as illustrated, we have altered the conventional longhand division format by moving the residue to the right and the quotient to the place where the residue is ordinarily put. For large numbers, the conventional format might be less error-prone.

Decimal to Binary*

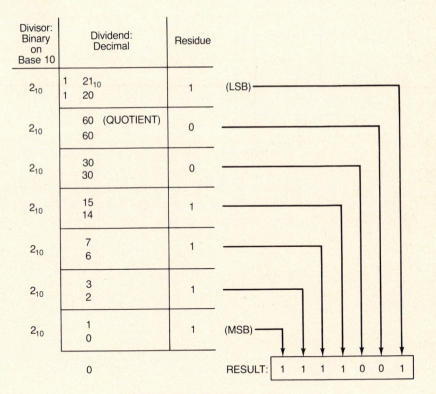

Binary to Decimal

Since the binary representation of base 10 is 1010_2, we divide the given binary number by 1010_2 as follows:

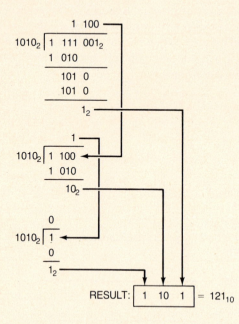

Note that in this example, the divisor is the base of 10 in binary because the dividend is in binary format. The subtract process in this longhand division is similar to that in the decimal system except that a "borrow" from a left digit has a value of 2 instead of a value of 10, as in the decimal system.

Decimal to Octal

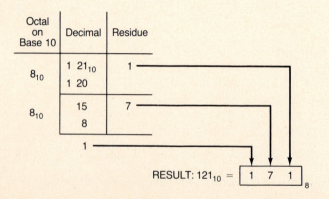

Octal to Decimal

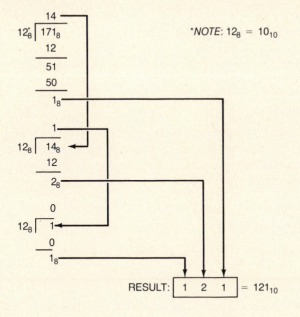

*NOTE: $12_8 = 10_{10}$

Octal to Binary to Octal

Although longhand division is also applicable here, the conversion can easily be done by inspection for both-way conversions. Using Table 3.1, the conversion for this example can be done by inspection, as follows:

$$1 \quad 7 \quad 1_8 \rightarrow 1 \ 111 \ 001_2$$
$$1 \ 111 \ 001_2 \rightarrow 1 \quad 7 \quad 1_8$$

The longhand division algorithm can now be generalized as follows:

$$X_{b1} = (b2)_{b1} \, Q_0 + R_0$$
$$Q_0 = (b2)_{b1} \, Q_1 + R_1$$
$$Q_i = (b2)_{b1} \, Q_{i+1} + R_{i+1}$$
$$Q_J = (b2)_{b1} \, 0 + R_{J+1} \tag{3.2}$$

where
b_1 = the radix or base of the original number
b_2 = the radix of the number system to be converted unto
Q_0 = the quotient of the initial level of division
R_0 = the residue of the initial level of division
Q_i = the quotient of ith level of division
R_i = the residue of ith level of division

By repeatedly substituting the lower line into the next higher one of Equation 3.2, we have

$$X_{b1} = R_{J+1} \, b_2^{J+1} + \cdots + R_1 \, b_2^1 + R_0 \, b_2^0$$

It is interesting to note that it might be easier to perform decimal-to-binary conversion via decimal-to-octal conversion.

3.3 NEGATIVE NUMBER REPRESENTATIONS

There are two ways of representing a negative number, by **sign magnitude** and by **complement.**

Sign Magnitude Representation

For a 16-bit machine (digital computer), the most significant bit (MSB) is assigned as the sign bit (1 = negative, 0 = positive), and the rest of it is the magnitude. For example, for the 16-bit binary number $b_{15}, \ldots, b_1, b_0$, we would have b_{15} as the sign bit and $b_{14}, \ldots, b_0$ as the magnitude. Its value can be evaluated as follows:

$$\text{value} = (1 - 2b_{15})\,(b_{14}\,2^{14} + \cdots + b_0\,2^0)$$

For example: $1\ 000\ 000\ 000\ 000\ 110_2$ is a negative number with the value

$$V = (1 - 2 \cdot 1)\,(1 \cdot 2^2 + 1 \cdot 2^1 + 0 \cdot 2^0) = -6_{10}$$

Complement Representation

Complement representation may appear to be somewhat complicated. It, however, requires only a hardware adder to perform either addition or subtraction. Furthermore, the complement representation of a positive number is the same as that of the sign magnitude; therefore, most digital computers use complement representation instead. Two kinds of complement representation are currently commonly used with digital computers, the twos complement and the ones complement. But there are also sevens, eights, nines, and tens complements for the programmer to use. We will first introduce the twos complement and then the others.

Twos Complement

Mathematical Derivation   The **twos complement** of an n-bit binary number in sign magnitude representation can be derived by the following formula:

$$\boxed{b_{n-1}}\ b_{n-2}, \ldots \ldots, b_0 \xrightarrow{\ \overline{2}\ } - b_{n-1}\,2^{n-1} + b_{n-2}\,2^{n-2} + \ldots + b_0\,2^0 \quad (3.3)$$

where the $\overline{2}$ riding on the arrow symbolizes the twos complement operation, and the sign bit b_{n-1} is enclosed in a rectangle for easy identification.

EXAMPLE 1 _____

Convert the sign magnitude number -6 to its twos complement equivalent.

$$\text{sign mag of } -6 \text{ in binary} = \boxed{1}\ 110$$

Here we have $n = 4$. From Equation 3.3, we have

$$-1 \cdot 2^3 + 1 \cdot 2^2 + 1 \cdot 2^1 + 0.2^0$$
$$= -8 + 4 + 2 = -2 \longrightarrow \boxed{1}\ 010$$

Thus the twos complement of the sign mag of -6 in binary, $\boxed{1}\ 110$ is $\boxed{1}\ 010$, or

$$\boxed{1}\ 110 \xrightarrow{\ \overline{2}\ } \boxed{1}\ 010$$

EXAMPLE 2 ──

Convert the sign magnitude number $+6$ to its twos complement equivalent.

$$\text{sign mag of } +6 = 0110$$

From Equation 3.3, we have

$$0 \cdot 2^3 + 1 \cdot 2^2 + 1 \cdot 2^1 + 0 \cdot 2^0 = +6 \longrightarrow \boxed{0}\ 110$$

Note that the complement of a positive number in sign mag representation is itself. This is obvious from Equation 3.3, since the b_{n-1}, the sign bit, is zero, which would not alter the value of the number. ■■

Examination of the complement process reveals that the calculation appears to be lengthy. One might question the real value of taking the complement route. Fortunately, the process can easily be implemented logically, as follows.

Complement by Logic Procedure

Step 1: Negate the *magnitude* of the number but leave the sign-bit alone.
Step 2: Add one to the negated number.
Step 3: Copy or restore original sign bit to the result of step 2.

Example: Convert -6 to its twos complement using logic procedure. (We leave the square blank until step 3 for convenience.)

Step 1: $\boxed{1}\ 110 \xrightarrow{\text{negate mag}} 001$

Step 2: $001 + 1 = 010$

Step 3: $\boxed{1}\ 010$

Ones Complement The **ones complement** of a number is simply the negation of each bit except the sign bit. Thus, logic procedures for ones complement are

Step 1: Negate the magnitude of the number, but leave the sign-bit alone.
Step 2: Copy or restore the original sign bit to the result of step 1.

Example: Convert -6 to its ones complement.

Step 1: $\boxed{1}\ 110 \xrightarrow{\text{negate mag}} 001$

Step 2: Ones complement is $\boxed{1}\ 001$

Note that the twos complement of a number can be obtained by adding one to that number's ones complement.

Other Complement Representations Procedures for other complements can also be logically derived in the similar manner, as follows:

The **sevens complement** for the octal system:

Step 1: Determine the sevens complement of each digit of the magnitude by subtracting the digit from 7.

Step 2: Copy or restore the sign bit.

Example: Convert the sign mag number -634_8 into its sevens complement.

$$\boxed{-}\ 634 \xrightarrow{\ \overline{7}\ } \boxed{-}\ 143$$

The **eights complement** for the octal system:

Step 1: Determine the sevens complement of the number.

Step 2: Add one to the sevens complement of that number.

Example: Convert the sign mag number -634_8 into its eights complement.

Step 1: $\boxed{-}\ 634 \xrightarrow{\ \overline{7}\ } \boxed{-}\ 143$

Step 2: $\boxed{-}\ 143 + 1 = \boxed{-}\ 144$

Since the PDP-11 uses the octal number system for input/output data, the eights complement is quite useful for checking some of the machine-assembled results. The following examples illustrate the parallelism between the ones complement and sevens complement, as well as the twos complement and eights complement.

EXAMPLE 1 _____

Let a byte of a binary number in sign mag $X = \boxed{1}\ 0\ 101\ 011_2$. Then the ones complement of X is

$$X(\overline{1}) = \boxed{1}\ 1\ 010\ 100_2$$

where $X(\overline{1})$ denotes the ones complement of X, whose sevens complement representation, by inspecting $X(\overline{1})$, is then

$$X(\overline{7}) = -124_8 = \boxed{1}\ 124_8 = 324_8 \text{ (if sign bit is included)}$$

However, $X(\overline{7})$ can be derived from the original number, as follows:
Since

$$X = -053_8$$

then

$$X(\overline{7}) = -124_8 = \boxed{1}\ 124_8 = 324_8 \text{ (if sign bit is included)}$$

which yields the same result.   ■ ■

Note that since the most significant digit of the octal representation here has only one bit, we take the ones complement for this digit instead of the sevens complement. Similarly, we can derive the twos complement of X as follows:

$$|X(\overline{2})| = |X(\overline{1})| + 1 = \boxed{\ }\ 1\ 010\ 101$$

and by restoring the sign bit, we have

$$X(\bar{2}) = \boxed{1}\ 1\ 010\ 101$$

where $|X(\bar{2})|$ denotes the magnitude of $X(\bar{2})$.

Its eights complement representation, by direct translation of $X(\bar{2})$, is:

$$X(\bar{8}) = -125_8 = \boxed{1}\ 125_8 = 325_8 \text{ (if sign bit is included)}$$

But

$$|X(\bar{8})| = |X(\bar{7})| + 1 = \square\ 124 + 1 = \square\ 125$$

Thus

$$X(\bar{8}) = 1\ 125 = 325_8 \text{ (if sign bit is included)}$$

As another example, let us examine a 16-bit binary number.

EXAMPLE 2

Let $X = 1\ 000\ 000\ 101\ 100\ 001_2$. Then the process can be carried out as follows:

$$\boxed{1}\ 000\ 000\ 101\ 100\ 001 \rightharpoondown$$
$$ \bar{1}$$
$$\boxed{1}\ 111\ 111\ 010\ 011\ 110 \leftharpoonup$$

Thus we have

$$X(\bar{1}) = \boxed{1}\ 111\ 111\ 010\ 011\ 110$$
$$|X(\bar{2})| = |X(\bar{1})| + 1 = \square\ 111\ 111\ 010\ 011\ 111$$
$$X(\bar{2}) = \boxed{1}\ 111\ 111\ 010\ 011\ 111$$
$$X(\bar{7}) = \boxed{1}\ 77236$$
$$|X(\bar{8})| = |X(\bar{7})| + 1 = \square\ 7\ 72\ 36 + 1 = \square\ 7\ 72\ 37$$

and

$$X(\bar{8}) = \boxed{1}\ 7\ 72\ 37 \qquad\qquad \blacksquare\blacksquare$$

If we derive the eights complement from the original number, we will have

$$X = \boxed{1}\ 000\ 000\ 101\ 100\ 001_2$$
$$= \boxed{1}\ 0\ 05\ 41_8$$

then

$$X(\bar{7}) = \boxed{1}\ 7\ 72\ 36$$

and

$$|X(\bar{8})| = |X(\bar{7})| + 1 = \square\ 7\ 72\ 36 + 1 = \square\ 7\ 72\ 37$$

or

$$X(\bar{8}) = \boxed{1}\ 7\ 72\ 37$$

The **nines** and **tens complements** for decimal system, and the **fifteens** and **sixteens complements** for the hexadecimal system can all be derived in the similar way. That is:

$$|X(\overline{10})| = |X(\overline{9})| + 1, \text{ and } |X(\overline{16})| = |X(\overline{15})| + 1, \text{ and so on.}$$

Properties of Complement Representation

Cyclic Property The complement of a complemented number is its original number representation. For example, let $X = \boxed{1}\ 0\ 101\ 011$. Then $X(\overline{2}) = \boxed{1}\ 1\ 010\ 101$.

If we take the twos complement of $X(\overline{2})$ again, it yields the original number:

$$X = \boxed{1}\ 0\ 101\ 011$$

Arithmetic Right Shift Copy the sign bit to the spaces or empty leftmost bits caused by the arithmetic right shift. For example, let $X = \boxed{1}\ 0\ 101\ 011$. Then, after two arithmetic right shift operations,

$$X = \boxed{1}\ 1\ 101\ 010$$

Arithmetic Left Shift The arithmetic left shift can be performed only if the most significant bit of the magnitude has the same value as the sign bit. For example, $X = \boxed{1}\ 0\ 101\ 011$ cannot be shifted left. However, if $X = \boxed{1}\ 1\ 101\ 001$, then it can be shifted left at most two times—that is, after two arithmetic left shifts, we have $X = \boxed{1}\ 0\ 100\ 100$.

The Complement of a Positive Number Is the Number Itself For example, the $X(\overline{2})$ of 00 101 011 is 00 101 011. Table 3.2 shows the representations of sign magnitude and their equivalent complements of different radixes.

TABLE 3.2

Binary-coded Signed Magnitude	Decimal Equivalent	Ones Complement	Twos Complement	Sevens Complement	Eights Complement
0 0 0 0	0	0 0 0 0	0 0 0 0	0 0	0 0
0 0 0 1	1	0 0 0 1	0 0 0 1	0 1	0 1
0 0 1 0	2	0 0 1 0	0 0 1 0	0 2	0 2
0 0 1 1	3	0 0 1 1	0 0 1 1	0 3	0 3
0 1 0 0	4	0 1 0 0	0 1 0 0	0 4	0 4
0 1 0 1	5	0 1 0 1	0 1 0 1	0 5	0 5
0 1 1 0	6	0 1 1 0	0 1 1 0	0 6	0 6
0 1 1 1	7	0 1 1 1	0 1 1 1	0 7	0 7
1 0 0 0	−0	1 1 1 1	0 0 0 0	1 7	1 0
1 0 0 1	−1	1 1 1 0	1 1 1 1	1 6	1 7
1 0 1 0	−2	1 1 0 1	1 1 1 0	1 5	1 6
1 0 1 1	−3	1 1 0 0	1 1 0 1	1 4	1 5
1 1 0 0	−4	1 0 1 1	1 1 0 0	1 3	1 4
1 1 0 1	−5	1 0 1 0	1 0 1 1	1 2	1 3
1 1 1 0	−6	1 0 0 1	1 0 1 0	1 1	1 2
1 1 1 1	−7	1 0 0 0	1 0 0 1	1 0	1 1

3.4 COMPLEMENT ARITHMETIC

Presently, most digital computers contain only one hardware adder; the subtract operation is thus implemented by complement arithmetic. Since the complement of a positive number is the number itself, we will focus on subtraction by adding numbers in complement representations. First, let us use a simple example to illustrate the basic concept.

Figure 3.1 shows the dial of a decimal meter somewhat like a household electric kilowatt-hour or gas or water meter. Let us say that for addition, the hand goes clockwise; for subtraction, it goes counterclockwise. The hand is now at 6. Let us subtract the current number 6 by 2, or move the hand counterclockwise by two. As a result, the hand will stop at 4. Now, let us use complement arithmetic as follows. Since this is a decimal system, we use the tens complement representation. Note that,

$$6 - 2 = 6 + (-2)$$

Here, the tens complement of -2 is 8. If we add the tens complement of -2 to it, we have 14. By ignoring the carry (because we have only one digit), we have the same answer as that by conventional subtraction: 4. By the same logic, referring to Figure 3.1, we can turn the hand clockwise by 8 positions and it will also stop at 4, which is the correct answer. Note that we can determine the tens complement of any number that is less than or equal to ten. For -2, we have 8; for -3, we have 7, and so on. This concept can be applied to any complement arithmetic.

Subtraction by Addition of Twos Complements

Figure 3.2 shows the process of implementing subtraction by adding the twos complement. The symbol of S/M denotes the sign magnitude number, and $\overline{2}$ implies the twos complement operation. The procedure follows:

Step 1: Convert the negative number or numbers in sign magnitude into their twos complements, but leave the number alone if it is positive.

Step 2: Apply binary addition operation and treat the sign bit in the same way as the others, but ignore the carry bit.

Step 3: If the sign bit of the sum is one, the result is a negative number in twos complement. To convert the complement form back to sign magnitude, it should be twos-complemented again.

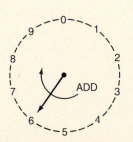

Figure 3.1 Complement arithmetic.

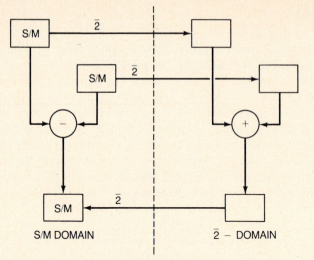

Figure 3.2 Process of subtraction by addition of twos complements.

EXAMPLE 1 _____

$$19_{10} - 14_{10} = ?$$

S/M:
$$19_{10} = \boxed{0}\ 10\ 011_2$$
$$-14_{10} = \boxed{1}\ 01\ 110_2$$

Step 1: Convert -14 to its twos complement.

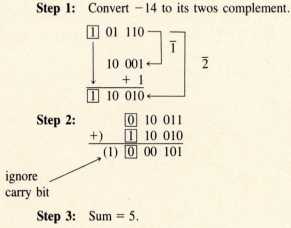

Step 2:
$$\boxed{0}\ 10\ 011$$
$$+)\quad \boxed{1}\ 10\ 010$$
$$(1)\ \boxed{0}\ 00\ 101$$

ignore
carry bit

Step 3: Sum = 5.

EXAMPLE 2 _____

$$7_{10} - 14_{10} = ?$$

S/M:
$$7_{10} = \boxed{0}\ 00\ 111_2$$
$$-14_{10} = \boxed{1}\ 01\ 110_2$$

Step 1: $-14_{10} \xrightarrow{\bar{2}} \boxed{1}\ 10\ 010$

Step 2:
$$\begin{array}{r} \boxed{0}\ 00\ 111 \\ +)\boxed{1}\ 10\ 010 \\ \hline \boxed{1}\ 11\ 001 \end{array}$$

Step 3: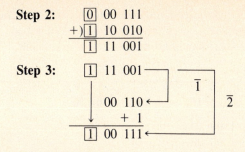

$\boxed{1}\ 11\ 001$ ⟶
$00\ 110$ ⟵ $\bar{1}$
$+\ 1$ ⟶ $\bar{2}$
$\boxed{1}\ 00\ 111$ ⟵

Answer in S/M: -7_{10}.

EXAMPLE 3 ────────────────────────────────────

$$-16_{10} - 14_{10} = ?$$

S/M:
$$-16_{10} = \boxed{1}\ 10\ 000$$
$$-14_{10} = \boxed{1}\ 01\ 110_2$$

Step 1: S/M → twos complement.

$\boxed{1}\ 10\ 000$ ⟶
$01\ 111$ ⟵ $\bar{1}$
$+\ 1$ $\bar{2}$
$\boxed{1}\ 10\ 000$ ⟵

$-14 \xrightarrow{\ \bar{2}\ } 1\ 10\ 010$

Step 2:
$$\begin{array}{r} \boxed{1}\ 10\ 000 \\ +\quad \boxed{1}\ 10\ 010 \\ \hline (1)\ \boxed{1}\ 00\ 010 \end{array}$$

ignore
carry bit

Step 3:
$\boxed{1}\ 00\ 010$ ⟶
$11\ 101$ ⟵ $\bar{1}$
$+\ 1$ $\bar{2}$
$\boxed{1}\ 11\ 110$ ⟵

Answer in S/M: -30_{10}

■ ■

Overflow in Complement Arithmetic

Overflow is an erroneous result of an arithmetic operation of which all programmers should be aware. It has often been confused with the result of a carry. Most computing systems have a system program routine to issue error messages and then halt the machine operation if overflow occurs. However, if the system software does not contain a program module for this service, it will be the programmer's responsibility to check for the overflow flag of the PSW. If it occurs, an error message should be issued, and the machine should be halted. The following examples demonstrate the problem.

EXAMPLE 1 ──

$$18_{10} + 16_{10} = ? \text{ for a six-bit ALU.}$$

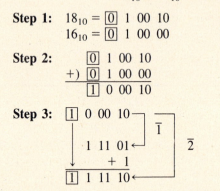

Step 1: $18_{10} = \boxed{0}\ 1\ 00\ 10$
             $16_{10} = \boxed{0}\ 1\ 00\ 00$

Step 2: $\boxed{0}\ 1\ 00\ 10$
            $+)\ \ \boxed{0}\ 1\ 00\ 00$
            ─────────────────
                 $\boxed{1}\ 0\ 00\ 10$

Step 3: $\boxed{1}\ 0\ 00\ 10$

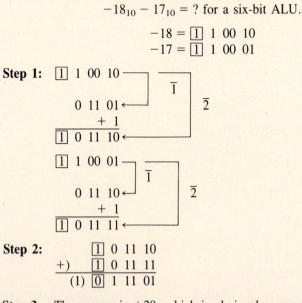

The answer is -30, while we expect it to be 34. Note that this is a 6-bit machine, which can only represent the numbers ranging from -31_{10} to $+31_{10}$. In this example, however, the expected result is outside the range of the ALU; thus, it will yield an erroneous or overflow result, and the machine should be halted.

EXAMPLE 2 ──

$$-18_{10} - 17_{10} = ? \text{ for a six-bit ALU.}$$

S/M: $-18 = \boxed{1}\ 1\ 00\ 10$
                                        $-17 = \boxed{1}\ 1\ 00\ 01$

Step 1: $\boxed{1}\ 1\ 00\ 10$
                 $0\ 11\ 01$
                  $+\ 1$
             ────────────
             $\boxed{1}\ 0\ 11\ 10$

             $\boxed{1}\ 1\ 00\ 01$
                 $0\ 11\ 10$
                  $+\ 1$
             ────────────
             $\boxed{1}\ 0\ 11\ 11$

Step 2: $\boxed{1}\ 0\ 11\ 10$
            $+)\ \ \ \boxed{1}\ 0\ 11\ 11$
            ───────────────────
            $(1)\ \boxed{0}\ 1\ 11\ 01$

Step 3: The answer is $+29$, which is obviously wrong.   ■ ■

With careful examination of the overflow process, one can conclude that if the values of the sign bits of two numbers are identical but the sign bit of the sum of those two numbers has a different value from the originals, an overflow has occurred. As we can see from the examples above, in Example 1 the original signs were positive, but it yielded a negative sign; in Example 2, the result bears a positive sign, whereas the originals were negative.

Subtraction by Addition of Ones Complements

Although PDP-11 families use twos complement arithmetic, a number of digital computers use ones complement arithmetic. The procedure for subtraction by addition of ones complements is as follows:

Step 1: Convert the negative number or numbers into ones complements.

Step 2: Apply the binary addition operation, including the sign bit. If carry occurs, add 1 to the resulting sum.

Step 3: If the sign bit of the result is 1, apply the ones complement operation again to obtain the sign magnitude representation; otherwise no conversion is necessary.

EXAMPLE 1 ───

$$34_{10} - 23_{10} = ? \text{ for an eight-bit ALU.}$$

S/M:
$$34_{10} = \boxed{0}\ 0\ 10\ 00\ 10_2$$
$$-23_{10} = \boxed{1}\ 0\ 01\ 01\ 11_2$$

Step 1:
$$\boxed{1}\ 0\ 01\ 01\ 11$$
$$\overline{1}$$
$$\boxed{1}\ 1\ 10\ 10\ 00$$

Step 2:
$$\boxed{0}\ 0\ 10\ 00\ 10$$
$$+)\quad \boxed{1}\ 1\ 10\ 10\ 00$$
$$(1)\ 0\ \ 0\ 00\ 10\ 10 \qquad \text{carry occurs}$$
$$+\ 1$$
$$0\ \ 0\ 00\ 10\ 11$$

Step 3: The answer = +11.

EXAMPLE 2 ───

$$17_{10} - 23_{10} = ? \text{ for an eight-bit ALU.}$$

S/M:
$$17_{10} = \boxed{0}\ 0\ 01\ 00\ 01_2$$
$$-23_{10} = \boxed{1}\ 0\ 01\ 01\ 11$$

Step 1:
$$\boxed{1}\ 0\ 01\ 01\ 11$$
$$\overline{1}$$
$$\boxed{1}\ 1\ 10\ 10\ 00$$

Step 2:
$$\boxed{0}\ 0\ 01\ 00\ 01$$
$$+)\boxed{1}\ 1\ 10\ 10\ 00$$
$$\boxed{1}\ 1\ 11\ 10\ 01$$

Step 3: $\boxed{1}$ 1 11 10 01 ⌐
                                        $\overline{1}$
              $\boxed{1}$ 0 00 01 10 ⌐

The answer is −6.

EXAMPLE 3 _____

$$-22_{10} - 8_{10} = ? \text{ for an eight-bit ALU.}$$

S/M: $-22_{10} = \boxed{1}$ 0 01 01 10
                                        $-8_{10} = \boxed{1}$ 0 00 10 00

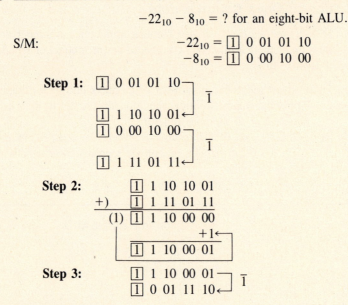

Step 1: $\boxed{1}$ 0 01 01 10 ⌐
                                        $\overline{1}$
              $\boxed{1}$ 1 10 10 01 ⌐
              $\boxed{1}$ 0 00 10 00 ⌐
                                        $\overline{1}$
              $\boxed{1}$ 1 11 01 11 ⌐

Step 2: $\boxed{1}$ 1 10 10 01
          +) $\boxed{1}$ 1 11 01 11
              (1) $\boxed{1}$ 1 10 00 00
                                    +1 ⌐
              $\boxed{1}$ 1 10 00 01

Step 3: $\boxed{1}$ 1 10 00 01 ⌐ $\overline{1}$
              $\boxed{1}$ 0 01 11 10 ⌐

The answer is −30.   ∎∎

Subtraction by Addition of Eights Complements

Since PDP-11 families use octal systems for input/output or user-machine communication, we will demonstrate how the following procedure can be applied to a 16-bit machine.

Step 1:   Convert the negative number or numbers into the eights complement.
Step 2:   Apply the octal addition operation, including the sign bit, and ignore the carry if it occurs.
Step 3:   If the sign bit is 1, apply the eights complement again to obtain the sign magnitude representation.

For example: $715_8 - 234_8 = ?$ for a 16-bit ALU.

Step 1: $\boxed{0}$ 0 07 15
              $\boxed{1}$ 0 02 34 ⌐
                                      $\overline{7}$
                   7 75 43 ⌐ $\overline{8}$
                          + 1
              $\boxed{1}$ 7 75 44 ⌐

Step 2:
$$
\begin{array}{r}
\boxed{0}\ 0\ 07\ 15 \\
+)\quad \boxed{1}\ 7\ 75\ 44 \\
\hline
(1)\ \boxed{0}\ 0\ 04\ 61
\end{array}
$$

ignore
carry

Remember we are using octal arithmetic here!

Step 3: The answer is 461_8.

Of course, this example can also be worked out using twos complement addition, as follows:

S/M:
$$715_8 = \boxed{0}\ 000\ 000\ 111\ 001\ 101$$
$$-234_8 = \boxed{1}\ 000\ 000\ 010\ 011\ 100$$

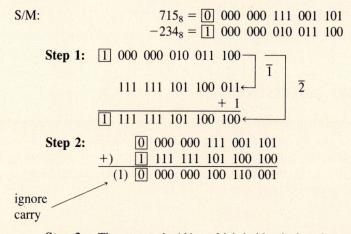

Step 1: $\boxed{1}\ 000\ 000\ 010\ 011\ 100$

$$111\ 111\ 101\ 100\ 011$$
$$+\ 1$$
$$\boxed{1}\ 111\ 111\ 101\ 100\ 100$$

Step 2:
$$
\begin{array}{r}
\boxed{0}\ 000\ 000\ 111\ 001\ 101 \\
+)\quad \boxed{1}\ 111\ 111\ 101\ 100\ 100 \\
\hline
(1)\ \boxed{0}\ 000\ 000\ 100\ 110\ 001
\end{array}
$$

ignore
carry

Step 3: The answer is 461_8, which is identical to the result of using eights complement arithmetic.

Subtraction by Addition of Hexadecimals Complements

Follow the same logic, we can easily derive the procedure of subtraction by addition of hexadecimal complements. A simple numeric example should be sufficient to demonstrate the process: $7C34_{16} - 1F96_{16} = ?$ for a 16-bit ALU.

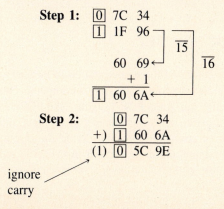

Step 1: $\boxed{0}\ 7C\ 34$
$\boxed{1}\ 1F\ 96$

$$60\ 69$$
$$+\ 1$$
$$\boxed{1}\ 60\ 6A$$

Step 2:
$$
\begin{array}{r}
\boxed{0}\ 7C\ 34 \\
+)\ \boxed{1}\ 60\ 6A \\
\hline
(1)\ \boxed{0}\ 5C\ 9E
\end{array}
$$

ignore
carry

Step 3:　The answer is 5C 9E.

Let us verify this example by the twos complement again.

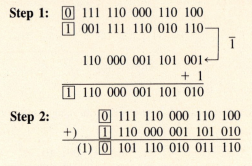

Step 1:
```
⓪ 111 110 000 110 100
① 001 111 110 010 110 ┐
                       │ 1̄
110 000 001 101 001 ←──┘
                + 1
① 110 000 001 101 010
```

Step 2:
```
     ⓪ 111 110 000 110 100
+)   ① 110 000 001 101 010
(1) ⓪ 101 110 010 011 110
```

Step 3:　The answer is identical to the result of using the hexadecimal operation.

3.5 FLOATING-POINT REPRESENTATION

What we have examined thus far for number representations is limited to integers. For fractions or real number representation, most digital computers use the binary **floating-point system.** In this system, the representation consists of three fields: (1) sign, (2) exponent, and (3) fraction. In the PDP-11, this system normally occupies two memory words and has the following format:

S	Exponent	Fraction
1	8 bits	23 bits

The hardware floating-point processor unit that executes the floating-point arithmetic instruction set is available as an option to the PDP-11 user. At this point we will deal with integers only, a more detailed description of floating-point representation will be described in the later chapter, Introduction to the VAX-11.

3.6 FIRST GLANCE AT THE INSTRUCTION SET

In the preceding sections we have described the representation of numbers, which is one of the key elements for conveying information to and from a computer. Next, we look at the other key element, the instruction set of the PDP-11. Since the PDP-11 is a powerful and flexible minicomputer, its instruction set is considered quite complex for a novice. To minimize unnecessary frustration or confusion, we will divide the discussion into two steps. That is, we will study the simple and more explicit instructions and their typical applications first and leave the more complicated ones to later sections.

Instruction Format and Machine Codes

For the PDP-11, some instructions have two operands and some have single or zero operands. As described in Chapter 1, a two-operands instruction has three fields: one for the operation code, and two for operands where the addresses of data are kept. The mnemonic operation code and operands are separated by one or more spaces; a comma is used to separate the operands. i.e.,

    ADD   R0, R1

In addition, for the sake of programming convenience, efficiency, and flexibility, two more optional fields can be defined by the programmer: **symbolic address** and **comment fields.** As far as the computer itself is concerned, the optional fields are meaningless because the CPU uses the numeric address at which this instruction statement is located in the memory. For example, if this instruction were stored at the address of 1000, the CPU would fetch and execute the instruction only when the content of the PC is pointing at this numeric address. In many cases, however, users prefer some symbolic addresses to which it is easier to refer. For example, if there is a shopping center at 1794 Sunrise Boulevard, we would rather refer to it with a specific name, say Sunrise Plaza, than as 1794 Sunrise Boulevard. Furthermore, for executing this instruction, all the CPU does is add the contents of R0 and R1 and put the sum in R1. It does not care what is in R0 and R1.

But we might use this same instruction in many places in a program. In many cases, we do wish to remind ourselves which action is for what purpose in the comment field. For instance, in one place we might have the price of merchandise in R0 and the tax value in R1. After execution of the instruction, we would have the total cost in R1. In another place, we might be referring to a savings account for which we have the principal in R0 and the interest in R1. Then we would have the total principal and interest in R1 after execution. We may have a program that looks like this:

Symbolic Address	Instructions		Comments
MER1:	ADD	R0, R1	;TOTAL COST
INCOME:	ADD	R0, R1	;PRINCIPAL AND INTEREST

Here, we use the PDP-11 convention; that is, we use the colon to separate the symbolic address from the mnemonic operation code, and the semicolon to separate the comment field from the operand. Note we have used MER1 for merchandise and INCOME for the calculation of the principal and interest as the symbolic addresses, respectively. Defining the symbolic address and comment fields is not an easy process. It requires some effort to make them useful to the programmer and to the user of the program.

What has been presented thus far are instructions in mnemonic form, but the computer understands only binary machine language. Therefore, for each instruction statement there is a unique corresponding machine code so that the CPU can interpret and execute the instruction. Each computer manufacturer has a unique set of instruction codes for each type of digital computer it produces. For PDP-11, there are about sixty-seven instructions plus a number of pseudoinstructions. The complete description of the **in-**

struction set for PDP-11 can be found in Appendix B or a programming card published by the Digital Equipment Corporation (DEC), the creator of PDP-11. For our example here, the machine code corresponding to the mnemonic instruction in binary and octal, respectively, can be shown as follows:

Mnemonic:	ADD	R0,	R1
		one memory word	

Binary:	0 1 1 0	0 0 0 0 0 0	0 0 0 0 0 1

Octal:	0 6	0 0	0 1

For discrimination purpose, the program written in mnemonic code is called the SOURCE program, while the latter two (binary and octal) are called OBJECT programs. Remember that the machine can read only the binary code; the octal code is the intermediate code for our convenience only.

Functional Classification of Instructions

A beginner might be fascinated with the availability of so many instructions and not know where to start. Therefore, it may be beneficial to classify instructions functionally so that one will have a clear idea of how many functions a given machine can offer a programmer.

Data Transfer This group of instructions is used to move or transfer data from one location to the other.

EXAMPLE 1 ————————————————————————————————

    MOV   R1, R3   ;   (R1) → R3

will move the contents of R1 to R3. The content of R1 will not be altered; however, the original content of R3 will be replaced by the original content of R1. Perhaps, to be more accurate, we should use COPY instead of MOV, but since this is defined by the designer of the machine, we will have to use MOV.

EXAMPLE 2 ————————————————————————————————

    MOV   #2, R5   ;   #2 → R5

will move the number 2 into R5.

Data Manipulation This group of instructions manipulates the data fetched from one or two locations on ALU and places the result into the designated address according to the instruction.   ■ ■

EXAMPLE 1 ————————————————————————————————

    SUB   A, R2   ;   (R2) − (A) → R2

will subtract the content at the symbolic memory address A from the content of R2 and place the difference in R2. The content of A is not altered, but the N, Z, V, and C flags of PSW will be set according to the result in R2.

EXAMPLE 2 _____

```
CMP     A, R2     ;(A) − (R2) and set
                  ;PSW according to
                  ;the result
```

will subtract the content of R2 from that of A and set the PSW flags accordingly. Note that at this time the contents of both A and R2 remain unchanged, and the content of A, or (A), the first operand, is subtracted by the second, (R2), which is just the reverse of the subtract instruction.   ∎ ∎

Logic Operation   This group of instructions logically manipulates the data fetched from one or two locations to ALU and places the result into the designated address according to the instruction.

EXAMPLE 1 _____

```
BIS     R4, A     ;     (R4) + (A) → A
```

will perform the OR-logical operation on the contents of R4 and A. To clarify the operation, let

$$(R4) = 1\ 000\ 000\ 000\ 000\ 101$$
$$(A)\ = 0\ 000\ 111\ 000\ 111\ 001$$

Then, after the execution,

$$(R4) = \text{no change}$$
$$(A)\ = 1\ 000\ 111\ 000\ 111\ 101$$

Note that wherever the bits in R4 are logic 1, the corresponding bits in A are set to logic 1, and the others are not altered. This is why the mnemonic code of this instruction is BIS, which stands for bit set.

EXAMPLE 2 _____

```
BIT     A, B     ;     (A)·(B) and SET PSW
```

will perform a logic AND operation on the contents of A and B, and set the flags in PSW accordingly. Let

$$(A) = 0\ 000\ 000\ 000\ 000\ 111$$
$$(B) = 1\ 101\ 111\ 110\ 001\ 000$$

Then after the execution,

$$(A) = \text{no change}$$
$$(B) = \text{no change}$$

But the flags in PSW are

$$\text{Carry: } C = \text{no change}$$
$$\text{Overflow: } V = 0$$
$$\text{Zero: } Z = 1$$
$$\text{Sign: } N = 0$$

■■

Note that in this example we wish to test whether the three least significant bits, $b_2b_1b_0$, of (B) are all zero or not. If yes, the zero flag will be 1; otherwise, $Z = 0$. This is why the mnemonic code for this instruction is BIT, which stands for bit or bits test.

Execution Sequence Control   This group of instructions allows the program to take a different course of execution according to the current condition or status of the PSW. This is the group of instructions for decision making. For example:

```
START:    MOV     #5, R0      ;INITIAL (R0) = 5
LOOP:     DEC     R0          ;(R0) − 1 → R0
          BNE     LOOP        ;IF Z FLAG OF PSW IS NOT 1,
                              ;BRANCH TO LOOP, OTHERWISE
                              ;CONTINUE
QUIT:     HALT                ;STOP THE COMPUTER OPERATION
```

This program uses the format described previously. Here, we use three symbolic addresses: START, LOOP, and QUIT. The action of the program can be described by the

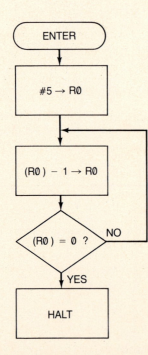

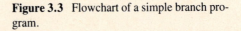

Figure 3.3 Flowchart of a simple branch program.

flowchart shown in Figure 3.3. The ellipsis symbols denote the entry or exit port of the program; the diamond symbol denotes the branch or decision-making process. The program operates as follows:

1. Initial the content of R0 to 5.
2. Decrement (R0) by one. The result can be either zero or not zero, and the Z flag of PSW will be set accordingly.
3. The sequence control instruction BNE (branch if not equal to zero) causes the CPU to examine the Z flag of PSW and act accordingly. Recall that $Z = 1$ (1 = true) implies that the result of executing the preceding instruction is TRUE zero, and $Z = 0$ (0 = false) implies that the result is not zero. Thus at this point, if $Z = 0$, then it is not zero. The program branches back to location, LOOP, and executes the DEC (decrement by 1) instruction again. This loop will be repeated until (R0) = 0 and $Z = 1$. The next instruction, HALT, is executed and the machine operation is stopped.

Pseudoinstructions or Directives   This group of instructions is quite different in nature from what we have described up to now. These instructions are not executable during program execution. Instead, they are executed by the system software, ASSEMBLER, before the program is set for execution. It may sound confusing, but some samples of this kind of instruction will make the idea clear.

EXAMPLE 1 _____

```
              .
              .
              .
    DATA:    .WORD    7, 16, 63    ;NOTE THE PERIOD SYMBOL
              .                    ;PRECEDES WORD. IT SHOULD
              .                    ;NOT BE NEGLECTED.
              .
```

Example 1 shows a program in which the pseudoinstruction .WORD has been used to place the data 7, 16, and 63, consecutively at the location, starting at the label DATA. If DATA = 1020, then the memory map for this section will be:

Numeric Address	Contents
.	.
.	.
.	.
10 20	00 00 07
10 22	00 00 16
10 24	00 00 63
.	.
.	.
.	.

Note that in many cases a program will consist of some data the programmers wish to be included within the program so that the program can use it during execution. The operands for this instruction are nothing but numbers, which we do not want the CPU to treat as a sequence of mnemonic instruction codes and try to execute. Therefore we should have some way to tell the CPU not to act upon these ''numbers,'' but just to use them as data for calculation. The instruction .WORD instructs the system software, assembler, to put these operands or data starting at the desirable location—say DATA in this example. Another simple example will illustrate a different kind of operation, but in the same class, pseudoinstruction.

EXAMPLE 2 _____

```
                  .
                  .
                  .
    RESULT:   .BLKW    n      ;N IS SOME DESIRABLE POSITIVE
                  .                 ;INTEGER
                  .
                  .
```

Example 2 shows that the programmer wishes the assembler to reserve n numbers of memory words, starting at the location labeled RESULT, for the program to place its results into these places during execution. Before execution, however, the system software will reserve a block of n words where zeros are placed initially.

EXAMPLE 3 _____

```
          .
          .
          .
    .END
```

Again, this is not an executable instruction during the program execution. It allows the programmer to communicate with the system program, assembler, to tell it that this is the end of the program so that the assembler knows where and when to stop its service.

Program Execution

In order to familiarize ourselves with how a program is executed, let us pretend to be the CPU and hand execute the simple example shown above under sequence control. For convenience, let us reproduce the program here.

```
    START:   MOV    #5, R0
    LOOP:    DEC    R0
             BNE    LOOP
    QUIT:    HALT
```

Basically, there are two essential cycles for executing a program: (1) the fetching cycle and (2) the executing cycle. First we have to be sure that the program we wish to execute is in the main memory waiting for action. Here, let us assume that the system software has loaded this program from the disk to the main memory, and that the designer of the system has decided that the first instruction of the program is always placed at a fixed location—say, 1000. Then, for our example we would have START = 1000, or the instruction MOV #5, R0 will be starting at location 1000 of the main memory. You will learn later in the addressing mode section that this instruction will occupy two memory words. However, the rest will occupy one word for each instruction. Thus, the whole program here will require five memory words or ten memory bytes. By consulting the instruction coding table, which you will learn in a later section on hand assembling, we can construct the machine codes or memory map of the program. For convenience, the program in mnemonics and the corresponding machine codes in the main memory, called the memory map, are shown below:

Source Program		Object Program in Main Memory (Memory Map)	
Symbolic Address	Instruction (mnemonic)	Numeric Address	Contents
START	MOV #5, R0	001000	012700
		001002	000005
LOOP	DEC R0	001004	005300
	BNE LOOP	001006	001376
QUIT	HALT	001010	000000

Note that the values shown in the numeric address column are in steps of two bytes, so they are always shown in even numbers. Unless an instruction is specifically on byte operation, the machine is addressed on a word basis.

For execution, we have to issue a command to one of the system programs that we wish it to execute the program starting at 1000. The format of the command varies from one system to the other. Typically, it can be 1000G, where G stands for GO. This command will cause the machine to put the value 1000 in PC; then the fetching and executing cycles follow.

Fetch Cycle

1. The contents of PC 1000 goes to MAR and (PC) is automatically incremented by 2.
2. The contents at the location specified by MAR goes to MDR then IR.
3. The control unit decodes the information in IR and determines if the instruction occupies one or two words. If the latter is true, then steps 1 and 2 are repeated.

In this example, the latter is true. Thus, the current contents of PC, 1002, goes to MAR; (PC) becomes 1004, and the contents at 1002, which is 000005, will go to MDR and then to ALU.

Execution Cycle   Since the whole instruction is now in CPU, the control unit starts to execute and place 5 in R0. As the execution cycle is completed, another fetch/execute cycle follows. Note that on executing the BNE   LOOP instruction, the CPU examines the Z flag. If Z = 0, the value of LOOP, which is 1004, is placed in PC, although the (PC) has been automatically incremented to 1010 during the fetching and executing of the instruction BNE   LOOP. However, if Z = 1, then the next instruction, HALT at 1010, will be fetched and executed. The machine will thus stop operation, and the value in PC will be updated to 1010 + 2 = 1012.

A Simple Application Program

In this section we will demonstrate how the instructions highlighted above can be put together to perform a specific task. The program shown below can pick out the bigger odd number of the two numbers located in N1 and N2, respectively, and store it at the location labeled ODDBIG. That is, if both numbers in N1 and N2 are odd, the bigger one is picked and stored in ODDBIG; if only one of the two numbers is odd, then the odd one is stored; and if none of the two is odd, then nothing should be done. The flowchart shown in Figure 3.4 suggests how the program can be developed.

An analysis of the problem specifications is now in order. First, since we do not normally wish to alter or accidentally alter the raw data, we will initially move the data to the general-purpose registers in the CPU for examination. There is another advantage of using general-purpose registers for data manipulation, that is, speed is a lot faster if the operation is kept within the CPU. Next, we will use the instruction BIT (bit test) to examine the least significant bit (LSB) of the number under examination. If the LSB is zero, then it is an even number. The source program to implement this task is shown as follows:

```
        ;This is a simple application program which
        ;demonstrates how a sequence of instructions with different
        ;functions can be put together to put the bigger odd
        ;number in a specific memory location.
D-1) ODDBIG: .BLKW 1          ;RESERVE ONE SPACE FOR RESULT
D-2) N1:      .WORD x         ;DATA SPACE, X IS AN INTEGER
D-3) N2:      .WORD y         ;DATA SPACE, Y IS AN INTEGER
 1) START:   MOV N1, R1       ;(N1) → R1
 2)          MOV N2, R2       ;(N2) → R2
 3)          MOV #1, R0       ;R0 AS THE LSB EXAMINATION MASK
 4) LOOK1:   BIT R0, R1       ;INSPECT LSB OF N1
 5)          BNE ODD2         ;(N1) IS ODD, GO AND CHECK N2
 6) LOOK2:   BIT R0, R2       ;INSPECT LSB OF N2
 7)          BNE STOREN2      ;STORE N2
 8)          BR QUIT          ;GO TO QUIT
 9) ODD2:    BIT R0, R2       ;IS BOTH (N1), (N2) ODD?
10)          BNE COMPR        ;YES, GO TO COMPARE
11) STOREN1:MOV R1, ODDBIG    ;STORE (N1)
12)          BR QUIT          ;GO TO QUIT
13) COMPR:   CMP R1, R2       ;COMPARE (N1), (N2)
14)          BGE STOREN1      ;(N1) ≥ (N2), STORE (N1)
15) STOREN2:MOV R2, ODDBIG    ;(N2) > (N1), STORE (N2)
16) QUIT:    HALT             ;FINISH
17) .END     START            ;END OF THE PROGRAM
```

Note that in lines 1, 2, 3, 11, and 15, we used a data transfer instruction (MOV) to initialize the registers R1, R2, R0 and store the result in ODDBIG, respectively. In lines 4, 6, 9, and 13, we used the logic operation instruction (BIT) for LSB inspection and the data manipulation instruction (CMP) to compare (N1) and (N2), respectively. In lines 5, 7, 10, and 14, we used the conditional sequence control instruction (BNE) to conditionally change the execution sequence. In lines 8 and 12, the unconditional branch instruc-

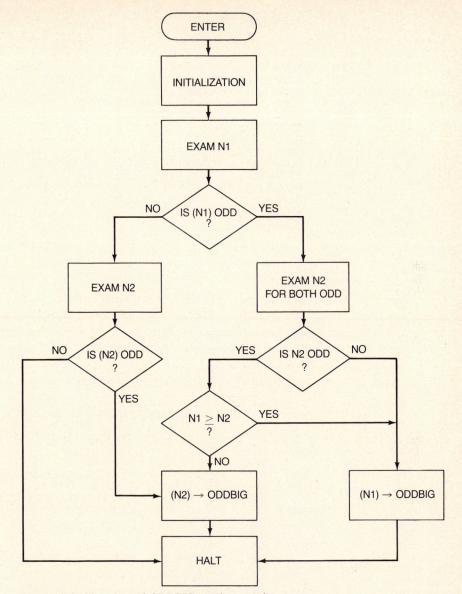

Figure 3.4 Flowchart of ODDBIG number search.

tion (BR) is used to terminate the execution. In line 16 we used the zero operand instruction HALT to stop the machine operation. In lines (D-1), (D-2), (D-3), and 17, we used pseudoinstructions to request the assembler to reserve a space called ODDBIG for result storage; put data x and y in N1, N2; and end the assembly process at line 17.

We have been using symbolic address technique here, since we do not really know where the system program is supposed to LOAD (put) this program in the memory. Actually, we don't really care where it puts the program if we are not interested in line-by-line **debugging** (trouble-shooting). You will learn later that there are several ways

```
                        ;THE BIG ODD NUMBER SEARCH
                        ;
                        ;
        START:   MOV     N1,R1           ;(N1) → R1
                 MOV     N2,R2           ;(N2) → R2
                 MOV     #1,R0           ;R0 IS THE LSB EXAMINATION MASK
        EXAM1:   BIT     R0,R1           ;EXAMINE LSB OF N1
                 BNE     ODD2            ;IF N1 IS ODD, CHECK N2
        EXAM2:   BIT     R0,R2           ;EXAMINE LSB OF N2
                 BNE     STON2
                 BR      QUIT
        ODD2:    BIT     R0,R2
                 BNE     COMPR           ;BOTH N1 N2 ARE ODD, SO COMPARE
        STON1:   MOV     R1,ODDBIG
                 BR      QUIT
        COMPR:   CMP     R1,R2
                 BGE     STON1
        STON2:   MOV     R2,ODDBIG
        QUIT:    HALT
        ODDBIG:  .BLKW  1
        N1:      .WORD 145
        N2:      .WORD 111
                 .END    START
```

Figure 3.5 Source file of the program ODDBIG with numeric example.

to pass the data x and y into the program. For the time being, we assume that the data is put in N1, N2 while we are preparing the program. The .END START instruction in the last line implies the pseudoinstruction; .END belongs to this program, which starts to execute at the address labeled START. Furthermore, since we know that in each line the

```
1                               ;THE BIG ODD NUMBER SEARCH
2                               ;
3                               ;
4   000000  016701  000050  START:   MOV    N1,R1        ;(N1) → R1
5   000004  016702  000046           MOV    N2,R2        ;(N2) → R2
6   000010  012700  000001           MOV    #1,R0        ;R0 IS THE LSB EXAMINATION MASK
7   000014  030001          EXAM1:   BIT    R0,R1        ;EXAMINE LSB OF N1
8   000016  001003                   BNE    ODD2         ;IF N1 IS ODD, CHECK N2
9   000020  030002          EXAM2:   BIT    R0,R2        ;EXAMINE LSB OF N2
10  000022  001010                   BNE    STON2
11  000024  000411                   BR     QUIT
12  000026  030002          ODD2:    BIT    R0,R2
13  000030  001003                   BNE    COMPR        ;BOTH N1 N2 ARE ODD, SO COMPARE
14  000032  010167  000014  STON1:   MOV    R1,ODDBIG
15  000036  000404                   BR     QUIT
16  000040  020102          COMPR:   CMP    R1,R2
17  000042  002373                   BGE    STON1
18  000044  010267  000002  STON2:   MOV    R2,ODDBIG
19  000050  000000          QUIT:    HALT
20  000052                  ODDBIG:  .BLKW  1
21  000054  000145          N1:      .WORD 145
22  000056  000111          N2:      .WORD 111
23          000000'                  .END    START
```

Result: Location ODDBIG contains 145

Figure 3.6 List file of the example ODDBIG number search.

CPU ignores the statement or comment following the semicolon symbol, we have freely put in message, comments, or notes preceded by the semicolon to remind ourselves all about the program we have created. This is a very useful option for the program user and creator.

Figure 3.5 shows the source file of this example with numeric data in N1 and N2; Figure 3.6 shows the corresponding list file and the execution result.

EXERCISES

3.1 Convert the following unsigned binary numbers into
   a. Octal number representations.
   b. Hexadecimal number representations.
   c. Decimal number representations.
   d. Binary code decimal (BCD) number representations.

$$1\ 1\ 0\ 0\ 1\ 0\ 0\ 0$$
$$1\ 1\ 1\ 0\ 0\ 1\ 0\ 1$$
$$1\ 1\ 1\ 0\ 1\ 1\ 0\ 0$$
$$1\ 1\ 1\ 0\ 1\ 1\ 0\ 0$$
$$1\ 1\ 1\ 0\ 1\ 1\ 1\ 1$$
$$0\ 0\ 1\ 0\ 0\ 0\ 0\ 0$$
$$1\ 0\ 1\ 0\ 0\ 0\ 0\ 1$$

3.2 Repeat 3.1, but treat the data as sign magnitude binary numbers.

3.3 Using Appendix A, convert the data given in 3.1 into characters. You may assume that the data given are in ASCII and that the most significant bit is the odd parity bit.

3.4 Convert the following decimal numbers into octal, binary, and hexadecimal number representations, respectively.

64000	32000	16000	-128	-256
121	-12	8	20	-10

3.5 Convert the numbers given in 3.4 into ones complement, twos complement, and eights complement representations, respectively.

3.6 Use twos complement and eights complement to perform the following arithmetic operations.
   a. $64000_{10} - 63210_{10} = ?$
   b. $20_{10} - 128_{10} = ?$
   c. $-12_{10} + 8_{10} = ?$
   d. $-256_{10} - 128_{10} = ?$
   e. $16000_{10} + 32121_{10} = ?$

3.7 Express the results of 3.6 in the PDP-11 16-bit memory word frame. Your answers should be packed into 16-bit binary forms; also show them in their equivalent octal number representations. You do not need to change them into sign magnitude representations.

3.8 Write a program in PDP-11 assembly language to search for the smaller number of an array of two elements which can be any integer, and place it at the location labeled SMALL. Show your work in both flowchart and source file formats.

3.9 Write a program in PDP-11 assembly language that will rearrange an array of four ASCII characters in alphabetic order and store it at the location, with its starting address labeled DIRECT, as in "directory." Show your work in flowchart format, and then the corresponding source program.

Chapter 4

A Close Look at the Instruction Set

This chapter describes the instruction set for the PDP-11 in great detail. First, we describe the important and potentially confusing subject of addressing modes, with many examples. Next, a set of examples is used as the vehicle to illustrate the applications of the instruction set. Finally, the concepts of relocatable address and position independent code are introduced. It is however strongly recommended that the reader reads the appendix on RSX-11 operating system concurrently with this chapter.

KEY WORDS

absolute addressing	memory address reference
branch instruction	PIC
direct addressing	push/pop operation
effective address	register reference
execution map	relative addressing
hand assemble	relocatable address
immediate mode	SOB-instruction
indirect or deferred addressing	stack memory

4.1 INTRODUCTION

In Chapter 3, we briefly noted the characteristics of the instruction set in the functional sense. We are somewhat familiar with two-operand instructions such as ADD A,B. Now, let us take a closer look at this instruction. Recall that we have religiously accepted that this instruction occupies two memory words, and that we never have a chance to ask why. We were able to code this instruction by a 16-bit word, as follows:

$$b_{15}..b_{12} \qquad b_{11}......b_6 \qquad b_5........b_0$$

OP. CODE   1ST OPERAND   2ND OPERAND

Note that there are three fields: (1) operation code, 4 bits; (2) first or source operand, 6 bits; and (3) second or destination operand, 6 bits. As it is, we could have only $2^4 = 16$ different operation codes, $2^6 = 64$ locations for source operands, and $2^6 = 64$ locations for destination operands. It is obvious that a computer with such a limited capacity would not be acceptable, even as a toy. The solution to this limitation is that, instead of putting the actual address values in the operand fields, we merely provide the information for determining address in the operand fields and request the CPU to calculate the actual or **effective address** by a set of rules. The price we have to pay is to expand the fetching cycle into two steps: (1) fetch instruction, and (2) calculate the effective addresses of the operands. Thus the entire fetch and execute cycles will be:

1. $(PC) \rightarrow MAR$.
   $(PC) + 2 \rightarrow PC$.
2. $(MDR) \rightarrow IR$.
3. Calculate the effective address for the source operand.
4. Calculate the effective address for the destination operand.
5. Execute the instruction.

The rules used for calculating effective addresses vary from one machine to another. Usually, the more powerful a machine is, the more complex rules it has. As expected, the addressing rules for the PDP-11 are fairly complex. However, investing a bit of effort in learning the addressing rules for PDP-11 instruction set brings rich rewards later in programming PDP-11 with assembly language. This set of rules is called the addressing modes for PDP-11.

4.2 ADDRESSING MODES

There are three general classes of addressing techniques: (1) register reference, (2) memory address reference, and (3) mixed register and memory address reference. For each class, there are a number of addressing modes. In general, the **register reference** is faster in operational speed, while the **memory reference** consists of a significantly larger addressing space. For PDP-11, there are three different formats, defined below.

EXAMPLE 2 _____

| Mnemonic code: | COMB R4 | ;(LO-BYTE of R4)→R4 |
| Octal machine code: | 1051 | ;0-Mode, Rn = R4 |

BEFORE	AFTER
R4:	R4:
00 010 010 ¦ 10 010 010	00 010 010 ¦ 01 101 101
←HI BYTE→¦←LO BYTE→	←HI BYTE→¦←LO BYTE→
(PC) ──────────────→	PC = (PC) + 2

This is a byte-complement operation, which needs special attention. First, note that the MSB of the machine code always is 1 for byte operation, and the instruction here implies the low-byte of R4, therefore only the low-byte of R4 is complemented.   ■ ■

Mode 1: Indirect Addressing   Indirect, also known as **deferred addressing,** is somewhat like the "care of" operation in the U.S. Postal Service system. That is, the address shown is not the real address of the receiver, but that of the receiver's friend or relative.

EXAMPLE _____

| Mnemonic code: | CLR @R5 | ;@R5 = (R5) |
| Octal machine code: | 0050 15 | ;MODE-1, Rn = R5 |

Note that the address of the operand shown is not R5 but @R5, which is equal to (R5). That is, the @R5 is equivalently equal to "C/O R5" in U.S. Postal Service notation. Thus the real address of the operand is the content of R5, not R5. The execution map will show the action.

BEFORE		AFTER	
(PC) ──────────→		PC = (PC) + 2	
(R5): 00 17 00 ─┐		(R5) = N.C.	
Memory Map:			
Address	Contents	Address	Contents
•	•	•	•
•	•	•	•
•	•	•	•
•	•	•	•
•	•	•	•
00 17 00	00 11 00	00 17 00	00 00 00
•	•	•	•
•	•	•	•
•	•	•	•
•	•	•	•
•	•	•	•

(CLR)

For this instruction, the CPU first discovers that it is an indirect addressing mode via R5, so that it will copy the contents of R5 into MAR and clear the contents at that location.

■■

Mode 2: Indirect Addressing with Post Auto Increment This is an indirect addressing process plus a *post* auto increment of the register involved. That is, the content of the register involved is automatically incremented by 2 (by 1 if it is a byte operation) *afterward*. It is important to point out that the PDP-11 does not provide a "pre auto increment" addressing mode. Here the symbol "( ) + " denotes the post increment and indirect addressing.

EXAMPLE 1: ───────────────────────────────────────

Mnemonic code: CLR (R5) +
Octal machine code: 00 50 25   ;Mode-2, Rn = R5

As shown in the execution map below, first the CPU discovers that it is a mode-2 operation. Thus, it would copy the content of R5 into MAR, clear the content of the memory word addressed by (R5), and finally increment the contents of R5 by 2.

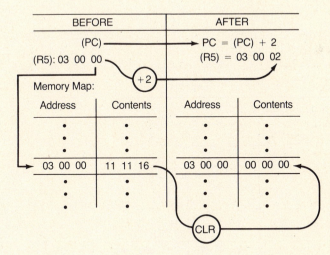

■■

EXAMPLE 2 ───────────────────────────────────────

Mnemonic code: ADD (R2) + , R4
Octal machine code: 06 22, 04

Note that this instruction involves mode 2 and mode 0 addresses. The source operand field has mode 2, while the destination operand has mode 0. The execution map follows:

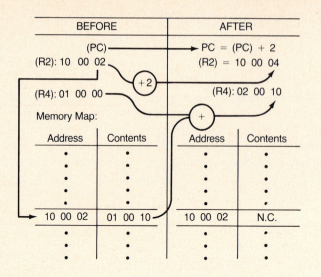

EXAMPLE 3: Operation on Byte _____

This example shows the byte operation of the auto increment. Here, the content of the register involved is auto-incremented by 1 instead of 2 after the operation code is executed.

Mnemonic code: CLRB (R5) +
Octal machine code: 1050 25

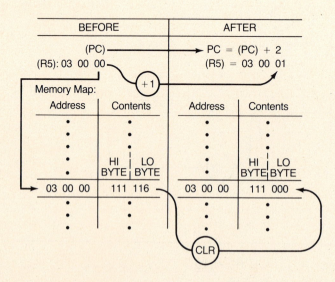

Note that the address of low-byte is 03 00 00, while that of hi-byte is 03 00 01.

Mode 3: Double Indirect Addressing with Post Auto Increment This mode has two levels of indirect addressing. The content of the register involved is automatically incremented by 2 (by 1 if it is a byte operation) afterward. If we use the U.S. Postal Service analogy again, we would have "C/O" twice. Notice that the symbol "@( ) + " is used, since it is a double indirect addressing plus post auto increment.

EXAMPLE

Mnemonic code: INC @(R2) +

Octal machine code: 0052 32

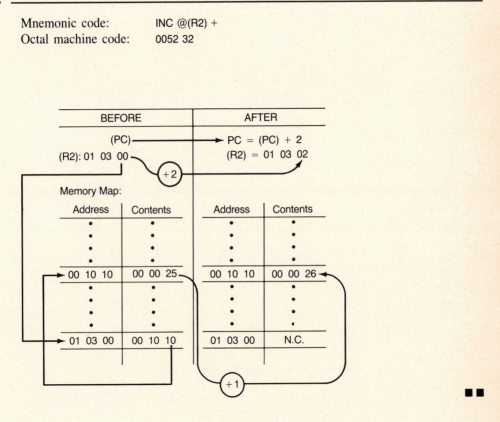

Mode 4: Indirect Addressing with Pre Auto Decrement In this mode, an auto-decremented action is taken before any other operation. That is, the content of the register involved is decremented by 2 (by 1 for byte operation) before any other action. Here the symbol "−( )" is used. It is important to point out that PDP-11 does not provide "Post auto decrement" addressing mode.

EXAMPLE 1

Mnemonic code: INC − (R0)

Octal machine code: 0052 40

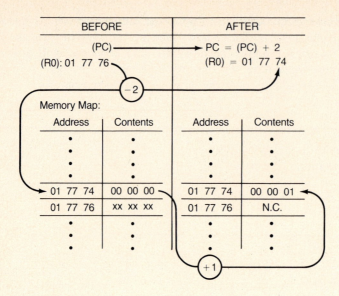

EXAMPLE 2: Operation on Byte _____

Mnemonic code: INCB − (R0)   ;BYTE OPERATION
Octal machine code: 1052 40

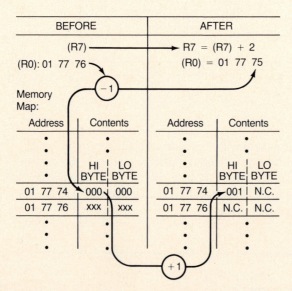

where (PC), the original

de

The execution map can t

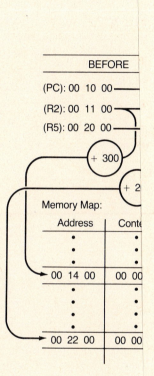

	BEFORE	
(PC): 00 10 00		
(R2): 00 11 00		
(R5): 00 20 00		

+ 300

+ 2

Memory Map:

Address	Conte
00 14 00	00 00
00 22 00	00 00

Mode 7: Double Indirect A
ment, the index mode has

EXAMPLE

Mnemonic code: A

Octal machine code: 0(
                       0(

Note that the source oper
thus the octal code is 71.
code is 02.

Mode 5: Double Indirect Addressing with Pre Auto Decrement   In this mode, there is two-level indirect addressing with pre auto decrement. That is, the content of the register involved is first decremented by 2 (by 1 for byte operation) and the double indirect addressing follows; thus the notation "$@ - (\ )$" is used.

EXAMPLE

Mnemonic code: COM @ − (R0)
Octal machine code: 0051 50

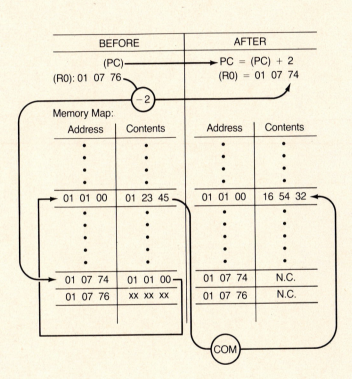

BEFORE		AFTER	
(PC)		PC = (PC) + 2	
(R0): 01 07 76		(R0) = 01 07 74	

−2

Memory Map:

Address	Contents	Address	Contents
01 01 00	01 23 45	01 01 00	16 54 32
01 07 74	01 01 00	01 07 74	N.C.
01 07 76	xx xx xx	01 07 76	N.C.

COM

Mode 6: Indirect Addressing with Index Mode   In this mode, the instruction occupies two memory words, with the value of the index in the second word and the instruction code in the first.

EXAMPLE 1

Mnemonic code: CLR 300(R5)
Octal machine code: 0050 65   ;IN FIRST MEMORY WORD
                       0003 00   ;IN SECOND MEMORY WORD

Here, the CPU woul

e

where   INDEX = a
         Rn =

and since this instru
would always be in
original content of th
is at 1000. Then the

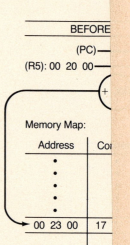

BEFORE
(PC)—
(R5): 00 20 00—

Memory Map:

Address	Co
⋮	⋮
00 23 00	17

EXAMPLE 2

Mnemonic code:
Octal machine code:

Since this instruction
ing, it must occupy
second for the index
contents of the PC w

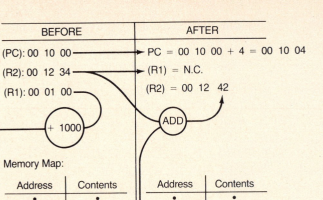

BEFORE	AFTER
(PC): 00 10 00	PC = 00 10 00 + 4 = 00 10 04
(R2): 00 12 34	(R1) = N.C.
(R1): 00 01 00	(R2) = 00 12 42

Memory Map:

Address	Contents	Address	Contents
⋮	⋮	⋮	⋮
00 10 50	00 00 06	00 10 50	N.C.
⋮	⋮	⋮	⋮
00 11 00	00 10 50	00 11 00	N.C.

Program Counter (PC)/Memory References Modes

The addressing modes discussed thus far have never directly involved the content of R7 or PC in the effective address calculation. In what follows, we present another group of addressing modes that use nothing but the content of PC to determine the effective address of the operand or operands. Since the value of PC is continuously being updated, it is somewhat difficult to keep track of it. However, because of the flexibility and power of these types of addressing techniques, it is worth investing the effort to learn them. Recall that there are six bits for each operand field to provide the information for address calculation: 3 leftmost bits for mode and 3 rightmost bits for the register involved. In this case we use only PC or R7, so it is obvious that the second octal digit would always be 7.

Mode 2: Immediate Mode   The **immediate mode** is normally used in the source operand field. Its expression is used to evaluate the data, not the effective address. This is useful when the programmer wishes to have some constant number or value placed next to the instruction concerned. For instance, when we want to initialize some register or memory location with a constant, we normally use this mode to achieve it.

EXAMPLE 1 _____

Mnemonic code: MOV   #1000, R1
Octal machine code: 01 27 01   ;OCCUPIES 2 MEMORY WORDS
                        00 10 00

Note that this instruction occupies two words, with the instruction code in the first and the number or constant, 1000, in the second. The source operand is using immediate mode (mode 2) and the register involved is R7. Thus the code is 27. The destination operand uses mode 0 and involves R1; thus the code is 01. A few words about the former are in order. Examine the instruction. It reveals no R7. Then why did we say that the R7 or PC is involved? Recall that while the machine is fetching a memory word, the (PC) is automatically incremented by 2. In this example, when the MOV instruction is in the CPU, the (PC) is already pointing at the next word, which in this case is the number 1000. For execution, having realized the code 27 in the source operand field, the CPU just "blindly" fetches whatever the (PC) is pointing at into R1. Here, PC is in fact the "underground hero" who has the "intelligence" to know where to get the data for action. Of course, while the CPU is getting the number 1000, the (PC) is again automatically incremented by 2. The execution map follows:

BEFORE		AFTER	
(PC): 00 11 00		PC = 00 11 00 + 4 = 00 11 04	
(R1): xx xx xx		(R1) = 00 10 00	
Memory Map:			
Address	Contents	Address	Contents
•	•	•	•
•	•	•	•
•	•	•	•
•	•	•	•
00 11 00	01 27 01	00 11 00	N.C.
00 11 02	00 10 00	00 11 02	N.C.
•	•	•	•
•	•	•	•
•	•	•	•
•	•	•	•

■■

EXAMPLE 2 _____

Mnemonic code: ADD #100, R2
Octal machine code: 06 27 02
                        00 01 00

and

$$RD = A - UD(PC) = 1100 - 1004 = 74$$

The execution map can then be shown as follows:

BEFORE		AFTER	
(PC): 00 10 00		PC = 00 10 04	
A: 00 11 00		A = N.C.	
Memory Map:			
Address	Contents	Address	Contents
•	•	•	•
•	•	•	•
•	•	•	•
00 10 00	00 52 67	00 10 00	N.C.
00 10 02	R.D. = 74	00 10 02	N.C.
•	•	•	•
•	•	•	•
•	•	•	•
•	•	•	•
00 11 00	00 10 07	00 11 00	00 10 10
•	•	•	•
•	•	•	•
•	•	•	•
•	•	•	•

INC

Here, the effective address of the operand is calculated during the fetching cycle, as follows:

$$\text{effective address} = UD(PC) + RD = 1004 + 74 = 1100$$

Case 2. The value of A is less than (PC), or the destination address is behind the address of the instruction:

(PC):   1000
   A: 0120
 (A):   1007

then the RD will be a negative number whose twos complement equivalent value can be calculated as follows: Since

$$UD(PC) = 1000 + 4 = 1004$$
$$RD = 120 - 1004$$

let us now convert the sign magnitude of UD(PC) into an eights complement, as follows:

$$
\begin{array}{ll}
\text{S/M:} & \boxed{1}0\ 10\ 04 \\
\overline{7}: & \quad 7\ 67\ 73 \\
& \qquad +1 \\
\overline{8}: & \boxed{1}7\ 67\ 74
\end{array}
$$

Then RD is calculated as shown below:

$$
\begin{array}{r}
00\ 01\ 20 \\
+\ \boxed{1}7\ 67\ 74 \\
\hline
\boxed{1}7\ 71\ 14
\end{array}
$$

And the execution map is:

BEFORE	AFTER
(PC): 00 10 00	PC = 1000 + 4 = 00 10 04
A: 00 01 20	A = N.C.

Memory Map:

Address	Contents	Address	Contents
•	•	•	•
•	•	•	•
•	•	•	•
00 01 20	00 10 07	00 01 20	00 10 10
•	•	•	•
•	•	•	•
•	•	•	•
•	•	INC	•
•	•	•	•
00 10 00	00 52 67	00 52 67	N.C.
00 10 02	17 71 14	17 71 14	N.C.

Here, the effective address of the operand is calculated during the fetching cycle as follows:

$$
\begin{aligned}
\text{effective address} &= UD(PC) + RD \\
&= 1004 + 17\ 71\ 14 = 00\ 01\ 20
\end{aligned}
$$

which agrees with the destination address A. ■ ■

EXAMPLE 2 _____

This example shows how a program starting at location 0000 can be hand assembled.

```
START:    MOV A, B
          HALT
A:        .WORD 6
B:        .BLKW 1
          .END START
```

First, let us determine how many memory words are required for this program:

1. The first instruction has two operands, and both use the relative addressing mode, so it requires three words.
2. The rest of the instructions all require one word each.
3. Since START = 0000, then we have A = 10; B = 12.

Next, let us determine the RD for A and B, respectively: The RD for A is

$$A - UD(PC)$$

where A = 10.

$$UD = (PC) + 4 = 0 + 4 = 4$$

Since, while the CPU is fetching (A), the (PC) is already incremented and pointing at the next word, whose address is 4, the RD for A is

$$A - UD(PC) = 10 - 4 = 4$$

Similarly, the RD for B is

$$B - UD(PC) = B - [(PC) + 6]$$
$$= 12 - [0 + 6] = 4$$

By consulting the machine code of the instruction set, the list file of this program, specified as ⟨example2.LST⟩, can be hand assembled as follows:

Memory Map		Source Code	
Address	Contents	Address	Mnemonic Instruction
00 00 00	01 67 67	START	MOV A, B
00 00 02	00 00 04		
00 00 04	00 00 04		
00 00 06	00 00 00		HALT
00 00 10	00 00 06	A	.WORD 6
00 00 12	00 00 00	B	.BLKW 1

EXAMPLE 3

This example shows the effects of different addresses of the destination operands on the calculation of the relative distance values. Let us place the data before the first instruction, as follows:

```
A:          .WORD 6
B:          .BLKW 1
START:      MOV A, B
HALT
.END START
```

Here, we have

```
A = 0         ,     (A) = 6
B = 2         ,     (B) = 0
START = 4
```

Thus, the RD for A and B can be calculated as follows:

$$A - UD(PC) = 0 - [4 + 4]$$
$$= 0 - 10 = -10(S/M) = 17\ 77\ 70\ (\bar{8})$$

Similarly, the RD for B = $177770(\bar{8})$.
Accordingly, the list file can be constructed:

Memory Map		Source Code	
Address	Contents	Address	Contents
00 00 00	00 00 06	A	.WORD 6
00 00 02	00 00 00	B	.BLKW 1
00 00 04	01 67 67	START	MOV A, B
00 00 06	17 77 70		
00 00 10	17 77 70		
00 00 12	00 00 00		HALT

■ ■

It is interesting to point out that for both Examples 2 and 3, if we assume that the beginning address of the program is 1172 instead of zero, we could calculate the RD values in the same way as shown above. That is, for examples 2 and 3, respectively, we would have the following.

For Example 2:

$$RD \text{ for } A = 1202 - (1172 + 4) = 4$$
$$RD \text{ for } B = 1204 - (1172 + 6) = 4$$

For Example 3:

$$RD \text{ for } A = 1172 - (1176 + 4) = 4 = -10 \text{ (S/M)} = 17\ 77\ 70\ (\bar{8})$$
$$RD \text{ for } B = 1174 - (1176 + 6) = -10 \text{ (S/M)} = 17\ 77\ 70\ (\bar{8})$$

Note that the RD values are independent of where the program begins in the memory. This is most helpful for the "task building" or "linking" process (TKB) in program development. Another good feature of the relative addressing mode is that the programmer does not have to worry about changing the operand address expression if, between the instruction in question and the destination address, some instructions have to be deleted or inserted. The programmer can still use the same symbolic address while letting the assembler readjust the RD values. The next two examples illustrate.

EXAMPLE 4 _____

Let us use the absolute addressing mode to implement the same program shown in Example 3.

Numeric Address	Source Code
00 00 00	.WORD 6
00 00 02	.BLKW 1
00 00 04	MOV @#0, @#2
00 00 06	
00 00 10	
00 00 12	HALT

This program would serve the same function until the beginning address is changed. For instance, if we load the program beginning at 1172, then we must change the operands of MOV from @#0, @#2 to @#1172, @#1174. Otherwise, it would never work.

EXAMPLE 5 _____

Using Example 2, let us pretend that we wish to divide the contents of B after the MOV operation.

```
START:   MOV A,B
         ASR B          ;ARITHMETIC RIGHT SHIFT HAS
                        ;THE EFFECT OF DIVIDE-BY-2
         HALT
A:       .WORD 6
B:       .BLKW 1
         .END START
```

Here, the instruction of ASR B would occupy two words, and thus the address values of A and B would be pushed 4 bytes higher. That is, A would change from 00 00 10 to 00 00 14, while B would change from 00 00 12 to 00 00 16. Since we are using the relative addressing mode here, we have nothing to worry about. We simply reassemble it by calling the assembler, which would put the proper RD values in the proper places. Had we used the absolute addressing mode, we would have had to change the operand expression of the MOV instruction. ■ ■

Mode 7: Relative Deferred (Indirect) Addressing This mode is nothing but an extension of mode 6 by adding an indirect addressing level to the operand.

EXAMPLE _____

Mnemonic code:	CLR @A
Octal machine code:	0050 77
	RD

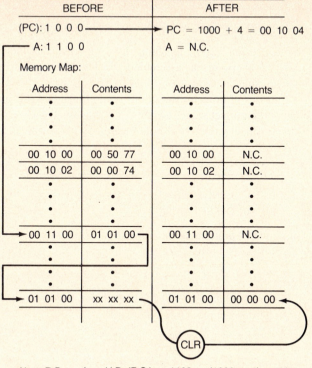

BEFORE		AFTER	
(PC): 1 0 0 0		PC = 1000 + 4 = 00 10 04	
A: 1 1 0 0		A = N.C.	

Memory Map:

Address	Contents	Address	Contents
•	•	•	•
•	•	•	•
•	•	•	•
•	•	•	•
00 10 00	00 50 77	00 10 00	N.C.
00 10 02	00 00 74	00 10 02	N.C.
•	•	•	•
•	•	•	•
•	•	•	•
•	•	•	•
00 11 00	01 01 00	00 11 00	N.C.
•	•	•	•
•	•	•	•
•	•	•	•
•	•	•	•
01 01 00	xx xx xx	01 01 00	00 00 00

CLR

Note: R.D. = A − U.D. (P.C.) = 1100 − (1000 + 4) = 74

■ ■

Addressing of Branch Instructions

A **branch instruction** is a single address instruction that commonly uses the relative addressing mode but occupies only one memory word. The high-byte is the operation code field, and the low-byte is the offset field:

$b_{15} \bullet \ \bullet \ \bullet \ \bullet \ \bullet \ b_8 | b_7 \bullet \ \bullet \ \bullet \ \bullet \ \bullet \ b_0$

OP CODE	OFFSET (2)

The offset value is one-half of the relative distance between the updated (PC) and the destination. The offset value is in twos complement representation. Positive implies "ahead" of the updated (PC), whereas negative implies "behind" the updated (PC):

$$\text{destination} = \text{UD(PC)} + \text{RD} = \text{UD(PC)} + 2(\text{OFFSET})$$

the starting address of the destination data array, to R2. Instruction 6, using the auto increment addressing mode, copies data from A array to B array, one at a time. Each time a datum is transferred, the pointers R1 and R2 are incremented by 2 and pointing to the next datum. Following each datum transfer, instruction 7 decrements (R0) by one. Instruction 8, branch to loop if not equal to zero, uses a conditional branch instruction and the relative addressing mode. It examines the result of the DEC instruction by checking the Z flag of PSW. If the result of execution of the DEC instruction is nonzero (that is, if $Z = 0$), it implies that the data transfer is not finished. Therefore the execution branches to the symbolic address, LOOP. The data transfer operation repeats itself until $(R0) = 0$, at which time the program moves to instruction 9 and stops the program execution. Figure 4.1 shows the list file of this program. The student should check the octal codes for each addressing mode used, as well as the relative distance values for the relative addressing mode and the offset value for the branch instruction.   ■ ■

Addressing of SOB Instruction   This instruction is particularly useful for writing a LOOP program. It is a two-address instruction:

SOB   Rn, dst

where

Rn = nth register for $n = 0, 1, \ldots, 5$

dst = destination that must be ''behind'' or whose value must be less than the UD(PC)

The instruction functions as follows: Subtract Rn by one; if not zero, branch to dst; otherwise execute the next instruction. It has the following format:

OFFSET − field = $b_0 \ldots b_5$, R$_n$ − field = $b_6 b_7 b_8$,
OP code − field = $b_9 \ldots b_{15} = 077$

Note that in this instruction the offset value is unsigned, because it always branches backward so that the maximum range is $2^6 - 1 = 63$. Thus the maximum RD value is 126 bytes.

```
 1                                                      ;THIS EXAMPLE USES 'BNE' TO CONTROL A LOOP
 2                                                      ;
 3                                                      ;
 4 000000  000000  000001  000002   A:       .WORD   0,1,2,3,4,5,6,7
    000006  000003  000004  000005
    000014  000006  000007
 5 000020                            B:       .BLKW   10
 6 000040  012700  000010            START:   MOV     #10,R0           ;R0 IS THE COUNTER
 7 000044  012701  000000'                     MOV     #A,R1            ;R1 IS THE POINTER TO ARRAY A
 8 000050  012702  000020'                     MOV     #B,R2            ;R2 IS THE POINTER TO ARRAY B
 9 000054  012122             LOOP:   MOV     (R1)+,(R2)+      ;COPY ARRAY A TO ARRAY B
10 000056  005300                              DEC     R0
11 000060  001375                              BNE     LOOP
12 000062  000000                              HALT
13          000040'                            .END    START
```

Figure 4.1   Copy data array using branch loop.

```
 1                                              ;THIS EXAMPLE USES 'SOB' TO CONTROL A LOOP
 2                                              ;
 3                                              ;
 4 000000  000000  000001  000002  A:          .WORD 0,1,2,3,4,5,6,7
   000006  000003  000004  000005
   000014  000006  000007
 5 000020                          B:          .BLKW 10
 6 000040  012700  000010  START:  MOV    #10,R0          ;R0 IS THE COUNTER
 7 000044  012701  000000'         MOV    #A,R1           ;R1 IS THE POINTER TO ARRAY A
 8 000050  012702  000020'         MOV    #B,R2           ;R2 IS THE POINTER TO ARRAY B
 9 000054  012122           LOOP:  MOV    (R1)+,(R2)+     ;COPY ARRAY A TO ARRAY B
10 000056  077002                  SOB    R0,LOOP
11 000060  000000                  HALT
12         000040'                  .END START
```

Figure 4.2 Copy data array using SOB-instruction.

EXAMPLE ───

This instruction can be used to replace instructions 7 and 8 of Example 3 in the preceding subsection. Figure 4.2 shows its list file. ■ ■

Limitations of the Branch Instruction Since the branch instruction requires only one memory word, the branching range or distance is limited by the 8-bit offset value. Therefore we must be sure that the branching distance is within the limit before using a branch instruction. Figure 4.3 shows the list file of a program that illustrates the problem. Note that the distance between location A and the updated (PC) of the instruction at location B is $1002 - 400 = 402$, which is greater than 400, the branching-backward limit. Thus the ASSEMBLER detected the error and classified it as an ''A-error'' as marked. An A-error is defined in the PDP-11 user's manual as: ''Address in instruction incorrect or relocation error.'' However, the distance between START: and B: is within the limit; therefore line 9 of the list file has no problem. To avoid this kind of problem, we could use a JUMP instruction instead of BRANCH. The next section describes the use of the JUMP instruction.

Addressing of JMP Instruction This is somewhat like the unconditional branch instruction except that it occupies two memory words, with the relative distance value stored in the second word. Thus it has a range of ± 32 thousand bytes or ± 16 thousand words. When the branch instruction fails, the JMP instruction should be used.

```
  1                                   ;THIS EXAMPLE SHOWS THE LIMIT OF BRANCH INSTRUCTIONS
  2                                   ;
  3                                   ;
  4 000000            BLOCK1:  .BLKW  200
  5 000400  000000    A:       HALT              ;A IS TOO DISTANT FROM B
  6 000402            BLOCK2:  .BLKW  177
A 7 001000  000777    B:       BR     A
  8 001002            BLOCK3:  .BLKW  37
  9 001100  000737    START:   BR     B
 10         001100'            .END   START
```

Figure 4.3 Limitation of branch instruction.

EXAMPLE _____

Mnemonic code: JMP A
Octal machine code: 0001 dst
                       RD

Where dst field specifies the addressing mode and the register involved, and RD△ relative distance value.

EXAMPLE _____

```
            .
            .
            .
        JMP A
            .
            .
            .
A:      HALT
            .
            .
        .END
```

Upon execution of the jump instruction, the effective address or the value of A is loaded into PC, and the program then starts to execute the instruction located at A.   ■■

Addressing of Stack Memory Using R6   When we gain some experience in programming, we all become more and more appreciative of the availability of general-purpose registers and even feel that we wish there were more than just R0, R1, . . . , R5. When we are doing calculations on paper, we often use scratch paper to do some side calculation to keep the main calculation neat. The stack memory concept is somewhat like a "scratch pad" in a computer. It can be used to store short-term data. We may think of the stack memory as an extension of the general-purpose register bank except that the registers reside in the CPU, whereas the stack memory is in the main memory. Here is how it works.

In the main memory we reserve an area, say 256 words, which we use exclusively for short-term purposes. For it, a register, R6, is assigned to be the pointer of this special area. This area is called **stack memory,** also known as scratch pad or cache memory. R6 is thus called the **stack pointer (SP).** The SP functions like the PC,(R7), but the former is the pointer for stack memory, while the latter is the pointer for the general memory area. For a typical PDP-11 system, the main memory has a capacity of 64K bytes and is addressed by a 16-bit register. The memory area with the address form 00 00 00 to some value, say 00 11 72, is reserved for system software. The rest of the main memory is for programs.

The stack memory is usually assigned to the area with an address from, say, 00 11 72, backward for 256 words. Accordingly, the SP is initialized by the system to 1172 and then progresses backward, while PC would start from 1172 and progress forward. When the main memory is configured this way, the SP is normally initialized by the system to 00 11 72; otherwise, initialization would be the programmer's responsibility.

Now, let us try to store (write) and retrieve (read) information into and from the stack memory through R6 or SP. We need only two instructions, one for WRITE and the other for READ. Since for WRITE we are really "pushing" information into the stack and for READ we are really "popping" information out of the stack, the operations are also known as PUSH and POP.

For PUSH, we use:

MOV src, −(SP)

That is, the contents of the source operand is being copied into the memory located at the current (SP) minus 2. Assume that the SP has been initialized with 1172. Then the source operand would be PUSHED into 1170.

EXAMPLE 1 _____

The program that follows will save the contents of the registers R0, R1, and R2 in the stack:

```
START:    MOV R0, −(SP)    ;PUSH (R0)
          MOV R1, −(SP)    ;PUSH (R1)
          MOV R2, −(SP)    ;PUSH (R2)
          HALT
          .END START
```

Its execution map follows:

Before Program Execution	After Program Execution
(PC): 00 11 72	(PC) = 00 12 02
(SP): 00 11 72	(SP) = 00 11 64
(R0): 00 10 10	(R0) = N.C.
(R1): 00 11 00	(R1) = N.C.
(R2): 00 12 34	(R2) = N.C.

	Address	Contents	Address	Contents
	.	.	.	.
	.	.	.	.
	.	.	.	.
	.	.	.	.
	00 11 60	xx xx xx	00 11 60	xx xx xx
	00 11 62	xx xx xx	00 11 62	xx xx xx
	00 11 64	xx xx xx	00 11 64	00 12 34 ←— (SP)
	00 11 66	xx xx xx	00 11 66	00 11 00
	00 11 70	xx xx xx	00 11 70	00 10 10
(SP) (PC)	00 11 72	01 00 46	00 11 72	N.C.
	00 11 74	01 01 46	00 11 74	N.C.
	00 11 76	01 02 46	00 11 76	N.C.
	00 12 00	00 00 00	00 11 00	N.C.
	00 12 02	xx xx xx	00 11 02	N.C. ←——— (PC)
	.	.	.	.
	.	.	.	.
	.	.	.	.

Note that after execution, (SP) is pointing at the address of 00 11 64, whereas (PC) is pointing at 00 12 02. In the stack memory, three "layers" of information have been stored; the last piece of information, (R2), is on the top layer.   ■ ■

For POP, we use

MOV (SP)+, dst

where dst $\underline{\Delta}$ destination operand. That is, the contents of the top layer in the stack is copied into destination, and the (SP) is auto incremented by 2.

EXAMPLE 2

Let us use the result of the preceding example as the initial condition, but let us assume that for some reason, the contents of R0, R1, and R2 have been changed. We wish to restore the original contents of R0, R1, and R2 which were saved in the stack. We may write the following program to achieve it.

```
START:   MOV (SP)+, R2    ;POP
         MOV (SP)+, R1    ;POP
         MOV (SP)+, R0    ;POP
         HALT
         .END START
```

The execution map follows:

Before Program Execution		After Program Execution	
(PC): 00 11 72		(PC) = 00 12 02	
(SP): 00 11 64		(SP) = 00 11 72	
(R0): xx xx xx		(R0) = 00 10 10	
(R1): xx xx xx		(R1) = 00 11 00	
(R2): xx xx xx		(R2) = 00 12 34	
Address	Contents	Address	Contents
.	.	.	.
.	.	.	.
.	.	.	.
00 11 60	xx xx xx	00 11 60	xx xx xx
00 11 62	xx xx xx	00 11 62	xx xx xx
(SP) → 00 11 64	00 12 34	00 11 64	xx xx xx
00 11 66	00 11 00	00 11 66	xx xx xx
00 11 70	00 10 10	00 11 70	xx xx xx
(PC) → 00 11 72	01 26 02	00 11 72	N.C. ←——(SP)
00 11 74	01 26 01	00 11 74	N.C.
00 11 76	01 26 00	00 11 76	N.C.
00 12 00	00 00 00	00 12 00	N.C.
00 12 02	xx xx xx	00 12 02	N.C. ←——(PC)
.	.	.	.
.	.	.	.
.	.	.	.
.	.	.	.

Note that initially the (SP) = 00 11 64. (PC) = 00 11 72, and after execution the (SP) goes back to 1172. All saved information is popped back to the registers. With this configuration, (PC) and (SP) would not invade each other's territories. ■ ■

Examination of the PUSH/POP process examples reveals that the (R2) was pushed into the stack last, whereas it was popped from the stack first. Memory with this kind of configuration is known as **last-in–first out (LIFO)** memory.

Summary of Addressing Techniques

Addressing Modes   In this chapter we have studied in detail about the addressing modes available for the PDP-11 system. Table 4.1 summarizes the register reference addressing modes, which exclude the use of R7 or PC. Column 3 describes the changes in the register contents before, during, and after the operand fetching process. For example, in mode 0, the Rn is the address and the content (Rn) is the operand, so no change will be made in this process. However, for mode 4, the (Rn) is decremented by 2 before fetching the operand. Columns 4 and 5 are the memory maps for one-level and two-level indirect addressing. The last column shows the real operand to be fetched for action. Table 4.2 summarizes the addressing process that involves PC only.

The Hand-Assembly Procedure   We have illustrated by several examples how to hand assemble a source program into its object program in octal machine code. Here we summarize the procedure.

TABLE 4.1   A SUMMARY OF PDP-LSI-11 (PDP 11/03) ADDRESSING MODE WITHOUT PC

Operand Address Field Notation	Mode	Addressing Operation Register R_n, $n = 0, 1, 2, \ldots, 5$			Memory		Memory		
		Before	During	After	Address	Content	Address	Content	Operand
R_n	0	(R_n)	(R_n)	(R_n)	R_n	(R_n)			(R_n)
@ R_n	1	(R_n)	(R_n)	(R_n)	(R_n)	A_1			A_1
				$(R_n)+2$					
$(R_n)^+$	2	(R_n)	(R_n)	$(R_n)+1$**	(R_n)	A_2			A_2
$@(R_n)^+$	3	(R_n)	(R_n)	$(R_n)+2$	(R_n)	C_1	C_1	D_1	D_1
			$(R_n)-2$	$(R_n)-2$	$(R_n)-2$				
$-(R_n)$	4	(R_n)	$(R_n)-1$**	$(R_n)-1$**	$(R_n)-1$**	A_3			A_3
$@-(R_n)$	5	(R_n)	$(R_n)-2$	$(R_n)-2$	$(R_n)-2$	C_2	C_2	D_2	D_2
$X(R_n)$	6	(R_n)	(R_n)	(R_n)	$(R_n)+X$	A_4			A_4
$@X(R_n)$	7	(R_n)	(R_n)	(R_n)	$(R_n)+X$	C_3	C_3	D_3	D_3

**Denotes byte operation.
A_1, A_2, A_3, A_4
C_1, C_2, C_3 } $\triangle$ some binary code
D_1, D_2, D_3

TABLE 4.2　A SUMMARY OF THE PC-BASED ADDRESSING MODE

Operand Address Field Notation	Name	Mode	Addressing Operation P_C or R_7			Memory		Memory		Operand
			Before	During	After (updated)	Address	Content	Address	Content	
#n	Immediate	2	(R_7)	$(R_7)+2$	$(R_7)+4$					n
@#A	Absolute deferred immediate	3	(R_7)	$(R_7)+2$	$(R_7)+4$	A	C_1			C_1
A	Relative	6	(R_7)	$(R_7)+2$	$(R_7)+4$	$(R_7)+4*+B$	C_2			C_2
@A	Relative deferred	7	(R_7)	$(R_7)+2$	$(R_7)+4$	$(R_7)+4*+B$	C_3	C_3	D_3	D_3

*Can be 6 if both operand addresses are in the relative mode.
$n \triangleq$ some number
$B \triangleq$ content at the location, $(R_7)+2$

Hand assembly code:

Step 1:　Decide how many words each instruction will need.

Step 2:　Assign consecutive memory locations for all the instructions, starting at location 0.

Step 3:　Determine the octal binary code for each instruction.

Determination of number of words for each instruction: Each instruction occupies one memory word location except for the addressing modes: index, index deferred, immediate, absolute, relative, and relative deferred, where one additional word per each operand per instruction is required. See the summary table for addressing modes.

Determination of the offset value or relative distance in twos complement:

1. For the relative addressing mode with the destination symbolic address A, offset value = A − (updated PC).
2. For the branch instruction, A = (updated PC) + 2 (offset value), or offset value = (½) [A − (updated PC)].
3. For instruction, SOB　　R,A　　　;subtract (R) by one if not zero, branch to A. Offset value = (½) [(updated PC) − A].

Restriction: (Updated PC) is always greater than A; that is, the offset value is always a positive 6-bit binary number.

Sample Programs Using Different Addressing Modes

Examples to clarify what has been described in this chapter are shown in Figures 4.4 through 4.8. Although Examples 1 through 3 are self-explanatory, Examples 4 and 5 need special attention. Note that in Example 4 we have begun to use system-defined MACRO instructions, .WRITE and .EXIT, for convenience. Since you will learn about the MACRO instructions in Chapter 6, here we will only briefly describe the functions of

```
                              ;EXAMPLE 1 : THIS EXAMPLE SHOWS THE NUMBER OF MEMORY
                              ;WORDS REQUIRED FOR INSTRUCTION WITH DIFFERENT
                              ;ADDRESSING MODE.
 1
 2
 3
 4
 5
 6 000000  010100  000020    START:  MOV   R1,R0          ;NEEDS 1 WORD
 7 000002  012702  177370            MOV   #20,R2         ;NEEDS 2 WORDS
 8 000006  010177  177370            MOV   R1,@177370     ;NEEDS 2 WORDS
 9 000012  012777  000010  177372    MOV   #10,@177372    ;NEEDS 3 WORDS
10 000020  000000'                   HALT                 ;NEEDS 1 WORD
11                                    .END  START
```

Figure 4.4 Determination of number of memory words required.

```
                              ;EXAMPLE 2: RELATIVE-ADDRESSING MODE. FIND THE LARGER
                              ;ONE OF TWO NUMBERS STORED IN N1 AND N2 AND PUT IT IN
                              ;BIG.
 1
 2
 3
 4
 5
 6 000000  000017           N1:     .WORD  15.        ;DECIMAL 15 IS STORED HERE
 7 000002  177744           N2:     .WORD  -28.       ;DECIMAL -28 IS STORED HERE
 8 000004                   BIG:    .BLKW  1
 9 000006  026767  177766  177766  START:  CMP   N1,N2
10 000014  002004                          BGE   POS    ;BRANCH IF (N1) >= (N2)
11 000016  016767  177760  177760          MOV   N2,BIG
12 000024  000000                          HALT
13 000026  016767  177746  177750  POS:    MOV   N1,BIG
14 000034  000000                          HALT
15         000006'                         .END  START
```

Result: Location BIG contains 15.

Figure 4.5 Relative addressing mode.

```
 1                                   ;EXAMPLE 3: DEMONSTRATION OF IMMEDIATE, RELATIVE
 2                                   ;AND INDEX ADDRESSING MODES.
 3                                   ;
 4                                   ;
 5 000000  012701  000002   START:   MOV    #2,R1
 6 000004  000411            L1:      BR     L2
 7 000006  062701  000002             ADD    #2,R1
 8 000012  016103  000006'            MOV    L1+2(R1),R3    ;L1+2 = 4+2
 9 000016  016100  177560             MOV    177560(R1),R0
10 000022  022701  000004             CMP    #4,R1
11 000026  001402                     BEQ    STOP
12 000030  000161  000004'   L2:      JMP    L1(R1)
13 000034  000000   STOP:    HALT
14         000000'                    .END   START
```

Figure 4.6 Immediate, index, and relative modes.

these two macros. The .EXIT instruction is used to replace the instruction HALT; and .WRITE is used to display the contents of specified memory or register without using ODT. For instance, the .WRITE instruction in line 6, each time after its execution, will display the contents of R0 on the CRT as follows:

$$(R0) = \text{content in octal}$$

Example 5 is an attempt to clarify some of the nontrivial or confusion-prone addressing modes. Here for convenience we use one more system-defined MACRO instruction, .RAD, which defines the radix of the number system we want to use. For example, in Figure 4.8a, the instruction on line 13 indicates that we wish the display following it to be in octal (8) radix and left-justified. The following are the results after execution of the program in Figure 4.8(a).

1. After line 13, the lines 11, 12, and 13 yielded the following:

$$(R0) = 3000, \ (R1) = 2000, \ (R2) = 123, \ (R3) = 3000$$

```
 1                                   ;EXAMPLE 4: DEMONSTRATION OF INSTRUCTION 'SOB'
 2                                   ;
 3                                   ;
 4                                   .MCALL  .WRITE,.EXIT
 5 000000  012700  000003   START:   MOV     #3,R0
 6 000004            L1:    .WRITE  '.__(R0) = , R0   ;CRT WILL SHOW THE CONTENT
 7                                                    ;OF R0
 8 000010  077003                    SOB     R0,L1    ;DECREMENT BY ONE UNTIL
 9                                                    ;(R0) = 0
10 000012                   .WRITE  '\\AFTER_COMPLETING_SOB_(R0) = ,R0
11 000016                   .EXIT
12         000000'                  .END     START
```

Result: (R0) = 3 (R0) = 2 (R0) = 1
*   AFTER COMPLETING SOB UNTIL (R0) = 0*

Figure 4.7 SOB instruction.

```
 1
 2                                ;EXAMPLE 5(A): DEMONSTRATION OF SOME NONTRIVIAL ADDRESSING
 3                                ;MODES.
 4                                ;------
 5                                        .MCALL  .WRITE,.EXIT,.RAD
 6 000000 012737 003000 003000  002000    START:  MOV  #3000,@#2000  ;INITIAL LOCATION 2000
 7 000006 012737 000123 002000  003000            MOV  #123,@#3000   ;INITIAL LOCATION 3000
 8 000014 013700 002000                           MOV  @#2000,R0
 9 000020 012701 002000                           MOV  #2000,R1
10 000024 017702 002000                           MOV  @2000,R2
11 000030 016703 002000                           MOV  2000,R3
12 000034                                          .WRITE \_\AS_A_RESULT_WE_HAVE:__
13 000040                                          .RAD   8L
14 000044                                          .WRITE \_(R0) = ,R0,'_(R1) = ,R1,'_(R2) = ,R2,'_(R3) = ,R3
15 000050 013703 000144'                          MOV  @#DATA,R3
16 000054 013704 000140                           MOV  @#140,R4
17 000060 012702 000144'                          MOV  #DATA,R2
18 000064 017701 000054                           MOV  @DATA,R1
19 000070 016700 000050                           MOV  DATA,R0
20 000074 016767 000046 000050                    MOV  A,C
21 000102 016767 000042 000044                    MOV  B,C+2
22 000110 016767 000032 000032                    MOV  A,B
23 000116                                          .WRITE \_\NOW_WE_HAVE:__
24 000122                                          .WRITE \_(R0) = ,R0,'_(R1) = ,R1,'_(R2) = ,R2,'_(R3) = ,R3,'
25 000126                                          .WRITE _(R4) = ,R4
26 000132                                          .WRITE \_(A) = ,A,'_(B) = ,B,'_(C) = ,C,'_(C+2) = ,C+2
27 000136                                          .EXIT
28 000144 002000                           DATA:  .WORD 2000
29 000146 000003                           A:     .WORD 3
30 000150 000007                           B:     .WORD 7
31 000152                                   C:     .BLKW 1000
32 000000'                                          .END  START
```

Result: AS A RESULT WE HAVE:
(R0) = 3000 (R1) = 2000 (R2) = 123 (R3) = 3000
NOW WE HAVE:
(R0) = 2000 (R1) = 3000 (R2) = 1336 (R3) = 2000 (R4) = −1
(A) = 3 (B) = 3 (C) = 3 (C+2) = 7
*Location 140 contains −1

Figure 4.8(a) Illustration of nontrivial addressing mode.

```
                                    ;EXAMPLE 5(B): DEMONSTRATION OF SOME NONTRIVIAL ADDRESSING
                                    ;MODES.
                                    ;....
 1                                          .MCALL  .WRITE,.EXIT,.RAD
 2
 3
 4
 5
 6  000146                          A = 146
 7  000000  012737  003000  003000  START:  MOV     #3000,@#2000    ;INITIAL LOCATION 2000
 8  000006  012737  000123  002000          MOV     #123,@#3000     ;INITIAL LOCATION 3000
 9  000014  013700  002000                  MOV     @#2000,R0
10  000020  012701  002000                  MOV     #2000,R1
11  000024  017702  002000                  MOV     @2000,R2
12  000030  016703  002000                  MOV     2000,R3
13  000034                                  .WRITE  <\AS_A_RESULT_WE_HAVE:__
14  000040                                  .RAD    8L
15  000044                                  .WRITE  <\(R0) = ,R0,'_(R1) = ,R1,'_(R2) = ,R2,'_(R3) = ,R3
16  000050  013703  000144'                 MOV     @#DATA,R3
17  000054  013704  000140                  MOV     @#140,R4
18  000060  012702  000144'                 MOV     #DATA,R2
19  000064  017700  000054                  MOV     @DATA,R1
20  000070  016700  000050                  MOV     DATA,R0
21  000074  016767  000146  000050          MOV     A,C
22  000102  016767  000042  000044          MOV     B,C+2
23  000110  016767  000146  000032          MOV     A,B
24  000116                                  .WRITE  <\NOW_WE_HAVE:__
25  000122                                  .WRITE  <\(R0) = ,R0,'_(R1) = ,R1,'_(R2) = ,R2,'_(R3) = ,R3,'
26  000126                                  .WRITE  <\_(R4) = ,R4
27  000132                                  .WRITE  <\(A) = ,A,'_(B) = ,B,'_(C) = ,C,'_(C+2) = ,C+2
28  000136                                  .EXIT
29  000144  002000                  DATA:   .WORD   2000
30  000146  000003                  B:      .WORD   3
31  000150  000007                  C:      .WORD   7
32  000152  000000'                          .BLKW   1000
33                                          .END    START
```

Result: AS A RESULT WE HAVE:

  (R0) = 3000   (R1) = 2000   (R2) = 123   (R3) = 3000
    NOW WE HAVE:
  (R0) = 2000   (R1) = 3000   (R2) = 1336   (R3) = 2000   (R4) = −1
  (A) = −1   (B) = −1   (C) = −1   (C+2) = 7
∗location 146 contains −1
  location 140 contains −1

Figure 4.8(c) Illustration of nontrivial addressing mode.

TST (R1)+

The original intent of the TST instruction is to examine the operand and set the PSW accordingly. However, here we wish only to increment the contents of R1 by 2. Although we can achieve the same result by using the instruction ADD #2,R1, the ADD instruction here will require two memory words, whereas the TST instruction requires only one.

ASR A

This instruction will divide the content of A by 2, although it is not obviously for this kind of application. Similarly, the instruction ASL A will multiply the (A) by two.

BIT #10,A

This instruction executes the logical AND operation of the two operands, which can be used to examine specific bit or bits of the destination operand. Here, the contents of A, (A), is AND with #10, as follows:

#10	= 0	000	000	000	001	000
(A)	= b_{15}	$b_{14}b_{13}b_{12}$	$b_{11}b_{10}b_9$	$b_8b_7b_6$	$b_5b_4b_3$	$b_2b_1b_0$
RESULT	= 0	000	000	000	$00b_3$	000

Here, if $b_3 = 1$, the Z-flag of PSW will be zero (FALSE); otherwise it will be one (TRUTH). However, both operands remain unchanged before and after the execution. This is a convenient way to find out the value of b_3.

BIC   src, dst

This instruction executes the operation in two steps:

1. Complements or ones complements the source operand (src).
2. Executes logical AND of the result of step 1 with the destination operand (dst), and places the result in dst. It can be used to clear one or more specific bits of the destination operand.

For example, if we wish to clear the b_3 bit of the content of A, B, and C, the following program can be used:

```
MOV #10,R1    ;INITIALIZE (R1)
BIC  R1,A     ;CLEAR b3 OF (A)
BIC  R1,B     ;CLEAR b3 OF (B)
BIC  R1,C     ;CLEAR b3 OF (C)
```

Similarly, we can SET any one or more bits of the destination by using the bit set (BIS) instruction, since BIS executes the logical OR operation. For example, if we wish to set $b_5b_4b_3$ of A, B, C to logical 1, the following can be done:

```
MOV #70,R1
BIS  R1,A
BIS  R1,B
BIS  R1,C
```

Instructions COM vs Neg

The complement instruction COM is a ones complement operation, whereas the negate instruction NEG is a twos complement operation. For example:

```
1) MOV #31,R1    ;INITIALIZATION
   COM R1        ;ONES COMPLEMENT OF (R1) → R1
```

As a result, (R1) = 177746

```
2) MOV #20,R1
   NEG R1
```

As a result, (R1) = 177760.

Instruction CMP vs SUB

The compare instruction, CMP, compares the source operand (src) and destination operand (dst) by

$$(\text{src}) - (\text{dst})$$

and sets the PSW flags or condition code accordingly. But the contents of src and dst remain unchanged.

However, the instruction subtraction, SUB, operates as follows:

$$(\text{dst}) - (\text{src})$$

The difference of the two goes to dst, and thus the original content of dst is lost. Note also that the order of the subtraction is reversed in comparison with the compare operation. For example:

```
1) MOV #31,A
   MOV #20,B
   CMP A,B
```

As a result: (A) = No change
            (B) = No change
In PSW, N = 0, Z = 0, V = 0, C = 1

```
2) MOV #31,A
   MOV #20,B
   SUB A,B
```

As a result: (A) = No change
            (B) = 177767
In PSW, N = 1, Z = 0, V = 0, C = 1

Signed vs. Unsigned Conditional Branch Instructions

The major difference between the two groups is in that the signed deal with the twos complement numbers, while the unsigned deal with the number that has no sign bit. That is, for a 16-bit word, 077777 is the largest number and 100000 the smallest for signed representation; 177777 is the largest and 000000 is the smallest for unsigned. The example illustrates the difference:

```
N1:        .WORD −2
N2:        .WORD 7
RESULT:    .BLKW 1
START:     CMP N1,N2
           BGE POS              ;SIGNED CONDITIONAL BRANCH
           MOV N2, RESULT
           HALT
POS:       MOV N1, RESULT
           HALT
.END START
```

Here, we use the signed conditional branch. Therefore, after execution, this program would place 7 into location RESULT. However, if the instruction BGE POS is replaced by the unsigned conditional branch instruction BHI POS, the program would place −2 into location RESULT. This is because of the fact that −2 was translated by the assembler into the twos complement, 177776, which is "higher" than 7, if it is not considered as a signed number. One typical application for unsigned conditional branch is if we wish to compare the address value of two symbolic addresses. Obviously, the address value of 177750, for example, is "higher" than that of 000010.

NOP Instruction

This instruction will cause the (PC) steps through it and yet have no effect on the program; however, it occupies one memory word and takes approximately 3.5 microseconds to execute. This instruction can be used in the ODT mode to check if the system operates normally. That is, it can be inserted in any desired place or places of a program as a dummy instruction for ODT debugging. For instance, if we suspect a logical error could be in a certain section of the program, we could pre-insert NOP in that place and then use ODT to replace the NOP we "planted" in the program by HALT. Then the program would stop at this location so we could investigate.

4.4 RELOCATABLE ADDRESS

Recall that the function of the task builder (TKB) described earlier is to link one or a group of object files into one file defined as the memory image TSK file, which is ready to be loaded into main memory from the disk for execution. But the starting address of any object file is always equal to zero. Without the linking process, all the object files would be loaded into the main memory starting at location zero, which would result in overwriting one onto the other and destroying the final executable file. Therefore, it is the TKB system software's responsibility to resolve this problem. That is, (1) if three object files A, B, and C are to be linked into one; (2) if file A requires 4 memory words; file B, 10; and file C, 20; and (3) if the system is configured such that all executable program would start at the location 1000; then file A would be loaded from 1000 to 1006; file B, from 1010 to 1026; and file C, from 1030 to 1066. Note that none of the subprograms would begin at zero. That is, the starting address for each file has now changed to 1000, 1010, and 1030 from 0000, respectively.

In other words, the subprograms are relocated to different, nonoverlapping, but consecutive memory areas for execution purposes. This, however, may cause problems if the subprogram uses symbolic address. Since the value of the symbolic address is normally assigned assuming the program starts at a zero location, it has to be added to the base value at which the subprogram begins. To make this modification simple for the TKB, the assembler would normally mark the address value related to the symbolic address that needs to be relocated with an apostrophe so that all the TKB has to do is to modify the base value to all numbers marked with an apostrophe by the assembler.

As an example, let us examine Example 3 (Figure 4.6). There, we have four symbolic addresses—namely, START, L1, L2, and STOP, with the original address values 000000, 000004, 000030, and 000034, respectively. From the text or the source code, we found that only the instructions of lines 6, 8, 11, 12, and 14 refer to the symbolic addresses. But lines 6 and 11 use the relative distance concept, so they are not a direct function of the address value of the symbolic addresses L2 or STOP. However, in line 8 the index value = L1 + 2. Here, as the value of L1 changes, the index value will change accordingly, and so does the instruction of line 12. Similarly, in line 14 the pseudo instruction .END refers to the symbolic address START, which has an original address value equal to zero. But after TKB has relocated the starting address, it would be different and thus have to be modified also. Assume that this program is to be loaded starting at 1000. Then the critical symbolic addresses that affect the text would be L1 and START. Their address values would be 1004 for L1 and 1000 for START. The index values in lines 8 and 12 have to be changed from 000006' to 001006 and 000004' to 001004, respectively, and the value in line 11 from 000000' to 001000. Note the apostrophes were marked only at those critical numbers. The addresses that can be modified in this way are called relocatable addresses.

4.5 POSITION-INDEPENDENT CODE (PIC)

A program that does not require address modification by TKB regardless of its starting address after it is assembled is known as a **position-independent code (PIC)** program. Obviously, programs that use only register reference instructions are PIC except for the index mode whose index is a symbolic address. The advantage of a PIC program is that it can be relocated anywhere in the main memory without address modification. Typical examples are shown below.

EXAMPLE 1 _____

The following are PICs:

```
1) A:      .WORD   16
   B:      .BLKW   1
           MOV     A,B
2)         MOV     R0,-(SP)
           MOV     R1,-(SP)
           MOV     (SP)+,R1
           MOV     (SP)+,R0
3) LOOP:   MOV     @#177756,B
           BR      LOOP
   B:      .BLKW   1
```

EXAMPLE 2

The following, however, is non-PIC:

```
A:    .WORD 16
B:    .BLKW 1
      MOV @#A,B
```

Compare this example with item 3 of the preceding example. Both use the absolute addressing mode. However, the contents of the second word of the MOV instruction of the former is 177756; that of the latter would be the current value of A, and as the program has been relocated, the value of A would change accordingly. Therefore, the TKB has to modify the value of the second memory word of the instruction, MOV @#A,B.

EXERCISES

4.1 Hand assemble the following sets of independent instruction statements. You may assume that each set is an independent one and that the values of the symbolic address labels are defined as follows:

$$START = 2000$$
$$A = 1770$$
$$B = 2760$$

a.
```
START: MOV #61, R0
       INC R0
       HALT
```

b.
```
START: MOV #1200, R1
       MOV #1717, R2
       SUB R1, R2
       HALT
```

c.
```
START: MOV #1200, R1
       MOV #1717, R2
       CMP R1, R2
       HALT
```

d.
```
START: MOVB #1200, R1
       MOVB #1717, R2
       CMPB R1, R2
       HALT
```

e.
```
    A: .WORD 1200
START: CMP A,B
       HALT
    B: 1717
```

f.
```
    A: .WORD 10, 12, 7, 3
START: MOV #A, R1
       CMP (R1)+, (R1)
       CMP (R1)+, (R1)+
       SUB (R1), −(R1)
       HALT
```

g.
```
    A: .WORD 0, 1, 2, 3, 4, 0, −1, −2
START: MOV #A, R0
       MOV #B, R1
       MOV #10, R2
 LOOP: MOV (R0)+, (R1)+
       SOB R2, LOOP
       HALT
    B: .BLKW 10
```

5.1 INTRODUCTION

In the preceding chapters, you learned the workings of the PDP-11 instruction set and gained some experience in developing a simple program. To develop any program, be it simple or complex, we have to go through the procedure of EDITOR → ASSEMBLER → TASKBUILDER → LOAD AND GO → DEBUGGING, shown in Figure E.5. Since program development is a time-consuming process, no one wants to have to redevelop a program if it is already a good one, and of course we would like to use a good program again and again.

For example, suppose we have developed a good program that can multiply two numbers. In an application program where we need to multiply two numbers many times, we would definitely want to insert the "good program" into this program as many times as necessary. To do this, we have to retype this "subprogram" into the main program as many times as required. In retyping, we would probably make a mistake somewhere. This is frustrating, not to mention the cost of the extra time required. Furthermore, every time we insert the subprogram, it will cost us a block of memory space. Consider a subprogram that required, say, 1,000 memory words. If we need it 10 times in our main program, it would require 10,000 extra memory spaces. This can be costly. Fortunately, there is a way out of these difficulties: the subroutine. Figure 5.1 depicts the solution.

We can reserve a memory area for the subprogram, use JUMP instruction to get to that area whenever the main program needs the operation, and return to the main program when the subprogram has finished. The main program is often known as the **host**

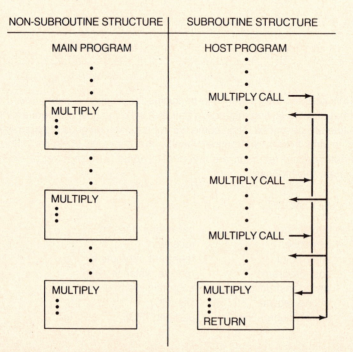

Figure 5.1 Memory map for the concept of subroutine.

program and the subprogram as the **subroutine.** The process of JUMP is known as **subroutine call.**

Basic Concepts

Figure 5.2 depicts the execution process of a host program calling subroutines. Note that there are two essential steps in calling a subroutine: entering the subroutine from the host program, and leaving the subroutine to return to the host program. Although the concept is quite straightforward, the details need to be clarified. Recall that in the instruction set, there is a class called program sequence control instructions, such as BRANCH and JUMP. However, the BRANCH instruction has a limited branching distance, from -256 to $+254$ words. So it is obvious that the JUMP instruction should be chosen for leaving the host and entering the subroutine.

Another important problem is how the computer will know where to return when the operation is finished. Recall that we use PC as the program counter or pointer to execute the program step by step. Both the host and the subroutine would need to use the same PC to execute the program. To resolve the problem, the computer must have a way temporarily to store the old contents of PC until the subroutine has finished. Thus, we need a pair of instructions to work together, one for leaving and the other for returning. Normally, the leaving instruction is included in the host program and the return instruction is included in the subroutine.

The last problem for calling a subroutine is passing parameters through which the data for the subroutine can be supplied. The data for a routine naturally change from time to time. For example, if a MULTIPLY subroutine is called, the host would need to be able to provide different data at different times. Therefore, how the host passes parameters to a subroutine is an essential problem.

So in utilizing subroutine call, we should be aware of the following problems:

1. The **entry point** or the starting address of the subroutine.
2. Selection of the **linking instruction pair.**
3. Saving of the content of the PC for returning to the host program.
4. The means of **passing parameters** for data transfer from the host to the subroutine and back.

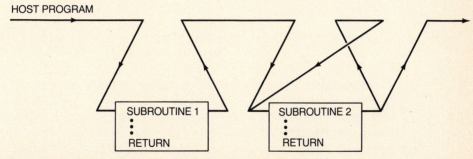

HOST PROGRAM

SUBROUTINE 1
⋮
RETURN

SUBROUTINE 2
⋮
RETURN

Figure 5.2 Execution of host program containing subroutines.

Key Instruction Pairs for Linking Host and Subprogram

Using Rn ($n = 0, \ldots, 5$) as the Linking Register

Leaving Instruction

Mnemonic code: JSR Rn, dst

Octal machine code: 0 04 Rn, dst

                              RD

where   Rn $\underline{\Delta}$ nth register for $n = 0,1,\ldots,5$ occupies 3 bits, b_8, b_7, b_6.

           dst $\underline{\Delta}$ symbolic starting address of the subroutine, or simply the name of the subroutine, occupies 6 bits, $b_5\ldots b_0$.

           RD $\underline{\Delta}$ **relative distance** between **updated (PC)** and the destination.

Note that this is a JUMP instruction specifically for a subroutine. That is, *JSR* stands for *jump to subroutine*. It requires two memory words, and the relative addressing mode is used for dst.

Although we do not need to know how the CPU executes this instruction internally, we do need to understand the execution process. As an example, let us execute the instruction JSR R5, dst. The action follows:

$$1\text{st fetch cycle:} \quad (PC) \rightarrow MAR$$
$$(PC)+2 \rightarrow PC$$
$$JSR\ CODE \rightarrow IR$$
$$2\text{nd fetch cycle:} \quad (PC) \rightarrow MAR$$
$$(PC)+2 \rightarrow PC$$
$$RD \rightarrow CPU$$

Note that since there are two memory words for this instruction, it requires two fetching cycles. Next, for execution, the old content of R5 is saved by pushing it into the stack memory. This is necessary because basically the JSR instruction is "borrowing" R5 here. The host program may have some important information in R5 which may need it after subroutine execution. After the old contents of R5 have been saved, the CPU can use R5 for tentative storage of the updated PC, which will be the returning address for resumption of the executing host program. Finally, the address value of the dst, which is the sum of RD and updated (PC), is loaded into PC. Then the CPU starts to execute the subroutine. This process is summarized as follows:

$$(R5) \rightarrow -(sp)$$
$$UD(PC) \rightarrow R5$$
$$RD + UD(PC) \rightarrow PC$$

Fortunately, all these actions are carried out internally within the CPU. It is not the programmer's responsibility to implement them. However, we do have to understand what information is where when. At this point, some keen readers may wonder why we bother with R5. Why not just simply PUSH the UD(PC) into stack? This method of pushing (PC) will come next, but here R5 serves dual functions: holding the return address and passing parameters to and from the subroutine. The detail of utilizing R5 will be described in the later section.

Returning Instruction

Mnemonic code: RTS Rn

Octal machine code: 00020 Rn ; Rn requires 3 bits, $b_2b_1b_0$

This Rn must be the same Rn used in the JSR instruction described above. The execution process follows.

    The UD(PC) or the return address, which was saved in R5, is loaded into PC, and the top layer of information in the stack is POPed back to R5. That is, the old content of R5 which was PUSHed onto the stack is restored to R5, and the host program can continue normally. Again, this is done by CPU hardware, not the program.

EXAMPLE

Assume that the JSR instruction is at location 2000; that the subroutine named LOAFER is at 3000; and that the stack memory starts at 1172 backward. We would have the source program as follows:

```
STACK RANGE = 00 07 14 → 00 11 70
START       = 00 11 72
```

Symbolic Address	Numeric Address	Source Codes
START	-- -- --	----
	00 20 00	JSR R5, LOAFER
	-- -- --	----
	-- -- --	----
	-- -- --	----
LOAFER	00 30 00	NOP
	00 30 02	RTS R5
	-- -- --	----
	-- -- --	----

Note that we use a dummy subroutine to illustrate the principle. The execution maps for both instructions follow:

    [JSR R5, LOAFER] execution map:

Before		After	
(PC) : 00 20 00		(PC) = 00 30 00	
(SP) : 00 11 72	−2	(SP) = 00 11 70	
(R5) : 00 01 32		(R5) = 00 20 04	
LOAFER : 00 30 00	+4	LOAFER = N.C.	

Memory Map :

Address	Contents	Address	Contents
00 11 70	XX XX XX	00 11 70	00 01 32 ◄(SP)
(SP)► 00 11 72	XX XX XX	00 11 72	N.C.
— — —	— — —	— — —	— — —
(PC)► 00 20 00	00 45 67	00 20 00	N.C.
00 20 02	00 07 74	00 20 02	N.C.
00 20 04	XX XX XX	00 20 04	N.C.
— — —	— — —	— — —	— — —
— — —	— — —	— — —	— — —
— — —	— — —	— — —	— — —
— — —	— — —	— — —	— — —
00 30 00	00 02 40	00 30 00	N.C. ◄(PC)
00 30 02	00 02 05	00 30 02	N.C.

[RTS R5] execution map:

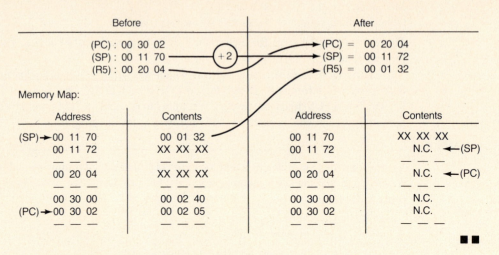

Memory Map:

Address	Contents	Address	Contents
(SP)→00 11 70	00 01 32	00 11 70	XX XX XX
00 11 72	XX XX XX	00 11 72	N.C. ←(SP)
— — —	— — —	— — —	— — —
00 20 04	XX XX XX	00 20 04	N.C. ←(PC)
— — —	— — —	— — —	— — —
00 30 00	00 02 40	00 30 00	N.C.
(PC)→00 30 02	00 02 05	00 30 02	N.C.
— — —	— — —	— — —	— — —

■■

Using PC as the Linking Register

Leaving Instruction

Mnemonic code: JSR PC, dst
Octal machine code: 0 04 7   dst
                         RD

Execution process:
  1st fetch cycle: (PC) → MAR
                          (PC)+2 → PC
                          JSR CODE → IR
  2nd fetch cycle: (PC) → MAR
                          (PC)+2 → PC
                          RD → CPU
  Execution cycle: (PC) → −(SP)
                          RD + UD(PC) → PC

Note that the action is quite similar to that described above except that the return to host address value is here PUSHed into stack instead of R5.

Returning Instruction

Mnemonic code: RTS   PC
Octal machine code: 00020 7

This instruction is executed by simply POPing the return address value, which was saved in stack, back to PC from the top layer of the stack. An example follows.

EXAMPLE   _____

[SOURCE PROGRAM]:

Symbolic Address	Numeric Address	Source Codes
STACK	00 11 70	——
	00 11 72	——
	—— —	——
	00 20 00	JSR PC, LOAFER
	—— —	——
	—— —	——
LOAFER	00 30 00	NOP
	00 30 02	RTS PC
	—— —	——
		——

[JSR PC, LOAFER] execution map:

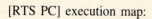

	Before			After	
	(PC) : 00 20 00			(PC) = 00 30 00	
	(SP) : 00 11 72	−2		(SP) = 00 11 70	
	LOAFER : 00 30 00				

Memory Map: +4

Address	Contents		Address	Contents
00 11 70	XX XX XX		00 11 70	00 20 04 ◄(SP)
(SP)►00 11 72	XX XX XX		00 11 72	N.C.
—— —	— — —		—— —	— — —
(PC)►00 20 00	00 47 67		00 20 00	N.C.
00 20 02	00 07 74		00 20 02	N.C.
00 20 04	XX XX XX		00 20 04	N.C.
—— —	— — —		—— —	— — —
00 30 00	00 02 40		00 30 00	N.C. ◄(PC)
00 30 02	00 02 07		00 30 02	N.C.
—— —	— — —		—— —	— — —

[RTS PC] execution map:

	Before			After	
	(PC) : 00 30 02			(PC) = 00 20 04	
	(SP) : 00 11 70	+2		(SP) = 00 11 72	

Memory Map:

Address	Contents		Address	Contents
00 11 70	00 20 04		00 11 70	XX XX XX
00 11 72	XX XX XX		00 11 72	N.C.
—— —	— — —		—— —	— — —
00 20 00	00 47 67		00 20 00	N.C.
00 20 02	00 07 74		00 20 02	N.C.
00 20 04	XX XX XX		00 20 04	N.C.
—— —	— — —		—— —	— — —
00 30 00	00 02 40		00 30 00	N.C.
00 30 02	00 02 07		00 30 02	N.C.
—— —	— — —		—— —	— — —

Coroutine Linking Instruction This is a special instruction for linking coroutines instead of linking host and subroutine. The difference between them is in that for coroutines, both routines are equal in rank. They can call each other, whereas the host-subroutine process has one-way calling. Because of this equal rank feature, the return instruction is not necessary. Instead, one just calls the other routine, and vice versa. In other words, the calling and returning instructions are identical; namely:

Mnemonic code: JSR PC, @(SP)+
Octal machine code: 004 7   36

Note that this instruction requires only one memory word, where the dst field uses the auto increment deferred mode or addressing mode 3. Many students appear to have difficulty understanding this instruction at the beginning. Let us analyze it.

First, remember that no matter what is in the dst field, the CPU eventually puts the address value into PC. Let us examine the preceding example, where we have JSR PC, LOAFER. The CPU eventually puts the address value, LOAFER = 3000, into PC. Similarly, we need to determine the address value of @(SP)+, and to put it into PC. Now, we know that SP = R6, (SP) = the contents of R6, and @(SP) = the contents of the stack memory word whose address is the content of SP. Remember, this is a double-level indirect addressing mode. To evaluate @(SP)+, the CPU eventually puts the top layer of information in the stack memory into PC and auto increments (SP) by 2 afterward. Meanwhile, the CPU puts the updated (PC) into the stack. Therefore this instruction basically exchanges the updated (PC) for the top layer of information in the stack. Let us use two dummy routines, LOAFER 1 and LOAFER 2, to illustrate the operation.

Symbolic Address	Numeric Address	Source Code	Comments
INITIAL	00 11 72	MOV #LOAFER2, −(SP)	;NOTE 1
LOAFER1	00 11 74	NOP	
	00 11 76	JSR PC, @(SP)+	;NOTE 2
	00 12 00	NOP	
	00 12 04	JSR PC, @(SP)+	
	00 12 06	NOP	
	00 12 10	JSR PC, @(SP)+	
	00 12 12	HALT	
LOAFER2	00 12 14	NOP	
	00 12 16	JSR PC, @(SP)+	;NOTE 3
	00 12 20	NOP	
	00 12 22	JSR PC, @(SP)+	
	00 12 24	NOP	
	00 12 26	JSR PC, @(SP)+	

1. The top layer of the stack is initialized with 00 12 14. That is, @(SP) = 00 12 14, the address value of LOAFER 2, is now in the stack.
2. This instruction gets the address value of LOAFER 2, 00 12 14, which was placed in the stack, and places it into PC; meanwhile the updated (PC), which is 00 12 00, is put into the stack. The program jumps to execute the instruction at 00 12 14.

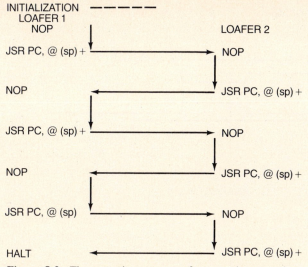

Figure 5.3 The execution sequence for coroutine operation.

3. Here, the contents of updated (PC) and that of the stack are being swapped again, and the program thus jumps back to 00   12   00, and so on.

The execution sequence of these two coroutines is shown in Figure 5.3.

5.2 TRANSMISSION OF PARAMETERS OR ARGUMENTS

The means of linking host and subroutine having been decided, the next important step is to choose the proper way for passing the data into the subroutine and the result back to the host. There are a number of ways to achieve this goal. Here we describe three different popular ones.

Parameters Next to JSR Instruction

For this technique, we must place the data or the addresses of the data next to the JSR instruction for the host program. Then it is the subroutine's responsibility to use its linking register to get the data and put the result back to that place. Figure 5.4(a) and (b) depict the concept. In Figure 5.4(a), the data are placed next to the instruction; in Figure 5.4(b), the addresses are placed next instead of the data. In the figures, the solid arrows denote the instruction linkages of the two programs and the dashed lines the data or parameter passing paths. The following two examples illustrate the concepts.

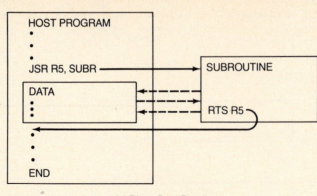

(a) Direct Data Passing

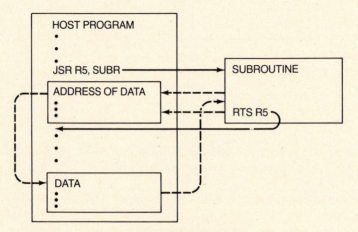

(b) Passing Parameters of Addresses

Figure 5.4 Parameters next to JSR instruction.

EXAMPLE 1 _____

```
START:
                .
                .
                .
                JSR     R5, SUM
DATA:           .WORD   3,4
TOTAL:          .BLKW   1
                .
                .
QUIT:           HALT
SUM:            MOV     (R5)+, R0    ;   3 → R0
                ADD     (R5)+, R0    ;   4 + (R0) → R0
                MOV     R0, (R5)+    ;   RESULT → TOTAL
                RTS     R5
                .END    START
```

In this example, the host program calls the subroutine by the name of SUM and provides it with data, 3 and 4, and requests it to calculate the sum of the given data and place the result into the memory word with the symbolic address TOTAL.

Let us put the program and Figure 5.4(a) side by side and execute by assuming that the address value of the JSR instruction is 2000.

1. Execution of JSR R5, SUM will result in:

$$(R5) \rightarrow STACK$$
$$(PC)+4 \qquad\qquad \text{or} \qquad\qquad \#DATA \rightarrow R5$$
$$\#SUM \rightarrow PC$$

2. Following the solid line in Figure 5.4(a), the program jumps to execute the first instruction of the subroutine: Here, $(R5) = \#DATA$ is pointing at the first datum, 3. Thus, $3 \rightarrow R0$ as depicted by the dashed line; and then $(R5)+2 = \#DATA+2 \rightarrow R5$. As a result, (R5) is pointing at the datum 4 at the end of the execution. Recall that in the previous chapter we defined

$$\#DATA \underline{\Delta} \text{ the address value of the symbolic address, DATA}$$

3. After execution of the next instruction, we have

$$4+(R0) = 4 + 3 = 7 \rightarrow R0$$
$$(R5) + 2 = \#DATA + 4 = \#TOTAL \rightarrow R5$$

That is, at the end of this instruction, (R5) is pointing at the symbolic address TOTAL.

4. The next instruction copies (R0), which is the sum of 3 and 4, or 7, into location TOTAL. Then it auto increments (R5). As a result, $(R5) = \#TOTAL + 2$ is pointing at the location at which the host wishes to resume its operation.

5. Next, the RTS instruction is executed as follows:

$$(R5) \qquad\qquad \text{or} \qquad\qquad \#TOTAL + 2 \rightarrow PC$$
$$\text{top} \qquad \text{layer} \qquad \text{of} \qquad \text{the} \qquad \text{stack} \rightarrow R5$$

Remember that the JSR instruction has saved the old (R5) on the stack.

6. The host program resumes its operation at $\#TOTAL + 2$.

EXAMPLE 2

In this example, the addresses of the data are placed next to the JSR instruction.

```
START:          .
                .
                .
                .
         JSR R5, SUM
PARAM:   .WORD    A, B
TOTAL:   .BLKW    1
                .
                .
                .
                .
```

```
QUIT:      HALT
 A:        .WORD 3
 B:        .WORD 4
SUM:       MOV @(R5)+, R0
           ADD @(R5)+, R0
           MOV R0, (R5)+
           RTS R5
           .END START
```

■ ■

The difference between Examples 1 and 2 is in that the latter uses the auto increment deferred addressing mode so that the linking register, R5, can get the data in A and B, respectively. Since the result is expected to be put in TOTAL, as in Example 1, that instruction still uses the auto increment mode.

Note that this technique of parameter passing has the merit of simplicity. The CPU automatically saves the (R5) and makes it available for the subroutine to "borrow" the R5 as its linking register. However, the technique has the drawback of mixing the data with the instructions.

Another important issue we should bring to your attention is that the subroutine in these examples has also "borrowed" R0 as a data register. This may cause a problem if the host program has important information in R0, because the old content of R0 will be lost as the program enters the subroutine. In order to make the subroutine general for any host program, it would be wise to save the (R0) on stack before the subroutine "borrows" R0 and to restore the old (R0) near the end of the subroutine. That is, the subroutine, SUM, can be modified as follows:

```
SUM:       MOV R0, -(SP)      ;PUSH (R0) to stack
           MOV (R5)+, R0
           ADD (R5)+, R0
           MOV R0, (R5)+
           MOV (SP)+, R0
           RTS R5
```

If we assume the (SP) is initially 1172 before the JSR instruction, the memory map of the stack before, during, and after execution of the subroutine can be shown as follows:

Before		During		After	
(R0) = OLD (R0)		(R0) = VARIABLE		(R0) = OLD (R0)	
(R5) = OLD (R5)		(R5) = LINKING REG.		(R5) = OLD (R5)	
Address	Contents	Address	Contents	Address	Contents
00 10 62	XX XX XX	00 10 62		00 10 62	XX XX XX
00 10 64	XX XX XX	00 10 64		00 10 64	XX XX XX
00 10 66	XX XX XX	00 10 66	OLD (R0)	00 10 66	XX XX XX
00 11 70	XX XX XX	00 11 70	OLD (R5)	00 11 70	XX XX XX
00 11 72	XX XX XX	00 11 72	XX XX XX	00 11 72	XX XX XX

Parameters in a Specific Exclusive Area

For this technique, the data are placed in a specific and exclusive area; they do not mix with instructions. Here, the technique uses JSR   PC, SUBR, and RTS   PC as the in-

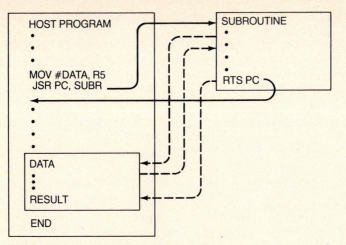

Figure 5.5 Parameter in a specific exclusive area.

struction pair linking the host and subroutine, but uses a general register, say R5, as the data linking register. Figure 5.5 depicts the action. Again, we use the dashed lines for data paths and the solid lines for the program links. In the following material, Example 1 is a program that describes the general operation and Example 2 is a numeric example.

EXAMPLE 1

```
START:
            .
            .
            .
INIT:    MOV  #DATA, R5    ;INITIAL R5 WITH THE ADDRESS
                           ;VALUE OF DATA
         JSR   PC, SUBR    ;(PC) → STACK, #SUBR → PC
                   .
                   .
                   .
QUIT:    HALT      .
DATA:    d₁
         d₂
          .
          .
          .
         dₙ
SUBR:    MOV  (R5)+, dst    ;dst = AREA OF THE DESTINATION
                           ;WHERE THE DATA ARRAY OR
                   .        ;PARAMETERS ARE TO BE COPIED
                   .        ;INTO
                   .
         MOV  (R5)+, dst
                   .
                   .
                   .
         RTS  PC
         .END  START
```

EXAMPLE 2 _____

In this example let us use the subroutine SUM to determine the total of an array of data and let us assume that the total will not exceed ± 32000; that is, it would not overflow the ALU. Furthermore, we assume that the first element or member of the data array is the total number of the members or the size of the array—say, 10.

```
START:    MOV #DATA, R5         ;INITIAL R5 AS DATA
                                ;POINTER
          JSR PC, SUM           ;(PC) + 4 → PC, (PC) →
                                ;STACK, #SUM → PC
QUIT:     HALT
DATA:     .WORD 10              ;SIZE OF DATA ARRAY
          .WORD 1,−2,3,−4,5,−6,7,10;DATA d₁,d₂,..,dₙ
TOTAL:    .BLKW1                ;RESERVED SPACE FOR
                                ;RESULT
SUM:      CLR R0                ;INITIAL R0 AS
                                ;ACCUMULATOR
          MOV (R5)+, R1         ;INITIAL R1 AS DATA
                                ;COUNTER
LOOP:     ADD (R5)+, R0         ;BEGIN ADDING DATA
          SOB R1, LOOP          ;SUBTRACT R1 BY ONE IF
                                ;NOT ZERO BRANCH TO
                                ;LOOP

          MOV R0, TOTAL         ;RESULT → TOTAL
          RTS PC                ;TOP LAYER OF STACK--
                                ;PC

          .END START
```

Figure 5.6 shows the list file of this program and its execution result.

Transmission of Parameters Through Stack Memory

This technique is best for subroutine nesting or interrupt service. The operation basically is this: (1) The host copies the data to the stack memory; (2) the subroutine fetches data from the stack and puts the result into stack; and (3) the host copies the result from the stack to the destination. In this way, the subroutine is never concerned with where to get data, since the data are always in the stack for it to operate on. Figure 5.7 shows the operation of this technique. Note that the solid lines show the program linkage and the dashed lines the data flow paths.

Here, before the JSR instruction and after the RTS instruction, we need to push all data into stack for the subroutine to operate on, and then to pop the result into the destination. While executing, the subroutine fetches data from, and leaves the result in, the stack. This technique appears quite straightforward; however, there are some details that need to be considered. Remember that the JSR instruction normally pushes the updated (PC) into stack for the subroutine return process, but here we also push and pop data into and out of the stack. Obviously, if we are not careful there will be some conflict between the two kinds of information. Let us use an example similar to Example 2 in the preceding section to clarify the process.

```
 1                                    ;EXAMPLE
 2                                    .................
 3
 4                                    ;EXAMPLE 2:
 5
 6
 7
 8
 9  000000  012705  000012'  START:  MOV   #DATA,R5    ;INITIAL R5 AS DATA POINTER
10  000004  004767  000026           JSR   PC,SUM      ;(PC)+4 → PC,(PC) → STACK,#SUM → PC
11  000010  000000          QUIT:    HALT
12  000012  000010          DATA:    .WORD 10          ;SIZE OF THE DATA ARRAY
13  000014  000001  177776  000003   .WORD 1,-2,3,-4,5,-6,7,10
    000022  177774  000005  177772
    000030  000007  000010
14  000034                  TOTAL:   .BLKW 1           ;STORE RESULT HERE
15  000036  005000          SUM:     CLR   R0          ;INITIAL R0 AS ACCUMULATOR
16  000040  012501                   MOV   (R5)+,R1    ;INITIAL R1 AS DATA COUNTER
17  000042  062500          LOOP:    ADD   (R5)+,R0    ;SUMMING UP THE DATA
18  000044  077102                   SOB   R1,LOOP     ;(R1)-1 → R1, IF NOT ZERO GOTO LOOP
19  000046  010067  177762           MOV   R0,TOTAL    ;RESULT → TOTAL
20  000052  000207                   RTS   PC          ;TOP LAYER OF STACK → PC
21  000000'                          .END  START
```

Execution Result: Location TOTAL contains 14 (octal)

Figure 5.6 Example of parameter transmission with data in an exclusive area.

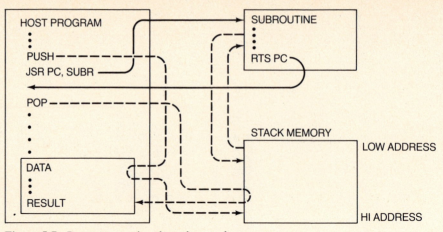

Figure 5.7 Parameter passing through a stack.

EXAMPLE 1

```
 1) START:    MOV SP, R4          ;COPY (SP) → R4
 2)           TST −(R4)           ;(R4) − 2 → R4
 3)           MOV #DATA, R5       ;R5 AS DATA POINTER
 4)           MOV (R5)+, R3       ;INITIAL R3 AS DATA
                                  ;COUNTER WITH THE SIZE
                                  ;OF THE DATA ARRAY
 5)           MOV R3, R2          ;INITIAL R2 AS DATA
                                  ;COUNTER FOR THE STACK
 6) PUSH:     MOV (R5)+, −(R4)    ;PUSH DATA INTO STACK
 7)           SOB R3, PUSH        ;IF NOT FINISH PUSHING
                                  ;DATA, BRANCH TO PUSH.
                                  ;IF FINISH, (R5) POINTS
                                  ;AT TOTAL, AND EXECUTE
                                  ;NEXT INSTRUCTION
 8) CALLSB:   JSR PC, SUM         ;(PC) + 4 → PC, (PC)--
                                  ;STACK, #SUM → PC
 9)           MOV (R4), TOTAL     ;RESULT → TOTAL
10) QUIT:     HALT
11) DATA:     .WORD n
12)           .WORD d₁,d₂,..,dₙ
13) TOTAL:    .BLKW 1
14) SUM:      CLR R0              ;INITIAL R0 AS
                                  ;ACCUMULATOR
15) LOOP:     ADD (R4)+, R0       ;POP DATA FROM STACK
                                  ;FOR ADDITION
16)           SOB R2, LOOP        ;FINISH ADDING?
17)           MOV R0, −(R4)       ;RESULT TO STACK
18)           RTS PC
              .END START
```

To resolve the conflict between the data and the updated (PC) for returning to host from subroutine, first we copy the value of SP into R4, which is to be used as the data pointer for the stack. Next, we decrement (R4) by 2 to skip one word, which will be used for storing the updated (PC) in the near future. Then we assign R5 as the data pointer for the data array, and R3 and R2 as the data counters, respectively, for the original data array and stack. Having finished data pushing, we are ready to call the subroutine SUM. The

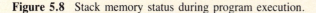

Register Status After Instruction 5	STACK Memory Status									
	After Instruction 7		After Instruction 8		After Instruction 17		After Instruction 18		After Instruction 9	
	Address	Contents	Address	Contents	Address	Contents	Address	Contents	Address	Contents
(SP) = 1172		dn		dn		xx xx xx		xx xx xx		xx xx xx
(R4) = 1170	•	•	•	•	•	•	•	•	•	•
(R5) = #DATA	•	•	•	•	•	•	•	•	•	•
(R3) = n	•	•	•	•	•	•	•	•	•	•
(R2) = n	•	•	•	•	00 11 64	xx xx xx	•	•	•	•
	00 11 66	d1	00 11 66	d1	00 11 66	RESULT	00 11 66	RESULT	00 11 66	xx xx xx
	00 11 70	xx xx xx	00 11 70	#CALLSB+4	00 11 70	#CALLSB+4	00 11 70	xx xx xx	00 11 70	xx xx xx
	00 11 72	xx xx xx	00 11 72	xx xx xx	00 11 72	xx xx xx	00 11 72	xx xx xx	00 11 72	xx xx xx

Figure 5.8 Stack memory status during program execution.

subroutine then sums up all the data in the stack and leaves the result in the stack. As the process returns from the routine, the host fetches the result from the stack and puts it into the destination, TOTAL.

Figure 5.8 depicts the stack memory maps showing the status of the stack before, during, and after the program execution, assuming the stack pointer (SP) was initialized to 1172. The first column shows the condition of the registers listed at the completion of instruction 5. The second column shows the status of the stack memory after instruction 7. Here, the program used the data pointers R5 and R4 to copy the data into stack from the original data array. The third column shows that instruction 8 puts the updated (PC) into stack at 00 11 70 through SP, and the program jumps to the subroutine starting at SUM. The fourth column shows that at the end of subroutine execution, instruction 17 puts the total sum from R0 into location 00 11 66 through R4. The fifth column shows that instruction 18 puts the updated (PC) at 00 11 70 into PC, and the program then returns to instruction 9. The sixth column shows the result after execution of instruction 9. The stack finally returns to its original status. ■■

Figure 5.9 contains a numerical example that illustrates the parameters or data transmission through the stack. Note that in this parameter transmission technique, the subroutine deals only with the stack memory.

5.3 GENERAL FORMATS FOR SUBROUTINE AND HOST PROGRAM DOCUMENTATION

Thus far we have been describing the basic principles of operation for subroutine programming techniques. For convenience, in our examples the host program is shown containing the subroutine. In practice, however, the host program does not normally contain the subroutine or subroutines. In fact, the subroutines most likely were written by other programmers, and they can be in source file or object file forms.

When we want to use subroutines written by others, we must know (1) the names, or the starting address labels, or the entry points of the subroutines; (2) the linking registers used by the subroutines; and (3) the parameter transmission techniques expected to be used by the subroutines. Therefore it is quite reasonable that there should be general formats for both the subroutines and host programs for us to follow. Here is a description of the format normally used for the RSX-11M operating system.

```
 1                                      ;EXAMPLE
 2                                      ;........
 3                                      ;EXAMPLE 2:
 4
 5
 6 000000 010604           START:  MOV   SP,R4          ;COPY (SP) → R4
 7 000002 005744                   TST   -(R4)          ;(R4)-2 → R4
 8 000004 012705 000032'           MOV   #DATA,R5       ;R5 AS DATA POINTER
 9 000010 012503                   MOV   (R5)+,R3       ;INITIAL R3 AS DATA COUNTER WITH
10                                                      ;    THE SIZE OF THE DATA ARRAY
                                                        ;INITIAL R2 AS DATA COUNTER
11 000012 010302           PUSH:   MOV   R3,R2          ;
12 000014 012544                   MOV   (R5)+,-(R4)    ;PUSH DATA INTO STACK
13 000016 077302                   SOB   R3,PUSH        ;IF NOT FINISH BRANCH TO PUSH
14 000020 004767 000032    CALLSB: JSR   PC,SUM         ;(PC)+4 → PC,(PC) → STACK,#SUM → PC
15 000024 011467 000024            MOV   (R4),TOTAL     ;RESULT → TOTAL
16 000030 000000           QUIT:   HALT
17 000032 000010           DATA:   .WORD 10
18 000034 000001 177776 000003     .WORD 1,-2,3,-4,5,-6,7,10
   000042 177774 000005 177772
   000050 000007 000010
19 000054                  TOTAL:  .BLKW 1
20 000056 005000           SUM:    CLR   R0             ;INITIAL R0 AS ACCUMULATOR
21 000060 062400           LOOP:   ADD   (R4)+,R0       ;POP DATA FROM STACK FOR ADDITION
22 000062 077202                   SOB   R2,LOOP        ;FINISH ADDING ?
23 000064 010044                   MOV   R0,-(R4)       ;RESULT TO STACK
24 000066 000207                   RTS   PC
25        000000'                  .END  START
```

Execution Result: Location TOTAL contains 14 (octal)

Figure 5.9 Example of parameter transmission through a stack.

Subroutine

Let us use a typical subroutine with which we are familiar to illustrate the principle. The following is a typical **subroutine format** using the parameter transmission technique described above.

```
                    ;subroutine calling vector
                    ;JSR R5, SUM
                    ;.WORD n, the size of the data array
                    ;.WORD DATA, starting address of the data array
                    ;In addition, the subroutine uses R0 as accumulator
                    ;R1 as the data counter.
                    ;R2 as the data pointer.
                    .GLOBL SUM
      SUM:          CLR R0              ;INITIAL ACCUMULATOR
                    MOV (R5)+, R1       ;INITIAL DATA COUNTER,
                                        ;n → R1
                    MOV (R5)+, R2       ;R2 AS THE DATA POINTER, OR
                                        ;#DATA → R2
      LOOP:         ADD (R2)+, R0       ;R0 AS THE ACCUMULATOR
                    SOB R1, LOOP
                    RTS R5
                    .END SUM
```

Note that we use a semicolon to start each comment line. This is necessary because the semicolon tells the computer that what follows is merely comment for program documentation purposes. It is for the convenience of the user, and the computer should ignore it. As a result, the assembler would not assemble the comment lines headed by the semicolons. The pseudoinstruction or the directive .GLOBL is another vital means to communicate with the operating system. It allows us to place the entry point of the subroutine or the address label of the starting address of the subroutine after it, since it tells the computer and the user that SUM is a global address label for linking the host and the subroutine. Here, SUM is a global label; LOOP is a local label.

Host Program

With the subroutine documentation given in the preceding section, we could write our host program as follows:

```
      ; This is a host program which calls the subroutine SUM,
      ; to calculate the total sum of an array of data with n
      ; elements and place the result into destination, TOTAL.
                    .GLOBL    SUM
      DATA:         .WORD d₁, d₂, . . . ,dₙ
      TOTAL:        .BLKW 1
      START:        JSR R5, SUM         ;JUMP TO SUBROUTINE
                    .WORD n             ;PASSING ARRAY SIZE
                    .WORD DATA          ;PASSING STARTING
                                        ;ADDRESS OF DATA
                                        ;ARRAY
                    MOV R0, TOTAL       ;RESULT → TOTAL
                    HALT
                    .END START
```

Note that we also use the .GLOBL pseudoinstruction here to point out to the assembler that the label SUM is a global address symbol. Although not defined in the host program, it is defined in the subroutine. By using the directive .GLOBL in both the host and the subroutine, the task builder (TKB) will be able to take care of the "confusion." Otherwise, the assembler will consider it an error of undefined symbol, since the label SUM is not defined in the host program.

It is also worthwhile to point out that in this example, we move the data section to the beginning of the program. This configuration has some merit in restarting the program, since after execution the program is normally stopped one word ahead of the HALT instruction. Here, the final (PC) would be pointing at the START label if the HALT instruction is replaced by .EXIT. However, if a data section follows the .EXIT instruction, the computer would not know what to do next.

In addition, we know from the subroutine documentation that the subroutine needs to borrow the registers R0, R1, R2, and R5 during its operation. But we know that the instruction JSR R5, SUM does automatically save the old (R5). If the old contents of R0, R1, and R2 are important to the host program, then before calling the subroutine, the host program must save (R0), (R1), and (R2) in the stack and retrieve them after the subroutine is done. In this example, the host program does not need to save them, so the save-retrieve steps have been omitted.

5.4 LINKING OR TKB SUBROUTINES WITH THE HOST PROGRAM

There are two ways to link or TKB the subroutine with the host program to generate the executable memory image or TSK file, depending on what type of the subroutine file is available. If only the source file of the subroutine is available, then we may assemble the subroutine and the host program at the same time, using the following command:

≥MAC <HOST.OBJ>,<HOST.LST> = <SUBR.MAC>,<HOST.MAC>

As a result, we would have both the object and list files of the combined program. To generate the TSK file, we simply use the following command:

≥TKB HOST = HOST

and we have the executable HOST.TSK file ready for load and go (LGO) command.

However, if the object file of the subroutine is available, we may assemble the host alone to generate <HOST.OBJ> by the assembler. Then we could use TKB command to create the TSK file of the linked program:

≥TKB HOST = <SUBR.OBJ>, <HOST.OBJ>

Two examples will illustrate the procedure in detail.

EXAMPLE 1 ————————————————————————————————

Write a host program that will call for a subroutine named SCREEN. The host program is to select a group of males from an array of n candidates for a football team by their weights. Only candidates who weigh within the range of from 180 to 220 pounds inclusive are qualified. If a candidate is qualified, nothing will be done to his old data; if not, his original data will be replaced by a zero weight. First we must study the subroutine SCREEN carefully and see whether modification is necessary. Assume we have found the information about the subroutine.

[SUBROUTINE]
```
;This is a subroutine which will examine an array of data of
;n elements. If a datum is outside the range, from LOW-LIMIT
;to HIGH-LIMIT, it will be replaced by zeros, otherwise no
;modification will be made. It is expected that the array is
;arranged in such a way that the first three data, respectively,
;is data-array size, upper-limit and lower-limit, which is
;followed by an n-element data array to be examined. Further-
;more, the subroutine uses R5 as the data pointer, and
;registers R0, R1, and R2 to hold the transient data. The
;calling vector is,
;       SCREEN:    MOV #DATA, R5      ;DATA =STARTING DATA ARRAY
;                                     ;ADDRESS
;                  JSR PC, SCREEN
                   .GLOBL SCREEN
        SCREEN:    MOV (R5)+, R0      ;ARRAY SIZE → R0
                   MOV (R5)+, R1      ;HI-LIMIT → R1
                   MOV (R5)+, R2      ;LO-LIMIT → R2
        LOOP:      CMP (R5), R1       ;TOO HEAVY?
                   BGT REJECT         ;YES, REJECT
                   CMP (R5), R2       ;TOO LIGHT?
                   BLT REJECT         ;YES, REJECT
                   TST (R5)+          ;ADVANCE DATA POINTER
                   BR CHECK           ;CHECK IF IT IS DONE
        REJECT:    CLR (R5)+          ;CLEAR DATA, ADVANCE
                                      ;DATA POINTER
        CHECK:     SOB R0, LOOP       ;CHECK IF IT IS DONE
                   RTS PC
                   .END
```

[HOST PROGRAM]
```
                   .GLOBL    SCREEN
        DATA:      .WORD n, 220., 180.
                   .WORD d₁, d₂, . . . , dₙ
        START:     MOV #DATA, R5
                   JSR PC, SCREEN
                   HALT
                   .END START
```

Figure 5.10 (a) and (b) show a numerical example of this program.

```
 1                          ;EXAMPLE
 2                          ;
 3                          ;
 4                          ;
 5                          ;
 6                          ;<SUBROUTINE : SCREEN >
 7                          .GLOBL SCREEN
 8 000000 012500 SCREEN: MOV    (R5)+,R0   ;ARRAY SIZE → R0
 9 000002 012501         MOV    (R5)+,R1   ;HIGH-LIMIT → R1
10 000004 012502         MOV    (R5)+,R2   ;LOW-LIMIT → R2
11 000006 021501 LOOP:   CMP    (R5),R1    ;TOO HEAVY ?
12 000010 003004         BGT    REJECT
13 000012 021502         CMP    (R5),R2    ;TOO LIGHT ?
14 000014 002402         BLT    REJECT
15 000016 005725         TST    (R5)+      ;INCREMENT DATA COUNTER BY 2
16 000020 000401         BR     CHECK      ;CHECK IF IT IS DONE
17 000022 005025 REJECT: CLR    (R5)+      ;ZERO THE DATA AND ADVANCE POINTER
18 000024 077010 CHECK:  SOB    R0,LOOP    ;CHECK IF IT IS DONE
19 000026 000207         RTS    PC
20        000001         .END
```

Figure 5.10(a) Numerical example of screening football players.

```
 1                              ;EXAMPLE
 2                              ; ......... THIS IS THE HOST PROGRAM FOR SUBROUTINE SCREEN
 3
 4
 5
 6                              ;<HOST PROGRAM >
 7                              .GLOBL  SCREEN
 8 000000  000010  000334  000264  DATA:   .WORD  10,220.,180.
 9 000006  000310  000226  000276          .WORD  200.,150.,190.,230.,210.,170.,215.,240.
   000014  000346  000322  000252
   000022  000327  000360
10 000026  012705  000000'      START:  MOV   #DATA,R5      ;INITIAL DATA POINTER
11 000032  004767  000000G              JSR   PC,SCREEN     ;JUMP TO SUBROUTINE
12 000036  000000                       HALT
13 000026'                              .END  START
```

Execution Result: DATA: 10, 220., 180., 200., 0, 190., 0, 210., 0, 215., 0
note that values (<180.) or (>220.) have been reset to 0

Figure 5.10(b) Numerical example of screening football players.

EXAMPLE 2 _____

Modify Example 1 and generate a separate array to show the result of screening so that the original data array remains unchanged. For illustration purposes, use a different parameter passing technique.

```
        <SUBROUTINE: SCREEN>
        ;           CALLING VECTOR
        ;           JSR R5, SCREEN
        ;           .WORD    DATA        ;STARTING ADDRESS LABEL VALUE OF
        ;                                ;DATA ARRAY
        ;           .WORD    n           ;DATA ARRAY SIZE
        ;           .WORD    HI-LIMIT
        ;           .WORD    LO-LIMIT
        ;           .WORD    RESULT      ;STARTING ADDRESS VALUE OF RESULT
        ;                                ;ARRAY
                    .GLOBL   SCREEN
        SCREEN:     MOV (R5)+, R0        ;#DATA → R0, AS DATA POINTER
                    MOV (R5)+, R1        ;ARRAY SIZE → R1, AS DATA COUNTER
                    MOV (R5)+, R2        ;HI-LIMIT → R2
                    MOV (R5)+, R3        ;LO-LIMIT → R3
                    MOV (R5)+, R4        ;RESULT → R4 AS RESULT DATA
                                         ;POINTER
        LOOP:       CMP (R0), R2         ;TOO HEAVY?
                    BGT REJECT           ;YES, REJECT
                    CMP (R0), R3         ;TOO LIGHT?
                    BLT REJECT           ;YES, REJECT
                    MOV (R0)+, (R4)+     ;COPY ORIGINAL DATA TO RESULT
                    BR CHECK             ;CHECK IF FINISH
        REJECT:     CLR (R4)+            ;SET THIS RESULT ELEMENT ZERO
                    TST (R0)+            ;ADVANCE DATA POINTER
        CHECK:      SOB R1, LOOP         ;CHECK IF FINISH
                    RTS R5
                    .END

        <HOST PROGRAM>
                    .GLOBL   SCREEN
        DATA:       .WORD d₁, d₂, . . . , dₙ
        RESULT:     .BLKW n
        START:      JSR R5, SCREEN
                    .WORD    DATA, n, HI-LIMIT VALUE, LO-LIMIT VALUE
                    .WORD    RESULT
                    HALT
                    .END START
```

Figure 5.11 (a) and (b) show a numerical example of this program.

5.5 MORE EXAMPLES

In this section we present examples that illustrate how we can convert a general program into a subroutine and how the different parameter passing techniques described in the preceding sections can be applied to the same host-subroutine program with some modification. For convenience, we define the parameter passing techniques as follows:

technique 1 Δ parameters placed next to JSR instruction
technique 2 Δ parameters in a specific exclusive area
technique 3 Δ parameter transmission through stack memory

```
1                         ;EXAMPLE
2
3                         ......................
4
5                         ;<SUBROUTINE SCREEN >
6                         .GLOBL  SCREEN
7  000000 012500  SCREEN: MOV  (R5)+,R0     ;#DATA → R0 AS DATA POINTER
8  000002 012501          MOV  (R5)+,R1     ;ARRAY SIZE → R1 AS DATA COUNTER
9  000004 012502          MOV  (R5)+,R2     ;HIGH-LIMIT VALUE → R2
10 000006 012503          MOV  (R5)+,R3     ;LOW-LIMIT VALUE → R3
11 000010 012504          MOV  (R5)+,R4     ;#RESULT → R4,AS ARRAY POINTER
12 000012 021002  LOOP:   CMP  (R0),R2      ;TOO HEAVY ?
13 000014 003004          BGT  REJECT
14 000016 021003          CMP  (R0),R3      ;TOO LIGHT ?
15 000020 002402          BLT  REJECT
16 000022 012024          MOV  (R0)+,(R4)+  ;COPY DATA TO RESULT ARRAY
17 000024 000402          BR   CHECK
18 000026 005024  REJECT: CLR  (R4)+        ;SET THIS RESULT ELEMENT TO ZERO
19 000030 005720          TST  (R0)+        ;ADVANCE DATA POINTER
20 000032 077111  CHECK:  SOB  R1,LOOP      ;CHECK IF FINISH
21 000034 000205          RTS  R5
22        000001          .END
```

Figure 5.11(a)   Modified numerical example of screening football players.

```
1                              ;EXAMPLE
2                              ;   THIS IS THE HOST PROGRAM FOR SUBROUTINE SCREEN
3
4                              ......................
5
6                              ;<HOST PROGRAM >
7                              .GLOBL  SCREEN
8  000000 000310 000226 000276 DATA:   .WORD 200.,150.,190.,230.,210.,170.,215.,240.
   000006 000346 000322 000252
   000014 000327 000360
9  000020                      RESULT: .BLKW 10
10 000040 004567 000000G       START:  JSR  R5,SCREEN
11 000044 000000' 000010 000334         .WORD DATA,10,220.,180.,RESULT
   000052 000264 000020'
12 000056 000000                        HALT
13        000040'                        .END START
```

Execution Result: DATA: *(the 8 values are unchanged)*
                  RESULT: *200., 0, 190., 0, 210., 0, 215., 0*

*note that DATA array is unchanged, while in RESULT, the rejected data has been reset to 0.

Figure 5.11(b)   Modified numerical example of screening football players.

For each technique, the programmer is allowed to have a small logical variation. Figures 5.12 through 5.16 are examples in source program form that show the details. First, we show how the program BIGNUM can be converted into a subroutine that itself contains general data areas, N1 and N2, for temporary data storage. Although this technique makes the program easier to follow, it has some drawbacks. Compare the examples using techniques 1 and 1A against that using 1B.

First of all, the subroutine of the latter uses more memory space. Second, the subroutine of the latter cannot be stored in a ROM, or it is not "ROMable." Third, it is not a **reentrant subroutine.** That is, for a multitask application, there are cases in which a host program may call a subroutine, but it might temporarily quit before finishing. In the meantime another host program might call the same subroutine, and then the data in N1 and N2 would be lost. It is therefore not advisable to have a general data area within a subroutine.

```
        ;PROGRAM THAT COMPARES TWO NUMBERS AND
        ;STORES THE BIGGER ONE.
        ;
        ;
        .TITLE      BIGNUM
START:  CMP         N1,N2                   ;COMPARE TWO NUMBERS
        BGE         POS
        MOV         N2,RESULT
        HALT
POS:    MOV         N1,RESULT
        HALT
N1:     .WORD       11
N2:     .WORD       7
RESULT: .BLKW       1
        .END        START

        ;CONVERTING THE PROGRAM INTO A GENERAL SUBROUTINE,
        ;THE SUBROUTINE CALLING VECTOR IS AS FOLLOWS:
        ;
        ;       JSR         R5,SUB
        ;       .WORD       N1
        ;       .WORD       N2
        ;RESULT: .BLKW      1
        ;
        .GLOBL      SUB
SUB:    MOV         @(R5)+,N1
        MOV         @(R5)+,N2
        CMP         N1,N2
        BGE         POS
        MOV         N2,(R5)+                ;(N2) → RESULT
        RTS         R5
POS:    MOV         N1,(R5)+                ;(N1) → RESULT
        RTS         R5
N1:     .BLKW       1
N2:     .BLKW       1
        .END
```

Figure 5.12 Example of writing a subroutine.

```
                ;PROGRAM THAT CONVERTS BIGNUM TO A SUBROUTINE USING
                ;NO. 1 PARAMETER PASSING TECHNIQUE.
                ;
                ;
START:    NOP                              ;SIMULATING ANY INSTRUCTION
          NOP                              ;SIMULATING ANY INSTRUCTION
          JSR       R5,SUB
N1:       .WORD     11
N2:       .WORD     7
RESULT:   .BLKW     1
          NOP                              ;SIMULATING ANY INSTRUCTION
          HALT
          ;
SUB:      CMP       (R5)+,(R5)
          BGE       POS
          MOV       (R5)+,(R5)+            ;(N2) → RESULT
          RTS       R5
POS:      TST       (R5)+                  ;(R5) = (R5)+2 SO THAT (R5) IS
                                           ;POINTING TO RESULT
          MOV       -4(R5),(R5)+           ;(N1) → RESULT
          RTS       R5
          .END      START


                ;PROGRAM THAT CONVERTS BIGNUM TO A SUBROUTINE USING
                ;NO. 1A PARAMETER PASSING TECHNIQUE.
                ;
START:    NOP                              ;SIMULATING ANY INSTRUCTION
          NOP                              ;SIMULATING ANY INSTRUCTION
          JSR       R5,SUB
A:        .WORD     N1
B:        .WORD     N2
C::       .WORD     RESULT
          NOP                              ;SIMULATING ANY INSTRUCTION
          HALT
N1:       .WORD     -2
N2:       .WORD     7
RESULT:   .BLKW     1
          ;
          ;
SUB:      CMP       @(R5)+,@(R5)
          BGE       POS
          MOV       @(R5)+,@(R5)+
          RTS       R5
POS:      TST       (R5)+                  ;(R5) = (R5)+2 SO THAT (R5) IS
                                           ;POINTING TO RESULT
          MOV       @-4(R5),@(R5)+         ;(N1) → RESULT
          RTS       R5
          .END      START
```

Figure 5.13 Examples of subroutine parameter passing.

5.6 NESTED SUBROUTINES

Because of the stack memory configuration, the PDP-11 system makes the subroutine nesting operation very simple. That is, a subroutine can call another subroutine and another subroutine, and so on, as long as the capacity of the stack memory is large enough to hold all the return address information. Figure 5.17 illustrates the nested subroutine

```
                ;PROGRAM THAT CONVERTS BIGNUM TO A SUBROUTINE
                ;USING NO. 1B PARAMETER PASSING TECHNIQUE.
                ;
                ;
                ;
START:  NOP                     ;SIMULATING ANY INSTRUCTION
        NOP                     ;SIMULATING ANY INSTRUCTION
        JSR     R5,SUB
D1:     .WORD   11
D2:     .WORD   7
RESULT: .BLKW   1
        NOP                     ;SIMULATING ANY INSTRUCTION
        HALT
        ;
SUB:    MOV     (R5)+,N1        ;BRING DATA IN
        MOV     (R5)+,N2
        CMP     N1,N2
        BGE     POS
        MOV     N2,(R5)+        ;(N2) → RESULT
        RTS     R5
POS:    MOV     N1,(R5)+        ;(N1) → RESULT
        RTS     R5
N1:     .BLKW   1
N2:     .BLKW   1
        .END    START


                ;PROGRAM THAT CONVERTS BIGNUM TO A SUBROUTINE
                ;USING NO. 1C PARAMETER PASSING TECHNIQUE.
                ;
                ;
                ;
START:  NOP                     ;SIMULATING ANY INSTRUCTION
        NOP                     ;SIMULATING ANY INSTRUCTION
        JSR     R5,SUB
A1:     .WORD   D1
A2:     .WORD   D2
RESULT: .BLKW   1
        NOP                     ;SIMULATING ANY INSTRUCTION
        HALT
D1:     .WORD   −2
D2:     .WORD   7
        ;
SUB:    MOV     @(R5)+,N1       ;BRING DATA IN
        MOV     @(R5)+,N2
        CMP     N1,N2
        BGE     POS
        MOV     N2,(R5)+        ;(N2) → RESULT
        RTS     R5
POS:    MOV     N1,(R5)+        ;(N1) → RESULT
        RTS     R5
N1:     .BLKW   1
N2:     .BLKW   1
        .END    START
```

Figure 5.14 Examples of subroutine parameter passing.

operation and the memory map of the stack memory while the system is executing the nth subroutine. Assume the stack memory was initialized with 1172. The return address to the host was pushed into the stack first, and those of the subroutines 1, 2, . . . , $n-1$ followed. When the subroutines are finished one by one, the return addresses stored are popped back to PC in the right order.

```
                ;PROGRAM THAT CONVERTS BIGNUM TO A SUBROUTINE
                ;USING NO. 2 PARAMETER PASSING TECHNIQUE.
                ;
                ;
START:   NOP                       ;SIMULATING ANY INSTRUCTION
         NOP                       ;SIMULATING ANY INSTRUCTION
         MOV      #DATA,R5
         JSR      PC,SUB
         NOP                       ;SIMULATING ANY INSTRUCTION
         HALT
DATA:    .WORD    -11
         .WORD    -3
RESULT:  .BLKW    1
SUB:     CMP      (R5)+,(R5)
         BGE      POS
         MOV      (R5)+,(R5)+      ;(DATA+2) → RESULT
         RTS      PC
POS:     TST      (R5)+            ;(R5) = (R5)+2 SO THAT (R5) IS
                                   ;POINTING TO RESULT
         MOV      -4(R5),(R5)+     ;(DATA) → RESULT
         RTS      PC
         .END     START

                ;PROGRAM THAT CONVERTS BIGNUM TO A SUBROUTINE
                ;USING NO. 2A PARAMETER PASSING TECHNIQUE.
                ;
                ;
START:   NOP                       ;SIMULATING ANY INSTRUCTION
         NOP                       ;SIMULATING ANY INSTRUCTION
         MOV      #DATA,R5
         JSR      PC,SUB
         NOP                       ;SIMULATING ANY INSTRUCTION
         HALT
DATA:    .WORD    -11
         .WORD    -3
RESULT:  .BLKW    1
SUB:     MOV      (R5)+,N1         ;(DATA) → N1
         MOV      (R5)+,N2         ;(DATA+2) → N2
         CMP      N1,N2
         BGE      POS
         MOV      N2,(R5)+         ;(DATA+2) → RESULT
         RTS      PC
POS:     MOV      N1,(R5)+         ;(DATA) → RESULT
         RTS      PC
N1:      .BLKW    1
N2:      .BLKW    1
         .END     START
```

Figure 5.15 Examples of subroutine parameter passing.

5.7 COROUTINES

Earlier we introduced the special instruction that links coroutines. In this configuration, the leaving and returning instruction are identical, and there is no host program per se. Instead, the two programs can call each other. Thus one is the other's subroutine, and the configuration is known as a **coroutine configuration.** A typical application is in the assembling process, where one routine may process the symbolic address and the other the mnemonic operation code.

```
                    ;PROGRAM THAT CONVERTS BIGNUM TO A SUBROUTINE
                    ;USING NO. 3 PARAMETER PASSING TECHNIQUE.
                    ;
                    ;
START:      NOP
            NOP
PREP:       MOV     N2,-(SP)        ;(N2) → STACK
            MOV     N1,-(SP)        ;(N1) → STACK
JMPSUB:     JSR     PC,SUB
            MOV     (SP)+,RESULT
            NOP
            HALT
N1:         .WORD   13
N2:         .WORD   -13
RESULT:     .BLKW   1
            ;
SUB:        MOV     (SP)+,R0        ;SAVE 'RETURN PC'
            CMP     (SP)+,(SP)      ;COMPARE (N1),(N2)
            BGE     POS
            MOV     R0,-(SP)        ;RESTORE 'RETURN PC'
            RTS     PC
POS:        TST     -(SP)           ;DECREMENT SP BY 2
            MOV     R0,-(SP)        ;RESTORE 'RETURN PC'
            RTS     PC
            .END    START


                    ;PROGRAM THAT CONVERTS BIGNUM TO A SUBROUTINE
                    ;USING NO. 3A PARAMETER PASSING TECHNIQUE.
                    ;
                    ;
START:      NOP
            NOP
PREP:       MOV     D2,-(SP)        ;(D2) → STACK
            MOV     D1,-(SP)        ;(D1) → STACK
JMPSUB:     JSR     PC,SUB
            MOV     (SP)+,RESULT
            NOP
            HALT
D1:         .WORD   13
D2:         .WORD   -13
RESULT:     .BLKW   1
            ;
SUB:        MOV     (SP)+,R0        ;SAVE 'RETURN PC'
            MOV     (SP)+,N1        ;(D1) → N1
            MOV     (SP)+,N2        ;(D2) → N2
            CMP     N1,N2           ;COMPARE (N1),(N2)
            BGE     POS
            MOV     N2,-(SP)
            MOV     R0,-(SP)        ;RESTORE 'RETURN PC'
            RTS     PC
POS:        MOV     N1,-(SP)
            MOV     R0,-(SP)        ;RESTORE 'RETURN PC'
            RTS     PC
N1:         .BLKW   1
N2:         .BLKW   1
            .END    START
```

Figure 5.16 Examples of a subroutine parameter.

HOST

JSR PC,
SUBR 1

RTS PC

SUBR 1

SUBR 2

SUBR n

STACK MEMORY MAP

ADDRESS	CONTENTS
	x x x x x x
	x x x x x x
. . . .	
	RETURN TO SUBR (n − 1)
. . . .	
0 0 1 1 6 4	RETURN TO SUBR 2
0 0 1 1 6 6	RETURN TO SUBR 1
0 0 1 1 7 0	RETURN TO HOST
0 0 1 1 7 2	x x x x x x

Figure 5.17 Nested subroutine operation.

5.8 RECURSION

Recursion is a process in which a subroutine calls itself. It can be best understood through an example.

EXAMPLE

Calculation of n-factorial using stack memory as the parameter transmission medium. Let us first define:

$n \geq 1$

n-factorial $= n! = n(n − 1)! = n(n − 1) \ . \ . \ . \ . \ . \ 1$

$0! = 1! = 1$

The program follows:

```
   ; SECTION I: INITIALIZATION FOR FACTORIAL OPERATION
1) START:    MOV #n, R0      ;INITIAL R0 AS DATA COUNTER
2)           CLR R2          ;INITIAL REGISTER-PAIR (R2,R3)
                             ;AS DESTINATION
3)           MOV #1, R3      ;FOR THE PRODUCT, R3 = LOW-ORDER
                             ;WORD
4)           JSR PC, FACTOR  ;JUMP TO SUBROUTINE FACTORIAL
5) QUIT:     HALT
   ; SECTION II: GENERATE DATA ARRAY IN STACK MEMORY
6) FACTOR:   TST R0          ;CHECK IF (R0)=0, OR IF ARRAY HAS
                             ;BEEN CREATED IN STACK
7)           BEQ BEGIN       ;YES, BEGIN TO MULTIPLY
8)           MOV R0, -(SP)   ;NO, CONTINUE CREATE DATA ARRAY
9)           DEC R0          ;DECREMENT DATA COUNTER
10)          JSR PC, FACTOR  ;SUBROUTINE CALLS ITSELF
```

```
          ; SECTION III: MULTIPLICATION PROCESS
11) SETSRC:     MOV (SP)+, R1   ;SET UP SOURCE OPERAND FOR
                                ;MULTIPLICATION
12)             JSR PC, MULT    ;CALL MULTIPLY ROUTINE, PUSH
                                ;#BEGIN INTO STACK
13) BEGIN:      RTS PC          ;JUMP TO SETSRC IF NOT DONE
                                ;OTHERWISE #QUIT → PC
14) MULT:       MUL R1, R2      ;(R1) × (R2,R3) → (R2,R3)
15)             RTS PC          ;#BEGIN → PC
16)             .END START
```

Note that the program consists of three sections. The first section is for initialization, the second for setting up the data array in the stack, and the third for the multiplication process.

In section I, we initialize R0 with $\#n$, which is to be used as data counter for setting up the data array in the stack memory, and the register pair R2, R3 to 0, 1, which is to be used to store the product of the multiplication. Thus, after instruction 3, we have:

$$(R0) = \#n$$
$$(R2),(R3) = 0,1$$

Instruction 4 jumps the operation to instruction 6. Instructions 6, 7, 8, and 9 eventually set up a data array in the stack in a desirable order, as shown below:

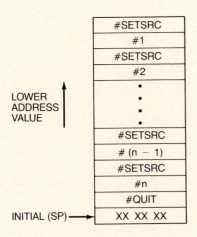

LOWER ADDRESS VALUE

INITIAL (SP) →

Let us trace this map for a few steps. Note that instruction 4 puts the updated (PC), which has the address value #QUIT, into stack, and the program jumps to instruction 6. Since initially $(R0) = \#n$, which is not zero, the program goes to instruction 8 and thus $\#n \to$ STACK, as shown. Instruction 10 then pushes #SETSRC into stack and the program jumps to instruction 6 again. But (R0) is now $\#(n - 1)$, and as a result instruction 8 pushes $\#(n - 1)$ into stack. The process is repeated until $(R0) = 0$.

The final stack map is thus created; in it we have numbers interlaced with the address value #SETSRC. At this point, the program, ordered by instruction 7, jumps to

```
 1                                      ;EXAMPLE
 2                                      ;
 3                                      ;
 4                                      ;
 5                                      ;
 6 000000  012700  000005  START:   MOV   #5,R0         ;INITIAL R0 AS DATA COUNTER
 7 000004  012702  000001           MOV   #1,R2         ;DESTINATION FOR THE PRODUCT
 8 000010  004767  000002           JSR   PC,FACTOR
 9 000014  000000          QUIT:    HALT
10 000016  005700          FACTOR:  TST   R0            ;CHECK IF (R0) = 0 (ARRAY CREATED?)
11 000020  001407                   BEQ   BEGIN         ;YES, BEGIN TO MULTIPLY
12 000022  010046                   MOV   R0,-(SP)      ;NO, CONTINUE TO CREATE ARRAY
13 000024  005300                   DEC   R0            ;DECREMENT DATA COUNTER
14 000026  004767  177764           JSR   PC,FACTOR     ;SUBROUTINE CALLS ITSELF
15 000032  012601          SETSRC:  MOV   (SP)+,R1      ;SETUP SOURCE OPERAND
16 000034  004767  000002           JSR   PC,MULT       ;CALLS MULTIPLY ROUTINE
17 000040  000207          BEGIN:   RTS   PC            ;JUMP TO "SETSRC" IF NOT DONE,
18                                                      ;   OTHERWISE #QUIT → PC
19 000042  010204          MULT:    MOV   R2,R4         ;R4 CONTAINS MULTIPLICATION
20 000044  005002                   CLR   R2
21 000046  060402          LOOP:    ADD   R4,R2
22 000050  077102                   SOB   R1,LOOP
23 000052  000207                   RTS   PC
24          000000'                  .END  START
```

Execution Result: R2 contains 170 (octal)

Figure 5.18 Numerical example of recursion to determine 5!

instruction 13, which in turn moves the top layer of the stack, #SETSRC, into PC. The CPU begins to execute instruction 11. This instruction pops the top layer of the stack, which is #1 at this time, into R1. Basically this instruction sets up the source operand for the multiply subroutine, or instruction 14, which multiplies (R1) with (R2, R3) and places the product in register pair R2 and R3, with the least significant word in R3. Since instruction 12 has put the address value of #BEGIN into stack, instruction 15 will bring the program to instruction 13, which in turn puts #SETSRC into PC. This process repeats until the bottom layer of the stack, which is #QUIT, shows in PC. The program thus ends at instruction 5 and leaves the final product in register pair R2, R3.   ■ ■

Figure 5.18 shows a numerical program for this example. For simplicity, we use $n = 5$ here.

5.9 BUBBLE SORT PROGRAM

A sort program is one that arranges a randomly ordered data array into a numeric order. A **bubble sort** program, as its name implies, is one that will sort an array such that the one with the lower value will "bubble up" to the lower address and the one with the lowest value will settle at the lowest address or the top of the array. This is also a useful program for sorting an array in alphabetic order, since the ASCII's values of the alphabet are in numeric order, with the letter A having the lowest numeric value.

Figure 5.19(a) shows the memory map of a data array of n elements. Let us define the parameters as follows:

ARRAY $\underline{\Delta}$ starting address of the array
ARRAY $+ 2(n - 1)$ $\underline{\Delta}$ maximum address of the array
TOP $\underline{\Delta}$ pointer, pointing at the top element of the unsorted portion of the data array
BOT $\underline{\Delta}$ pointer, pointing at the bottom element of the data array
IDX $\underline{\Delta}$ address for initial index value

Note that in the address column we use the indexed address symbol; that is, ARRAY$(2(n - 1))$ has an address value of #ARRAY $+ 2(n - 1)$. Remember that each datum occupies one memory word or two bytes, which is why we multiply $n - 1$ by 2.

Now we start to compare the bottom two elements, namely, d_{n-1} and d_{n-2}, with the addresses ARRAY$(2(n - 1))$ and ARRAY$(2(n - 2))$, respectively. If $d_{n-1} < d_{n-2}$ then the two elements are swapped; otherwise they are left untouched. The comparison continues on d_{n-2} and d_{n-3}, and so on. Eventually the element with the smallest value will bubble up to the top and stay there "forever." Since once the smallest one gets to the top we do not need to compare it any more, we can move the TOP pointer one word higher in value toward the bottom to avoid comparing the smallest one against the others repeatedly. The process will be finished as the TOP = BOT.

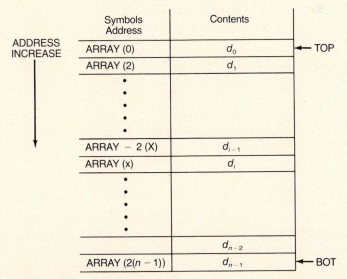

Figure 5.19(a) Memory map.

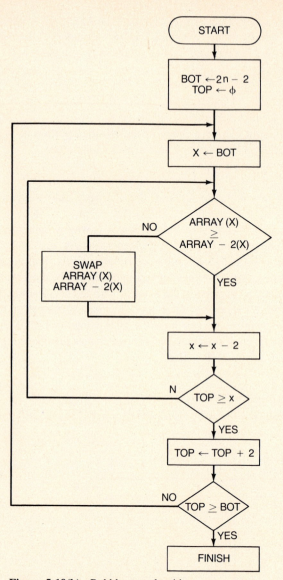

Figure 5.19(b)   Bubble sort algorithm.

Figure 5.19(b) shows the flowchart of this algorithm, and its list file program for $n = 10_8$ is shown in Figure 5.19(c). This program is quite straightforward and easy to follow. However, it is not in a subroutine format. As an exercise, let us modify it to make it a subroutine. Figure 5.19(d) shows the host and subroutine program. Figure 5.19(e) shows another alternate.

```
                                    ; EXAMPLE OF A SORTING PROGRAM.
 1
 2
 3                          .MCALL  .WRITE,.EXIT
 4
 5  000000  000000  TOP:    .WORD   0                      ;INITIAL R1 AS TOP DATA POINTER
 6  000002  000016  BOT:    .WORD   16                     ;INITIAL R2 AS BOTTOM POINTER
 7  000004  000016  IDX:    .WORD   16                     ;INITIAL R0 AS THE INDEX
 8  000006  000006  ARRAY:  .WORD   6,-5,-1,0,3,7,-6,1
    000010  177773
    000012  177777
    000014  000000
    000016  000003
    000020  000007
    000022  177772
    000024  000001
 9  000026  016701          MOV     TOP,R1        177746   ;INITIAL R1 AS TOP DATA POINTER
10  000032  016702  START:  MOV     BOT,R2        177744   ;INITIAL R2 AS BOTTOM POINTER
11  000036  016700  LOOP1:  MOV     IDX,R0        177742   ;INITIAL R0 AS THE INDEX
12  000042  026060  LOOP2:  CMP     ARRAY(R0),ARRAY-2(R0)  ;COMPARE ADJACENT DATA ELEMENTS
                                          000006'  000004'
13
14  000050  002007          BGE     INDEX
15  000052  016003  SWAP:   MOV     ARRAY(R0),R3  000006'  ;SMALLER NUMBER → R3
16  000056  016060          MOV     ARRAY-2(R0),ARRAY(R0)  ;LARGER ONE SUNK DOWN ONE WORD
                                          000004'  000006'
17
18  000064  010360          MOV     R3,ARRAY-2(R0) 000004' ;SMALLER ONE BUBBLE-UP ONE WORD
19  000070  005740  INDEX:  TST     -(R0)                  ;(R0) POINTS TO LOWER ADDRESS
20  000072  020067          CMP     R0,TOP        177702   ;BUBBLE UP TO TOP ?
21  000076  003361          BGT     LOOP2                  ;COMPARE NEXT ADJACENT DATA
22  000100  005721          TST     (R1)+                  ;(TOP)+2 → TOP
23  000102  020102          CMP     R1,R2                  ;ALL DONE ?
24  000104  002754          BLT     LOOP1                  ;DO NEXT ROUND
25  000106  005000          CLR     R0
26  000110          OUTPUT: .WRITE  ARRAY(R0)              ;OUTPUT THE ARRAY
27  000114  005720          TST     (R0)+
28  000116  020067          CMP     R0,BOT        177660   ;OUTPUT FINISHED ?
29  000122  003772          BLE     OUTPUT
30  000124          .EXIT
31  000026'                 .END    START
```

Execution Result: -6 -5 -1 0 1 3 6 7

Figure 5.19(c) A bubble sort program for an array of 10_8 element.

6.1 INTRODUCTION

Macro or macro instruction is basically a provision that offers the user or system programmer flexibility and convenience. It practically allows users to make or create their own "composite instructions" based on the basic instructions available for the PDP-11 computing system. Macros are often confused with subroutines. Although both allow the user to use them repeatedly without rewriting the routine, there are great differences in structure and in properties with respect to memory space and execution time.

The subroutines described in the preceding chapter are normally known as **close routines,** while the macros are called **open routines.** Recall that for calling a subroutine, the host program must use a linking instruction pair—namely, JSR and RTS—to jump into and return from that subroutine. In addition, it is the responsibility of the host program to pass the proper set of parameters to and from the subroutine. All these processes require extra memory space and executing time, so they are known as the "overhead cost" of using a subroutine. A subroutine itself, however, does not require more memory spaces, regardless of whether it is called one or a hundred times. As far as the memory space is concerned, besides the overhead, it is a "once-only" situation.

A Macro instruction, in contrast, is merely a group of basic PDP-11 instructions that make up one "super" or "Macro" instruction. Since it belongs to the instruction category, a macro has the fields for operation code and operands. Each time a macro is used, the assembler will "translate" its corresponding basic instructions into machine code to yield the object file. That is, if a specific macro whose machine code occupies 10 memory words is used 10 times in a program, it will be "expanded" or "translated" 10 times and thus require 100 memory words.

Figure 6.1 shows the difference between a subroutine and a macro in reference to

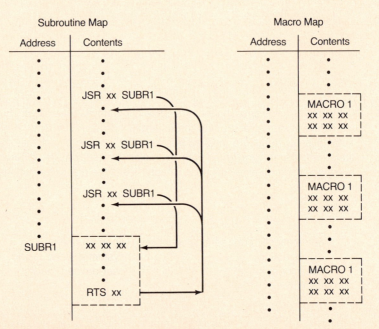

Figure 6.1 Memory maps for subroutine and macros.

their memory maps. It is evident that the memory space required by a macro is linearly proportional to the frequency of that macro being used, whereas in the case of subroutine, the memory space requirement is practically independent of the calling frequency. However, the latter would require more time for execution. As a general rule, the subroutine approach is better for a longer subprogram with high calling frequency, and the macro approach is suitable for a short one. Basically, we consider the tradeoff between executing time and memory space when we want to determine which approach is better for our application.

6.2 CLASSIFICATIONS OF MACRO INSTRUCTONS

There are two essential kinds of macros: system-defined and user-defined. A **system-defined macro** is a macro instruction normally defined by the system designer and provided by the manufacturer. Or it is a macro instruction defined by a system programmer who then installs it into the system for the application programmer to use. For example, for a basic PDP-11 system, we might have the following system-defined macros:

1. .PNUM N, which would print the signed octal value at location N to an output terminal or CRT.
2. .RNUM N, which would read a signed octal digital into location N from a keyboard.
3. .Exit, which can be used to replace the HALT instruction so that the program would exit from the program after execution.

Users can refer to the user manual to find out how many and what system-defined macros are available so that they do not have to reinvent them in application programs. In many cases, however, system programmers may create some system-defined macros for their own application programs. If so, the system programmer would first define the macros and then install them into the system for all users. For example, in our laboratory, we have created and installed system-defined macros such as .WRITE, .RAD, and .READ for our own convenience. For consistency and less possibility of confusion, a system-defined macro always has a dot or a period symbol preceding its mnemonic name once it is created and installed in the system.

The procedure for using system-defined macros is as follows:

1. In the first line of the program, we write: .MCALL .PNUM .EXIT .WRITE if in our program we are going to use them as macro instructions. Here, .MCALL is a pseudoinstruction to inform the assembler that we will be using those system macros.
2. We then use the macros in the same way we would use other basic instructions.

For example:

```
        .MCALL .PNUM, .EXIT
START:  .PNUM N             ;USE SYSTEM MACRO AS AN
                            ;INSTRUCTON
        .EXIT
N:      .WORD 6
```

This program after execution would display the number 6 on the CRT. In the next section we describe how a user-defined macro can be created.

6.3 USER-DEFINED MACROS

Format

The general format of a user-defined macro is shown below. The *xs* denote the basic instruction statement.

```
. MACRO _____   _____ , _____ , _____
x x x x ┐                Fields for dummy arguments or parameters
x x x x │                Field for the mnemonic name of the macro
x x x x │                A collection of basic instructions
x x x x │
x x x x │
x x x x ┘
.ENDM
```

For example:

```
        .MACRO SUMINC A,B,C      ;A MACRO FOR SUM AND INCREMENT
        ADD A,B
        INC B
        ADD B,C
        .ENDM
;MAIN PROGRAM
START:  MOV #4, R0
        MOV #1, R1
        SUMINC #10, R0, R1
        SUMINC X,Y,Z
        HALT
X:      .WORD 10.
Y:      .WORD 4
Z:      .WORD 2
        .END START
```

After it is assembled, this program will generate an object file. For convenience, the mnemonic equivalent of the object file can be shown as follows:

```
START:  MOV #4, R0
        MOV #1, R1
        ADD #10, R0      ;FIRST EXPANSION OF THE MACRO
                         ;SUMINC

        INC R0
        ADD R0, R1
        ADD X,Y          ;SECOND EXPANSION OF THE MACRO
                         ;SUMINC

        INC Y
        ADD Y,Z
        HALT
X:      .WORD 10
Y:      .WORD 4
Z:      .WORD 2
        .END START
```

Note that whenever the macro is used, it is replaced or "expanded" by the assembler with three basic instructions. After execution, we will find:

$$(R0) = 15$$
$$(R1) = 16$$
$$(X) = 10$$
$$(Y) = 15$$
$$(Z) = 17$$

Automatically Created Local Symbols

In some cases, we must use one or more symbolic address labels within a macro. These local symbolic addresses, however, would cause problems when the macro is being used more than once.

For example, this program uses the macro technique to copy a block of data from one place to the other:

```
          .MACRO COPY ARRAY1, ARRAY2, M
                               ;M IS A POSITIVE INTEGER
                MOV #ARRAY1, R0    ;R0 AS SOURCE-DATA POINTER
                MOV #ARRAY2, R1    ;R1 AS DESTINATION-DATA POINTER
                MOV #M, R2         ;INITIAL DATA COUNTER, (R2)=M
LOOP:           MOV (R0)+, (R1)+   ;TRANSFER DATA
                SOB R2, LOOP       ;CONTINUE
                .ENDM
;MAIN PROGRAM
A1:             .WORD d1, d2, ..., dm
B1:             .BLKW m
A2:             .WORD b1, b2, ..., bn
B2:             .BLKW n
START:          COPY A1,B1,m
                COPY A2,B2,n
                .END START
```

After expansion, the program can be shown as follows:

```
;MAIN PROGRAM
   A1:          .WORD d1,d2,...,dm
   B1:          .BLKW  m
   A2:          .WORD b1,b2,...bn
   B2:          .BLKW  n
   START:   MOV  #A1, R0
            MOV  #B1, R1
            MOV  #m, R2       ;FIRST EXPANSION
   LOOP:    MOV  (R0)+, (R1)+
            SOB  R2, LOOP
            MOV  #A2, R0
            MOV  #B2, R1
            MOV  #n, R2       ;SECOND EXPANSION
   LOOP:    MOV  (R0)+, (R1)+
            SOB  R2, LOOP
            .END   START
```

Note that the program, after macro expansion, has two identical symbolic address labels—namely, LOOP. This of course would cause problems since the assembler would consider it as an error because the address value of LOOP is not uniquely defined. There are two ways to solve the problem. One is quite straightforward but somewhat cumbersome, and the other is more convenient to the user. The following examples illustrate the two methods. The simple one is first.

EXAMPLE 1 ───

```
.MACRO     COPY ARRAY1, ARRAY2, M, LOOP
           MOV  #ARRAY1, R0
           MOV  #M, R2
           MOV  #ARRAY2, R1
LOOP:      MOV  (R0)+, (R1)+
           SOB  R2,LOOP
.ENDM
```

Note that originally the LOOP is a "local" address label within the macro. Here we treat it as an operand of the macro or an external address label so that the user can control it as follows:

```
;MAIN PROGRAM
A1:        .WORD d1, d2,...,dm
B1:        .BLKW  m
A2:        .WORD b1, b2,...,bn
B2:        .BLKW  n
START:     COPY  A1, B1, m, L1
           COPY  A2, B2, n, L2
           .END   START
```

After expansion, we would have:

```
A1:        .WORD d1,d2,...,dm
B1:        .BLKW  m
A2:        .WORD b1, b2,..., bn
B2:        .BLKW  n
START:     MOV    #A1, R0
           MOV    #B1, R1
           MOV    #m, R2
L1:        MOV    (R0)+, (R1)+
           SOB    R2,L1
           MOV    #A2, R0
           MOV    #B2, R1
           MOV    #n, R2
L2:        MOV    (R0)+, (R1)+
           SOB    R2, L2
           .END START
```

Note that each address label is uniquely defined.

EXAMPLE 2 ───

This example shows how we can use the automatically created local symbol feature provided by the PDP's RSX-11M operating system to cope with the problem. That is, we just inform the assembler what and how many local address symbols are used within the macro, and let the assembler make all the local address symbols unique.

```
.MACRO     COPY ARRAY1, ARRAY2, M, ?LOOP
           MOV  #ARRAY1, R0
           MOV  #ARRAY2, R1
           MOV  #M, R2
LOOP:      MOV  (R0)+, (R1)+
           SOB  R2, LOOP
.ENDM
```

Note that here we use a question mark to precede the local address symbol to request the assembler to assign a unique address label each time the macro is called.

```
;MAIN PROGRAM
A1:        .WORD d1, d2, ..., dm
B1:        .BLKW  m
A2:        .WORD b1, b2,...,bn
B2:        .BLKW  n
START:     COPY   A1, B1, m
           COPY   A2, B2, n
           HALT
           .END START

;MAIN PROGRAM AFTER EXPANSION
   A1:        .WORD d1,d2,...,dm
   B1:        .BLKW  m
   A2:        .WORD b1,b2,...,bn
   B2:        .BLKW  n
   START:     MOV    #A1, R0
              MOV    #B1, R1
              MOV    #m, R2
   64$:       MOV    (R0)+,(R1)+  ;FIRST AUTOMATIC LOCAL ADDRESS
                                  ;ASSIGNED

              SOB    R2,64$
              MOV    #A2, R0
              MOV    #B2, R1
              MOV    #n, R2
   65$:       MOV    (R0)+, (R1)+ ;SECOND AUTOMATIC LOCAL
                                  ;ADDRESS ASSIGNED

              SOB    R2, 65$
              HALT
              .END START
```

Note that the local address symbols are automatically assigned by the assembler with a format of n$, where $64 \leq n \leq 127$ in decimal.

EXAMPLE 3

In many applications, we would like temporarily to save the contents of all general purpose registers—R0, . . . , R5—in the stack and retrieve or unsave them afterward. Since these processes are simple and short, the macro approach would be appropriate. The following procedure shows how we can enrich Example 2 with SAVE and UNSAVE macros. Here, we assume that the main program has important information in R0, R1, and R2 before we use COPY-MACRO.

```
.MACRO SAVREG              ;SAVE REGISTERS
        MOV R0,-(SP)
        MOV R1,-(SP)
        MOV R2,-(SP)
.ENDM SAVREG
.MACRO RETRREG             ;RETRIEVE REGISTERS
        MOV (SP)+, R2
        MOV (SP)+, R1
        MOV (SP)+, R0
.ENDM RETRREG
```

Note that since we are saving the contents in the stack, which is a last-in–first-out memory, we must write the unsave process in reverse order.

```
        .MACRO COPY ARRAY1, ARRAY2, N, ?LOOP
                MOV #ARRAY1, R0
                MOV #ARRAY2, R1
                MOV N, R2          ;TO SHOW AN ALTERNATIVE, WE
                                   ;TREAT N AS AN ADDRESS LABEL HERE
LOOP:           MOV (R0)+, (R1)+
                SOB R2, LOOP
        .ENDM COPY

        ;MAIN PROGRAM
          A1:           .WORD d1, d2, . . . , dm
          B1:           .BLKW m
          A2:           .WORD b1, b2, . . . , bm
          B2:           .BLKW m
          N:            .WORD m
          START:        .
                        .
                        .
                        SAVREG
                        COPY A1, B1, N
                        COPY A2, B2, N
                        RETRREG
                        .
                        .
                        .
                        .END START
```

EXAMPLE 4 ——

In this example, we show the application of both system macros and user-defined macros. The program uses the system macros (1) .WRITE to display the contents of the specific memory locations on the CRT, and (2) .RAD to let the user specify the radix system to be used. Therefore, the program is user-machine interactive.

```
        .MCALL .RAD, .READ, .WRITE,.EXIT
                                   ;CALL SYSTEM MACROS
        .MACRO SAVREG              ;USER DEFINED MACROS
                MOV R0,-(SP)
                MOV R1,-(SP)
                MOV R2,-(SP)
        .ENDM   SAVREG
        .MACRO  RETREG
                MOV (SP)+,R2
                MOV (SP)+,R1
                MOV (SP)+,R0
        .ENDM   RETREG
        .MACRO  COPY    ARRAY1, ARRAY2, N, ?LOOP
                MOV     #ARRAY1, R0
                MOV     #ARRAY2, R1
                MOV     N, R2
LOOP:           MOV (R0)+, (R1)+
                SOB R2, LOOP
        .ENDM COPY
        ;MAIN PROGRAM
          1) START: .WRITE "\\INPUT_DESIRED_RADIX_AND_FORMAT_OPTION:
          2) .RAD
          3) .WRITE "\\INPUT_3_NUMBERS:_
          4) .READ A1
          5) .WRITE "INPUT_3_CHARACTERS:_
```

```
 6) .READ 'A2
 7) SAVREG
 8) COPY A1, B1, N
 9) RETREG
10  .WRITE B1, B1+2, B1+4
11) SAVREG
12) COPY A2, B2, N
13) RETREG
14) .WRITE 'B2
15) .EXIT
16) A1: .BLKW 3
    A2: .BLKW 3
    B1: .BLKW 3
    B2: .BLKW 3
    N:  .WORD 3
    .END START
```

■ ■

If your system does not have the system macros we have used here, you will not be confused if you just accept the format as shown. Let us work through the program and find out how these system macros function.

Line 1 would display on the CRT the following message: INPUT DESIRED RADIX AND FORMAT OPTION:

Line 2 would cause the computer continuously to check the keyboard input. If the user at the keyboard does not do anything, the computer will just wait for input. Suppose the user types 8L <CR>. Then the computer would interpret this to mean that the user would like to use octal radix and left-justified format, and execute the next line.

Line 3 displays the message: INPUT 3 NUMBERS:

Line 4 waits for the user to input three numbers at the keyboard. Suppose the user types 1, 2, 3. Then the .READ macro would take in the numbers 1, 2, 3 and store them at locations A1, A1+2, and A1+4, respectively.

Line 5 displays the following message: INPUT 3 CHARACTERS:

Line 6 waits for input from the keyboard. Suppose the user types LIN. Then the .READ macro would take in the three characters typed and store them in A2, A2+2, and A2+4, respectively.

Line 7 saves (R0), (R1), (R2) into stack.

Line 8 copies (A1), (A1+2), and (A1+4) to B1, B1+2, and B1+4.

Line 9 retrieves (R2), (R1), (R0).

Line 10 displays contents at B1, B1+2, and B1+4. Here we expect to see on CRT the following: 123.

Line 11 saves (R0), (R1), (R2) into stack.

Line 12 copies (A2), (A2+2), (A2+4) to B2, B2+2, B2+4.

Line 13 retrieves (R2), (R1), (R0).

Line 14 displays content at B2, B2+2, B2+4. Here we expect to see on the CRT the following: LIN.

Line 15 is EXIT for the program.

```
                ;EXAMPLE TO SHOW THE MIXED USE OF USER AND SYSTEM DEFINED MACROS.
                ;
                ;
                .MCALL .RAD,.READ,.WRITE,.EXIT
                .MACRO SAVREG
                MOV         R0,-(SP)
                MOV         R1,-(SP)
                MOV         R2,-(SP)
                .ENDM SAVREG
                .MACRO RETRREG
                MOV         (SP)+,R2
                MOV         (SP)+,R1
                MOV         (SP)+,R0
                .ENDM RETRREG
                .MACRO COPY ARRAY1,ARRAY2,N,?LOOP
                SAVREG
                MOV         #ARRAY1,R0
                MOV         #ARRAY2,R1
                MOV         N,R2
LOOP:           MOV         (R0)+,(R1)+
                SOB         R2,LOOP
                RETRREG
                .ENDM COPY
                ;
                ;MAIN PROGRAM
START:   .WRITE       "\\INPUT_DESIRED_RADIX_AND_FORMAT_OPTION:__
         .RAD
         .WRITE       "\\INPUT_3_NUMBERS:__
         .READ        A1
         .WRITE       "\\INPUT_3_CHARACTERS:__
         .READ        'A2
         .LIST
         COPY         A1,B1,N
         .WRITE       B1,B1+2,B1+4
         COPY         A2,B2,N
         .WRITE       'B2
         .EXIT
A1:      .BLKW        3
A2:      .BLKW        3
B1:      .BLKW        3
B2:      .BLKW        3
N:       .WORD        3
         .END         START
```

Execution Result: INPUT DESIRED RADIX AND FORMAT OPTION: 10
INPUT 3 NUMBERS: 1 3 4
INPUT 3 CHARACTERS: LIN
1 3 4 LIN

Figure 6.2(a)   An example of mixed use of system-and user-defined macros.

Figure 6.2(a) shows the source program and its execution as a result of the above example. Figure 6.2(b) shows the source program after macro expansion.

Nesting of Macros

Just like the subroutine, a macro can contain another macro and another macro, and so on. The following example shows **nesting macros.**

```
                    ;EXAMPLE TO SHOW THE NESTING OF MACROS.
                    ;
                    ;
                    .MCALL .RAD,.READ,.WRITE,.EXIT
                    .MACRO SAVREG
                    MOV         R0,-(SP)
                    MOV         R1,-(SP)
                    MOV         R2,-(SP)
                    .ENDM SAVREG
                    .MACRO RETRREG
                    MOV         (SP)+,R2
                    MOV         (SP)+,R1
                    MOV         (SP)+,R0
                    .ENDM RETRREG
                    .MACRO COPY ARRAY1,ARRAY2,N,?LOOP
                    SAVREG
                    MOV         #ARRAY1,R0
                    MOV         #ARRAY2,R1
                    MOV         N,R2
LOOP:               MOV         (R0)+,(R1)+
                    SOB         R2,LOOP
                    RETRREG
                    .ENDM COPY
                    ;
                    ;MAIN PROGRAM
START:              .WRITE      "\\INPUT_DESIRED_RADIX_AND_FORMAT_OPTION:__
                    .RAD
                    .WRITE      "\\INPUT_3_NUMBERS:__
                    .READ       A1
                    .WRITE      "\\INPUT_3_CHARACTERS:__
                    .READ       'A2
                    COPY        A1,B1,N
                    SAVREG
                    MOV         R0,-(SP)
                    MOV         R1,-(SP)
                    MOV         R2,-(SP)
                    MOV         #A1,R0
                    MOV         #B1,R1
                    MOV         N,R2
64$:                MOV         (R0)+,(R1)+
                    SOB         R2,64$
                    RETRREG
                    MOV         (SP)+,R2
                    MOV         (SP)+,R1
                    MOV         (SP)+,R0
                    .WRITE      B1,B1+2,B1+4
                    COPY        A2,B2,N
                    SAVREG
                    MOV         R0,-(SP)
                    MOV         R1,-(SP)
                    MOV         R2,-(SP)
                    MOV         #A2,R0
                    MOV         #B2,R1
                    MOV         N,R2
64$:                MOV         (R0)+,(R1)+
                    SOB         R2,64$
                    RETRREG
                    MOV         (SP)+,R2
                    MOV         (SP)+,R1
                    MOV         (SP)+,R0
                    .WRITE      'B2
                    .EXIT
A1:                 .BLKW       3
A2:                 .BLKW       3
B1:                 .BLKW       3
B2:                 .BLKW       3
N:                  .WORD       3
                    .END        START
```

Figure 6.2(b)   Source program at Figure 6.2(a) after macro expansion.

In this example, we show how a realtime macro of one second, one minute, and one hour can be defined with the time information of the basic instruction set provided by the PDP-11 user's manual or Appendix C.

```
.MACRO    SEC ?L1
          MOV    R0, -(SP)      ;SEE NOTE 1
          CLR R0,               ;SEE NOTE 2
L1:       INC R0                ;SEE NOTE 3
          CMP #0, R0            ;SEE NOTE 4
          NOP                   ;SEE NOTE 5
          BNE L1                ;SEE NOTE 6
          MOV (SP)+,R0          ;SEE NOTE 7
.ENDM     SEC
```

In reference to the execution time information given in the user's manual, for each instruction for LSI-11, we can use this macro to make a "realtime" clock of one second. The time calculation follows.

In general, the time required to execute an instruction can be estimated by the following formula:

$$T(i) = t1 + t2 + t3 \quad ;\text{ALL IN MICROSECOND}$$

where $t1 = t10 + t11 + t12$

- $T(i)$ = total time for fetching and executing ith instruction
- $t1$ = basic time
- $t10$ = fetch time
- $t11$ = decode time
- $t12$ = execute time
- $t2$ = source operand processing time
- $t3$ = destination processing operand time

The times required for the instructions shown above are calculated as follows:

> Note 1: save old (R0)
> $$T(1) = 2.45 + 0 + 2.8 = 5.25$$
> Note 2: $T(2) = 3.85 + 0 + 0 = 3.85$
> Note 3: Start counting
> $$T(3) = 4.2 + 0 + 0 = 4.2$$
> Note 4: $T(4) = 3.5 + 1.4 + 0 = 4.9$
> Note 5: $T(5) = 3.5$
> Note 6: $T(6) = 3.5 + 0 + 0 = 3.5$
> Note 7: $T(7) = 3.5 + 1.4 + 0 = 4.9$

Notice that the third, fourth, fifth, and sixth instructions compose a time loop. The program would not leave the counting loop until (R0) becomes zero again. Since the time required for the first, second, and seventh instructions is insignificant in comparison with the loop time for the third, fourth, fifth, and sixth instructions, we can neglect it. Thus, the total loop time can be estimated as follows:

Total loop count for a "full-scale" of R0 $\simeq 2^{16} = 65.5 \times 10^3$

Each loop count time

$$= T(3) + T(4) + T(5) + T(6)$$
$$= 4.2 + 4.9 + 3.5 + 3.5 = 16.1$$

Total loop time elapsed

$$\simeq 65.5 \times 10^3 \times 16.1 \simeq 1054 \text{ millisec}$$
$$\simeq \text{one second}$$

Now we can easily define minute macro and hour macro by the technique of nesting macros, as follows:

```
.MACRO MIN ?L2
               MOV R1,-(SP)     ;SAVE (R1)
               CLR R1           ;INITIAL R1
       L2:     SEC              ;NESTING OF SECOND-MACRO
               INC R1
               CMP #60., R1     ;REACH 60 (IN DECIMAL) SECOND?
               BNE L2
               MOV (SP)+, R1    ;RETRIEVE (R1)
       .ENDM   MIN
       .MACRO  HOUR ?L3
               MOV R2, (-SP)    ;SAVE (R2)
               CLR R2           ;INITIAL R2
       L3:     MIN              ;NESTING OF SECOND AND MINUTE MACROS
               INC R2
               CMP #60., R2     ;REACH 60 MINUTES?
               BNE L3
               MOV (SP)+, R2    ;RETRIEVE R2
       .ENDM   HOUR
```

Conditional Macros

In practice, we may wish to write macros that are very flexible and cover a lot of features. To achieve this goal, the macro would become larger and thus require more memory space, plus assemble and execute time. We may have a macro that possesses a great many features, but in practice we seldom use all the features at one time. Thus, it is somewhat a waste of memory space and process time if the macro contains some features we do not really need in specific applications. For this reason, the PDP-11 system offers **conditional macros.** As a simple example, let us define macros for general register saving and retrieving. We shall deal with all registers, but provide conditions so that the user can selectively save and retrieve the registers he or she really needs and leave the other registers alone. First, we need the general format for defining a conditional macro:

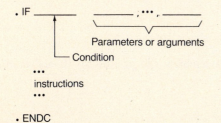

```
. IF _____    _____ ;•••, _____
        |              Parameters or arguments
        |___ Condition
   •••
instructions
   •••
. ENDC
```

EXAMPLE 1 Conditional Save/Retrieve Register ─────────────────────────

```
.MACRO SAVE R0, R1, R2, R3, R4, R5
.IF NB R0            ;ASSEMBLE THE FOLLOWING IF R0
                     ;IS NOT BLANK (NB)
MOV R0, -(SP)        ;PUSH (R0)
.ENDC
.IF NB R1
MOV R1, -(SP)
.ENDC
.IF NB R2
MOV R2, -(SP)
.ENDC
.IF NB R3
MOV R3, -(SP)
.ENDC
.IF NB R4
MOV R4, -(SP)
.ENDC
IF NB R5
MOV R5, -(SP)
.ENDC
.ENDM SAVE
```

In a similar manner, we can define a companion macro called RTRV to retrieve the registers:

```
.MACRO RTRV R5, R4, R3, R2, R1, R0
.IF NB R5
MOV (SP)+, R5     ;POP R5
.ENDC
.
.
.
.IF NB R0
MOV (SP)+, R0
.ENDC
.ENDM RTRV
;MAIN PROGRAM
START:
.
.
.
SAVE R0,R5
.
.
.
RTRV R5,R0
.
.
.
.END START
```

After the main program is assembled, the macros SAVE and RTRV would be expanded, respectively, as follows:

```
MOV R0, -(SP)
MOV R5, -(SP)
```

for SAVE and

```
MOV (SP)+, R5
MOV (SP)+, R0
```

for RTRV.

EXAMPLE 2 ─────────────────────────────────

In this example, we modify the time macro to illustrate the use of nested conditional macros. Figure 6.3 shows the source program of the user-defined macro that can be used to generate a time delay in hours, minutes, and seconds, as specified by the operands. Note that in the main program we use the directives .LIST and .NLIST to control the listing and not listing of the specific macros. Since we are not interested in seeing the expansion of the system macro .WRITE, we precede them with .NLIST.

However, in this example we do want to see how the conditional macro of time delay is being expanded under different conditions. Therefore we precede them with .LIST. Figure 6.4 shows the conditional time delay macro after expansion. Here we can see clearly how local symbolic addresses and macros affect the expansion under different conditions. ■ ■

```
            ;THIS PROGRAM SHOWS HOW TO USE CONDITIONAL NESTED MACROS.
            .MCALL   .WRITE.,.EXIT
            .MACRO DELAY S,M,H,?LS,?LM,?LH    ;SECONDS,MINUTES,AND HOURS
            .MACRO SEC ?L1
            MOV      R0,-(SP)
            CLR      R0
L1:         INC      R0
            CMP      #0,R0
            BNE      L1
            MOV      (SP)+,R0
            .ENDM    SEC
            ;
            .MACRO   MIN ?L2
            MOV      R1,-(SP)
            CLR      R1
L2:         SEC
            INC      R1
            CMP      #60.,R1
            BNE      L2
            MOV      (SP)+,R1
            .ENDM    MIN
            ;
            .IF NB S
                MOV  R2,-(SP)
                MOV  #S,R2
LS:             SEC
                SOB  R2,LS
                MOV  (SP)+,R2
            .ENDC
            .IF NB M
                MOV  R3,-(SP)
                MOV  #M,R3
```

```
LM:        MIN
           SOB     R3,LM
           MOV     (SP)+,R3
        .ENDC
        .IF NB H
           MOV     R4,-(SP)
           MOV     #H,R4
           MOV     R5,-(SP)
           CLR     R5
LH:        MIN
           INC     R5
           CMP     #60.,R5
           BNE     LH
           SOB     R4,LH
           MOV     (SP)+,R5
           MOV     (SP)+,R4
        .ENDC
        .ENDM DELAY
        ;MAIN PROGRAM
START:  .LIST
        DELAY    1          ;ONE SECOND DELAY
        .NLIST
        .WRITE   "\\1_SECOND_HAS_PASSED
        .LIST
        DELAY    ,1         ;ONE MINUTE DELAY
        .NLIST
        .WRITE   "\\1_MINUTE_HAS_PASSED
        .LIST
        DELAY    , ,1       ;ONE HOUR DELAY
        .NLIST
        .WRITE   "\\1_HOUR_HAS_PASSED
        .LIST
        DELAY    1,1,1      ;1 HOUR,1 MIN AND 1 SEC DELAY
        .NLIST
        .WRITE   "\\1_HOUR_1_MIN_1_SEC_HAS_PASSED
        .EXIT
        .END     START
```

Execution Result: 1 SECOND HAS PASSED   *; after 1 sec*
                      1 MINUTE HAS PASSED   *; after 1 min*
                      1 HOUR HAS PASSED   *; after 1 hr*
                      1 HOUR 1 MIN 1 SEC HAS PASSED; after 1 hr 1 min 1 sec

Figure 6.3 Time delay using nested conditional macros.

```
        ;THIS PROGRAM SHOWS HOW TO USE CONDITIONAL NESTED MACROS.
        .MCALL   .WRITE,.EXIT
        .MACRO DELAY S,M,H,?LS,?LM,?LH ;SECONDS,MINUTES,AND HOURS
        .MACRO SEC ?L1
        MOV      R0,-(SP)
        CLR      R0
L1:     INC      R0
        CMP      #0,R0
        BNE      L1
        MOV      (SP)+,R0
        .ENDM    SEC
        ;
        .MACRO MIN ?L2
        MOV      R1,-(SP)
        CLR      R1
```

```
          L2:     SEC
                  INC       R1
                  CMP       #60.,R1
                  BNE       L2
                  MOV       (SP)+,R1
                  .ENDM     MIN
                  ;
                  .IF NB S
                     MOV    R2,-(SP)
                     MOV    #S,R2
          LS:        SEC
                     SOB    R2,LS
                     MOV    (SP)+,R2
                  .ENDC
                  .IF NB M
                     MOV    R3,-(SP)
                     MOV    #M,R3
          LM:        MIN
                     SOB    R3,LM
                     MOV    (SP)+,R3
                  .ENDC
                  .IF NB H
                     MOV    R4,-(SP)
                     MOV    #H,R4
                     MOV    R5,-(SP)
                     CLR    R5
          LH:        MIN
                     INC    R5
                     CMP    #60.,R5
                     BNE    LH
                     SOB    R4,LH
                     MOV    (SP)+,R5
                     MOV    (SP)+,R4
                  .ENDC
                  .ENDM DELAY
                  ;MAIN PROGRAM
                  DELAY    1             ;ONE SECOND DELAY
                  .MACRO SEC ?L1
                  MOV       R0,-(SP)
                  CLR       R0
          L1:     INC       R0
                  CMP       #0,R0
                  BNE       L1
                  MOV       (SP)+,R0
                  .ENDM     SEC
                  ;
                  .MACRO MIN ?L2
                  MOV       R1,-(SP)
                  CLR       R1
          L2:     SEC
                  INC       R1
                  CMP       #60.,R1
                  BNE       L2
                  MOV       (SP)+,R1
                  .ENDM     MIN
                  ;
                  .IF NB 1
                     MOV    R2,-(SP)
                     MOV    #1,R2
          64$:       SEC
                     MOV    R0,-(SP)
                     CLR    R0
```

```
67$:      INC     R0
          CMP     #0,R0
          BNE     67$
          MOV     (SP)+,R0
          SOB     R2,64$
          MOV     (SP)+,R2
          .ENDC
          .IF NB
          MOV     R3,-(SP)
          MOV     #,R3
65$:      MIN
          SOB     R3,65$
          MOV     (SP)+,R3
          .ENDC
          .IF NB
          MOV     R4,-(SP)
          MOV     #,R4
          MOV     R5,-(SP)
          CLR     R5
66$:      MIN
          INC     R5
          CMP     #60.,R5
          BNE     66$
          SOB     R4,66$
          MOV     (SP)+,R5
          MOV     (SP)+,R4
          .ENDC
          .WRITE  "\\1_SECOND_HAS_PASSED
          DELAY   ,1              ;ONE MINUTE DELAY
          .MACRO  SEC ?L1
          MOV     R0,-(SP)
          CLR     R0
L1:       INC     R0
          CMP     #0,R0
          BNE     L1
          MOV     (SP)+,R0
          .ENDM   SEC
          ;
          .MACRO  MIN ?L2
          MOV     R1,-(SP)
          CLR     R1
L2:       SEC
          INC     R1
          CMP     #60.,R1
          BNE     L2
          MOV     (SP)+,R1
          .ENDM   MIN
          ;
          .IF NB
          MOV     R2,-(SP)
          MOV     #,R2
64$:      SEC
          SOB     R2,64$
          MOV     (SP)+,R2
          .ENDC
          .IF NB 1
          MOV     R3,-(SP)
          MOV     #1,R3
65$:      MIN
          MOV     R1,-(SP)
          CLR     R1
```

```
      67$:  SEC
            MOV     R0,-(SP)
            CLR     R0
      68$:  INC     R0
            CMP     #0,R0
            BNE     68$
            MOV     (SP)+,R0
            INC     R1
            CMP     #60.,R1
            BNE     67$
            MOV     (SP)+,R1
              SOB   R3,65$
              MOV   (SP)+,R3
            .ENDC
            .IF NB
              MOV   R4,-(SP)
              MOV   #,R4
              MOV   R5,-(SP)
              CLR   R5
      66$:    MIN
              INC   R5
              CMP   #60.,R5
              BNE   66$
              SOB   R4,66$
              MOV   (SP)+,R5
              MOV   (SP)+,R4
            .ENDC
            .WRITE  "\\1_MINUTE_HAS_PASSED
            DELAY   , ,1            ;ONE HOUR DELAY
            .MACRO SEC ?L1
            MOV     R0,-(SP)
            CLR     R0
      L1:   INC     R0
            CMP     #0,R0
            BNE     L1
            MOV     (SP)+,R0
            .ENDM   SEC
            ;
            .MACRO MIN ?L2
            MOV     R1,-(SP)
            CLR     R1
      L2:   SEC
            INC     R1
            CMP     #60.,R1
            BNE     L2
            MOV     (SP)+,R1
            .ENDM   MIN
            ;
            .IF NB
              MOV   R2,-(SP)
              MOV   #,R2
      64$:    SEC
              SOB   R2,64$
              MOV   (SP)+,R2
            .ENDC
            .IF NB
              MOV   R3,-(SP)
              MOV   #,R3
      65$:    MIN
              SOB   R3,65$
              MOV   (SP)+,R3
```

```
                .ENDC
                .IF NB 1
                MOV     R4,-(SP)
                MOV     #1,R4
                MOV     R5,-(SP)
                CLR     R5
        66$:    MIN
                MOV     R1,-(SP)
                CLR     R1
        67$:    SEC
                MOV     R0,-(SP)
                CLR     R0
        68$:    INC     R0
                CMP     #0,R0
                BNE     68$
                MOV     (SP)+,R0
                INC     R1
                CMP     #60.,R1
                BNE     67$
                MOV     (SP)+,R1
                INC     R5
                CMP     #60.,R5
                BNE     66$
                SOB     R4,66$
                MOV     (SP)+,R5
                MOV     (SP)+,R4
                .ENDC
                .WRITE  "\\1_HOUR_HAS_PASSED
                DELAY   1,1,1           ;1 HOUR, 1 MIN AND 1 SEC DELAY
                .MACRO SEC ?L1
                MOV     R0,-(SP)
                CLR     R0
        L1:     INC     R0
                CMP     #0,R0
                BNE     L1
                MOV     (SP)+,R0
                .ENDM   SEC
                ;
                .MACRO MIN ?L2
                MOV     R1,-(SP)
                CLR     R1
        L2:     SEC
                INC     R1
                CMP     #60.,R1
                BNE     L2
                MOV     (SP)+,R1
                .ENDM   MIN
                ;
                .IF NB 1
                MOV     R2,-(SP)
                MOV     #1,R2
        64$:    SEC
                MOV     R0,-(SP)
                CLR     R0
        67$:    INC     R0
                CMP     #0,R0
                BNE     67$
                MOV     (SP)+,R0
                SOB     R2,64$
                MOV     (SP)+,R2
```

```
              .ENDC
              .IF NB 1
                 MOV    R3,-(SP)
                 MOV    #1,R3
      65$:    MIN
                 MOV    R1,-(SP)
                 CLR    R1
      68$:    SEC
                 MOV    R0,-(SP)
                 CLR    R0
      69$:  INC    R0
                 CMP    #0,R0
                 BNE    69$
                 MOV    (SP)+,R0
                 INC    R1
                 CMP    #60.,R1
                 BNE    68$
                 MOV    (SP)+,R1
                 SOB    R3,65$
                 MOV    (SP)+,R3
              .ENDC
              .IF NB 1
                 MOV    R4,-(SP)
                 MOV    #1,R4
                 MOV    R5,-(SP)
                 CLR    R5
      66$:    MIN
                 MOV    R1,-(SP)
                 CLR    R1
      70$:    SEC
                 MOV    R0,-(SP)
                 CLR    R0
      71$:  INC    R0
                 CMP    #0,R0
                 BNE    71$
                 MOV    (SP)+,R0
                 INC    R1
                 CMP    #60.,R1
                 BNE    70$
                 MOV    (SP)+,R1
                 INC    R5
                 CMP    #60.,R5
                 BNE    66$
                 SOB    R4,66$
                 MOV    (SP)+,R5
                 MOV    (SP)+,R4
              .ENDC
              .WRITE   "\\_HOUR_1_MIN_1_SEC_HAS_PASSED
              .EXIT
              .END     START
```

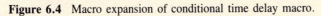

Figure 6.4 Macro expansion of conditional time delay macro.

Conditions Available The PDP-11 system provides many more conditions other than the NB (not blank) illustrated here. Consult the user's manual for details. An excerpt of the conditions available is shown in the following table:

Conditions	Arguments	Expand the Block if Arguments are:
NB	EXPRESSIONS	NOT BLANK
B	EXPRESSIONS	BLANK
EQ	EXPRESSIONS	EQUAL ZERO
NE	EXPRESSIONS	NOT EQUAL ZERO
GT	EXPRESSIONS	GREATER THAN ZERO
LT	EXPRESSIONS	LESS THAN ZERO
DF	EXPRESSIONS	DEFINED
NDF	EXPRESSIONS	NOT DEFINED

Example:

```
.IF EQ ALPHA + 1        ;THIS BLOCK IS EXPANDED IF AND ONLY IF
.                       ;ALPHA + 1 = 0
.
.
.ENDC
.IF DF SYMBL1 & SYMBL2  ;THIS BLOCK IS EXPANDED IF AND ONLY IF
.                       ;BOTH SYMBL1 and SYMBL2 ARE DEFINED.
.
.
.ENDC
```

EXERCISES

6.1 With respect to execution time and memory space, briefly discuss the differences between subroutines and macro instructions.

6.2 Briefly discuss the differences between system- and user-defined macro instruction.

6.3 Using Appendix C, write a user-defined macro that has one millisecond delay of time.

6.4 Write a conditional macro that will append the parity bit to the most significant bit of a 7-bit ASCII-coded character in a byte representation. The condition can be set either ODD or EVEN, as the user wishes.

Chapter 7

Input/Output Programming

In this chapter, we describe the process of creating an input/output program. This process involves the hardware structure of the I/O interface board and the I/O software created by the programmer. The hardware structure of a general purpose I/O interface board is presented first. Based on the structure of the I/O board, the programmer creates I/O software. A set of examples is used to show the process in detail, including the "handshaking" and data transfer steps.

KEY WORDS

A/D converter
D/A converter
data transfer
handshaking

7.1 INTRODUCTION

Input/output (popularly known as I/O) programming is one application in which the assembly language is mostly used for efficiency and high-speed operation. Basically, it is the software that links the peripherals or I/O devices with the CPU. Without an I/O device a CPU is useless, no matter how powerful it is. There are many kinds of I/O devices. Depending on the nature of the application, they vary from special purpose ones, such as the optical character recognizer and the speech recognizer/synthesizer to general purpose ones, such as the terminal, the lineprinter, and the magnetic disk drive.

But any I/O device can be viewed as a piece of hardware or a black box that converts the information of the physical world into logical signals of ones and zeros which are fed into a computing system for data processing. Conversely, the computing system yields information in logical ones and zeros to the I/O devices, which reconstruct the information into physical world signals. The I/O device can simply be a relay that is enabled by a logic one or disabled by a logic zero; or it can be a sophisticated, colorful graphic terminal that can produce natural pictures on a CRT screen.

As programmers, we need not be concerned with the detailed hardware structure of the device. Instead, we need only know the format of data and the time for data transfer. Based on this information, we can develop input/output programs and install them for application purposes. In this chapter, we describe the I/O programming technique in detail, with examples.

General Input/Output Devices

There is a set of I/O devices currently considered the most basic or general to any computing system: the CRT/keyboard terminal, paper tape drive, magnetic tape drive, magnetic disk drive, and lineprinter. Among them, the CRT/keyboard terminal is the one we are most familiar with. It generates and receives ASCII code on a one character per byte basis.

A paper tape drive is a device that can punch and read paper tape in ASCII or other codes. Magnetic tape is considered a mass storage device, since a lot of information can be stored on and retrieved from it. However, the information for both paper and magnetic tape drives can only be accessed serially. That is, if we want to access information that happens to be stored near the end of the tape, it would take a long time to retrieve it.

Magnetic disk drive is also a mass storage device, but it is considered a random access memory device. It operates like a record player. Information is stored on a magnetic coated plate or record and addressed by sector and track number. The device can "read" and "write" information by means of a set of fixed-position magnetic heads or a head moving radially. Because the cost of the device has been decreasing continuously, currently almost anyone can afford at least one floppy disk drive. All system software and program files are stored on the disk. They can be "called" and "loaded" by software into main memory for execution. The input/output programs for a disk drive are usually developed in assembly language and installed in the system by the manufacturer.

Lineprinters are another important device if we want to keep a printed hard copy for permanent record purposes. Analog to digital converter (A/D/C) and digital to analog converter (D/A/C) are other devices gaining popularity. Once considered special devices,

A/D/C and D/A/C on a board are now available as general or standard I/O equipment in many systems. This is because we are really living in an analog physical world, and most physical transducers or sensors generate electrical signals only in analog form. To have the digital computer process these signals, an analog-to-digital converter is required at the input port of the system; conversely, it would require a digital-to-analog converter to output the results of processed data to the real world. As an obvious example, if a computer system requires direct voice or speech input/output, it would need the A/D/C and D/A/C as its I/O terminal. Currently, the voice I/O terminal is beginning to revolutionize the computing industry.

Communication Between CPU and Input/Output Devices

All these devices require interface hardware and software to support them so that they can operate smoothly with the CPU. Since each type of I/O device has its own electrical characteristics, interfacing it to the CPU may require some basic hardware knowledge. However, for the general I/O devices described in the preceding section, there are standard interface boards with appropriate connectors. For example, a set of interface boards is available for PDP-11 system users. Once they are properly connected, we can develop I/O software to transfer data into and out of the system.

There are two basic kinds of formats for I/O data transfer: (1) serial and (2) parallel. For example, the CRT/keyboard terminal uses the serial format. Since most computer systems are bus-structured and data are transferred to and from the CPU in parallel, the interface board for the serial format needs circuitry for parallel-to-serial and serial-to-parallel conversions. Although this is not the programmer's concern, it is important that programmers be aware of the process, since it requires some time to collect the serial data and convert it into parallel for CPU, or to convert parallel data from CPU into serial for the I/O device.

As a typical example, let us examine the serial transmission of ASCII data from a terminal. Although an ASCII character requires only 7 bits, for the serial format it normally would use 11 bits. That is, 7 bits for ASCII code, 1 parity bit for error detection purposes, and 3 frame bits (one for signaling the beginning, and one and one half or two for the ending of the incoming data frame). Figure 7.1 shows respectively a general transmission signal in the serial format and the typical character, A, in serial format. Currently, most computing systems have the so-called RS-232-C port ready for the connection of an RS-232-C-compatible CRT/keyboard terminal. The RS-232-C communication link uses the serial data format. It is normally the responsibility of the circuitry on the I/O interface board to convert the serial data format into parallel and deposit it into a data register for parallel data transfer into CPU through the system data bus. Similarly, it is also responsible for converting the parallel data from the CPU into serial format for data transmission to the CRT terminal.

The drawback of serial data communication is the speed of transmission. Many applications would require high-speed operation. Therefore, the parallel format is used instead. In this system, all the data bits would be available at the same time, and no serial-parallel or parallel-serial conversion circuitry is required. Obviously, the parallel format would require more transmission lines in parallel, which would not be economical for long-distance data links.

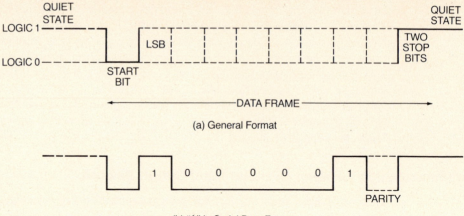

(a) General Format

(b) "A" in Serial Data Format

Figure 7.1 Communication in serial format.

Finally, it is important to point out that most I/O devices consist of electrical-mechanical components. As a result, operational speed varies from one device to another. Obviously, the operational speed of any electrical-mechanical I/O device is far slower than that of the CPU. Because of this, communication between the CPU and the I/O device is asynchronous. That is, whenever a datum, say a character in ASCII, is to be transferred, it requires a "precheck" or the so-called **handshaking** process. Basically, the CPU has to check if the data are ready in the data register before taking in data. Likewise, for outputting data the CPU has to check whether the preceding data in the data register have been transmitted. It is thus the programmer's responsibility to develop the input/output program so that it carries out the data transfer task asynchronously in two steps—namely, handshaking and data transfer.

7.2 INPUT/OUTPUT PROGRAMMING FOR THE PDP-11 SYSTEM

In the preceding section, we described the popular I/O devices and the basic principles of communication between the CPU and the I/O devices. In this section, we present I/O programming for the PDP-11 system. First, let us examine the general structure of a typical I/O interface board from a programmer's viewpoint.

General Structure of an I/O Interface Board

As a programmer, one might be fascinated by looking at an I/O interface board, which is full of chips, resisters, and capacitors. One might wonder how one could program with it. Fortunately, we do not have to know the details of the hardware. An understanding of the basic structural concepts is sufficient to develop the necessary software. Figure 7.2 depicts a bus-structured PDP-11 system. There are two kinds of bus structures for the PDP-11 system, Unibus and Q-bus. The major difference between the two is that the former has separate address lines and data lines, whereas the latter has the address and

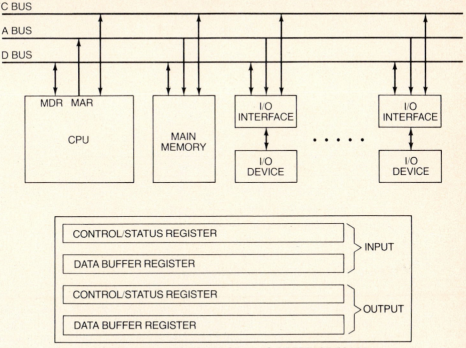

FUNCTIONAL STRUCTURE OF AN I/O INTERFACE BOARD

Figure 7.2   Bus structure of a PDP-11 system.

data bus sharing the same physical lines. Conceptually however, they are both structured in three groups, address bus (A bus), data bus (D bus), and control bus (C bus), as shown.

Fortunately, from a programmer's viewpoint the I/O interface board can be considered as nothing but a group of two or more registers. For a simple CRT/keyboard terminal, the I/O interface board would need four registers, two for input operation and two for output operation, as shown. Here, the interface board communicates with the CPU by an I/O program, and with the I/O device by electronic circuitry. Recall that we can communicate with a register as if it is one location of a memory word. Thus, to deal with an I/O board with four registers, all we have to do is assign four unique memory locations or addresses to these registers, respectively, and then the CPU can communicate with them as if they were memory words. This concept is called the **memory mapping I/O addressing technique.** Of course, we must avoid assigning the same addresses to the main memory.

Now let us examine the registers in more detail. As shown in the inset of Figure 7.2, a typical I/O board has four registers, two for input and two for output. For both input and output, there is one register dedicated to the functions of control and status and another to data buffer. They are therefore called the control-status register and the data buffer register, respectively.

Figure 7.3 shows the general format of the I/O registers, which have the I/O device connected to them. The detailed definition of each bit of the registers may vary, but the general format still holds. As shown in Figure 7.3, the data buffer register is 16 bits wide,

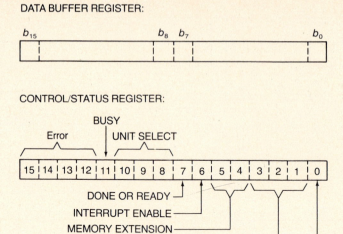

Figure 7.3 General format of I/O registers.

so it can accommodate any data of 16 or fewer bits. Currently, most I/O devices have an 8-bit format, so the upper byte of the register is not frequently used. The control-status register is not so straightforward. Generally speaking, control bits indicate the commands provided by the CPU, and status bits indicate the status of the I/O devices. Here, for example, we have b_6 and b_0 defined as the control bits. When $b_6 = 1$, it implies that the system has been evoked to accept an interrupt request signal. When $b_0 = 1$, it implies that the CPU wishes to enable whichever device has been connected to this bit. It could be a relay, a buzzer, a red light, and so on. In addition, we have three subsets of bits controlled by CPU: function bits, b_1, b_2, b_3; memory extension bits, b_4, b_5; and I/O unit-select bits, b_8, b_9, and b_{10}. For some I/O devices, their functions can be specified by the CPU through b_1, b_2, and b_3.

Memory extension bits can be used to expand memory space, and I/O unit-select bits can be used to select I/O devices if several devices share the same control-status register. Bits b_7, b_{11}, and b_{12}, . . . , b_{15} are defined as the status bits. These bits indicate the current state of the I/O device. For example, if $b_{11} = 1$, it indicates to the CPU that the I/O device is currently "busy" and requests the CPU to leave it alone. The status of the data buffer register is shown by b_7. As an input device, $b_7 = 1$ implies that the input data buffer register is full of data that can be transferred into CPU. As an output device, however, $b_7 = 1$ implies that the output data buffer is currently empty and waiting for the CPU to load new data into it. The error bits indicate to the CPU that some kind of error specified by the error bit code has occurred and requests the CPU to respond to the error indicated.

Input/Output Programming

In this section we deal with some typical I/O devices and interface boards. Here we will see how one can write specific I/O programs with the hardware.

EXAMPLE 1 I/O Programs for a Teletype ─────────────────────────────

A teletype actually contains four devices—keyboard, printer, paper tape puncher, and paper tape reader. The keyboard and tape reader are input devices that normally share the same control-status register and data buffer register; the printer and tape punch are output devices sharing another pair of registers. The symbolic connection of the devices and the I/O registers is shown in Figure 7.4. The teletype uses the serial data transmission format, and the I/O process is carried out asynchronously. The input/output registers are defined as follows:

Input Registers

Data buffer register $\underline{\Delta}$ TKB, symbolic address of tape-keyboard buffer register

$b_0, \ldots, b_7 \underline{\Delta}$ data
$b_8, \ldots, b_{15}$, not used

Control-status register $\underline{\Delta}$ TKS, symbolic address of tape-keyboard control-status register

$b_0 \underline{\Delta}$ read enable: set by CPU through software, which requests one character be read and cleared by the start bit of the serial input signal through hardware.

$b_7 \underline{\Delta}$ done: set by hardware when a character has been converted into parallel format and is available in the data buffer register and waiting to be transferred into CPU.

$b_{11} \underline{\Delta}$ busy: set by "read-enable" while a character code (ASCII) is serially being loaded into buffer register, and cleared by done bit.

Other bits not used.

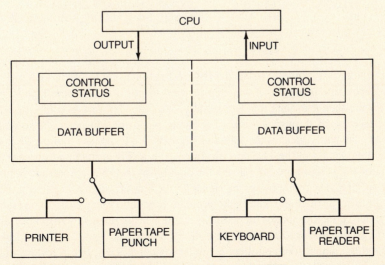

Figure 7.4 Communication between a teletype and CPU.

Output Registers

Data buffer registers Δ TPB, symbolic address of tape-printer buffer register

$b_0, \ldots, b_7 \Delta$ data

$b_8, \ldots, b_{15}$, not used

Control-status register Δ TPS, symbolic address of tape-printer control-status register

$b_0 \Delta$ punch enable

$b_2 \Delta$ maintenance: connects TPB serial output directly to TKB serial input for checking if the device itself is functioning normally

$b_7 \Delta$ ready: set by the TPB through hardware indicating that TPB is empty and ready to accept new data from CPU; cleared as new data is loaded into TPB

Figure 7.5 depicts the flowcharts of the I/O process, assuming that the paper tape unit is currently active. The corresponding programs follow:

```
;Paper tape reader
TKS = 177560              ;I/O REGISTER ADDRESS ASSIGNMENTS:
TKB = 177562              ;THIS IS PDP-11 CONVENTIONAL ADDRESS
TPS = 177564              ;VALUES FOR TELETYPE I/O REGISTERS.
TPB = 177566
1)  INPUT:      INC TKS   ;SET READ-ENABLE BIT b0 = 1 TO ADVANCE
                          ;PAPER TAPE ONE STEP AND START
                          ;TO SEND DATA TO TKB SERIALLY
2) LOOP1:       TSTB TKS  ;EXAMINE b7 (DONE-BIT) = 1?
3)              BPL  LOOP1 ;IF NOT GO TO LOOP1 AND EXAMINE AGAIN
4)              MOV  TKB,R0 ;DATA → R0, OR CPU
5)              HALT
6)              .END INPUT
;PAPER TAPE PUNCH
7) OUTPUT:      INC  TPS   ;SET b0 = 1
8) LOOP2:       TSTB TPS   ;EXAMINE b7 (READY-BIT) = 1?
9)              BPL  LOOP2 ;IF NOT, GO TO LOOP2 AND EXAMINE AGAIN
10)             MOV  R0,TPB ;(R0) → TPB
11)             HALT
12)             .END OUTPUT
```

Note that in line 1 we use the INC instruction to set b_0 of the TKS to 1. As a result, the paper tape is advanced one step forward to position the paper tape to be read. The hardware then transmits the data serially, with the start and stop bits added, to the I/O interface board through a cable. The circuitry on the I/O board, if so equipped, then checks the parity, deletes the start and stop bits, loads the data into the TKB register, and sets the done bit of the TKS to 1. In line 2, the TSTB instruction examines the low-byte data of the (TKS) register and sets the sign bit of the PSW (processor status word) to 1 if b_7 of (TKS) is 1; otherwise, the sign bit = 0. This is a simple way to examine b_7. In line 3, the BPL instruction controls the program execution route: If the test result of line 2 is negative, it implies that b_7 (done bit) = 1 and data are ready in TKB to be transferred into CPU, so line 4 is executed; otherwise, line 2 is executed again and again. Lines 7 through 12 and the output routine follow a similar logical process, but in reverse order. The I/O device eventually punches the paper tape according to the data in R0.

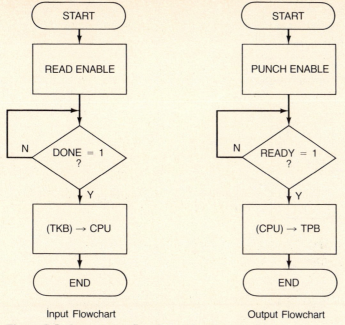

Input Flowchart   Output Flowchart

Figure 7.5 Input-output flowcharts of paper tape drive.

EXAMPLE 2 I/O Program for Reading the Paper Tape and Echoing What Has Been Read to the Printer

The flowchart of this program is shown in Figure 7.6. The program follows:

```
                TKS = 177560
                TKB = 177562
                TPS = 177564
                TPB = 177566
ECHO:    INC    TKS
LOOP1:   TSTB   TKS
         BPL    LOOP1
LOOP2:   TSTB   TPS
         BPL    LOOP2
         MOVB   TKB,TPB
         BR     ECHO
```

Note that the program assumes that the "symbolic switch" for the output device in Figure 7.4 was on the printer side. However, this program would never stop executing even when there is no tape to read. As an exercise, it is left to you to modify this program so that it will stop at the end of the tape.

EXAMPLE 3 High-Speed Tape Reader Subroutine with Error-Checking Capability _____

The teletype in Examples 1 and 2 is considered slow in operation speed (10 characters per second), and might not require the error-checking feature in our program. However, for the high-speed paper tape read and punch—say, 300 characters per second—we may

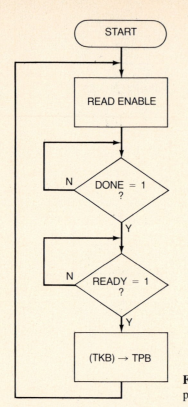

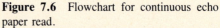

Figure 7.6 Flowchart for continuous echo
paper read.

want to have the error-checking capability. Let us say that b_{15} of TRS, the tape reader control-status register, is an error indicator bit. Figure 7.7 shows the flowchart of this routine, and its source program is as follows:

```
               PRS = 177550
               PRB = 177552
1) READ:       INCB PRS              ;PRS = SYMBOLIC ADDRESS OF
                                     ;PAPER READER CONTROL/STATUS
                                     ;REGISTER
2) TEST:       BIT #100200,PRS       ;EXAMINE b15 AND b7 of PRS
3)             BEQ TEST              ;BRANCH TO TEST IF BOTH b15 AND
                                     ;b7 ARE ZERO.
4)             BMI ERROR             ;IF b15 = 1, BRANCH TO ERROR.
5)             MOVB PRB,R0           ;IF b15 = 0, b7 MUST BE 1, THE
                                     ;TRANSFER DATA SUBROUTINE
                                     RETURN.
6)             RTS PC
7) ERROR:      (MESSAGE DISPLAY ROUTINE)
8)             HALT
```

Note that in this program there is nothing new except lines 2, 3, and 4. In line 2, since we wish to examine b_{15} and b_7, a mask, 100200, is used to examine the contents of PRS. Here, the mask is in octal representation, which in binary representation is 1 000 000 010 000 000. That is, the mask will mask out every bit except b_7 and

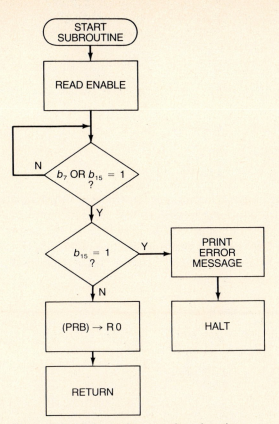

Figure 7.7 High-speed tape reader subroutine.

b_{15}. Therefore, if either b_7, or b_{15}, or both is 1, the program will proceed. Line 4 is to check if b_{15} is set. If so, the sign flag of PSW will be set, which means that the data under examination are negative, or $b_{15} = 1$; otherwise b_7 must be 1 at this point. As a result, line 5 of the program is executed. You may ask at this point who sets b_{15} if error occurs. The answer is that it is usually done by the hardware on the I/O board.

EXAMPLE 4   Display a Message on CRT or Printer by Means of the ASCII Directive ⎯⎯⎯⎯⎯

Let us write a macro to implement this routine.

```
.MACRO      CHAROUT     R, ?L1
L1:         TSTB        177564      ;177564 IS THE ADDRESS OF CONTROL/
                                    ;STATUS REGISTER.
            BPL         L1          ;DONE-BIT = 1? IF NOT, GO TO L1
            MOVB        R,177566    ;177566 IS THE ADDRESS OF OUTPUT
                                    ;DATA
                                    ;BUFFER REGISTER
.ENDM       CHAROUT
.MACRO      DISPLAY INFO,?L2
            MOV         #INFO,R5    ;R5 AS THE DATA POINTER
```

```
L2:          CHAROUT    (R5)+    ;MACRO NESTING
             TSTB       (R5)     ;EXAMINE IF THE DATA AT WHICH R5
                                 POINTS
                                 ;EQUALS ZERO
             BNE        L2       ;IF NOT, MORE MESSAGE COMING,
                                 OTHERWISE
                                 ;NO MORE MESSAGE

.ENDM DISPLAY
;MAIN PROGRAM
START:       DISPLAY    MESSAGE
             HALT
MESSAGE:     .ASCIZ     /HI !/
             .EVEN
             .END       START
```

In this program we have two macros, one for writing or outputting one character at a time, and the other for displaying messages. Note that two directives, .ASCIZ and .EVEN, are new to us. The format of .ASCIZ is to spell out the message we wish to display within a pair of slash symbols. Here we have four characters, H, I, space, and !, in the four consecutive bytes in the memory. The assembler automatically appends the message with a byte of zeros, as follows:

| Symbolic Address | Contents | |
	High Byte	Low Byte
Message	1 1 1 (I)	1 1 0 (H)
	0 4 1 (!)	0 4 0 (space)
	0 0 0	0 0 0
	.	.
	.	.
	.	.

The directive .EVEN requests the assembler to check whether the total message occupies an even number of bytes, and if not, to add one more byte of zeros to it so that it will be even eventually. This is important, because otherwise the next instruction would be split into two bytes. That is, half of the instruction would be in the high byte of a memory word and the other half in the low byte of the next memory word.

Returning to the macro of display of this example, note that we use R5 as the data pointer. It initially points at H, then is auto incremented by one byte at a time. The BNE instruction checks if the "zero byte" has been encountered. If so, it is the end of the message, and it will stop the display macro. PDP-11 provides another similar directive, .ASCII. For the latter, however, the assembler would not append a byte of zeros to the message automatically. It is the programmer's responsibility to provide some means, such as a counter, to sense the end of the message display. Figure 7.8 shows a list file similar to this example, but with two more friendly messages added. ■ ■

7.3 MORE DETAILED EXAMPLES

In this section, we show examples that are somewhat more practical or complete than what we have illustrated so far. These examples should help to build your self-confidence.

```
 1                      ;EXAMPLE OF MESSAGE DISPLAY USING .ASCIZ DIRECTIVE
 2                      ;.........
 3                      ;.........
 4                      .MACRO CHAROUT R,?L1
 5                      TSTB    177564
 6              L1:     BPL     L1
 7                      MOVB    R,177566
 8                      .ENDM   CHAROUT
 9
10                      .MACRO DISPLAY INFO,?L2
11                      MOV     #INFO,R5
12              L2:     CHAROUT (R5)+
13                      TSTB    (R5)
14                      BNE     L2
15                      .ENDM   DISPLAY
16
17                      .MACRO NEWLINE
18                      CHAROUT #12      ;#12 IS THE ASCII OF LINEFEED
19                      CHAROUT #15      ;#15 IS THE ASCII OF CARRIAGE RETURN
20                      .ENDM   NEWLINE
21
22                      ;MAIN PROGRAM
23 000000              START:  DISPLAY  MESS1
24 000022                      DISPLAY  MESS2
25 000044                      NEWLINE
26 000074                      DISPLAY  MESS3
27 000116 000000               HALT
28 000120 110 111      MESS1:  .ASCIZ /HI !/        ;THERE IS A 'SPACE' BETWEEN I AND !
   000123 041 000 040
29 000125 040 117      MESS2:  .ASCIZ / GOOD MORNING/
   000130 117 104 122
   000133 115 117 116
   000136 116 111
   000141 107 000
30 000143 115 131      MESS3:  .ASCIZ /MAY I HELP YOU ?/
   000146 040 101 040
   000151 110 111 114
   000154 120 105 131
   000157 117 040 040
   000162 077 125
          000 000
31                      .EVEN
32 000000'              .END    START
```

Execution Result: HI ! GOOD MORNING
MAY I HELP YOU ?

Figure 7.8 Example of using ASCIZ directive for information display.

SYSTEM BUS

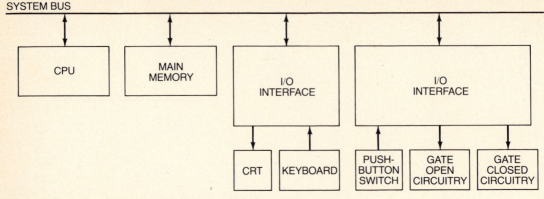

Figure 7.9 Conceptual system structure for a security gate controller.

Simulation of a Security Gate Controller

In this example, we wish to show the PDP-11 can be used to simulate a security gate controller. Figure 7.9 shows the conceptual system structure. The visitor is instructed to ring the doorbell by pressing the push-button switch. The computer responds on the CRT with the message: YOUR NAME PLEASE. The visitor enters his or her name through the keyboard. If the name matches with the prestored name, the computer requests the PASS-WORD. If everything goes right, the gate will be opened and then closed. Otherwise the computer will display: SORRY, NO ADMITTANCE.

For simulation in the lab, we would not have the hardware for the doorbell or the motor that opens and closes the gate. Instead, we use the B-character key on the keyboard to simulate the doorbell and messages on the CRT, such as OPEN THE GATE and CLOSE THE GATE, to simulate the motor action. Figure 7.10(a) shows the flowchart of the program, and Figure 7.10(b) the source program. Here, we assume the name is L and the password is P, for simplicity. By now you should be able to modify the program so that a group of characters, instead of just a single character, can be used for name and password.

I/O Programming for A/D and D/A Converters

In many cases, we wish to be able to process analog signals on the PDP-11 and output the result in analog form. To do this, we must install an I/O board that has the hardware circuitry for analog-to-digital (A/D/C) and digital-to-analog conversion (D/A/C). Fortunately, this type of board is now available at a fairly reasonable cost. However, we would still have to write I/O programs to take in the digitized data from the **A/D converter** and send the processed digital data to the **D/A converter** to produce the analog signal.

Figure 7.11 shows a functional block diagram of an A/D and D/A conversion interface. Although the I/O hardware structure and circuitry for the conversion interface is quite different from that for the peripherals described in the preceding sections, its I/O programming is still implemented in two steps, handshaking and data transfer. For instance, to perform A/D/C, the CPU must issue a ''start to convert'' command signal that initiates the conversion process. As soon as the digital signal is ready and loaded into the

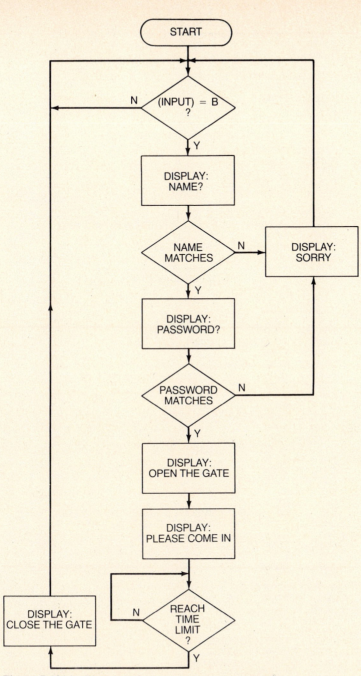

Figure 7.10(a) Flowchart for the security gate controller.

data buffer register, the A/D/C would send an ''end of conversion'' signal to inform the CPU that the input data are ready for transfer. For output or D/A/C, the converter must first issue the ''request for new data'' signal to inform the CPU that it can take new digital

```
                        ;EXAMPLE OF A PROGRAM WHICH CONTROLS A GATE OF A
                        ;BUILDING. AS THE PROGRAM IS BEING EXECUTED, IT
                        ;EXPECTS THE VISITOR TO PRESS THE 'B' KEY WHICH
                        ;SIMULATES THE DOOR BELL.
                        ;
                        .TITLE GATE CONTROLLER
                        .MACRO    READ  R,?L1
          L1:           TSTB      177560
                        BPL       L1
                        MOVB      177562,R
                        .ENDM     READ
                        ;
                        .MACRO    PRINT  R,?L2
          L2:           TSTB      177564
                        BPL       L2
                        MOVB      R,177566
                        .ENDM     PRINT
                        ;
                        .MACRO    DISPLAY INFO,?L3
                        MOV       #INFO,R5       ;R5 AS A POINTER STARTS AT INFO
          L3:           PRINT     (R5)+
                        TSTB      (R5)           ;END OF MESSAGE ?
                        BNE       L3
                        PRINT     #12            ;LINEFEED
                        PRINT     #15            ;CARRIAGE RETURN
                        .ENDM     DISPLAY
                        ;
                        ;MAIN PROGRAM
          START:        READ      TEMP           ;TAKE IN DATA
                        DISPLAY   TEMP           ;ECHO THE INPUT
                        CMP       #102,TEMP      ;(TEMP) = B ?
                        BNE       START
                        DISPLAY   NAME
                        READ      TEMP
                        DISPLAY   TEMP
                        CMP       #114,TEMP      ;(TEMP) = L ?
                        BNE       S
                        DISPLAY   PASSWD
                        READ      TEMP
                        DISPLAY   TEMP
                        CMP       #120,TEMP      ;(TEMP) = P ?
                        BNE       S
                        DISPLAY   OPEN
                        DISPLAY   WELCOM
                        CLR       R0
                        CLR       R1
          T:            INC       R0             ;SIMULATES A TIME PERIOD BEFORE
                        BNE       T              ;CLOSING THE GATE
                        INC       R1
                        CMP       TLIMIT,R1
                        BNE       T
                        DISPLAY   CLOSE
                        BR        AGAIN
          S:            DISPLAY   SORRY
          AGAIN:        JMP       START
          TEMP:         .BLKB     1
                        .EVEN
          TLIMIT:       .WORD     4
          NAME:         .ASCIZ / YOUR NAME PLEASE. /
          PASSWD:       .ASCIZ / PASSWORD PLEASE. /
          SORRY:        .ASCIZ / SORRY, NO ADDMITTANCE /
          OPEN:         .ASCIZ / OPEN THE GATE /
          WELCOM:       .ASCIZ / PLEASE COME IN /
          CLOSE:        .ASCIZ / CLOSE THE GATE /
                        .EVEN
                        .END      START
```

Figure 7.10(b) Source program for gate controller.

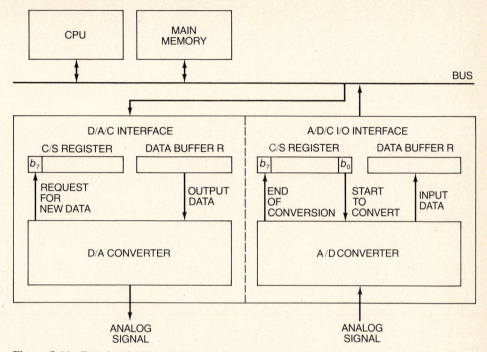

Figure 7.11 Functional block diagram of an A/D/A interface.

data from the CPU. Then the CPU would transfer data to the output data buffer register. The corresponding I/O program follows:

```
;A/D/C/ SUBROUTINE
    ADC: CLR    ADCSR       ;INITIAL CONTROL/STATUS REGISTER
         INC    ADCSR       ;SET b₀ TO START CONVERSION
    L1:  TSTB   ADCSR       ;END OF CONVERSION ? SEE NOTE 1
         BPL    L1          ;NO, CHECK DONE-BIT b₇ AGAIN
         MOV    ADBUF,R0    ;INPUT DATA TO CPU
         RTS    PC
;NOTE: WE ASSUME THAT THE END OF CONVERSION SIGNAL WILL SET b₇
;D/A/C SUBROUTINE
    DAC: TSTB   DACSR       ;REQUEST FOR NEW DATA?
         BPL    DAC         ;NO, CHECK READY-BIT (b₇) AGAIN
         MOV    R0,DABUF    ;CPU OUTPUTS DATA TO BUFFER REGISTER
         RTS    PC
```

where $\quad$ ADCSR $\underline{\Delta}$ A/D/C $\quad$ control-status register
$\qquad$ ADBUF $\underline{\Delta}$ A/D/C $\quad$ data buffer register
$\qquad$ DACSR $\underline{\Delta}$ D/A/C $\quad$ control-status register
$\qquad$ DABUF $\underline{\Delta}$ D/A/C $\quad$ data buffer register

Thus far, we have described the basic principles of operation of the I/O interface of A/D/C and D/A/C. In order to convey the principles, the structure has been simplified. In practice, an A/D/A I/O board would normally consist of a channel multiplexer that can multiplex up to 64 channels of analog signal lines into a single A/D/C so that they can "time share" on a good A/D/C. In addition, the board would also provide the interrupt capability. We will show a practical example using a typical PDP-11 A/D/A I/O interface board in the next chapter, after we have learned the interrupt process.

EXERCISES

7.1 List the essential information you need to write an I/O program.

7.2 What is a handshaking process, and why do we need the handshaking process for writing asynchronous I/O programs?

7.3 Write an output routine that will display a specific visual pattern specified by the CPU on an 8×8 matrix of an LED light panel. You may use two output ports whose registers have the addresses specified as follows:

      Port 1.   Status-control register = 177570
                 Data buffer register = 177572

      Port 2.   Status-control register = 177574
                 Data buffer register = 177576

Of course, you may assume that the interface hardware has already been designed and is functioning.

7.4 Can you write an output macro that will "decode" any ASCII character from CPU and use the routine you created in Problem 7.3 to display that specific ASCII character? Yes? No? Give it a try.

7.5 Assume that a typewriterlike keyboard that can generate ASCII code is connected to an input port of your PDP-11 system. The addresses of the input registers are as follows:

      Status-control register = 177560
      Data buffer register = 177562

Write an I/O program that will "echo" the input character at the display panel described in Problem 7.3.

7.6 Write a main or host program to display HI! in sequence on the LED light panel by keying in the characters through the keyboard described in Problem 7.5. For reading purposes, each character should be displayed for at least one second, and the whole message should repeat by itself until the user presses the CR (carriage return) key on the keyboard.

7.7 Modify the program of Example 2 (page 171) such that the process will stop at the end of the tape. You may assume that at the end of the tape the reader will continuously read in "all zero" data for 10 steps.

7.8 Modify the program for the security gate controller in such a way that the system will allow up to three characters for each name and password, respectively. It will also allow the user to have a list of 10 authorized persons.

Chapter 8

Interrupts and Traps

In this chapter, we introduce the external and internal interrupt processes. First, the principle of operation that involves both hardware and software is presented. Then a typical example follows the description of the general procedure. Next, three practical and more sophisticated examples are used to demonstrate the power of the interrupt process. Finally, the trap and trap instruction procedures are presented, with examples.

KEY WORDS

interrupt	priority rank
interrupt grant	trap
interrupt request	trap handler
interrupt service routine	trap instruction
interrupt vector	trap vector
polling	

8.1 INTRODUCTION

The concept of interrupt was one of the great inventions in computer architecture, especially for dealing with input/output devices. Before the adoption of the concept, a computing system would normally use the **polling** technique. That is, the CPU would normally ''go around'' to check each I/O port one by one and ''see'' if any peripheral device connected to it needed service. If so, the CPU would jump to a proper subroutine and serve that device; otherwise it would continue checking devices. This process is somewhat like a door-to-door salesperson who does nothing but poll potential customers and hope that someone will be interested in buying his or her products.

The drawback of the polling technique is the inefficient use of the CPU's time, because while polling, the CPU can do nothing else. In particular, we are wasting CPU time if most of the I/O devices do not request service frequently. The **interrupt** technique is basically a concept of service by request. It is somewhat like a mail order system. No salesperson calls; if a customer wants to buy something, he or she orders it through the mail. With an interrupt-driven system, the CPU can do something else until a request for service, or an ''interrupt request,'' is initiated by an I/O device. To the CPU, the interrupt request is an unexpected event, since it can happen at any time. However, it is an efficient way to utilize CPU time.

8.2 PRINCIPLES OF OPERATION

Basically the interrupt is a process that handles unexpected events occurring internally or externally to a computing system. For instance, the internal interrupt process is evoked if events such as ALU overflow, power failure, or illegal instruction have occurred within the system. The external interrupt is usually related to events that signal some condition associated with the I/O devices. Let us examine the process of external interrupt in detail.

The following key steps must be taken for carrying out the external interrupt process originated by one or more I/O devices:

1. An I/O device issues an **interrupt request** signal to the CPU.
2. The rank of the interrupt priority of the device must be checked.
3. If the device has a higher rank than the current program, the CPU will send the **interrupt grant** or ''interrupt acknowledge'' signal to fetch the device's identification number.
4. The CPU pushes the current program status and the address for returning to the host program into stack. By host program, we mean the program which is currently being executed.
5. The CPU jumps to the service routine of that device and executes.
6. The CPU returns to the host program by popping back the status and return address to PSW and PC from stack.

Hardware Structure for an Interrupt-Driven System

To implement the interrupt process, we need special hardware equipped with proper software. Figure 8.1 shows the hardware structure of an interrupt-driven computer system. Here we see two new things: interrupt vectors in the main memory block and a

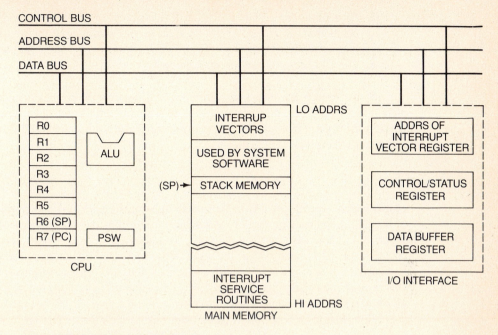

PSW = PROCESSOR STATUS WORD

Figure 8.1 Interrupt driven computer system diagram.

register holding information on the address of the interrupt vector on the I/O interface board. The former carries an array of information on the starting addresses of the **interrupt service routines** and the **priority ranks** of the I/O devices; the latter directs the CPU to where it can find information for the service routine and priority rank of the specific device associated with this I/O board. That is, the latter provides the "identification number" of the device. This kind of interrupt system is known as a **vector interrupt system.** In the interrupt vector block of the main memory, each I/O port (device) "owns" two consecutive memory words. The starting address of the interrupt service routine is stored in the first word, and the priority rank in the second or next higher address word.

General Procedure for an Interrupt Process

Assume the content in the address of the interrupt vector register of an I/O board is 60. The interrupt process will then start with the following steps:

1. The I/O board sends the interrupt request signal through the control bus.
2. Assuming the priority rank of the I/O device is higher than that of the current program, the CPU responds with the interrupt grant signal through the control bus, which gates the content of the ADDRESS of INTERRUPT VECTOR REG., 60, onto the data bus and then onto CPU.
3. The CPU pushes the current (PSW) and updated PC onto the stack.
4. The CPU fetches the interrupt vector at location 60 and loads the starting address of the interrupt service routine and the priority rank onto PC and PSW, respectively.

5. As soon as the CPU ''sees'' the RTI instruction, or the return from interrupt instruction, at the end of the interrupt service routine, the updated PC and the original PSW pop back to PC and PSW, respectively, from the stack.
6. The CPU resumes the original process.

Steps 3 and 5 are shown in Figure 8.2. All these steps are implemented by hardware. Therefore, all the programmer has to do is simply initialize the interrupt vector and develop the appropriate interrupt service routine. Figure 8.3 depicts the flowchart that summarizes the procedure.

A Typical Example

In this section we will use a typical example utilizing the DLV11-F I/O board (a product of Digital Equipment Corporation) as a vehicle to illustrate the interrupt process. Refer to Figure 8.1. There are three key registers: (1) address of interrupt vector register whose content is the ''I.D. number'' of the board or the address of the interrupt vector assigned to this board. It is a ''read-only-register''—that is, the CPU can read information from but cannot write information into the register; (2) the control-status (C/S) register; and (3) the data buffer register. Both C/S and buffer registers are read/write (R/W) registers; that is, the CPU can read or write information from or into the register through a sequence of instructions. For the DLV11-F, however, we have five key registers, as follows:

1. *Address of interrupt vector register*. This is implemented by an 8-bit dip switch whose contents can only be set manually by the customer. The original factory setting of the board is normally 60. That is, the default value of the identification number of the I/O board is set to 60.
2. *Input (receiver) control-status register*. Suggested symbolic address = RCSR, whose address value or default value is set to 177560 by the manufacturer, but can be changed manually by the customer. The bit pattern is defined as follows:
   b_0 = read-enable bit. Can be used to advance paper tape or other I/O device; cleared by the start bit of the serial input data.
   b_6 = interrupt enable bit. Usually set by the CPU through MOV instruction. Together with the done bit (b_7) set, it would generate the interrupt request signal to the CPU.
   b_7 = done bit. Indicates that the data in the buffer register are ready for transfer to the CPU.
   b_{11} = busy bit. Set by the start bit of the serial input signal or data, and cleared by the system done signal.
3. *Input (receiver) data buffer register*. Suggested symbolic address = RBUF. Default address value of RBUF = 177562.
   $b_7, b_6, \ldots, b_0$ = data byte.
   b_{12} = parity error. Parity received does not agree with expected.
   b_{13} = transmission frame error. Stop bit of the serial data missing.
   b_{14} = overrun error. Done bit was not cleared as expected.
   $b_{15} = b_{12} + b_{13} + b_{14}$, where + = logic OR operation.
4. *Output (transmitter) control-status register*. Suggested symbolic address = XCSR. Default address value of XCSR = 177564.

KEY OPERATIONS: PUSH/POP

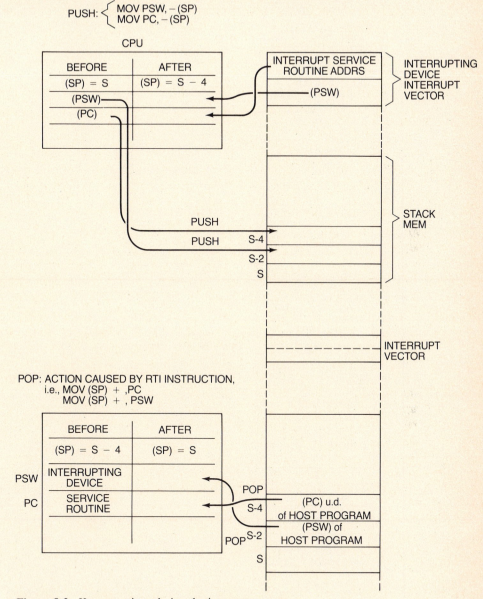

Figure 8.2 Key operations during the interrupt process.

b_0 = break bit. Transmits a continuous pace to the external device.

b_2 = maintenance bit. Connects the transmitter serial output to the receiver serial input.

b_6 = output interrupt enable. With ready bit (b_7) set, it generates the interrupt request signal.

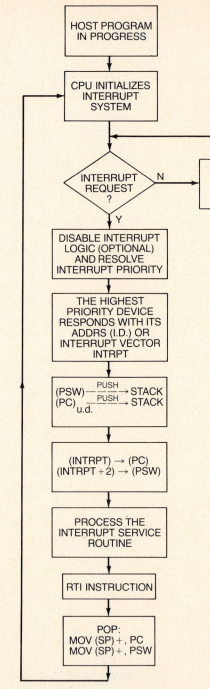

Figure 8.3 Flowchart of the interrupt process.

b_7 = ready bit. The buffer data register is empty and ready to accept new data from the CPU.

b_{11} = baud rate enable.

$b_{12}, \ldots, b_{15}$ = baud rate select. The baud rate, in bit-per-second, is a measure of how fast a digital signal is being transmitted serially.

5. *Output (transmitter) data buffer register.* Suggested symbolic address = XBUF. Default address value of XBUF = 177566.

$b_7, \ldots, b_0$ = data byte.

Now, let us write an interrupt-driven program using the DLV11-F interface board to read a block of 26 characters from a paper reader. For simplicity, we assume that the baud rate has been set properly. Recall that the PSW bit pattern is defined as follows:

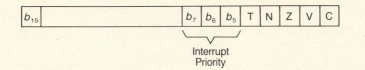

Figure 8.4 shows the flowchart of this program. Its corresponding source program is given below:

```
                    RCSR = 177560        ;ASSIGN THE ADDRESS VALUES TO
                    RBUF = 177562        ;THE KEY REGISTERS
      ARRAY:        .BLKW 26
      START:        .
                    .
                    .
1)                  MTPS  #0             ;CLEAR CURRENT PSW SO THAT THE HOST
                                         ;PROGRAM HAS THE LOWEST PRIORITY.
                                         ;THIS STEP IS OPTIONAL
2)                  MOV   #ITRPTSR, 60   ;INITIAL INTERRUPT VECTOR
3)                  MOV   #200,62        ;INITIAL PRIORITY RANK OF 4 TO THE
                                         ;PAPER READER
4)                  MOV   #26,CNTR       ;SET CHARACTER COUNTER
5)                  MOV   #ARRAY,TEMP    ;INITIAL TEMP WITH DESTINATION ADDRESS
6)                  MOVB  #101,RCSR      ;SET READER ENABLE AND INTERRUPT ENABLE
                    .                    ;BITS
                    .                    ;INTERRUPT MAY OCCUR ANY TIME FROM
                    .                    ;HERE ON
7)                  .END   START
      ⟨Interrupt Service Routine Option No. 1⟩ Transfer one character per interrupt.
8) ITRPTSR:         MOV   TEMP,R0        ;INITIAL R0 AS THE DATA POINTER
9)                  MOVB  RBUF,(R0)+     ;CPU READS IN ONE CHARACTER AND STORES
                                         ;IT IN DESTINATION MEMORY
10)                 DEC   CNTR           ;COUNT DOWN
11)                 BEQ   QUIT
12)                 MOV   R0,TEMP        ;SAVE POINTER FOR NEXT CHARACTER
                                         ;INTERRUPT
13)                 INC   RCSR           ;ADVANCE PAPER TAPE ONE STEP
14) RETURN:         RTI                  ;RETURN TO HOST PROGRAM
15) QUIT:           CLR   RCSR           ;DISABLE THE INTERRUPT ENABLE BIT
16)                 BR    RETURN
17) CNTR:           .BLKW 1
18) TEMP:           .BLKW 1
                    .END
```

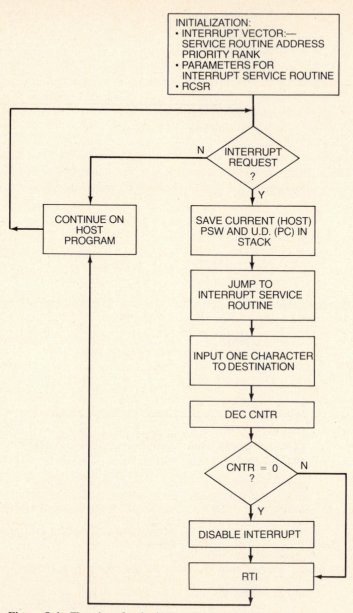

Figure 8.4 Flowchart for the interrupt driven paper tape reader.

Some of the less obvious lines in this program need clarification.

Line 2: Initial the first word of the interrupt vector, whose address is 60 for this I/O board, with the starting address of the interrupt service routine.

Line 3: Initial the second word of the interrupt vector, whose address is 62, with #200, which will set the $b_7b_6b_5$ to 4. When this word is loaded into PSW, it will result in a priority rank of 4.

Line 4: Interrupt service routine parameter passing.

Line 5: Interrupt service routine parameter passing.

Line 6: Initial RCSR with $b_0 = 1$ and $b_6 = 1$.

From here on, the CPU would continue executing the host program until the interrupt request signal is received. Note that the paper tape reader is an electrical-mechanical device which would require at least 50 milliseconds or more to respond to the enable command. That is, the CPU will not receive the interrupt request signal until tens or even hundreds of milliseconds after line 6. During this delay period, the CPU can execute hundreds of instructions of the host program.

Let us assume that the CPU has eventually received the interrupt request signal caused by the done bit, b_7, and the interrupt enable bit, b_6, of RCSR. Then the interrupt process is executed, as described in the preceding section, by the interrupt hardware logic. As a result, the CPU starts to execute line 8. The address value of ARRAY, the starting address of the data destination, is transferred to R0, which in turn becomes the data pointer. Line 9 transfers one character into destination. Line 10 keeps track of whether 26 characters have been read. If "yes," the program jumps to QUIT, line 15, which will disable the interrupt logic and then return to the host program. If "no," the routine goes to line 12, where the CPU saves the pointer value in TEMP so that the R0 can be released to be used in the host program. Line 13 reenables the reader enable bit to advance the paper tape one step to read another character. Since there again will be a delay, the CPU can use this time to execute the host program. Thus we have line 14 to return the interrupt process back to the host program. Here, we assume that once the interrupt enable bit (b_6) of RCSR has been set (line 6), it will remain set until line 15 is executed.

In this example we have "borrowed" one of the general purpose registers, R0, to serve as the data pointer. Since the interrupt process is an unexpected one, the host program has no idea at what instant the process will occur. So it is possible that R0 will be holding important data when the interrupt occurs. After the interrupt process is complete, the original contents of R0 will be lost. The programmer must be aware of this problem. The programmer should avoid using R0 as an important data storage register in the host program or avoid using R0 in the service routine. Or the pushing-popping of the R0 process should be included within the interrupt service routine. Although logically the pushing-popping of the contents of the general purpose registers is a general solution that will be illustrated in the later examples, let us for simplicity try to avoid using R0 in the interrupt service routine here. For this example, we could modify the interrupt service routine as follows:

```
INTRPTSR:    MOVB RBUF, @TEMP    ;USE TEMP AS THE DATA POINTER
             INC  TEMP
             DEC  CNTR
             BEQ  QUIT
             INC  RCSR
RETURN:      RTI
QUIT:        CLR  RCSR
             BR   RETURN
CNTR:        .BLKW 1
TEMP:        .BLKW 1
             .END
```

At this point, you may wonder why the interrupt service routine is designed to transfer one character per interrupt. Why not transfer the whole 26 characters per interrupt? What follows is the second option of the service routine, which will transfer the whole block within one interrupt: ⟨Interrupt Service Routine Option No. 2⟩ Transfer one set of data per interrupt.

```
INTRPTSR:   CLR   RCSR        ;DISABLE (OPTIONAL) THE INTERRUPT
                              ;-ENABLE-BIT
            MOV   TEMP,R0     ;INITIAL R0 AS THE DATA POINTER
L1:         MOV   RBUF,(R0)+
            DEC   CNTR
            BEQ   QUIT
            INC   RCSR
L2:         TSTB  RCSR        ;IS DONE-BIT SET?
            BPL   L2          ;IF NOT, BRANCH TO L2
            BR    L1          ;IF YES, TRANSFER DATA TO DESTINATION
QUIT:       MOV   #100,RCSR   ;RESUME (OPTIONAL) INTERRUPT ENABLE SYSTEM
            RTI
CNTR:       .BLKW 1
TEMP:       .BLKW 1
            .END
```

It is important to point out that in this option, the operation of loop L2 may take 50 or more milliseconds. During this time, CPU cannot execute the host program. Therefore, this option is a lot slower than option 1.

8.3 MORE EXAMPLES

Saving and Retrieving the Contents of Registers for the Interrupt Process

Since the instant at which the interrupt occurs is not predictable, it is important that we learn the techniques for saving and retrieving the contents of the general purpose registers, R0, R1, . . . , R5, before and after the interrupt process so that the interrupt service routine can freely use or "borrow" the general registers for its operation without destroying data in the register that may be important to the host program. Figures 8.5 (a), (b), (c), and (d) present examples illustrating the variety of techniques for these purposes. It is also a good review on the topics of subroutines, coroutines, macros, and conditional macros.

The examples are organized in four parts: (1) interrupt service routine, (2) program for saving the contents of the registers in the stack memory, (3) program for retrieving the contents of the registers from the stack memory, and (4) host (main) program for illustrating the actions. To demonstrate the actions in progress, we use the system macro .WRITE developed in our lab to carry out the process interactively, as shown. You may not have this convenience in your laboratory. However, you need not be concerned; in fact, by now you should be able to guess what is in the system macro .WRITE. It consists of a set of I/O macros illustrated in the preceding chapter, using the directive .ASCIZ for displaying messages and the routine of converting binary numbers into ASCII for number display. It is important that you trace the action of the program step by step to become familiar with the process. You can pretend that you have the .WRITE system macro in your laboratory.

```
                    ;THIS IS AN EXAMPLE SHOWING AN INTERRUPT ROUTINE THAT USES
                    ;SUBROUTINES TO SAVE & RETRIEVE THE CONTENTS OF REGS.
                    .TITLE    INTRPT(TECHNIQUE 1)
                    .GLOBL    SAVE,RTRV
                    .MCALL    .WRITE
INTRPT:  JSR        PC,SAVE        ;JUMP TO SUBROUTINE SAVE
         .WRITE     '\\INTRRUPT_IN_PROGRESS__
         MOV        SP,R5          ;SET UP DISPLAY POINTER
         MOV        #6,R4          ;R4 AS DISPLAY COUNTER
         .WRITE     '\\THE_(REGS)_SAVED_ON_STACK_ARE:\\
L1:      .WRITE     (R5)+          ;DISPLAY CONTENTS SAVED ON STACK
         SOB        R4,L1
DMS1:    JSR        PC,RTRV        ;JUMP TO SUBROUTINE RTRV
RTRN:    RTI
         ;
         ;THE FOLLOWING IS SUBROUTINE SAVE
         .GLOBL     SAVE
SAVE:    NOP
         MOV        R0,-(SP)       ;SAVE (REGS) ON STACK
         MOV        R1,-(SP)
         MOV        R2,-(SP)
         MOV        R3,-(SP)
         MOV        R4,-(SP)
         MOV        R5,-(SP)
DMS2:    MOV        14(SP),PC      ;RETURN TO INTRPT ROUTINE
         ;
         ;THE FOLLOWING IS SUBROUTINE RTRV
         .GLOBL     RTRV
RTRV:    TST        (SP)+          ;SKIP TOP LAYER OF STACK
         MOV        (SP)+,R5       ;RETRIEVE (REGS)
         MOV        (SP)+,R4
         MOV        (SP)+,R3
         MOV        (SP)+,R2
         MOV        (SP)+,R1
         MOV        (SP)+,R0
DMS3:    MOV        -16(SP),(SP)   ;SET RETURN ADDRS FOR RTS-INSTRUCTION
         RTS        PC             ;RETURN TO INTERRUPT ROUTINE
         ;
         ;MAIN PROGRAM
         .MCALL     .WRITE
MAIN:    MOV        #0,R0          ;STORE ABITRARY DATA IN REGS
         MOV        #1,R1
         MOV        #2,R2
         MOV        #3,R3
         MOV        #4,R4
         MOV        #5,R5
         MOV        #INTRPT,60     ;INITIAL INTERRUPT VECTOR
         MOV        #200,62        ;PRIORITY = 4
         MOV        #100,177560    ;ENABLE INTERRUPT
         .WRITE     'DEPRESS_ANY_KEY_TO_INTERRUPT_ME
         WAIT
         .WRITE     '\\THE_(REGS)_AFTER_INTERRUPT_ARE:\\
         .WRITE     R0,R1,R2,R3,R4,R5
         HALT
         .END       MAIN
```

Figure 8.5(a)   Interrupt with SAVE/RETRIEVE registers.

```
          ;THIS IS AN EXAMPLE SHOWING AN INTERRUPT ROUTINE THAT USES
          ;COROUTINES TO SAVE & RETRIEVE THE CONTENTS OF REGS.
          .TITLE INTRPT(TECHNIQUE 2)
          ;THE FOLLOWING IS THE COROUTINE INTRPT
          .MCALL  .WRITE
INTRPT:   MOV     #SAVE,-(SP)     ;INITIAL COROUTINE PROCESS
          .WRITE  '\\INTRRUPT_IN_PROGRESS__
          JSR     PC,@(SP)+       ;JUMP TO COROUTINE SAVE/RETRIEVE
                                  ;OR,#DS → TOP LAYER OF STACK & #SAVE → PC
DS:       MOV     SP,R5           ;SET UP DISPLAY POINTER
          TST     (R5)+           ;SKIP TOP LAYER OF STACK
          MOV     #6,R4           ;R4 AS DISPLAY COUNTER
          .WRITE  '\\THE_(REGS)_SAVED_ON_STACK_ARE:\\
L1:       .WRITE  (R5)+           ;DISPLAY CONTENTS SAVED ON STACK
          SOB     R4,L1
          JSR     PC,@(SP)+       ;JUMP TO COROUTINE SAVE/RETRIEVE
                                  ;OR,#DMS1 → TOP LAYER OF STACK & #RTRV → PC
DMS1:     TST     (SP)+           ;RESET (SP) TO INITIAL STATE
RTRN:     RTI
          ;
          ;THE FOLLOWING IS THE COROUTINE SAVE/RETRIEVE
SAVE:     NOP
          MOV     R0,-(SP)        ;SAVE (REGS) ON STACK
          MOV     R1,-(SP)
          MOV     R2,-(SP)
          MOV     R3,-(SP)
          MOV     R4,-(SP)
          MOV     R5,-(SP)
DMS2:     MOV     14(SP),-(SP)    ;PUT RETURN ADDRS ON TOP LAYER OF STACK
          JSR     PC,@(SP)+       ;JUMP TO COROUTINE INTRPT,OR #RTRV →
                                  ;TOP LAYER OF STACK AND #DS → PC
RTRV:     TST     (SP)+           ;SKIP TOP LAYER OF STACK
          MOV     (SP)+,R5        ;RETRIEVE (REGS)
          MOV     (SP)+,R4
          MOV     (SP)+,R3
          MOV     (SP)+,R2
          MOV     (SP)+,R1
          MOV     (SP)+,R0
DMS3:     MOV     -16(SP),(SP)    ;SET RETURN ADDRS TO INTRPT,#DMS1 → STACK TOP
          JSR     PC,@(SP)+       ;RETURN TO INTRPT,#MAIN → STACK ,#DMS1 → PC
          ;
          ;MAIN PROGRAM
          .MCALL  .WRITE
MAIN:     MOV     #0,R0           ;STORE ABITARY DATA IN REGS
          MOV     #1,R1
          MOV     #2,R2
          MOV     #3,R3
          MOV     #4,R4
          MOV     #5,R5
          MOV     #INTRPT,60      ;INITIAL INTERRUPT VECTOR
          MOV     #200,62         ;PRIORITY = 4
          MOV     #100,177560     ;ENABLE INTERRUPT
          .WRITE  'DEPRESS_ANY_KEY_TO_INTERRUPT_ME
          WAIT
          .WRITE  '\\THE_(REGS)_AFTER_INTERRUPT_ARE:\\
          .WRITE  R0,R1,R2,R3,R4,R5
          HALT
          .END    MAIN
```

Figure 8.5(b) Interrupt with SAVE/RETRIEVE registers.

```
                      ;THIS IS AN EXAMPLE SHOWING AN INTERRUPT ROUTINE THAT USES
                      ;MACROS TO SAVE & RETRIEVE THE CONTENTS OF REGS.
                      .TITLE   INTRPT(TECHNIQUE 3)
                      ;THE FOLLOWING IS THE MACRO SAVE-MODULE
                      .MACRO   SAVE
           SAVE:      NOP
                      MOV      R0,-(SP)        ;SAVE (REGS) ON STACK
                      MOV      R1,-(SP)
                      MOV      R2,-(SP)
                      MOV      R3,-(SP)
                      MOV      R4,-(SP)
                      MOV      R5,-(SP)
                      .ENDM    SAVE
                      ;
                      ;THE FOLLOWING IS THE MACRO RTRV-MODULE
                      .MACRO   RTRV
           RTRV:      NOP
                      MOV      (SP)+,R5        ;RETRIEVE (REGS)
                      MOV      (SP)+,R4
                      MOV      (SP)+,R3
                      MOV      (SP)+,R2
                      MOV      (SP)+,R1
                      MOV      (SP)+,R0
                      .ENDM    RTRV
                      ;
                      .TITLE   INTRPT(MODULE)
                      .MCALL   .WRITE
           INTRPT:    SAVE
                      .WRITE   '\\INTRRUPT_IN_PROGRESS__
                      MOV      SP,R5           ;SET UP DISPLAY POINTER
                      MOV      #6,R4           ;R4 AS DISPLAY COUNTER
                      .WRITE   '\\THE_(REGS)_SAVED_ON_STACK_ARE:\\
           L1:        .WRITE   (R5)+           ;DISPLAY CONTENTS SAVED ON STACK
                      SOB      R4,L1
           M1:        RTRV
           RTRN:      RTI
                      ;
                      ;MAIN PROGRAM
                      .MCALL   .WRITE
           MAIN:      MOV      #0,R0           ;STORE ABITARY DATA IN REGS
                      MOV      #1,R1
                      MOV      #2,R2
                      MOV      #3,R3
                      MOV      #4,R4
                      MOV      #5,R5
                      MOV      #INTRPT,60      ;INITIAL INTERRUPT VECTOR
                      MOV      #200,62         ;PRIORITY = 4
                      MOV      #100,177560     ;ENABLE INTERRUPT
                      .WRITE   'DEPRESS_ANY_KEY_TO_INTERRUPT_ME
                      WAIT
                      .WRITE   '\\THE_(REGS)_AFTER_INTERRUPT_ARE:\\
                      .WRITE   R0,R1,R2,R3,R4,R5
                      HALT
                      .END     MAIN
```

Execution Result: **DEPRESS ANY KEY TO INTERRUPT ME**
      INTERRUPT IN PROGRESS
      THE (REGS) SAVED ON STACK ARE:
      5 4 3 2 1 0
      THE (REGS) AFTER INTERRUPT ARE:
      0 1 2 3 4 5

Figure 8.5(c)   Interrupt with SAVE/RETRIEVE registers.

```
        ;THIS IS AN EXAMPLE SHOWING AN INTRRUPT ROUTINE THAT USES
        ;CONDITIONAL MACROS TO SAVE & RETRIEVE SELECTED REGISTERS.
        .TITLE INTRPT(TECHNIQUE 4)
        ;THE FOLLOWING IS THE CONDITIONAL MACRO SAVE-MODULE
        .MACRO  SAVE            R0,R1,R2,R3,R4,R5
.IF     NB      R0              ;NB = NON-BLANK
        MOV     R0,-(SP)
        .ENDC
.IF     NB      R1
        MOV     R1,-(SP)
        .ENDC
.IF     NB      R2
        MOV     R2,-(SP)
        .ENDC
.IF     NB      R3
        MOV     R3,-(SP)
        .ENDC
.IF     NB      R4
        MOV     R4,-(SP)
        .ENDC
.IF     NB      R5
        MOV     R5,-(SP)
        .ENDC
        .ENDM   SAVE
;
        ;THE FOLLOWING IS THE CONDITIONAL MACRO RTRV-MODULE
        .MACRO  RTRV    R5,R4,R3,R2,R1,R0
.IF     NB      R5
        MOV     (SP)+,R5
        .ENDC
.IF     NB      R4
        MOV     (SP)+,R4
        .ENDC
.IF     NB      R3
        MOV     (SP)+,R3
        .ENDC
.IF     NB      R2
        MOV     (SP)+,R2
        .ENDC
.IF     NB      R1
        MOV     (SP)+,R1
        .ENDC
.IF     NB      R0
        MOV     (SP)+,R0
        .ENDC
        .ENDM   RTRV
;
        .TITLE    INTRPT(MODULE)
        .MCALL    .WRITE
INTRPT: SAVE      R0,R5
        .WRITE    '\\INTRRUPT_IN_PROGRESS__
        MOV       SP,R5              ;SET UP DISPLAY POINTER
        MOV       #2,R4              ;R4 AS DISPLAY COUNTER
        .WRITE    '\\THE_(REGS)_SAVED_ON_STACK_ARE:\\
L1:     .WRITE    (R5)+              ;DISPLAY CONTENTS SAVED ON STACK
        SOB       R4,L1
M1:     RTRV      R5,R0
RTRN:   RTI
;
        ;MAIN PROGRAM
        .MCALL    .WRITE
```

```
MAIN:    MOV      #0,R0                ;STORE ABITARY DATA IN REGS
         MOV      #1,R1
         MOV      #2,R2
         MOV      #3,R3
         MOV      #4,R4
         MOV      #5,R5
         MOV      #INTRPT,60           ;INITIAL INTERRUPT VECTOR
         MOV      #200,62              ;PRIORITY = 4
         MOV      #100,177560          ;ENABLE INTERRUPT
         .WRITE   'DEPRESS_ANY_KEY_TO_INTERRUPT_ME
         WAIT
         .WRITE   '\\THE_(REGS)_AFTER_INTERRUPT_ARE:\\
         .WRITE   R0,R1,R2,R3,R4,R5
         HALT
         .END     MAIN
```

Execution Result: **DEPRESS ANY KEY TO INTERRUPT ME**
                    INTERRUPT IN PROGRESS
                    THE (REGS) SAVED ON STACK ARE:
                    5 0
                    THE (REGS) AFTER INTERRUPT ARE:
                    0 1 2 3 4 5

Figure 8.5(d)   Interrupt with SAVE/RETRIEVE registers.

Input/Output Data Queue Buffer Program

In this example, we will attempt to illustrate how we could use what we have learned to develop a useful application program for collecting data. We intend to demonstrate the following features:

1. Use of system macros, user-defined macros, macros with automatic local address assignment, subroutines, and interrupt to carry out a fairly complex task.
2. Use of software test points for debugging purposes.
3. Use of module concepts to break a complex program into modules and develop them one by one and then link them into one complete program for the task.

Problem Statement   Often we wish to collect data in a repeating burst format for data processing. During the burst, we wish to collect the data as fast as the data were generated. Between the bursts, we could store the collected data into a mass storage area for future processing. Obviously, in this application we would need fast memory to collect the burst data, whereas the access time for the mass storage device would not be so critical, provided that the time between bursts is reasonably long. In some cases, however, the requirement for access speed can be just the opposite of what we have just described. That is, the input data can be infrequent and the occurring time may not be predictable. In such cases, we do not want to tie up the mass storage device. We would rather provide a small block of main memory as a buffer to collect the data trickling in and then transfer them into a destination or mass memory at once. Figure 8.6(a) depicts the data flow of the process described. We will now show how the process can be implemented using interrupt and subroutine techniques. We will also use the concept of the buffer queue to enhance the buffering process.

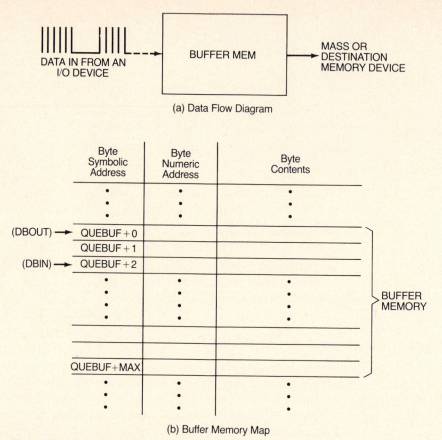

(a) Data Flow Diagram

(b) Buffer Memory Map

Figure 8.6 Data collection using buffer memory.

Structure of the Data Buffer   Figure 8.6(b) shows the buffer memory map in byte basis. The starting address of the buffer is QUEBUF, and it has a capacity of (MAX + 1) bytes or (1/2)(MAX + 1) words. We have also defined two data pointers—namely, DBIN (input to data buffer queue) and DBOUT (output from data buffer queue). The former is always pointing at the location at which the next input data are to be deposited, while the latter is pointing at the location whose content is to be transferred out of the buffer next. Intuitively, we might think one data pointer would be sufficient to serve the input and output purposes. For example, we could use a single data pointer to "fill up" the buffer first and then reset the pointer to the starting address and use it as the output pointer to transfer the data out of the buffer.

But although simple and straightforward, the single-pointer configuration has a serious drawback. What happens if new data arrive while the data are being moved out? Furthermore, how can we guarantee that the new data would not be written over the collected data that have not yet been moved out? What if some single burst of data requires a buffer capacity larger than the reserved capacity? Is it possible to move data out within the burst period during the brief break between two adjacent data?

The two-pointer configuration can best be explained by presenting the buffer in

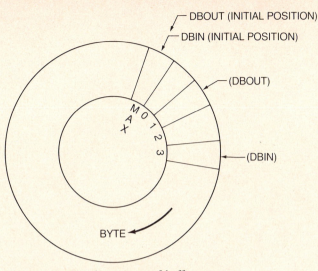

Figure 8.7 Circular concept of buffer memory.

circular form, as shown in Figure 8.7. Initially, both pointers are pointing at the MAXth byte. As the data enter the buffer, the (DBIN) increases clockwise, while the pointer DBOUT is standing still. When the input data stop coming, the collected data, which will be in the memory area between pointers, will be transferred out and the DBOUT pointer increased accordingly. As a result, the "gap" between the two pointers will be decreasing while data are moving out. In this way, we should have an infinite buffer capacity as long as the gap is always less than MAX but greater than zero number of bytes. We could use the buffer space over and over again without worrying about the valid data being written over or outputting nonvalid data. To maintain this ideal situation, we must consider the following conditions:

1. (DBIN) catching up with the (DBOUT), or (DBIN) = (DBOUT), implies that the buffer is full.
2. (DBOUT) catching up with the (DBIN), or (DBOUT) = (DBIN), implies that the buffer is empty.
3. When either of the pointers equals MAX, it must be reset or cleared to zero value so that it can start from the zero position again.

The Algorithm In this section we will develop an algorithm that can be implemented in the laboratory. For convenience, we assign another block of memory as the destined storage to simulate the destined mass storage device in our problem. Figure 8.8 shows the functional block diagram of the system. Here we use the interrupt approach for inputting data to the circular buffer and a subroutine for outputting data to the destination from the circular buffer, plus a host program to call the subroutine and display the results.

The subroutine will terminate its operation if (1) the data in the buffer have been completely removed to the destination, and (2) there are probably no further input data coming. It will check whether the buffer is empty for sensing the first condition, and

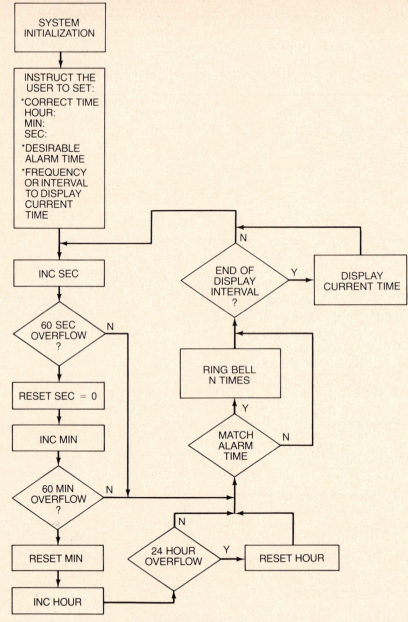

Figure 8.15 Flowchart for the alarm clock.

```
                    ;THIS PROGRAM SIMULATES AN ALARM CLOCK USING SYSTEM AND
                    ;USER DEFINED MACROS.
                    ;
          .MCALL    .WRITE,.READ,.RAD,.EXIT
          .MACRO    SEC ?L1
          MOV       R5,-(SP)              ;SAVE OLD (R5)
          CLR       R5
L1:       INC       R5
          CMP       #0,R5                 ;MAKING UP A SECOND
          BNE       L1
          MOV       (SP)+,R5
          .ENDM     SEC
          ;
          .MACRO    RBELL N,LOOP
          MOV       R5,-(SP)
          MOV       #N,R5                 ;RING BELL N TIMES
LOOP:     .WRITE    '#007                 ;STRIKE THE BELL
          SEC                             ;ONE SECOND DELAY
          SOB       R5,LOOP
          MOV       (SP)+,R5
          .ENDM     RBELL
          ;
          .MACRO    ALARMCK ALARMH,ALARMM,ALARMS,?NOTCK
          CMP       ALARMS,R0
          BNE       NOTCK
          CMP       ALARMM,R1
          BNE       NOTCK
          CMP       ALARMH,R2
          BNE       NOTCK
          RBELL     5,DLOOP
NOTCK:    NOP
          .ENDM     ALARMCK
          ;
          .MACRO OVRFLW ?QUIT
          CMP       #60.,R0
          BGT       QUIT
          CLR       R0
          INC       R1
          CMP       #60.,R1
          BGT       QUIT
          CLR       R1
          INC       R2
          CMP       #24.,R2
          BGT       QUIT
          CLR       R2
QUIT:     NOP
          .ENDM     OVRFLW
          ;
          ;MAIN PROGRAM
START:    .WRITE    '\\INPUT_RADIX_AND_FORMAT
          .RAD
SETIME:   .WRITE    '\\INPUT_CURRENT_HOUR__MIN__SEC:__
          .READ     R2,R1,R0
          .WRITE    '\\NOW_THE_TIME_IS:__,R2,'_:,R1,'_:,R0
SETALRM:  .WRITE    '\\SET_ALARM_HOUR__MIN__SEC:__
          .READ     ALARMH,ALARMM,ALARMS
          .WRITE    '\\ALARM_SET_TO::_,ALARMH,'_:,ALARMM,'_:,ALARMS
          .WRITE    '\\SET_TIME_DELAY_INTERVAL__IN_SECOND:__
          .READ     INTRVL
          MOV       INTRVL,R3
```

```
TICK:        SEC
             INC         R0
             OVRFLW
             ALARMCK     ALARMH,ALARMM,ALARMS,BELL
CONT:        DEC         R3
             BEQ         DISPLAY
             JMP         TICK
DISPLAY:     .WRITE      '\\NOW_THE_TIME_IS::__,R2,'_:,R1,'_:,R0
             MOV         INTRVL,R3
             JMP         TICK
INTRVL:      .BLKW
ALARMH:      .BLKW
ALARMM:      .BLKW
ALARMS:      .BLKW
             .END        START
```

Figure 8.16 Source program of the alarm clock module.

Macro That Takes One Character into CPU from Keyboard

```
.MACRO      KEYBRDIN R,?L2
L2:         TSTB  177560
            BPL   L2
            MOVB 177562,R
.ENDM       KEYBRDIN
```

Macro That Puts One Character into CRT from CPU

```
.MACRO      CRTOUT      R,?L3
L3:         TSTB        177564
            BPL         L3
            MOVB        R,177566
.ENDM       CRTOUT
```

Macro That Converts a 6-Bit Binary Number into Two-Digit Octal Numbers in ASCII Codes

```
.MACRO      ASCIOUT     R,TEMP1,TEMP2,?L5
            MOV R5,-(SP)
            MOV #3,R5                    ;R5 AS A COUNTER FOR SHIFT
                                         ;OPERATION
            MOV R,TEMP1                  ;USE TEMP1 AS A WORKING
                                         ;REGISTER
            BIC   #177770,TEMP1          ;MASK THE CONTENT IN TEMP 1
                                         ;EXCEPT THE 3 LEAST SIGNIFI-
                                         ;CANT BITS
            ADD #60,TEMP1                ;CONVERT BINARY TO ASCII CODE
            MOV R,TEMP2
L5:         ASR TEMP2                    ;SHIFT OUT THE 3 LEAST SIGNI-
                                         ;FICANT BITS
            DEC R5
            BNE L5
            BIC   #177770,TEMP2
            ADD #60,TEMP2
            CRTOUT      TEMP2            ;OUTPUT ASCII ON CRT BY THE
                                         ;MACRO DEFINED IN 3)
            CRTOUT      TEMP1
            MOV         (SP)+,R5
            .ENDM       ASCIOUT
TEMP1:      .BLKW       1
TEMP2:      .BLKW       1
```

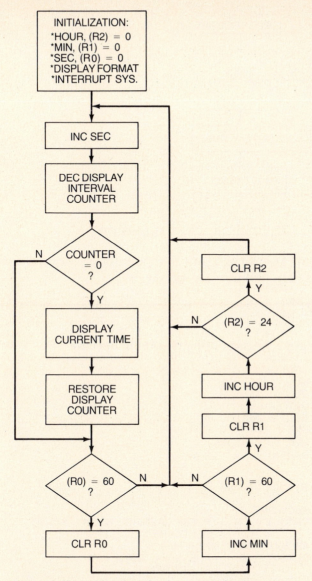

Figure 8.17(a) Flowchart for the stopwatch program.

Note that in this macro we have reserved two memory words, temp 1 and temp 2, for the temporary storage register. This, of course, has the disadvantage of requiring memory space external to the macro. As an alternative, we could use the technique of borrowing R5, as shown. That is, we could borrow R4 and R3, as we did R5, by saving (R4), (R3) as follows:

```
MOV     R4,−(SP)
MOV     R3,−(SP)
```

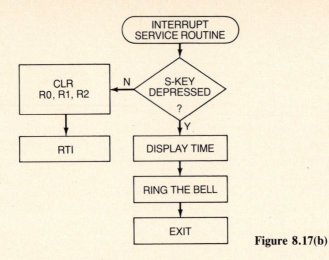

Figure 8.17(b)

and use R3 for TEMP 1 and R4 for TEMP 2. At the end of the macros, of course, we have to retrieve the old (R4), (R3) from the stack by

```
MOV     (SP)+,R3
MOV     (SP)+,R4
```

Macro That Displays a Message Using the .ASCIZ Directive

```
.MACRO    DISPLAY INFO, ?L4
          MOV     R5,-(SP)
          MOV     #INFO,R5
L4:       CRTOUT (R5)+
          TSTB    (R5)
          BNE     L4
          MOV     (SP)+,R5
.ENDM     DISPLAY
```

Macro That Displays the Current Time

```
.MACRO    SHOWTIME
          CRTOUT    CR     ;PRESS CARRIAGE RETURN KEY BY
                           ;SOFTWARE
          ASCIOUT   R2,TEMP1,TEMP2
          CRTOUT    BL     ;PRESS THE SPACE KEY
                           ;BY SOFTWARE
          CRTOUT    BL
          ASCIOUT   R1,TEMP1,TEMP2
          CRTOUT    BL
          CRTOUT    RL
          ASCIOUT   R0,TEMP1,TEMP2
.ENDM     SHOWTIME
```

If the current time in R2, R1, and R0 is 6, 20, and 6, respectively, this macro will display on the CRT in octal representation as follows: 06   24   06.

Having defined the necessary macros, we proceed to write the program. For the purpose of demonstrating the I/O macros, we will write a program slightly fancier than one an ordinary stopwatch would need. We want the CRT to display as follows:

Stopwatch

XX	XX	XX
(hour)	(min)	(sec)

and the display to change every 3 seconds. If the S key of the keyboard is depressed, the watch will stop operation, show the time at which it was stopped, and ring the bell at the keyboard. If any other key is depressed, the watch is reset to zero and will start to count again. Figure 8.17(c) shows the actual source program that implements the specifications described here.

```
          .TITLE      WATCH
          .MCALL      .EXIT
          ;THIS IS A STOP WATCH PROGRAM USING INTERRUPT TECHNIQUE
          ;AND NO SYSTEM MACROS (EXCEPT .EXIT) ARE TO BE USED.
          .MACRO      ASCIOUT R,TEMP1,TEMP2,?CONV,?OK
          MOV         R5,-(SP)              ;GENERATES A TWO DIGIT DECIMAL NUMBER
          MOV         R,TEMP1               ;FROM A BINARY NUMBER IN R
          CLR         TEMP2                 ;THE TWO DIGITS ARE PUT IN
CONV:     CMP         TEMP1,#10.            ;TEMP2 AND TEMP1 FOR OUTPUT
          BLT         OK
          SUB         #10.,TEMP1
          INC         TEMP2
          BR          CONV
OK:       ADD         #60,TEMP1
          ADD         #60,TEMP2
          CRTOUT      TEMP2
          CRTOUT      TEMP1
          MOV         (SP)+,R5
          .ENDM       ASCIOUT
TEMP1:    .BLKW
TEMP2:    .BLKW
          ;
          .MACRO      SEC     ?L1          ;MAKE UP 1 SEC
          MOV         R5,-(SP)
          CLR         R5
L1:       INC         R5
          TST         R5
          BNE         L1
          MOV         (SP)+,R5
          .ENDM       SEC
          ;
          .MACRO      KEYIN R
          MOVB        177562,R
          .ENDM       KEYIN
          ;
          .MACRO      CRTOUT R,?L2
L2:       TSTB        177564
          BPL         L2
          MOVB        R,177566
          .ENDM       CRTOUT
          ;
          .MACRO      DISPLAY INFO,?L4
          MOV         R5,-(SP)              ;DISPLAY MESSAGE
          MOV         #INFO,R5
```

```
L4:        CRTOUT     (R5)+
           TSTB       (R5)
           BNE        L4
           MOV        (SP)+,R5
           .ENDM      DISPLAY
           ;
           .MACRO     SHOWTIME              ;SHOW TIME STORED IN R2,R1,R0
           CRTOUT     CR
           ASCIOUT    R2,TEMP1,TEMP2
           CRTOUT     BL
           CRTOUT     BL
           ASCIOUT    R1,TEMP1,TEMP2
           CRTOUT     BL
           CRTOUT     BL
           ASCIOUT    R0,TEMP1,TEMP2
           .ENDM      SHOWTIME
CR:        .WORD      15                    ;ASCII FOR CARRIAGE RETURN
LF:        .WORD      12                    ;ASCII FOR LINEFEED
BELL:      .WORD      7                     ;ASCII FOR BELL
BL:        .WORD      40                    ;ASCII FOR BLANK
           .EVEN
TRMARK:    .ASCIZ     /STOP WATCH/
LINE:      .ASCIZ     /----------/
           ;
           ;MAIN PROGRAM
START:     CLR        R0                    ;INITIALIZATION
           CLR        R1
           CLR        R2
           CLR        R4
           CRTOUT     LF
           DISPLAY    LINE
           CRTOUT     CR
           CRTOUT     LF
           DISPLAY    TRMARK
           CRTOUT     CR
           DISPLAY    LF
           DISPLAY    LINE
           DISPLAY    CR
           CRTOUT     LF
           MOVB       #0,177560
           SHOWTIME                         ;SHOW INITIAL TIME
WAIT1:     TSTB       177560                ;WAIT FOR START SIGNAL
           BPL        WAIT1
           MOVB       177562,R4
           CMP        #122,R4
           BNE        WAIT1
           CRTOUT     BELL
           MTPS       #0                    ;SET INTERRUPT VECTOR
           MOVB       #100,177560
           MOV        #INTRPT,60
           MOV        #140,62
TIME:      NOP                              ;SIMULATE TIMER
           SEC
           INC        R0
CHK60:     CMP        #60.,R0
           BEQ        J2
           JMP        SHOW
J2:        CLR        R0
           INC        R1
           CMP        #60.,R1
           BEQ        J3
           JMP        SHOW
```

```
J3:       CLR       R1
          INC       R2
          CMP       #24.,R2
          BNE       SHOW
          CLR       R2
SHOW:     SHOWTIME
          JMP       TIME
          ;BEGINNING OF INTERRUPT ROUTINE
INTRPT:   KEYIN     R4
          MTPS      #340
          CMPB      #123,R4        ;CHECK FOR 'S' (STOP)
          BEQ       STOP
          RTI
STOP:     CRTOUT    BELL
          SHOWTIME
WAIT2:    TSTB      177560
          BPL       WAIT2
          MOVB      177562,R4
          CMP       #103,R4        ;CHECK FOR 'C' (CLEAR)
          BEQ       CLEAR
          CMP       #122,R4        ;CHECK FOR 'R' (RESTART)
          BNE       WAIT2
          CRTOUT    BELL
RET:      RTI
CLEAR:    CLR       R0
          CLR       R1
          CLR       R2
          CRTOUT    BELL
          SHOWTIME
          JMP       WAIT2
          .END      START
```

Execution Result:

STOP WATCH

00   00   00

WHEN "R" IS PRESSED, THE CLOCK STARTS TO TICK.
WHEN "S" IS PRESSED, THE CLOCK STOPS.
WHEN "C" IS PRESSED, THE CLOCK IS CLEARED.

Figure 8.17(c) Source of program for a stopwatch.

8.6 TRAPS

Thus far we have described an interrupt-driven system in which the interrupt source is normally one of the external devices. Once we have initialized for the interrupt process, the interrupt hardware logic will take over. The CPU may expect that it could receive an interrupt request at any moment, but does not know the exact time or moment. This class of interrupt is known as the external or hardware interrupt, for which the interrupt source identification, or the address of its unique interrupt vector, is provided by the I/O hardware through the data bus.

In the PDP-11 system, there is another kind of interrupt provision. That is, the system, in addition, contains a **trap** provision. Under abnormal conditions, such as illegal instruction, power failure, or nonexistent memory location, the system would get into a trap through a trap vector at a unique address. Like an interrupt vector, a **trap vector** consists of two memory words whose contents are, respectively, the starting address of the trap service routine and the PSW of that routine. The service routine could contain as little as one single instruction, such as HALT, or an error message to inform the user of what has happened internally. Therefore the trap process is considered an internal or software interrupt process.

When a trap occurs, the CPU (hardware) would push the (PSW) of the host program and the updated (PC) into the stack memory and place the starting address of the trap service routine into PC and its rank of interrupt priority into PSW. At the end of the trap service routine, the RTI instruction would pop the information saved in the stack back to the host program.

Unlike the case of the external interrupt process, the address of the trap vector for each internal interrupt is predefined, and the user cannot alter it as he or she wishes. The PDP-11 system has defined the trap vector addresses for different events as follows:

Trap Vector Address	Descriptions
00 00 00	(reserved)
00 00 04	CPU errors
00 00 10	Illegal and reserved instruction
00 00 14	BPT, breakpoint trap, or trace (T bit)
00 00 20	IOT, input/output trap
00 00 24	Power-fail
00 00 30	EMT (emulator trap) instruction
00 00 34	TRAP instruction

Among these trap processes, BPT, IOT, EMT, and TRAP are accessible to the user. However, the EMT and TRAP instructions require special attention if we wish to develop or use their service routines. That is, the contents of the vectors at 30 and 34 are not the starting addresses of the trap service routines; instead, they should be the starting addresses of the special purpose routines called **TRAP HANDLER.** Via these handlers, the specific trap service routine is called to service.

Both the EMT and **TRAP instructions** have an operand that is normally an integer. The mnemonic instruction format of each is shown below.

EMT n   In this case n is an integer that occupies the low-byte space of the 16-bit word: $n = 0 \sim 377$. Upon execution of this instruction, the system is interrupted or trapped and the following sequence of action is carried out by the CPU hardware:

$$\text{current or host-(PSW)} \rightarrow \text{stack}$$
$$\text{updated (PC)} \rightarrow \text{stack}$$

$(30) \rightarrow$ PC	;CONTENT AT 30 GOES TO PC
$(32) \rightarrow$ PSW	;CONTENT AT 32 GOES TO PSW

However, the content at memory location 30 is not the starting address of the interrupt service routine. Instead, it is the starting address of the service routine defined as the trap handler through which the system would jump to the nth interrupt service routine and then return to the host program through instruction RTI or RTT.

The EMT instruction is normally used by the system software of the PDP-11 system, so the EMT trap service routines from $n = 0$ to $n = 377$ may have already been defined and developed. Therefore it is not recommended for general use. However the TRAP instruction, which will be described next, is designed for general use.

TRAP n   Like in the EMT instruction, n is an integer that occupies the low-byte space of the 16-bit instruction word with a value ranging from 0 to 377. Upon execution, the CPU hardware carries out the following steps:

$$\text{current or host (PSW)} \rightarrow \text{stack}$$
$$\text{updated (PC)} \rightarrow \text{stack}$$
$$(34) \rightarrow \text{PC}$$
$$(36) \rightarrow \text{PSW}$$

Again the content at memory location 34 is not the interrupt service routine; it is the starting address of the trap handler. It is the user's or programmer's responsibility to write the trap handler and initialize its starting address at location 34 and its priority rank of interrupt at location 36. The trap handler must serve the following functions:

1. Save and retrieve all general purpose registers—R0, R1, . . . , R5.
2. Interpret the operand, n.
3. Call the specific or nth interrupt service routine.
4. Pass the necessary parameters to the interrupt service routine if applicable.
5. Return to the host program.

The following examples may clarify the process.

The Trap Handler

Since it is the trap handler's responsibility to interpret the TRAP instruction and call the desired nth interrupt service routine, it must consist of a section of program that would interpret the operand n of the trap instruction, TRAP n. Unfortunately, by the time the CPU is executing the trap handler, the instruction TRAP n is gone. That is, the information of operand n is no longer in the CPU. The handler must find some way to recover this information. Fortunately, the updated (PC) was PUSHed onto the stack and the (SP) was decremented by 2.

Therefore, we should be able to find the location for the TRAP n instruction by subtracting the updated (PC) by 2 and fetching for the number n. In addition, the trap handler should consist of a directory in which all the starting addresses of the n interrupt routines are listed. Figure 8.18 shows the flowchart for the trap handler routine, and its source program is shown below:

```
THDLR:      MOV       R0,-(SP)        ;SAVE GENERAL PURPOSE REGS(GPR)
            MOV       R1,-(SP)
            MOV       R2,-(SP)
            MOV       R3,-(SP)
            MOV       R4,-(SP)
            MOV       R5,-(SP)
```

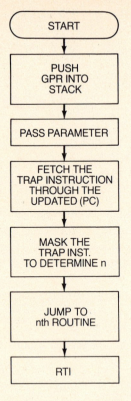

Figure 8.18 Trap handler routine flowchart.

```
            MOV        14(SP),R0         ;COPY UPDATED (PC) TO R0
            MOV        −(R0),R0          ;TRAP INSTRUCTION → R0
            BIC        #177400,R0        ;GET N BY MASKING R0
            ASL        R0                ;2 × (R0) → R0
            JMP        @SRVDIR(R0)       ;JUMP TO SERVICE ROUTINE
                                         ;DIRECTORY TO FETCH NTH ROUTINE
                                         ;AND BACK TO SYMBOLIC ADDRESS,
                                         ;"RETURN," SHOWN IN NEXT LINE
RETURN:     MOV        (SP)+,R5
            MOV        (SP)+,R4
            MOV        (SP)+,R3
            MOV        (SP)+,R2
            MOV        (SP)+,R1
            MOV        (SP)+,R0
            RTI
SRVDIR:     .WORD      SRVR0,...,SRV377
            .END       THDLR
```

A Typical Example Using TRAP Instruction

The following is a typical example using the TRAP instruction.

```
START:      MOV        #THDLR,34         ;INITIAL TRAP VECTOR
            MOV        #200,36           ;INITIAL PRIORITY RANK TO 4
            TRAP       2                 ;SOFTWARE OR INTERNAL INTERRUPT
            HALT
```

```
MESSG:    .ASCIZ    /HELLO/
          .EVEN
THDLR:    MOV       R0,-(SP)          ;FOR SIMPLICITY, ASSUME ONLY NECESSARY
          MOV       R1,-(SP)          ;TO SAVE (R0),(R1).
          MOV       4(SP),R0          ;COPY UPDATED (PC) TO R0
          BIC       #177400,R0        ;GET 2 BY MASKING R0
          ASL       R0                ;2 × 2 = 4 → R0
          JMP       @SRVDIR(R0)
RETURN:   MOV       (SP)+,R1          ;RETRIEVE (R1) FROM STACK
          MOV       (SP)+,R0          ;RETRIEVE (R0) FROM STACK
          RTI
SRVDR:    .WORD     SRVR0,SRVR1,SRVR2
SRVR0:    JMP       RETURN            ;DUMMY SERVICE ROUTINE
SRVR1:    JMP       RETURN
SRVR2:    MOV       #MESSG,R1         ;R1 AS DATA POINTER TO "MESSG."
L1:       TSTB      177564
          BPL       L1
          MOVB      (R1)+,177566
          TSTB      (R1)
          BNE       L1
          JMP       RETURN
```

The list file of this program is shown in Figure 8.19.

Comments on TRAP Instructions

We noted earlier that because the EMT instruction is generally used by the system programmer in the system software for PDP-11, it is not recommended for general use by users. If, however, we wish to use the nth system service routine created by the system programmer, we could of course use the instruction EMT n to enter the system. This is a sort of protection to the system software so that we as users will not accidentally enter the system software. Since we can freely define and develop the software for the TRAP instruction, we could confine ourselves to the TRAP instruction domain.

Note that the TRAP instruction is functionally quite similar to the instruction JSR R, SUBR, but there are some differences. That is, the former occupies only one single memory word, and it is an interrupt process, so it has the priority property. In addition, the service routines are specified by n, where $n = 0 \sim 377$. On the other hand, the JSR instruction occupies two memory words; its destination is normally a symbolic label; and there is no priority ranking involved in the process.

8.7 INTERRUPT NESTING AND PRIORITY RESOLVERS

Just like the macro or subroutine processes, an interrupt service routine can be nested within another interrupt service routine as long as they satisfy the priority condition. Figure 8.20 shows the concept of interrupt nesting. Here the interrupt routine n must have higher priority than the (n − 1)th interrupt routine. In general, the interrupt priority resolver is implemented by the hardware. Figure 8.21 depicts some typical hardware realizations of the priority resolvers.

```
 1                                          ;
 2                                          ;A TYPICAL EXAMPLE USING TRAP INSTRUCTION
 3 000000 012767 000020' 000034   START:    MOV   #THDLR,34       ;INITIAL TRAP VECTOR
 4 000006 012767 000200' 000036             MOV   #200,36         ;INITIAL PRIORITY RANK TO 4
 5 000014 104402                            TRAP  2               ;SOFTWARE OR INTERNAL INTERRUPT
 6 000016 000000                            HALT
 7                                          ;
 8 000020 010046                  THDLR:    MOV   R0,-(SP)        ;FOR SIMPLICITY,ASSUME ONLY NEED
 9 000022 010146                            MOV   R1,-(SP)        ;TO SAVE (R0) AND (R1)
10 000024 016600 000004                     MOV   4(SP),R0        ;COPY UPDATED (PC) TO R0
11 000030 014000                            MOV   -(R0),R0        ;THE CODE OF 'TRAP 2' → R0
12 000032 042700 177400                     BIC   #177400,R0      ;RECOVER THE INTEGER '2'
13 000036 006300                            ASL   R0              ;2 * 2 → R0
14 000040 000170 000052'                    JMP   @SRVDIR(R0)     ;JUMP TO APPROPRIATE ROUTINE
15 000044 012601                  RETURN:   MOV   (SP)+,R1        ;RETRIEVE (R1) AND (R2)
16 000046 012602                            MOV   (SP)+,R2
17 000050 000002                            RTI
18                                          ;
19 000052 000060' 000064' 000070' SRVDIR:   .WORD SRVR0,SRVR1,SRVR2   ;DUMMY SERVICE ROUTINES
20 000060 000167 177760          SRVR0:     JMP   RETURN
21 000064 000167 177754          SRVR1:     JMP   RETURN
22 000070 012701 000116'         SRVR2:     MOV   #MESSG,R1       ;R1 AS DATA POINTER TO 'MESSG'
23 000074 105767 177564          L1:        TSTB  177564
24 000100 100375                            BPL   L1
25 000102 112167 177566                     MOVB  (R1)+,177566
26 000106 105711                            TSTB  (R1)
27 000110 001371                            BNE   L1
28 000112 000167 177726                     JMP   RETURN
29 000116 105 110               MESSG:      .ASCIZ / HELLO /
   000120 114 114
   000122 040 117
   000124 000
30                                          .EVEN
31 000000'                                  .END  START
```

Figure 8.19 List file of the example for trap operation.

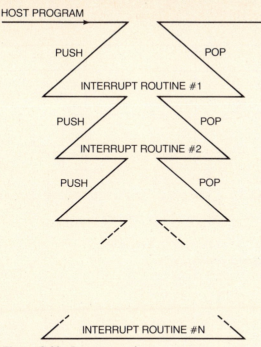

HOST PROGRAM

PUSH   POP

INTERRUPT ROUTINE #1

PUSH   POP

INTERRUPT ROUTINE #2

PUSH   POP

INTERRUPT ROUTINE #N

Figure 8.20   Interrupt nesting.

Figure 8.21(a) shows a simple daisy chain technique. Here, the interrupt request lines of the devices are logically OR-together. Thus, if one or more devices issue the interrupt request signal, the CPU would respond with the interrupt acknowledge signal. The acknowledge signal would then be sent throughout the devices one by one, but device 1 would receive the signal first. If device 1 did not request interrupt, it would pass the acknowledge signal to the next device, say 2, and so on. If device 1 did request interrupt, it would not pass the acknowledge signal to the next device. Instead, it would send its identification number, which is nothing but its interrupt vector address, to the CPU through the data bus, and the interrupt process would then be executed accordingly. Note that with this configuration, device 1 has the highest priority.

Figure 8.21(b) shows another typical configuration of an interrupt resolver that can be an interface board or a chip. The basic principle of operation is almost the same, except that the current CPU priority status is sent to the resolver and it is then compared against those devices that issue the request. Whichever has the highest priority would take over the operation and send out its interrupt vector address. In addition, this configuration normally allows the user to control it with a set of instructions, recognizable to the hardware, so this configuration is programmable. In other words, it offers flexibility so that the programmer can control the resolver.

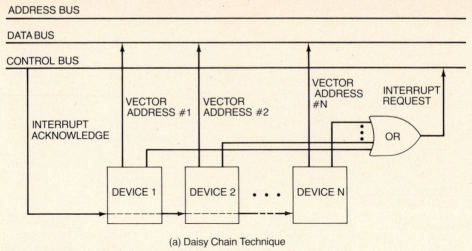

(a) Daisy Chain Technique

Figure 8.21(a)   Typical interrupt priority resolvers.

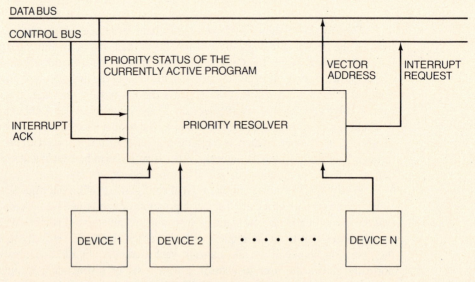

(b) Priority resolver chip or board

Figure 8.21(b)   Typical interrupt priority resolvers.

EXERCISES

8.1 Briefly discuss the differences between polling and interrupt techniques for input/output devices.

8.2 Discuss why in many cases it is important that a subroutine for SAVE/RETRIEVE the contents of the general registers is required for an interrupt-driven system.

8.3 Using the interrupt technique, write a program that will display on the CRT the message ''May I help you?'' whenever any key on the keyboard is depressed. You may assume that the address information of the I/O port for the terminal is as follows:

Input: Control-status register = 177560
         Data buffer register = 177562
Output: Control-status register = 177564
         Data buffer register = 177566
Interrupt vector: 60

8.4 Design a complete but simple PDP-11-based office automation system for an accounting office. The secretary is normally working at a CRT terminal connected to a PDP-11 system, on clients' accounts. Obviously, the contents of the general registers are always important at any instant. The supervisor's office needs another terminal connected to another I/O port of the system so that the boss can interrupt the secretary and demand service. They are supposed to talk to each other through their terminals. You must plan what kind of software to create, and also specify the address information for both terminals. Construct a detailed flowchart first and write the assembly language program accordingly. It is always helpful if you break your program into modules or subroutines.

Chapter 9

Direct Memory Access (DMA) Operation

In this chapter, we introduce the direct memory access (DMA) operation. First, we describe the objective of the DMA process and the transfer of bus control between the CPU and DMA device. Next, the hardware structure and the principles of operation for the DMA process are presented. Finally, a typical example is presented to illustrate the entire process.

KEY WORDS

analog-to-digital converter
cycle stealing
DMA
end of conversion

9.1 INTRODUCTION

Thus far we have described the hardware and software required for I/O interface programming and interrupt processes. Note that all these processes or operations have involved the CPU. It is the CPU that manages the handshaking and data transferring; and it is the PC of the CPU that sends out specific addresses to read or write the memory. Obviously the CPU is the master of the system; it has control of the buses at all times. However, in practice, we often wish only to collect data and deposit them into the memory without any manipulation. Likewise, in many cases we wish only to output the data in the memory to a peripheral as they are. With this kind of operation, it is obvious that the intervening of the CPU is a sort of wasting of its ''talent'' and ''time,'' because there is no data manipulation required.

To improve the efficiency of the CPU, and the speed of transferring data directly to and from the memory to I/O devices, it is desirable to have a technique that eliminates the CPU intervention in this kind of transfer. The technique known as **direct memory access (DMA)** does exactly this. It is apparent that just transferring one or two data between an I/O device and the memory may not save any significant machine operation time. However, when we wish to transfer a block of data, we could save a lot of computing time by means of DMA. Therefore, we would consider using the DMA technique only if there is a need to transfer data on a block by block basis. Otherwise, we would use the conventional I/O data transfer.

Like any other I/O process, the DMA does need a special hardware-software interface to carry out the mission. To eliminate the CPU intervention in the DMA process, we must determine what function or functions the CPU performs that we may or may not need to imitate. It is evident that we need a PC equivalent register to specify where in the memory we wish to transfer data, and the READ/WRITE control signals to specify whether we wish to transfer data out of or into the memory. Next, of course, we must specify how many words of a block of data we wish to transfer. Therefore we need a kind of counter equivalent to keep track of whether the whole block of data has been transferred. In addition, we must have some mechanism to do the handshaking so that the DMA interface board can ''kick out'' the CPU in the operation loop during the data transfer period and return the control back to the CPU when it finishes the task.

With these considerations in mind, we can now examine the DMA process. Figure 9.1 depicts the DMA process. The CPU first initializes the DMA interface board, and as the data are ready for transfer, the board issues the DMA request signal to the CPU. The CPU responds with the DMA request grant signal and ''disconnects'' itself from the buses. As a result, the DMA board becomes the master of the buses and executes the data transfer task. Depending on the specific configuration, the DMA board may hold the bus control for one data transfer cycle or more at a time. However, as soon as it has finished the block data transfer, the DMA board would initiate an interrupt request signal to inform the CPU that the transfer has been completed, and that the CPU may resume its control of the buses. Figures 9.1 (a) and (b), respectively, depict the data transferring to and from the main memory.

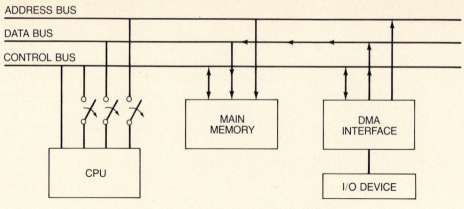

(A) DMA PROCESS FOR INPUT DATA TO MEMORY

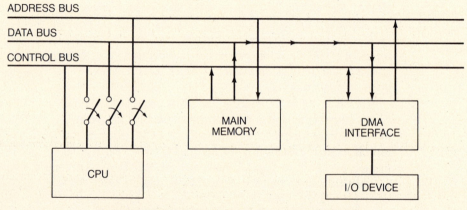

(B) DMA PROCESS FOR OUTPUT DATA FROM MEMORY

Figure 9.1   Functional diagram for DMA process.

9.2 HARDWARE ORGANIZATION AND PRINCIPLES OF OPERATION

Let us now examine the hardware configuration of a basic DMA interface board. In general, it consists of five registers, plus the interrupt identification number (interrupt vector) hardware:

1. *Word count register (WCR)*. This register keeps track of whether the whole block of data has been completely transferred.
2. *Bus address register (BAR)*. This register functions as the PC register of the CPU. It is usually initialized by the CPU with the starting address of the memory block in which the data are to be transferred into or out of that memory area.
3. *Control-status register (CSR)*. Just like any other I/O board, this register serves as the storage for the command to, and status from, the MDA board. It has the standard bit definitions, such as

b_7 = ready/done bit

b_6 = interrupt enable bit

b_4, b_5 = extend address

b_1, b_2, b_3 = function selection

b_0 = enable the DMA transfer

In addition, the typical definitions for b_8, . . . , b_{15} are as follows:

b_{15} = error

b_{14} = nonexistent memory

b_{13} = attention

b_{12} = maintenance

b_{11}, b_{10}, b_9 = device status

b_8 = cycle to prime a DMA bus cycle

4. *Input data buffer register (IDBR)*. This register holds data to be read into the memory.

5. *Output data buffer register (ODBR)*. This register receives data from the memory.

6. *Interrupt vector address information provider*. This register (not shown in Figure 9.2) provides the ID number of the board for interrupt purposes. Its contents can be set manually by an 8-bit dip switch.

The DMA operation is now in order. Refer to Figure 9.2. As a programmer, one should initialize the board by (1) loading the word count register (WCR) in negative twos complement with a count equal to the number of words to be transferred; (2) loading the bus address register (BAR) with the starting address of a block of memory where the data are to be transferred; and (3) loading the control-status register (CSR) with a suitable bit pattern.

The bit pattern of the CSR might be defined differently from one machine to the other, but the principle of operation would still be the same. Basically, there are bits that function as controls or commands to the board, while others indicate the status of the board or of the I/O device connecting to it. The former are normally programmable, and can be set or cleared to a desirable pattern through instructions. The latter are normally set or cleared by the on-board hardware logic indicating the status of the I/O device. Like the CSR of conventional I/O board, here we have b_0 as the device enable bit which activates the DMA process, b_6 as the interrupt enable bit, and b_7 as the done/ready bit. However, we deal with b_7 quite differently. Here we use this bit to indicate that the countdown of WCR has reached zero; if b_6 is set to logical 1, an interrupt is evoked as b_7 goes to logical 1. Therefore, b_7 should be initialized to zero and b_6 to 1 by the initialization program.

Having been initialized, the hardware on the DMA interface board would normally take over the data transfer operation in the following steps: (1) Issues a DMA request signal as the data in the buffer register are ready for transfer; (2) becomes the master of the bus, since the CPU is floating from the bus at this point. What follows is the data transfer process. That is, the BAR functions as the MAR of the memory, and depending on the specific mode of operation, we would have either (IDBR) → (BAR), the content of IDBR being copied to the memory at the location specified by the BAR, or @(BAR) → ODBR.

The DMA I/O board then returns control to the CPU, decrements the WCR, and increments the BAR. This cycle repeats until the (WCR) = 0. At this point, the ready/

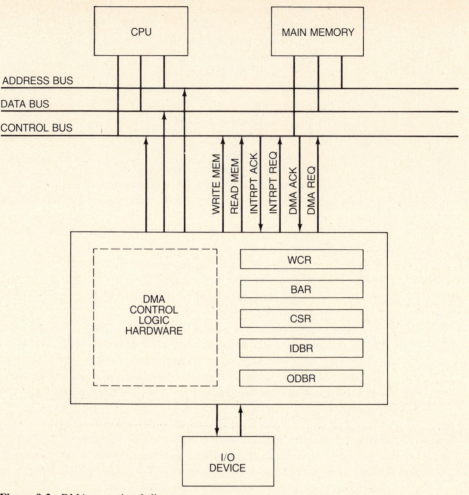

Figure 9.2 DMA operational diagram.

done bit of CSR (b_7) is set, which would initiate an interrupt process and place the vector address of the board on the data bus. The CPU would then jump to the interrupt service routine and execute accordingly.

It is the programmer's responsibility to write the interrupt service routine so that it will be suitable for the specific application. Note that the board issues an interrupt request by setting b_7 to 1, or b_{15} to 1. The former implies that the data transfer process has been finished, while the latter indicates that some errors have occurred on the board. So it is important that the interrupt service routine can recognize whether the interrupt request is a normal one or not by examining b_{15} first and then taking action accordingly.

This DMA data transfer method is known as **cycle stealing technique.** Since it takes over control of the bus only during the moment of transferring data, it is considered to "steal" a cycle from the CPU. If the "stealing" action can be synchronized to occur while the CPU is in its execution cycle, the system throughput would not be affected by the DMA process, since during the execution cycle the CPU does not normally require control of the external bus anyway.

9.3 A TYPICAL EXAMPLE

Let us assume that we want to collect a set of 200 data points through an analog-to-digital converter by means of the DMA technique. Figure 9.3 shows a simplified block diagram of the system. It operates as follows:

1. b_0 of CSR set by the CPU enables the local clock, which generates the start conversion pulse train.
2. The end of conversion (EOC) pulse of the A/D/C signals that the digital data in IDBP is ready and causes the board to generate the DMA request signal.
3. The DMA-GRANT signal arrives to cause the data transfer from IDBR to the memory, with the starting address label ADCDATA.
4. BAR is incremented.

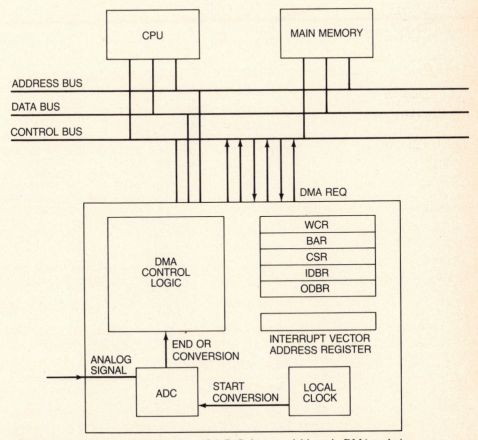

Figure 9.3 Simplified block diagram of A/D/C data acquisition via DMA technique.

5. WCR is incremented to decrement the word count, since WCR was loaded with the negative number of the total data count in twos complement. Here we have -200 or 177600_8.

6. The on-board hardware checks whether an error has occurred or (WCR) = 0. If (WCR) = 0 is true, b_7 of the CSR is set, and an interrupt request signal is generated. If an error has occurred, the error interrupt service routine would be evoked.

7. Upon receiving the INTERRUPT-GRANT signal, the board places the interrupt vector address VECTOR on the data bus.

8. The CPU jumps to the interrupt service routine, which will check b_{15} and b_7.

9. The CPU resumes executing the host program.

The source program for this sequence follows.

```
          .MACRO    CRTOUT    R,?L
L1:       TSTB      177564    ;CHECK C/S REGISTER OF CRT
          BPL       L1
          MOVB      R,177566  ;DISPLAY ONE CHARACTER
          .ENDM     CRTOUT
          .MACRO    DISPLAY INFO,?L2
          MOV       #INFO,R5
L2:       CRTOUT    (R5)+
          TSTB      (R5)
          BNE       L2
          .ENDM     DISPLAY
START:    .                   ;HOST PROGRAM

          .
          MOV #INTRPT, VECTOR
          MOV #ADCDATA, BAR   ;INITIAL BAR
          MOV #177600, WCR    ;LOAD -200 IN TWO'S COMPLEMENT INTO WCR
          MOV #101, CSR       ;SET INTERRUPT ENABLE BIT AND A/D/C
          .                   ;ENABLE BIT.
          .                   ;HOST PROGRAM IS BEING
          .                   ;EXECUTED UNTIL INTERRUPT OCCURS. AT
          .                   ;THE SAME TIME THE DMA STEALS CYCLES
          .                   ;FOR TRANSFERRING DATA BETWEEN
          .                   ;MEMORY AND THE DMA BOARD.

          .

          .
ADCDATA:  .BLKW 200           ;RESERVE MEMORY BLOCK FOR DATA
INTRPT:   TST CSR             ;INTERRUPT SERVICE ROUTINE BEGIN TO
                              ;EXAMINE IF b15 = 1
          BPL RETURN          ;B7 = 1, DATA HAS BEEN COLLECTED
                              ;NORMALLY
          DISPLAY MESSG       ;B15 = 1, ERROR HAS OCCURRED JUMP TO
                              ;ERROR MESSAGE MACRO
          HALT
MESSG:    .ASCIZ /ERROR ON DMA/
RETURN:   RTI                 ;RETURN TO HOST PROGRAM
          .END START
```

Note that the host program does not show the actual data transfer in the DMA process. This is because the DMA board takes over control of the buses during the DMA process. The real data transfer process is carried out by the hardware on the DMA board.

That is, the hardware of the DMA board would issue a DMA request signal whenever the end of conversion pulse of the A/D/C is generated. As a result, the CPU would "disconnect" itself from the bus, or temporarily give up its bus control, and issue by its hardware the DMA request grant signal to the DMA board.

Upon receiving the grant signal, the hardware of the DMA board would take over the bus control and transfer a datum from or to the memory specified by BAR, increment WCR by 1, and return the bus control to the CPU. The process repeats until (WCR) = 0, and the board then initiates the interrupt process to signal the CPU that the DMA process is completed. At this point, the CPU would respond to the interrupt request from the DMA board and jump to the interrupt serve routine, as shown.

EXERCISES

9.1 Briefly discuss the advantages and disadvantages, if any, of a digital computer system that has DMA capability.

9.2 Assume that the CPU of a digital computer system operates in the sequences shown below:
   a. Fetches instruction from the memory.
   b. Checks if the DMA-REQUEST signal is logically TRUE.
   c. If "yes," the CPU sends the DMA-ACKNOWLEDGE signal and transfer its BUS-MAS-TERSHIP to the device that requests DMA operation; otherwise the operation goes directly to step d.
   d. The CPU executes the instruction.
   e. The CPU checks again to see if the DMA-REQUEST signal is still TRUE.
   f. If "yes," the CPU would be idle until the REQUEST signal is logically FALSE.
   g. Returns to step a.
   Now, using Appendix C, plot two curves, one for non-DMA (straight asynchronous I/O) and the other for DMA operation, on a two-dimensional space where the x axis represents the number (MAX = 100) of data being transferred to or from the memory, and the y axis represents the execution speed in microseconds required to transfer the number of data. You may assume that the time required for fetching one memory word is half a microsecond and for transferring one memory word by DMA is also half a microsecond. Remember that the operation of DMA is done by hardware on the DMA control board which may require "overhead time" of 200 nenoseconds per word.

Chapter 10

An Introduction to the VAX-11 System

In this chapter we attempt to fill the knowledge gap between the PDP-11 and VAX-11 systems. Since the VAX-11 is a much more advanced machine, many sophisticated architectural concepts which are not included in the PDP-11 system have been implemented in the VAX-11. Therefore, simply studying the instruction set and addressing modes of the VAX-11 may not be adequate to understand the machine. In this chapter, the machine structure integrated with the principles of virtual memory, and memory management and multiprogramming are described. Concepts of virtual address space, physical address space, page table, context switching, data types, procedures, exceptions, and so on are presented. In addition, instruction format and addressing modes are also discussed.

KEY WORDS

exception	page
floating-point data representation	page table
longword	page table entry
memory management	physical address space
microprogramming	procedure
multiprogramming	quadword
octaword	virtual address space
operand specifier	virtual memory

10.1 INTRODUCTION

The preceding chapters have thoroughly covered the machine structure and assembly language programming for the PDP-11. According to our experience, students who have learned the machine structure and assembly language programming of the PDP-11 can easily adapt to machines other than the PDP-11. For example, our students have had no difficulty in adapting to the 8085 microprocessor-based system. Perhaps this is due to the fact that the structure of 8085 and its instruction set are a lot simpler than that of the PDP-11. To begin with, the 8085 microcomputer is an 8-bit machine, whereas the PDP-11 is a 16-bit machine. For the 8085, the addressing modes are simple and there are no powerful modes such as auto increment or auto decrement. Therefore, in using the 8085, students do not have difficulty, though they might feel its limitations in performance. We may consider designing with the 8085 instead of with the PDP-11 a "downgraded" environmental change, and we would not expect much difficulty. However, what would we expect in dealing with an "upgraded" machine? The obvious machine to select for upgrading would be the VAX-11.

In what follows, we will be dealing with that powerful machine, the VAX-11. The concepts and techniques we have developed in the preceding chapters can all be applied to this new and powerful machine. The objective of this chapter is to guide you smoothly through the transition from the PDP-11 to the VAX-11.

VAX stands for virtual address extension. Like the PDP-11, it is a product of the Digital Equipment Corporation. The VAX-11 is a 32-bit machine that operates in two modes, the native mode and compatibility mode. In the compatibility mode, the VAX-11 can run all PDP-11 developed programs with little modification; otherwise the machine will operate at its full capacity in the native mode. Since it is a 32-bit machine, the VAX-11 has an over 4 gigabytes possible address space. In the native mode, the VAX-11 can execute a large set (including 248 basic instructions) of variable-length instructions. Some of the instructions can have up to six operand specifiers. By **operand specifier,** we mean the portion in an instruction that specifies the address information for fetching the source or destination operands. For example, in the PDP-11, the instruction MOV   A,B has two operand specifiers, A and B. In addition, the instruction set of the VAX-11 can manipulate and transfer a variety of different data types, including floating point. With the operating system installed, the VAX-11 can be a multiprogramming multiuser and realtime digital computing system. A brief description of the unique features of the VAX-11 that are different from those of the PDP-11 is presented in the following sections.

10.2 MACHINE STRUCTURE

The System

Figure 10.1 shows a typical VAX-11 system. Note that there are two bus adapters, the unibus adapter and the massbus adapter. With this configuration, all the unibus-compatible peripherals or devices can be directly connected to the unibus, while the high-speed mass storage devices, such as disk drive and magnetic tape transports, can be connected to

For the second round, however, section 2 would be in slot 0 and section 1 still in slot 1, and for section 2, we would have

$$2000 \ (\textit{virtual}) = 2000 \ (\textit{physical})$$
$$2777 \ (\textit{virtual}) = 2777 \ (\textit{physical})$$

Note that the translation of the address is dynamic, and thus a dynamic address translation scheme, as shown in Figure 10.2, is necessary. With the "built-in" address translator, the user program can still reference to the virtual address without knowing that the CPU is actually executing the program within a limited physical memory space. Continuously feeding the user's program into the physical memory system and automatically translating the virtual memory address into the physical memory address are the responsibilities of the system software called **memory management.** We will examine the virtual memory system for VAX-11 in a little bit more detail in the later section on memory management.

The Principle of Multiprogramming

The main objective of **multiprogramming** is efficient utilization of the resources of the computing system. Obviously, among the user programs some may be number-crunching-based, which would use the CPU a lot; others may be I/O oriented, which most of the time would mean the CPU would be idling and waiting for the peripherals to respond; and still others may be short and need only a small area of physical memory space. In the multiprogramming system, while the I/O oriented programs are in process, the CPU could execute the number-crunching-based program. In addition, all or part of a set of user programs can reside in the primary (physical) memory at the same time so that there will be no, or very few, "unoccupied" memory spaces at any given moment. Memory utilization efficiency is thus improved. Figure 10.3 depicts the process. Note that the CPU time is segmented into slices of equal length and thus it is time-multiplexed to serve programs 1 and 2. Since the CPU execution speed is so fast, the user programs would seem to be served at the same time.

For clarity, let us use the analogy of several families living in a rented but unfurnished apartment to explain the principle of multiprogramming. The apartment building is furnished with a swimming pool, laundry facilities, health spa, tennis courts, and so on,

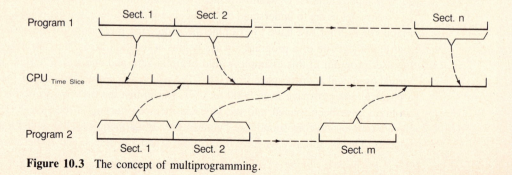

Figure 10.3 The concept of multiprogramming.

and each apartment consists of one or more bedrooms, kitchen, living room, and bathroom. Of course, there is an office from which the manager or the staff of the apartment run the building. We could imagine that a family living in an apartment is equivalent to a user's program, and the apartment is the physical memory space for the user's program; that the manager is the operating system residing in the physical memory space (office) for the system; that the swimming pool, health spa, and so on are the CPU, peripherals, and so on; and that each family consists of parents and some children, which are equivalent to the user's programs.

In a family, the parents normally have the highest priority for using the apartment's facilities; similarly, some routines in the user's programs have more privileges than others. In addition, it is the operating system's (manager's) responsibility to schedule the user programs (families, or members of families living in the building) to "time share" the resources (CPU, printer) of the system. So in a broad sense, the concept of the multiprogramming of a computing system is almost identical to the operation of an apartment building.

In a multiprogramming system, the operating system schedules the time slot for using the CPU for program execution and also schedules the use of the peripherals to improve system utilization efficiency. For example, let us assume we wish to execute a set of user programs in a multiprogramming system. First, the programs must be loaded into the physical memory from the disk. Next, the operating system would schedule the programs to be executed on the CPU in a time-sharing fashion. That is, each program will get a "slice" of time to use the CPU (Figure 10.3). Some short programs may be finished with execution with fewer time slices than the long ones. Since the operation speed of the CPU is so fast, all the programs being executed might think they were using the CPU alone. This is similar to the apartment manager scheduling each family a slice of time to use the health spa in the building. If the time scheduled is exactly what each family would wish, then the members of each family would feel that they "own" the health spa.

However, an examination of CPU time sharing would reveal one problem. That is, the "privacy" of one program may be destroyed by another if we are not careful. For example, the contents of the general purpose registers in the CPU for program 1, shown in Figure 10.3, would be destroyed if they were not saved while program 2 is executing in the CPU during its legitimate execution time. To prevent the invasion of privacy between programs, each program must save its key register contents, including that of the updated PC and PSW at the end of each execution time slice, and must bring them into the hardware registers in the CPU as its turn to use the CPU comes again. This concept is not really new.

Recall that in the interrupt-driven system described in a previous chapter, the contents of the updated PC and PSW of the host program must be pushed onto the stack, whereas the contents in the interrupt vector, the starting address as well as the PSW of the interrupt service routine, must be brought into the CPU for execution of the interrupt routine. Similarly, on a more sophisticated level, in a multiprogramming system each program must have its own specific and private memory area (similar to the interrupt vector) for storage of its key register contents and other important information.

At the beginning of the time slice scheduled for a program, the saved or initialized contents of the key registers, including updated PC and PSW for that program, must be brought into the CPU and loaded into the corresponding hardware registers (PC, PSW,

R0, R1) in the CPU for execution. At the end of the time slice, the current contents of the key registers must be saved again in that specific and private memory area reserved for that program until its turn to use the CPU arrives again. The contents of the key registers and other important information that is being saved from, and brought into, the CPU are collectively called the **state information of a process,** or the **context** of a process. The operation of bringing in and storing away of the context is called the **context switching of a process.** Now a definition of the term *process* is in order.

A **process** provided by the operating system is the environment in which the user can develop, run, and debug programs. Thus a process is specified by its context. Unlike the interrupt system in a simple PDP-11 system, where an interrupt service routine can be specified merely by a vector of two memory words, in a multiprogramming system the context of a process would consist of more than just the contents of the general purpose registers. It must also consist of information on the locations of instructions and data of a task in the physical memory. Clearly, for privacy each process should also have its own stack memory area; otherwise its information can easily be destroyed by other processes sharing the same CPU. Thus, the context of a process should also consist of information that specifies the location of stack memory in the physical memory. With the concept of context and the context switching operation, the objective of the multiprogramming system can be achieved.

In summary, we may think of a process as a "virtual" machine defined by its context, in which a task can be developed and executed. There is one virtual machine for each task, and the virtual machines are realized on the physical machine on a time-sharing basis. Each process shares the resources of the system and yet each process can still maintain its own privacy. With this introduction as a basis, we can examine the VAX-11 system in a little more detail.

The Central Processing Unit (CPU)

Figure 10.4 shows the major elements of the central processing unit of the VAX-11. In contrast to the PDP-11, here we have sixteen 32-bit registers and a 32-bit processor status longword. In VAX-11 convention, a binary representation of 8-bit, 16-bit, 32-bit, 64-bit, and 128-bit in length is respectively defined as **byte, word, longword, quadword,** and **octaword.**

For the processor status longword (PSL), the lower word, $b_0, \ldots, b_{15}$, is called PSW with the following bit definition, which is slightly different from that of the PDP-11:

b_0 = carry (borrow) condition code
b_1 = overflow condition code
b_2 = zero condition code
b_3 = negative condition code
b_4 = trace fault code
b_5 = integer overflow trap enable
b_6 = floating underflow fault trap
b_7 = overflow trap enable
$b_8, \ldots, b_{15}$ = not used

The upper word ($b_{16}, \ldots, b_{31}$) of the PSL, however, is described as follows:

$b_{16}, \ldots, b_{20}$ = interrupt priority level
b_{21} = not used
b_{22}, b_{23} = previous access mode
b_{24}, b_{25} = current access mode
b_{26} = executing on the interrupt stack
b_{27} = instruction first part done
b_{28}, b_{29} = not used
b_{30} = trace pending
b_{31} = compatibility mode

The registers R0, . . . , R11 are used as the general purpose registers. R12 and R13 are used in the procedure process, where R12 is used as the argument pointer (AP) and R13 as the frame pointer (FP). The **procedure** process is a more disciplined subroutine process. That is, for a procedure, the process of calling and returning is more rigid than that for a subroutine. In general, the frame pointer is used as the pointer to save the contents of the PSW and the general purpose registers of the host program, while the argument pointer is used as the pointer to an argument list or array for passing arguments or parameters to and from the routine being called. The difference between procedure and subroutine will be examined in a later section. The register R14 is the general system stack

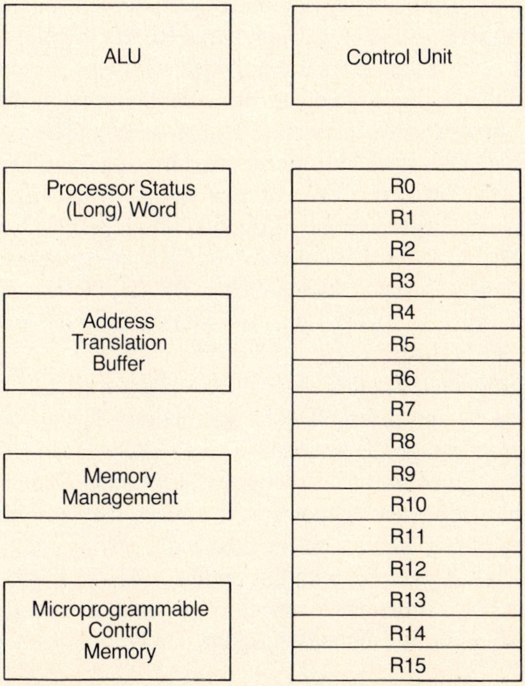

Figure 10.4 Central processor unit of VAX-11.

pointer (SP), and the R15 is the program counter (PC), which functions as the R7 in the PDP-11.

Note that in comparison with the PDP-11, there are three new blocks in the CPU diagram shown in Figure 10.4: address translation buffer, memory management, and an optional microprogrammable control memory. We will briefly describe the functions of these blocks here. Remember that the VAX-11 is a 32-bit machine. All the registers in the CPU are 32-bit in length. This means that we have a PC which can address 2^{32} or slightly over 4 billion memory locations. In other words, in terms of the virtual memory system described above, we have a virtual or logical memory address space of 4 billion bytes. Although in future years we might need and could afford to have such a huge physical memory space, we would be satisfied for now with a physical memory of a couple of million bytes. Thus, we would need the address translation mechanism, which would translate the virtual address specified by an instruction to the actual physical memory address. The block of the address translation buffer is a component of the virtual memory system of the VAX-11.

The **memory management** block is composed of both hardware and software modules. Its major functions are: (1) mapping or translating the virtual memory address to the physical address and giving each user program a transparent ''feeling'' that it is running not in a virtual memory space, but in a huge physical memory with contiguous address starting at zero; (2) assigning the available slots of the physical memory equitably among the programs; and (3) providing the privacy protection for each process. (More details on memory management will be given in a later section.)

Next, let us turn to the third special block, the **microprogrammable control memory.** In the publications of the Digital Equipment Corporation, this block is called the user control store (UCS). It is a 1024×80 high-speed READ/WRITE random access memory (RAM). When it is installed, users are provided with a set of very elementary instructions with which they are allowed to create or invent their own instruction set and store it in the UCS. The newly created instruction set can be completely different from that of the VAX-11. This process is called **microprogramming.** The basic concept of microprogramming is very similar to that of creating user-defined macros. Recall that a macro can be defined by the user based on the instruction set predefined by the manufacturer. For example, for the I/O macros we defined in Chapter 6, we used the format .MACRO . . . . .ENDM to create a set of macros such as READ, PRINT, and DISPLAY. There, we drew instructions such as TSTB, BPL, and MOVB from the instruction set of the PDP-11 to create the macro instructions.

It is evident that macros created in this way will be limited in efficiency and flexibility because we are limited by the given PDP-11 instruction set. In contrast, for the microprogramming process, although the user is also given a set of instructions on which to base new instructions, the given set of instructions is a lot more elementary and very flexible. This special set of instructions is known as the **micro instruction set.** With the micro instruction set, the user is free to invent practically any instruction efficiently according to his or her wishes. Therefore, with this option, VAX-11 users are allowed to make a family of special sets of instructions for specific applications. In addition, they can write a complete set of instructions to emulate a machine that is completely different from the VAX-11.

The Memory

Since the memory unit implemented for the VAX-11 is a virtual memory system, we need to discuss it in more detail.

Organization of the Physical (Primary) Memory   Although the physical memory unit of the VAX-11 still follows the traditional concept of address/content, it allows us to fetch instructions or data from the memory by the basic elements of byte, word, longword, quadword, and octaword. According to the specifications of the instruction, the operand or operands of different sizes of the basic unit are fetched and operated upon by the CPU. Actually, this is merely an extension of the operation of the PDP-11. For instance, in PDP-11 we have

```
MOVB  A,B
MOV   A,B
```

For the former, the operands are the low-bytes at locations A and B, respectively. For the latter, however, the whole word at locations A and B, respectively, is being operated on by the CPU. In a similar manner, for VAX-11, we would have

```
MOVB A,B      ;ON BYTE BASIS
MOVW A,B      ;ON WORD BASIS
MOVL A,B      ;ON LONGWORD BASIS
MOVQ A,B      ;ON QUADWORD BASIS
```

Figure 10.5 depicts the structures of an addressable basic memory element in different numbers of bytes. The figure is shown in increments of bytes, where A is the starting or the base symbolic address of the memory basic element. As a result, for updating the PC, the increment quantum will vary from one byte to a great number of bytes, depending on the size of the operand on which an instruction is to operate.

In addition, the VAX-11 also provides a set of special instructions that can operate on a variable-length bit field. That is, those instructions can operate on a specific group of contiguous bits specified by its operand specifier. The said group of contiguous bits is addressed by three variables: the position in number of bits offset from the address base, the group size in number of bits, and the address base. For example, if we wish to address an operand of 3-bit in size, 10 bits offset from location A, we specify the address by: position, 10; size, 3; and base, A. That is, the instruction will be operating on bits b_{12}, b_{11}, b_{10} of the longword located at address A.

Finally, it is important to mention here that for the VAX-11, the physical memory capacity can be as large as 2^{30} bytes, which can be addressed by the address bits $b_{29}, \ldots, b_0$. At the present time, this is, of course, an impressive and luxurious size for a physical memory unit.

Organization of the Virtual Memory   As we have pointed out, in the VAX-11 we have R15 as the program counter (PC), which is a 32-bit register. In other words, the PC can address a virtual memory space of 2^{32} (over 4 billion) bytes. Structurally, the virtual address space is subdivided into four regions defined by bits b_{31} and b_{30}. Figure 10.6 shows the definition of the four regions in the virtual address space. Note that each region has the address range, in HEX, as follows:

For simplicity, let us assume a page-oriented memory system, where a PC of 16-bit is used. Here, we would define the bits, $b_8, b_7, \ldots, b_0$, of the PC as the field for byte offset specification, and $b_{15}, b_{14}, \ldots, b_9$ as the field for page specification. Then, for example, for

	Page number field	Byte offset field
PC =	0 000 010	000 000 111

it implies that the PC is currently pointing at the address of the 7th byte on page 2. Note that for a 16-bit machine with a PC of 16 bits in length, we can have an address space of 256 pages. Let us now turn to the VAX-11 system.

Since the VAX-11 is a 32-bit machine, it will have a page field of 21 bits. However, since the VAX-11 uses the virtual memory system, it has a virtual address space and a physical address space. Figures 10.7(a) and (b), respectively, show the format of the address pointer and the address space organization of the virtual and physical memory schemes. It is important to remind ourselves that the virtual memory is merely an abstract memory space supported by a bank of disk memory which has a huge memory space

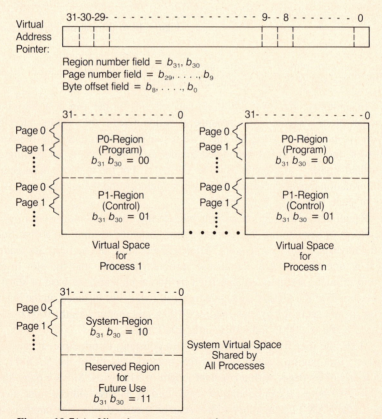

Virtual Address Pointer:

Region number field = b_{31}, b_{30}
Page number field = $b_{29}, \ldots, b_9$
Byte offset field = $b_8, \ldots, b_0$

Figure 10.7(a) Virtual memory space scheme.

whose address space is organized by drive number, track number, sector number, and byte number. The operating system is responsible for storing our program files systematically on the disks. Therefore, a programmer need only imagine that he or she has an infinite number of virtual memory spaces, one for each process, organized in contiguous bytes and pages, with addresses starting at location zero.

For example, suppose we have three tasks that we wish to implement on a VAX-11. For each task we would most likely have a host program, subroutines, and macros to edit, assemble, link, debug, and run in an environment (or a process) on the VAX-11. For each task, we would need to call on system programs such as EDIT, ASSEMBLER, ODT, and so on to assist us in developing the task program. Since these system programs are all residing in the system region (b_{31}, b_{30} = 10) and they are the same system software to be used for any task, each task can share the same system region of the virtual space.

Therefore, as shown in Figure 10.7(a), we must have P0 and P1 regions for each process in which a task can be developed and executed in the virtual space. However, we have only one system region, as shown. In other words, we have three pairs of P0 and P1 virtual memory regions, but only one system region. Let us return to our example. Since we have three tasks, say A, B, and C, we would have three processes, say No. 1, No. 2, and No. 3, in which to develop and run the tasks, respectively. Each process has its own context. Furthermore, task A might need only 100 or 200 of the virtual memory pages, whereas other tasks might require more or fewer pages. However, they would have their own P0 region and P1 region, with the program beginning at location page zero and byte zero in the P0 region and growing upward contiguously, and with control such as stack memory in the P1 region starting at the upper address limit and growing downward contiguously. As a result, we could logically imagine that each task has its own private VAX-11 to develop and run its programs.

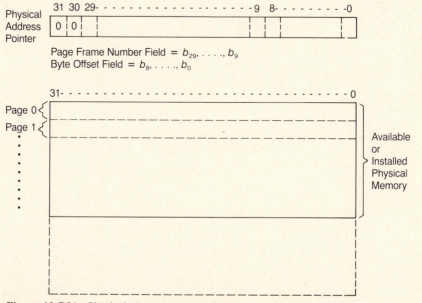

Figure 10.7(b) Physical memory space scheme.

Address Translation   With the concept of virtual memory, each task could have a memory space of 3 billion bytes, one for each of the three regions, the P0, P1, and system regions. If we wish to develop and run three tasks simultaneously, we would need 7 billion bytes of physical memory (remember that they share the same system region). Obviously, at the present time it is not practical to demand such a huge physical memory. Fortunately, since each program is being run one instruction at a time, we do not really need to store all the programs in the physical memory at the same time. The three tasks could share the same physical memory unit and CPU.

For simplicity, let us assume that all the three tasks have been debugged and linked, and are ready for execution. Initially, let us assume that the operating system had loaded, say, two pages, three pages, and four pages of tasks A, B, and C, respectively, into the physical memory, as shown in Figure 10.8. As the program execution progresses, the rest of the program for each task would be continuously fed into the physical memory to replace the old pages. Meanwhile, tasks A, B, and C would be executed on the CPU in

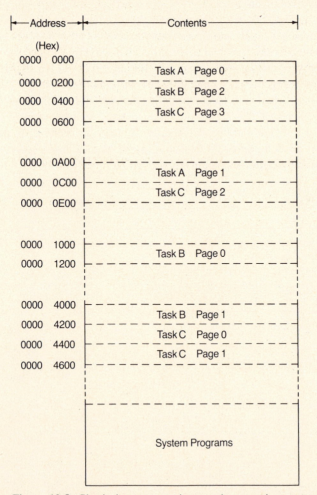

Figure 10.8 Physical memory assignment by operating system.

a time-multiplexing fashion. Note that the starting address in the physical memory space for task B, page 0, would be 0000   1000, as shown in Figure 10.8, while in the virtual space of task B, it would be 0000   0000. Therefore, as task B executes, the instruction would simply reference to its virtual space address.

However, a translation process that translates the virtual address into a physical address is needed before its operand is fetched. This is because during execution, the program is residing in the physical memory. The question then is how the address translator knows the physical location of the program in question. This is done in the VAX-11 by a unique address conversion table called a **page table.** The concept is shown in Figure 10.9. Note that any instruction of a program would originally provide the virtual address. In the virtual address, the byte offset value is the same as that of the physical address, but the information of the virtual page number (b_{29}, . . . , b_9) is not the real page number of the physical address, but is used to calculate the address of a specific location on the page table, where the information on its corresponding physical page number resides. Therefore the content of an element of the page table is called a **page table entry (PTE),** since it points to the entry for the physical page of interest.

Refer to Figure 10.8 again. For example, if an instruction for task C references to the virtual address of the 8th byte of page 0, its corresponding physical address will be 0000   4208, whereas its virtual address will be 0000   0008. Fortunately, the address translation process is carried out by the memory management system, so the user needs to be concerned only with the virtual address. However, we must realize that as soon as the contents of the virtual pages of a task have been loaded into the physical memory pages, the page table or the contents of the PTEs must be updated. The updating of the PTEs is also done by the memory management. Evidently, the total number of PTEs is determined by the length, in pages, of a task. That is, each page would require one PTE.

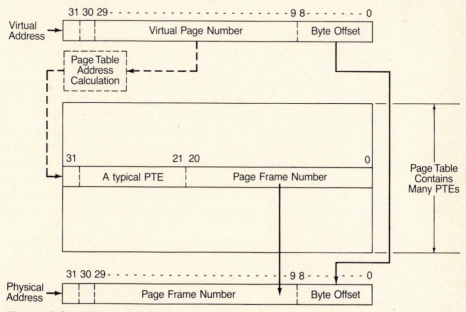

Figure 10.9 Address translation process.

Memory Management

As described briefly above, the major functions of the memory management block are: (1) virtual memory address to physical memory address translation, (2) assignment of the physical memory space for each process, and (3) protection of the privacy of each process. In this section, we will put all the pieces, such as context, page table, page table entry, and so on, together to show how the functions of memory management are achieved.

Basically, we wish to have several tasks run simultaneously on a computing system that has a CPU which can operate at high speed and has a high-speed primary (semiconductor) memory supported by a high-speed mass (secondary) memory device such as a disk memory system. In the VAX-11 system, we have one CPU and one good-sized physical memory. All the tasks are to time share the CPU and space share the physical memory in such a way that each task is being run as if it were operating on a machine of its own. Here the time scheduler of the operating system schedules the time slices of the CPU for each task, and the memory management, which is also a part of the operating system, manages the space-sharing process for each task. The physical memory is organized, in a general sense, as follows:

8 bits = a byte

2 bytes = a word

4 bytes = a longword

8 bytes = a quadword

16 bytes = an octaword

512 bytes = a page

The instructions normally reference byte, word, longword, quadword, or octaword, while the memory management transfers information between the secondary (disk) memory and the primary (semiconductor) memory on a page basis. A task that may consist of routines, macros, data, and so on is always in contiguous bytes in the virtual address space. However, it is loaded into available physical (primary) memory page by page. Therefore, in the physical memory, the page numbers of a task need not be contiguous, but the byte number within a page must be contiguous, as shown in Figure 10.8. Fortunately, once a virtual page is loaded into the physical memory, there is a unique physical starting address assigned to that virtual page. Therefore, the address values have a one-to-one correspondence between the virtual and the physical address. As shown in Figure 10.8, if an instruction for task C references to a location in the virtual address space (note that an instruction always references to a virtual address), say the 5th byte of page 1, or the virtual address

$$31\ 30\ 29\ .\ .\ .\ .\ .\ .\ .\ .\ .\ .\ .\ .\ .\ 9\ 8\ .\ .\ .\ .\ .\ .\ .\ 0$$

$$=\boxed{0\ 0\ 0\ 0\ .\ .\ .\ .\ .\ .\ .\ .\ .\ .\ 0\ 0\ 1\ 0\ 0\ 0\ 0\ 0\ 0\ 1\ 0\ 1}$$

= 00000205 HEX

then its corresponding physical address

$$
\begin{array}{cccccc}
31 & 30 & 29 & \ldots\ldots\ldots & 9\ 8 & \ldots\ldots & 0
\end{array}
$$

$$
= \boxed{0\ \ 0 \quad\quad 0\ \ldots\ldots\ 0\ 1\ 0\ 0\ 0\ 1\ 0\ 0\ 0\ 0\ 0\ 0\ 0\ 1\ 0\ 1}
$$

$$
= 00004405 \text{ HEX}
$$

Therefore the translation can be simply a table lookup process. Since the byte number within a page is contiguous, all we need to reference is the information of the starting address of each physical page. In other words, we only need a table that translates the virtual page number into a physical page number. This table is called the page table. It is evident that once each task is loaded, or partially loaded, into the physical memory, it must have a unique page table for itself. However, as shown in Figure 10.7(a), the virtual memory space is subdivided into the P0 region, the P1 region, and the system region. That is, a task would have its program in the P0 region, its stack memory in the P1 region, and may call for system software from the system region. Therefore, there must be three page tables for each task. But since the system region is common to each task, we can conclude that for each task there are two page tables, one in the P0 region and one in the P1 region. Additionally, all tasks share the same page table in the system region.

Let us examine the structure of a page table in detail. A page table is a block of contiguous longwords stored in a memory space. Thus it is specified by its starting address and the length of the block. The address of each longword of the page table is a function of the virtual page number specified in the virtual address, as shown in Figure 10.9. The content of each longword in the page table is called a page table entry (PTE). The PTE provides the following information: (1) the access mode of that page of a program for privacy protection purposes; (2) whether that virtual page has been loaded into the physical memory page; and (3) the corresponding physical page frame (base) number.

All the page tables are specified by based register and length register. For example, the system page table (SPT) is specified by its system base register (SBR), whose content is the starting address of the SPT, and its system length register (SLR). Similarly, P0BR (P0 region base register) and P0LR (P0 region length register) specify the page table in the P0 region, and P1BR and P1LR, those in P1 region.

As an example, let us assume that in an instruction, a specific system page is referenced in the virtual address specification in its operand specifier, as shown in Figure 10.9. The memory management would leave the byte offset alone, but extract the virtual page number and calculate the address of that PTE in the system page table via the SBR and SLR. As the specific PTE is located, the physical page number is found, and this physical page number is then concatenated with the byte offset to form the physical address. The operating process is somewhat similar to the one-level indirect addressing described in the addressing modes for the PDP-11 system. However, the PTEs of the P0 and P1 locations are calculated via the system page table, so the process is similar to a two-level indirect address process.

The format of a PTE is defined as follows:

Page frame number = $b_{20}, \ldots, b_0$

Field reserved for operating system = $b_{25}, \ldots, b_{21}$

Modify bit $= b_{26}$

Protection $= b_{30}, \ldots, b_{27}$

Valid bit $= b_{31}$

As the PTE is read, the CPU or the memory management checks the protection code for accessibility of that page. In the VAX-11, each instruction is assigned one of the four access modes: kernal, executive, supervisor, and user, whose accessing privileges are in descending order. In other words, the kernal mode has the highest privilege. That is, a "calling" page in the kernal mode can access any page, since the other three all have lower privilege ranks. If that page passes the protection test, the CPU checks the valid bit. If the valid bit $= 1$, it implies that that page of contents has been loaded into the physical memory and the page frame number, $b_{20}, \ldots, b_0$, of the PTE is the physical memory page number. The translation of the virtual memory address to physical memory address process is thus completed. Table 10.1 shows the PTE protection codes. For example, if the current instruction is in the kernal mode while the protection code of the PTE is 0011, the page of the PTE in question can only be read but not written by that instruction.

In summary, the memory management, based on the virtual address, fetches the right PTE; based on the information provided by the PTE, it checks accessibility and finally translates the virtual memory address into the physical memory address.

TABLE 10.1 PTE PROTECTION CODES

Binary code b_{30} b_{29} b_{28} b_{27}				Current access mode K	E	S	U	Comment
0	0	0	0	—	—	—	—	No access
0	0	0	1		unpredictable			reserved
0	0	1	0	RW	—	—	—	
0	0	1	1	R	—	—	—	
0	1	0	0	RW	RW	RW	RW	All access
0	1	0	1	RW	RW	—	—	
0	1	1	0	RW	R	—	—	
0	1	1	1	R	R	—	—	
1	0	0	0	RW	RW	RW	—	
1	0	0	1	RW	RW	R	—	
1	0	1	0	RW	R	R	—	
1	0	1	1	R	R	R	—	
1	1	0	0	RW	RW	RW	R	
1	1	0	1	RW	RW	R	R	
1	1	1	0	RW	R	R	R	
1	1	1	1	R	R	R	R	

Key to table symbols:
 — = no access
 R = read only
RW = read/write
 K = kernel
 E = executive
 S = supervisor
 U = user

The Multiprogramming Process

With the knowledge that we have obtained in the preceding sections, we should now be able to see the overall process of the multiprogramming system in the VAX-11 system. Consider a group of tasks to be executed on the VAX-11. The operating system would load a few pages of each task into the available physical memory and update all the PTEs of the page tables of each task. Next, the operating system would time-multiplex the CPU to execute the tasks. For each task, the operating system provides an environment called process in which the task runs. Every time a process is switched into the CPU for execution, it must bring in its own initial state, or the information of PC, R0, R1, . . . , page table specifications (based register and length register), processor status, longword, and so on. When the time slice expires, the process must be switched out of the CPU and its state information must be stored in some space for future operation. The state information of a process is the context, and the switching process is called context switching. The memory block where the state information is stored is called the **process control block (PCB).** Figure 10.10 shows the contents of the PCB of a process. In the CPU, there is a hardware process control block for context switching.

Kernal Stack Pointer
Executive Stack Pointer
Supervisor Stack Pointer
User Stack Pointer
R0
R1
R2
R3
R4
R5
R6
R7
R8
R9
R10
R11
R12 (Argument Pointer)
R13 (Frame Pointer)
PC
Processor Status Longword
P0-Based Register
P0-Length Register
P1-Based Register
P1-Length Register

Figure 10.10 Processor control block.

10.3 INSTRUCTIONS AND ADDRESSING MODES

Having studied the fundamentals of the machine structure, virtual memory system, and multiprogramming for the VAX-11, we should now be reasonably comfortable in gathering the basic information for assembly language programming. Again, we will pay more attention to the salient features in the VAX-11 that are different from the basic PDP-11. Obviously, we shall start with data types, instruction format, and addressing modes.

Data Types

As we noted in the memory section, the primary memory in the VAX-11 is fetched in byte, word, longword, quadword, and octaword, in contrast to the PDP-11, which has byte and word only. Thus, integers can be housed in all these units. Just like in the PDP-11 system, in the VAX-11 the integers are expressed in signed or unsigned representations, and the twos complement system is used for signed integers. However, since the floating-point number representation is a standard, not optional, installation in the VAX-11, we need to look at its fundamentals.

A floating-point number represented by a 32-bit longword is shown below.

31 16	15	14 7	6 0
Fraction (LSBs)	S	Exponent	Fraction (MSBs)

Note that the floating-point number is represented by a sign bit, b_{15}; an exponent, $b_{14}, \ldots, b_7$; and a fraction, where the most significant part (MSBS) resides in $b_6, \ldots, b_0$, while the least significant bits reside in $b_{31}, \ldots, b_{16}$, with b_{31} being concatenated to b_0. Since the most significant bit of the fraction after normalization is always one, in order to save a bit space, this redundant bit is always omitted in the representation.

For example, if a fraction in reality is .1010 0000 1100 0000 0000 1111, it will be packed in the fraction field as follows:

6 0

0 1 0	0 0 0 0

31 16

1 1 0 0	0 0 0 0	0 0 0 0	1 1 1 1

For exponent representation, the actual exponent value is first added to a constant of 128 and then placed into the exponent field. For example, if the actual exponent is -2, then in the exponent field we will find $-2 + 128 = 126$, which can be shown as follows:

14 7

0 1 1 1	1 1 1 0

In this excess of 128 representation, the exponent would always be a positive binary number, but the actual exponent = [number in exponent field] − 128

As another example, the number of 0.100101×2^{-3} can be stored in the VAX-11 as follows:

31 . . . . 16 15 14 . . . . 7 6 0

| 0 0 0 0   0 0 0 0   0 0 0 0   0 0 0 0 | 0 | 0 1 1 1   1 1 0 1 | 0 0 1 0 1 0 0 |

Here we have actual exponent $= -3$, and the value in the exponent field is equal to $-3 + 128 = 125 = 0111 \ 1101_2$.

What we have just described is the floating-point representation in single precision. In the VAX-11, users are allowed to use double-precision floating representation, whose format is defined as follows:

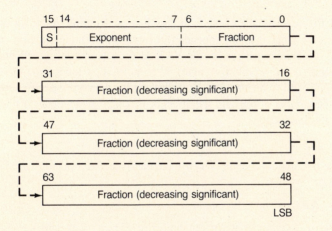

In addition to the integer, single-precision floating point, and double precision floating point, the VAX-11 offers other data types for the user. Table 10.2 shows the complete set of data types allowed in the VAX-11 system.

TABLE 10.2 VAX DATA TYPES

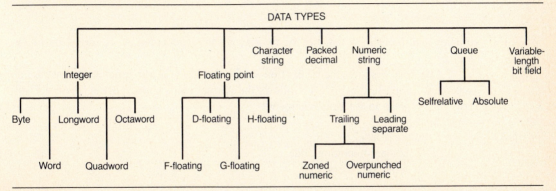

Instructions

The VAX-11 offers a very powerful set of instructions to users for developing simple and sophisticated programs. In addition to the huge virtual address space, it can operate on different types of data, and there are instructions that may allow the user to have up to six operand specifiers. For example, for the PDP-11, the instruction

ADD   A,B

has two operand specifiers. In the next subsection, we will examine the general format of the instruction set of the VAX-11.

Recall that in the basic PDP-11 system, we only have two data types of integers, byte and word. When an instruction is operating on a byte, a B is appended to the instruction. For example, the instruction

MOVB   A,B

instructs the CPU to copy the content of low-byte at location A into low-byte at B. However, when the letter B is not appended, it implies that the instruction operates on a word basis. As a logical extension, in the VAX-11 the instructions are appended with B, W, L, Q, F, and so on, where B = byte, W = word, L = longword, Q = quadword, F = floating point, and so on. In addition, following the data type specification, a number that indicates the number of operand specifiers is also appended whenever it is applicable. For example, the instruction

ADDB2   A,B

implies that the instruction operates on byte data and has two operand specifiers; and the instruction

ADDL3   A,B,C

implies that the instruction operates on longword (32-bit) data and has three operand specifiers. That is, in this example, it directs the CPU, adds longword data at A, and that at B, and places the result in C. The data at A and B are not altered.

In addition to appending the information of the data type and number of operand specifiers, the programmer is allowed to append the letters AL to the mnemonic to indicate that the operation is referring to address, not the content of the address. For example, the instruction

MOVAL   A,B

implies that the address value of A, or #A, not the contents of A, is copied into location B.

Appendix F shows the instruction set for the VAX-11. In general, the instruction statement format in the VAX-11 follows the normal convention. That is, there are still four fields for an instruction statement:

1. Address label
2. Mnemonic operation code
3. Operand specifiers
4. Comments

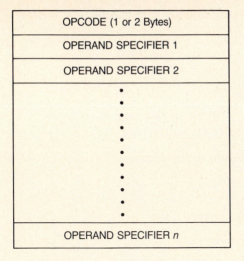

| OPCODE (1 or 2 Bytes) |
| OPERAND SPECIFIER 1 |
| OPERAND SPECIFIER 2 |
| · · · · · · · · · · · |
| OPERAND SPECIFIER n |

Figure 10.11 General VAX instruction format.

These are separated in the conventional way:

ADDRESS LABEL:OPCODE   SPECIFIER1,SPECIFIER2, . . .   ;COMMENT

Finally, it is important to point out that in contrast to the PDP-11 system, the literature from the Digital Equipment Corporation has eliminated octal numeric representation. In the VAX-11 system, only the binary, decimal, and hexadecimal representations are used.

Since the instructions for the VAX-11 are variable in length, the number of memory bytes varies depending on the type of opcode and the addressing modes used for the operand specifier. The general format of a VAX instruction is shown in Figure 10.11. Note that the opcode may require one or two bytes of memory space, and that each operand specifier may occupy one or more bytes.

Addressing Modes

We may examine the addressing modes for the VAX instructions in two general ways: (1) addressing modes involving general purpose registers, R0, R1, . . . , R11, excluding PC, R15; and (2) addressing modes involving PC. Let us examine these two types in detail. By now, we should all agree that a good programmer needs to know both the instruction set and all available addressing modes.

Non-PC Register Reference Addressing Modes

Register Mode This mode is the same as the direct addressing mode in the PDP-11 instruction, except that here we are dealing with 32-bit content instead of 16-bit. Example:

MOVW   R1,R2   ;   (R1) → (R2)

Here, only the low word of R1 is copied into the low word of R2. If, before execution, we have:

$$(R1) = A09A779B$$
$$(R2) = 00000000$$

then after execution, we have:

$$(R1) = A09A779B$$
$$(R2) = 0000779B$$

Remember that we are always using the hexadecimal representation instead of the octal.

CLRL   (R2)   ;   (R2) = contents of R2

Assume that before execution

$$(R2) = 00002120$$

and the content at the memory location 0000   2120 is AD9CF712. Then, after execution, at location 0000   2120, we have 0000   0000. Let us show the process using the memory map technique.

Before		After	
(R2) = 0000 2120		(R2) = N.C.*	
Address (Byte)	Content	Address (Byte)	Content
0000 2120	12	0000 2120	00
0000 2121	F7	0000 2121	00
0000 2122	9C	0000 2122	00
0000 2123	AD	0000 2123	00
•	•	•	•
•	•	•	•
•	•	•	•
•	•	•	•

*N.C. = No change.

Auto Increment Mode   Example:

MOVL   (R1)+,R3   ;   (R1)+4 → R1, incremented by 4 due to longword

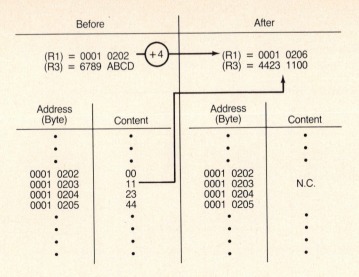

Auto Increment Deferred Mode   Example:

CLRW   @(R1)+   ;   (R1)+2 → R1, due to word

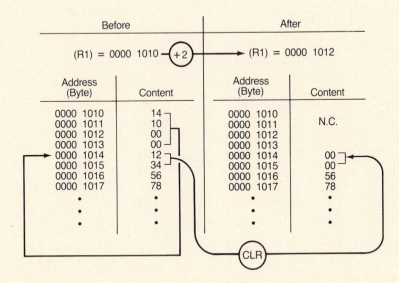

Auto Decrement Mode   Example:

ADDL   (R2)+,−(R3)   ;   (R2)+4 → R2, (R3)−4 → R3

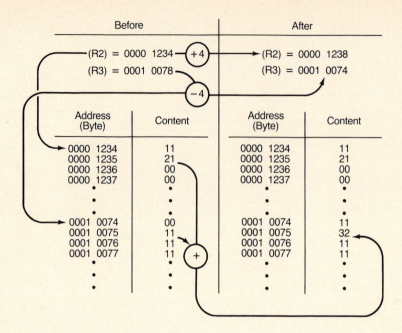

Displacement Mode This addressing mode is the same as the index mode in the PDP-11 system. Example:

        CLRB   5(R3)

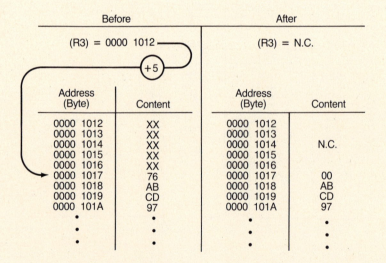

Displacement Deferred Mode This is the same as the indirect indexed mode of PDP-11. Example:

        INCW   @3(R2)

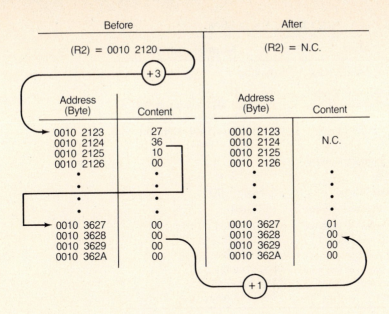

Note: In both displacement and deferred displacement modes, the programmer is allowed to use the symbols to inform the assembler that the displacement value must be placed in byte, word, or longword:

$B \uparrow D(R_n)$;forces byte displacement

$W \uparrow D(R_n)$;forces word displacement

$L \uparrow D(R_n)$;forces longword displacement

Index Mode The name of this mode is unfortunately confusing if one is used to the PDP-11, because this is not the index mode defined in the PDP-11 system. Table 10.3 describes the allowable formats for this mode.

EXAMPLE 1

    CLRW   (R2)[R5]

Here, the effective address = $x*[R5] + (R2)$

where $[R5]$ = content of R5

$(R2)$ = content of R2

$$x = \begin{cases} 1, \text{ for byte} \\ 2, \text{ for word} \\ 4, \text{ for longword, floating} \\ 8, \text{ for quadword, D-floating, G-floating} \\ 16, \text{ for octaword, H-floating} \end{cases}$$

TABLE 10.3   INDEX MODE ADDRESSING

Mode	Assembler notation
Register deferred index	(Rn)[Rx]
Auto increment indexed	(Rn) + [Rx]
Immediate indexed	|# constant [Rx] which is recognized by assembler but is not generally useful. Operand address is independent of value of constant.
Auto increment deferred indexed	@(Rn) + [Rx]
Absolute indexed	@#address [Rx]
Auto decrement indexed	−(Rn)[Rx]
Byte, word, or longword displacement indexed	B ↑ D(Rn)[Rx] W ↑ D(Rn)[Rx] L ↑ D(Rn)[Rx]
Byte, word, or longword displacement deferred indexed	@B ↑ D(Rn)[Rx] @W ↑ D(Rn)[Rx] @L ↑ D(Rn)[Rx]

Courtesy of Digital Equipment Corporation.

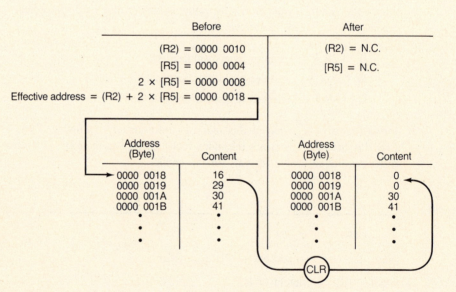

EXAMPLE 2

INCL   (R2)+[R3]   ;AUTOINCREMENT MIXED WITH INDEX MODE

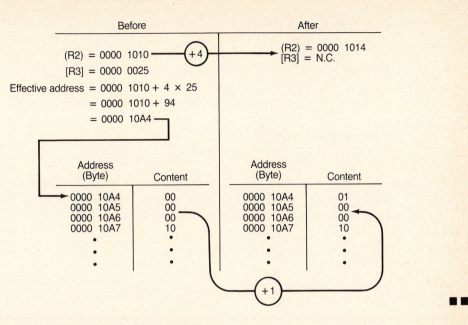

PC Register Reference Addressing Modes

Like the addressing modes in the PDP-11 system, there is a class of addressing modes that is PC-referenced. However, in the VAX-11 system, R15 is used as PC. But like the PDP-11, we have here the immediate mode, the absolute mode, the relative mode, and the relative deferred mode.

Immediate Mode   Example:

    A: MOVL #7,R1   ;   Let A = 00001172

This instruction simply moves integer 7 into longword of R1. However, the integer would occupy the 32-bit memory word (4 bytes) immediately following the instruction, as shown below.

Before		After	
(R1) = 0000 0000		(R1) = 0000 0007	
Address (Byte)	Content	Address (Byte)	Content
0000 1172	D0	0000 1172	
0000 1173	8F	0000 1173	
0000 1174	07	0000 1174	
0000 1175	00	0000 1175	N.C.
0001 1176	00	0001 1176	
0001 1177	00	0001 1177	
0001 1178	51	0001 1178	

where: D0 = opcode for MOVL instruction
         F = R15 or PC
         8 = addressing mode number for immediate mode
0000 0007 = integer 7 in 32-bit longword
         1 = R1
         5 = addressing mode No. 5 $\underline{\Delta}$ register mode

Absolute Mode   Example:

    A: CLRW @# ↑ X1234   ;   Let A = 0000   1172

This instruction clears the content at location 0000   1234; the notation ↑ X implies that the following number is a hexadecimal. This is necessary, since the VAX assembler would interpret an unspecified number as a decimal.

Before		After	
Address (Byte)	Content	Address (Byte)	Content
0000 1172	D4	0000 1172	
0000 1173	9F	0000 1173	
0000 1174	34	0000 1174	N.C.
0000 1175	12	0000 1175	
0000 1176	00	0000 1176	
0000 1177	00	0000 1177	
•	•	•	•
•	•	•	•
•	•	•	•
0000 1234	23	0000 1234	00
0000 1235	34	0000 1235	00
0000 1236	56	0000 1236	56
0000 1237	78	0000 1237	78
•	•	•	•
•	•	•	•
•	•	•	•

CLR

where: D4 = opcode for CLRW instruction
         F = PC or R15
         9 = code number for absolute addressing mode
0000 1234 = absolute address of the operand

Relative Mode   Example:

    A: MOVL ↑ X2176,R1   ;   Let A = 0000   1172

This instruction illustrates the relative addressing mode. Here the destination address is 2176, the updated PC is 1176, and therefore the relative distance between the updated PC and the destination is 1000. Again, in principle, this process is identical to that in the PDP-11 system. However, the VAX assembler is more intelligent in that it sees to it that the memory space for the relative distance is efficiently used. In other words, for short relative distances ($\le$ FF), it would allocate only one byte space for the relative distance value; for medium distances ($\le$ FFFF), one word space, and so on.

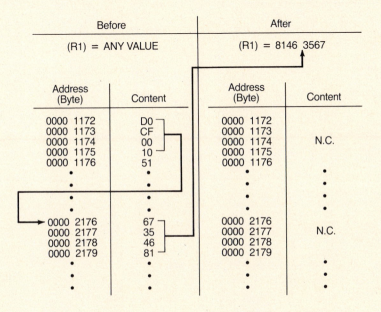

where: D0 = opcode for MOVL instruction
       F = PC or R15
       C = code for relative distance which requires a word space
  1000 = relative distance = destination − updated PC
      1 = R1
      5 = code for register mode

Relative Deferred Mode   Example:

   A: MOVL @ ↑ X1185, R3   ;   Let A = 1172

This is a relative indirect addressing mode. It is the same in principle as that for the PDP-11, except for the variable memory space allocated for relative distance value.

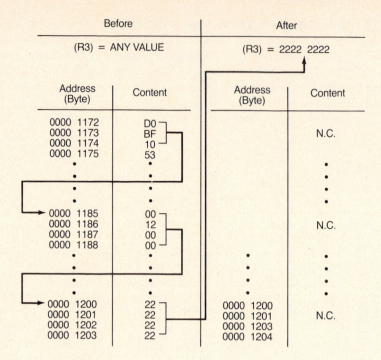

where: D0 = opcode for MOVL instruction
      F = PC or R15
      B = code for deferred relative distance which
            requires one byte space
     10 = relative distance
      3 = R3
      5 = code for register mode

Branch Addressing   The principle of branch addressing is the same in the PDP-11 as in the VAX-11. However, the range of relative distance in the PDP-11 is limited to −256 to 254, whereas in the VAX-11 the range of relative distance can be limited to one byte or one 16-bit word. For a 16-bit word, we will have a range of −32768 to 32766. Again, the assembler would calculate the relative distance value and store it next to the opcode. For example, BRB will allow a byte of relative distance, while BRW will allow a 16-bit word of relative distance. That is, the instruction

    A: BRW   LOOP

will allow the instruction to branch to LOOP, which can be as far as 32766 bytes forward or 32768 bytes backward from A.

10.4 MACROS, SUBROUTINES, AND PROCEDURES

Macros

Just like in the PDP-11 system, users are allowed to create macro instructions in the VAX-11, following the format shown below:

```
.MACRO     name      augment1,augment2,...,?L1,?L2,...
          .
          .
    macro body in VAX-11 instructions
          .
          .
    .ENDM      name
```

where ?L1,?L2,... are local address labels. Similarly, users are allowed to write conditional macros, as described in Chapter 6.

Subroutines

The principle of the subroutine process described in Chapter 5 for the PDP-11 is applicable in the VAX-11 system. That is, for the subroutine process in the VAX-11, we still need the instruction pair, jump to, and return from subroutine that links the host and the subroutine. In addition, we need a well-defined parameter passing mechanism to transmit the data into and out of the subroutine. In many cases, we may have to save and retrieve the old contents of some general purpose registers. It is the programmer's responsibility to implement all these requirements. However, instead of using the JSR and RTS as the linking instruction pair, in the VAX-11 programmers are allowed to use the instructions BSBB (branch subroutine byte) or BSBW (branch subroutine word) to enter a subroutine, depending on the relative distance between the calling instruction and the starting address of the called subroutine. For return, in the VAX-11, programmers are allowed to use the instruction RSB (return from subroutine). The following shows the general format for entering into, and returning from, a subroutine.

```
    ;Host program
START:      .
            .
            .
            BSBW SUBR      ;Branch to subroutine which can
            .              ;be ± 32K bytes or less away
            .
            .
SUBR:       .
            .
            .
    RSB
```

When the CPU executes BSBW or SUBR, it will push the updated PC into the stack and place the address value of SUBR into PC. For execution of RSB, the updated PC is popped from the stack and placed into PC. So except for the linking instruction pair, there is nothing new in the VAX-11.

Procedures

To PDP-11 users, the word "procedure" may be a new term. Actually, a procedure is a subroutine, but with a more rigid format. It is created for the user's convenience. Recall that, for writing a subroutine, the programmer is responsible for choosing and implementing a proper parameter passing technique. If applicable, it is also the programmer's responsibility to save and retrieve the contents of the general purpose registers through the stack memory. Although all these requirements or responsibilities are straightforward, they are somewhat wasteful of the programmer's time and talent, especially when saving and retrieving the contents of the registers are required in a process.

Normally, the saved contents of the registers are mixed with others on the same block of the stack memory, which refer to the same stack pointer the programmer has to keep track of. The process can be simplified a great deal if we have a pointer specifically assigned for the saving process, and a pointer for the data transfer. This idea is indeed implemented in the VAX-11, and it is called **procedure.** Now a user has the option of writing either subroutines or procedures.

In the VAX-11, the R12 is called the **augment pointer (AP),** which is used for parameter passing; and the R13 is called **frame pointer (FP),** which is used as the based register pointing to the base or starting address of a stack memory block exclusively reserved for the purpose of saving the key information of the host program, such as PSL, updated PC, the contents of all general purpose registers, and so on. The user can thus always find out where the information is stored by referencing FP instead of the system stack pointer, since the content of SP is usually changing with respect to time, while that of FP remains fixed. Let us examine how this idea is integrated into the format of calling a procedure.

In the VAX-11, users are provided with two sets of instruction pairs to link the host program and a procedure: CALLG and RET, and CALLS and RET. Basically, CALLG allows the host "automatically" to pass the starting address of the data array that the host program requests the called procedure to work with. CALLS requires the host program to push the data onto the system stack first, and then the procedure can work on the data in stack memory.

EXAMPLE 1 _____

```
                ;Host program
   ARRAY: .LONG n                    ;data array size in longword
          .LONG d₁d₂,...,dₙ          ;.LONG is the data directive similar
                                     ;to the .WORD, but it consists of longword
                                     ;data

   START:  .



          CALLG ARRAY, PROC          ;Call procedure
          .
          .

   PROC:  .WORD ↑M⟨R0,R1,...⟩        ;Format for saving registers
          .
          .
          .
   RET
   .END   START.
```

Note that the data array must be structured such that the first longword must be the size of the array. As the instruction

```
CALLG    ARRAY,    PROC
```

is executed, a sequence of steps is automatically carried out by the hardware. Among other essential steps, the hardware places the address value, #ARRAY, onto AP or R12; and the address value of the starting address of the procedure, #PROC, onto PC. Additionally, it saves the updated PC, PSL, and other information on the stack memory block defined by the FP, or R13.

Note that the first line of the procedure known as register masks is

```
.WORD      ↑ M⟨R0,R1,...⟩
```

which will be interpreted by the hardware as the programmer wishing to save the registers listed within the bracket. It pushes the contents of the registers listed onto the stack block defined by FP, or R13. The RET instruction at the end of the procedure will restore the registers and give control back to the host program. In summary, the instruction CALLG has two operands, one for the data array and the other for the starting address of the procedure.

EXAMPLE 2 _____

```
;Host program
ARRAY:.LONG d1,d2,...dn
START:PUSHL #dn
            .
            .
            .
       PUSHL #d2
       PUSHL #d1
       CALLS #n,PROC  ;calling instruction
            .
            .
            .
PROC:.WORD ↑ M⟨R0,...⟩
            .
            .
            .
       RET
       .END
```

In this example, we use CALLS, so the data array has to be pushed onto the stack before the calling. Note that there are also two operands for the CALLS instruction. While the second operand functions like that of CALLG instruction, the first operand is the number of data elements which have been pushed onto the stack. On executing the CALLS instruction, the hardware pushes onto the stack the first operand, #n, the registers, the updated PC, PSL, and so on. The AP and FP are fixed and used in the same way as for the CALLG instruction. However, the RET instruction, besides its normal operation, would also remove the arguments that were pushed onto the stack.

Actually, as an alternative, in this example one could just push the addresses of the data array and the array size onto the stack, and the procedure could use the address information pushed onto the stack to fetch the data by using the indirect addressing technique for the procedure. If so, we would have pushed only two longwords onto the stack, and the calling instruction would be CALLS   #2,PROC.

10.5 INTERRUPTS AND EXCEPTIONS

As described in Chapter 8, in the PDP-11 system we have loosely classified the interrupt processes into two classes: the hardware (external) interrupt, and the software (internal) interrupt. Strictly speaking, the software interrupts, such as the TRAP instruction and the like, cannot be called an interrupt. In the VAX-11, the software interrupts are called **exception.** For hardware (external) interrupts, the interrupting sources are normally external devices functionally independent from the current running program, and they request services likely to be independent of the host program. The exception processes are somewhat related to the host program. For example, if a fault occurs as a result of the execution of an instruction of the host program, the "normal" sequence of the host program would be stopped and the CPU would take an "exceptional" route to execute.

In the VAX-11, there are 32 levels of interrupt priority; the bits $b_{21}, \ldots, b_{16}$ of PSL define the levels, with the zero level as the lowest priority. For exceptions, there are three types: traps, faults, and aborts. For more details, refer to the *VAX Architecture Handbook,* published by the Digital Equipment Corporation.

REFERENCES FOR FURTHER READING

Lemone, Karen A., and Martin E. Kaliski. *Assembly Language Programming for the VAX-11*. Boston: Little, Brown, 1983.

Levy, Henry M., and Richard H. Eckhouse, Jr. *Computer Programming and Architecture: The VAX-11*. Bedford, Mass.: Digital Press, 1980.

VAX Hardware Handbook. Digital Equipment Corporation (1981).

VAX Architecture Handbook. Digital Equipment Corporation (1981).

VAX Software Handbook. Digital Equipment Corporation (1981).

EXERCISES

10.1 Repeat Problems 5.4 to 5.11 in the exercises of Chapter 5 (subroutines), but use the VAX-11 assembly language for different data types.

10.2 Repeat Problems 6.3 and 6.4 in the exercises of Chapter 6 (macros), but use the VAX-11 assembly language.

Chapter 11

Laboratory Exercises

11.1 INTRODUCTION

From our experience and the feedback from students, we have concluded that hands-on experience in the laboratory is the most important and efficient way to learn assembly language programming. As we noted in Chapter 1, there is an analogy between learning to swim and programming a computer. No one can be a swimmer by reading a number of books without getting into the water to practice what one has read. Therefore, if we are serious about assembly language programming, practice on a real machine is a vital step. Furthermore, we all know that lectures, laboratory work, and examinations are essential means to learning in any scientific/engineering discipline; therefore we believe that classroom examinations should be stressed in addition to laboratory exercises. In this chapter, we present some of the problems we have used for laboratory exercises.

Since there may still be differences in detail from one computing system to the other, it is important to point out that what is being described here may not be directly applicable to each and every system. However, with minor modifications, the problems should be useful to everyone.

11.2 SAMPLE PROBLEMS FOR LABORATORY EXERCISES

The following is a set of exercises designed to be done on the PDP-11 system. They involve the use of all the different features of the assembly language, and are arranged in order of increasing difficulty. By the last problem, students will be using everything they should have learned in class.

Problem 1

This is a simple exercise to guide a student in entering a program and simulating some typical human errors one can use the system software or text editor of the PDP-11 to correct. Figure 11.1 shows the actual interactive process between a programmer and the PDP-11 system in creating a new file and using the text editor to revise it until each editorial error has been corrected. To clarify the interactive action, all the computer responses are underlined, and the comments are in ***boldface italic*** type. Let us work through the exercise. First, we begin with the courtesy and security dialogues and get onto the system by noting the MCR (monitory) prompt, >; we then use the command PIP/LI to find out if there are any existing files on the disk. Here, the computer responds by saying NO SUCH FILE.

Next, we proceed to call the text editor, EDI, to assist us to create a program that will add two given numbers and test the result. What follows is the interactive process of using the commands provided by EDI to correct all the typical typo errors. Eventually we arrive at the point when we think everything is in proper order, and we are ready to call ASSEMBLER, MAC. to assemble our program.

The assembler then righteously points out all the programming errors we have made and forces us to go back to EDI to correct them. The example shows that the assembler finally reports that ERRORS DETECTED is zero, and the list file of the program is presented. At this point, we are ready to call the task builder or linker, TKB, to produce an executable program to be loaded into the main memory for execution. The rest of the example shows how we use the load-and-go command, LGO, and the ODT to examine the details and the result of execution.

For convenience in reading the example, we have used the symbol ⊡ to identify the major sections of the process: text editing, assembling, task building, and executing.

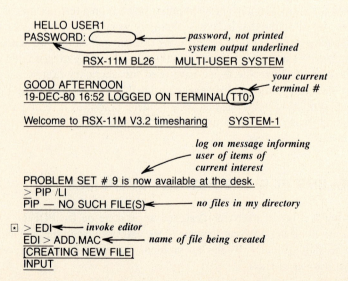

```
;THIS IS A VERY SIMPLE PDP-11 PROGRAM
;WHICH ADDS TWO NUMBERS AND TESTS THE RESULT.
;LITU\UTIL\IT IS USED TO EM\ME\DEMONSTRATE THE SIMPLE
;USE OF THE *U
USE OF THE EDITOR AND ASSEMBLER.
;
            .TITLE    ADD
A:          .BLKW               ;WORD RESERVED FOR A
B;\;\:      .WORD     299.      DECIMAL NUMBER
C:          .WORD     −476      ;OCTAL #
START:      MOVE      C,R0      ;R0 IS NAME FOR REGISTER 0
            ADD       B,R0      ;FORM SUM
            BMI       NEG
            HALT                ;HALT HERE IF POS
NEG:        HALT                ;HALT HERE IF NEG
            .END      START
```

4 ⟨rubouts⟩ typed to delete mistakes
⟨control u⟩ deletes line.

my input to file.

*TOP ⟵ *terminate input mode with ⟨CR⟩*
*LI ⟵ *command to list contents of page buffer*

```
; THIS IS A VERY SIMPLE PDP-11 PROGRAM
;WHICH ADDS TWO NUMBERS AND TESTS THE RESULT.
;IT IS USED TO DEMONSTRATE THE SIMPLE
USE OF THE EDITOR AND ASSEMBLER.
;
            .TITLE    ADD
A:          .BLKW               ;WORD RESERVED FOR A
B:          .WORD     299.      DECIMAL NUMBER
C:          .WORD     −476      ;OCTAL #
START:      MOVE      C,R0      ;R0 IS NAME FOR REGISTER 0
            ADD       B,R0      ;FORM SUM
            BMI       NEG
            HALT                ;HALT HERE IF POS
NEG:        HALT                ;HALT HERE IF NEG
            .END      START
```

*TOP
*LOC USE
*IT IS USED TO DEMONSTRATE THE SIMPLE
* ⟵ *⟨CR⟩ Causes editor to advance one line.*
USE OF THE EDITOR AND ASSEMBLER.

*C/U/;U ⟵ *change command corrects omission of ; at beginning of comment*
;USE OF THE EDITOR AND ASSEMBLER. ⟵ *corrected line*
*EXIT ⟵ *terminates editor, closes file*
[EXIT]

>PIP /LI

DIRECTORY DK0:[100,1]
19-DEC-80 16:59

size in blocks *when created*

name
ADD.MAC;1 *type*   1.   19-DEC-80 16:52
version

TOTAL OF 1./5. BLOCKS IN 1. FILE

⟨rubouts⟩ to correct typing error

⊡ ≥MAC ADD,TI: = MAC CAM ADD

assembler output
to file named ADD.OBJ   List to terminal

listing ↘

ADD   MACRO M113   19-DEC-80 16:59   PAGE 1

```
       1                                    ;THIS IS A VERY SIMPLE PDP-11 PROGRAM
       2                                    ;WHICH ADDS TWO NUMBERS AND TESTS THE RE
SULT ←   from previous line-(too long)
       3              error codes-          ;IT IS USED TO DEMONSTRATE THE SIMPLE
       4              forgot ; before DECIMAL ;USE OF THE EDITOR AND ASSEMBLER.
       5              used MOVE instead of MOV ;
       6                                             .TITLE     ADD
       7  000000                           A:        .BLKW                  ;WORD RESERVED F
OR A
  Ⓐ   8  000002  000453  000000G  000000G  B:        .WORD      299.        DECIMAL NUMBER
  Ⓐ   9  000010  177302                    C:        .WORD      −476        ;OCTAL #
      10  000012  000000G  000010'  000000  START:    MOVE       C,R0        ;R0 IS NAME FOR
REGISTER 0
      11  000020  066700  177756                      ADD        B,R0        ;FORM SUM
      12  000024  100401                              BMI        NEG
      13  000026  000000                              HALT                   ;HALT HERE IF PO
S
      14  000030  000000            NEG:              HALT                   ;HALT HERE IF NE
G
      15          000012'                             .END       START
```

tries to make
a label because   from comment
misspelled MOV   without ;

ADD   MACRO M1113   19-DEC-80 16:59   PAGE 1-1
SYMBOL TABLE

```
A        000000R        C        000010R      MOVE = ****** GX      NUMBER =
****** GX        START    000012R
B        000002R        DECIMA = ****** GX     NEG      000030R
```

```
.ABS.    000000        000
         000032        001
ERRORS DETECTED: 2
ERRORS DETECTED: 2
```

```
VIRTUAL MEMORY USED: 79 WORDS ( 1 PAGES)
DYNAMIC MEMORY: 3012 WORDS ( 11 PAGES)
ELAPSED TIME: 00:00:18
ADD,TI: = ADD
ADD,TI: = ADD
```

(all of the above is
computer generated output)

```
≥EDI ADD.MAC
[00015 LINES READ IN]
[PAGE 1]
*LI
```

(now we enter EDI
to correct our errors)

```
;THIS IS A VERY SIMPLE PDP-11 PROGRAM
;WHICH ADDS TWO NUMBERS AND TESTS THE RESULT.
;IT IS USED TO DEMONSTRATE THE SIMPLE
;USE OF THE EDITOR AND ASSEMBLER.
;
            .TITLE    ADD
A:          .BLKW                  ;WORD RESERVED FOR A
B:          .WORD     299.         DECIMAL NUMBER
C:          .WORD     −476         ;OCTAL #
START:      MOVE      C,R0         ;R0 IS NAME FOR REGISTER 0
            ADD       B,R0         ;FORM SUM
            BMI       NEG
            HALT                   ;HALT HERE IF POS        find line
NEG:        HALT                   ;HALT HERE IF NEG        with first
            .END      START                                error
*LOC B:
B:          .WORD     299.         DECIMAL NUMBER
*C/DEC/;DEC                                        change command
B:          .WORD     299.         ;DECIMAL NUMBER
*LOC MOVE
START:      MOVE      C,R0         ;R0 IS NAME FOR REGISTER 0
*C/MOVE/MOV                                        another change command
START:      MOV       C,R0         ;R0 IS NAME FOR REGISTER 0
*EX
[EXIT]                            (done editing)
```

>PIP /LI   first program file (with errors)
                            assembler output file from
DIRECTORY DK0:[100,1]   assembly with errors
19-DEC-80 17:01   corrected file

ADD.MAC;1   1.   19-DEC-80 16:52
ADD.OBJ;1   1.   19-DEC-80 16:59
ADD.MAC;2   1.   19-DEC-80 17:00

TOTAL OF 3./11. BLOCKS IN 3. FILES

>MAC ADD,TI: = ADD   *(Assemble the most recent*
                            version of ADD.MAC)

                   All below is Computer generated output

```
ADD        MACRO M1113  19-DEC-80 17:02   PAGE 1

      1                              ;THIS IS A VERY SIMPLE PDP-11 PROGRAM
      2                              ;WHICH ADDS TWO NUMBERS AND TESTS THE RE
SULT.
      3                              ;IT IS USED TO DEMONSTRATE THE SIMPLE
      4                              ;USE OF THE EDITOR AND ASSEMBLER.
      5                              ;
      6                                      .TITLE    ADD
      7  000000    A is not used    A:        .BLKW              ;WORD RESERVED F
OR A         in program!
      8  000002   000453            B:        .WORD     299.     ;DECIMAL NUMBER
      9  000004   177302            C:        .WORD     −476     ;OCTAL #
     10  000006   016700   177772   START:    MOV       C,R0     ;R0 IS NAME FOR
REGISTER 0
     11  000012   066700   177764             ADD       B,R0     ;FORM SUM
     12  000016   100401                      BMI       NEG
```

Fi

Problem 2

You are to write a program that finds the maximum value of three numbers, A, B, C, and puts the result in a variable MAX. Assemble the program by hand, assuming the first word will go into location 1172.

1. Use ODT to enter the machine language into the LSI-11.
2. Enter the following values for A, B, and C: (A) = −15.; (B) = −15; (C) = −100.
3. Run the program.
4. Use the ODT to inspect the result.
5. Have the T.A. (Teaching Assistant) verify operation.
6. Turn in a neat handwritten version of the assembly language and assembled program.

Problem 3

Write a program that computes the average, AV, of grades M1, M2, HW, and F, and then HALTs. You will need to set aside five memory locations at the end of your program (after the HALT!!) for these values, plus AV. (*Hint:* dividing by 2 may be accomplished with ASR). Assemble the program by hand, assuming the first word will go into location 1172_8. Your addresses should refer to the five memory locations reserved for the data M1, M2, HW, F, and AV.

1. Use ODT to enter the machine language into the LSI-11.
2. Use ODT to enter the values for M1, M2, HW, F: (M1) = 89, (M2) = 62, (HW) = 92, (F) = 75.
3. Run the program.
4. Use ODT to inspect the results.
5. Have the reader verify proper operations. Each member must have an 8½ × 11 sheet of paper with name, partner's name, account information, date, and assignment number for the reader to validate program execution. Turn this sheet in with your paper problems.
6. Also turn in a neat handwritten version of the assembly language and the hand assembly.

Problem 4

You must enter, assemble, and run the following program. Please add comments to show that you understand what the program is doing. Include your name in a comment line at the beginning of the program. The steps to follow are these:

1. Use EDI to enter the program with your comments.
2. Use MAC to assemble the program.
3. Use task builder (TKB) to task build.
4. Use GET to send the program to your LSI.
5. Execute the program for the reader.

6. Each partner should get a final listing of the program and have it validated by the T.A.

```
START:   CLR     R0
         MOV     #A,R1
LOOP:    ADD     (R1)+,R0
         CMP     #A+18.,R1
         BPL     LOOP
         MOV     R0,SUM
         HALT
A:       .WORD   1,2,3,4,5,6,7,8.,9.,10.
SUM      .BLKW
         .END
```

Problem 5

Write a program in assembly language that will take a number found in STD and put it into reverse order in REV. For example, if STD is 0   101   001   101   110   110, REV should be 0   110   111   011   001   010.

1. Enter the program into a file using EDI.
2. Assemble the program using MAC.
3. Task build the program using TKB.
4. Downline load the program using GET.
5. Use ODT to load a value of STD.
6. Execute the program.
7. Use ODT to inspect REV.
8. Repeat 5, 6, and 7 for several different numbers.
9. Have the T.A. verify proper operation.
10. Turn in a listing of the program.

Problem 6

Write a program that counts the number of 1 bits in the word X. Store the result in NUM. For X, use 170532: i.e., X: .WORD   170532

Problem 7

Write a program in assembly language to convert a 16-bit binary number in NUMBER into the ASCII code for the sign and 5 octal digits of the magnitude which describe the number. Put the six bytes so produced into the six successive bytes starting at the right byte of the word OUTPUT. The character for the sign should be first, since it would be the first typed. For example:

```
NUMBER:   173762   ( 1 111 011 111 110 010 )₂   ( −4016 )
OUTPUT:   055     (−)
          060
          060
          064
          060
          061
          066
```

1. Assemble the program.
2. Task build it.
3. Send it to the LSI-11.
4. Execute the program in the presence of a T.A.
5. Turn in a listing of the program.

Problem 8

Write a program in assembly language that will sort up to 30 numbers in the list ARRAY using a bubble sort. The numbers should be arranged in increasing order, with ARRAY containing the smallest number, and ARRAY + n − 2 containing the largest number. *Suggestion:* Use addressing modes 1 or 2 to refer to your array; it will make the next assignment easier.

1. Assemble the program and turn in a listing.
2. Task build and downline load the program.
3. Execute the program for a T.A. Use the following sample information (all numbers are octal).

```
    N:      20
ARRAY:     −10
           126
            15
           −30
             0
          5000
          −256
             0
```

Problem 9

The purpose of this problem is to have you gain experience with subroutine linkage on the PDP-11 and with system MACRO commands.

1. Convert your SORT program written for problem 8 into a subroutine. Calling the subroutine will be accomplished by the following sequence of commands.

```
JSR      R5,SORT
.WORD    N           ;ADDRESS OF SIZE OF ARRAY IN BYTES
.WORD    ARRAY       ;ADDRESS OF ARRAY TO BE SORTED
----------  --------------- ;FIRST INSTRUCTION EXECUTED UPON
                     ;RETURN
```

   SORT will be defined as .GLOBL in both the subroutine and the main program. Assemble and get a listing of your subroutine.
2. Write a main program which:
   a. Defines a 14_8 word array UNSRT (n = 30) of the following numbers: 0, −15, −256, −4123, +27, −1777, 0, −27, −15, +7775, +27, −101.
   b. Prints those numbers using .PNUM.
   c. Copies the array UNSRT into another array, SRTD.
   d. Calls SORT to sort array SRTD.

    e. Prints the sorted array.

    f. Returns to the monitor (MCR) using .EXIT.

3. Assemble and get a listing of the main program.

4. Task build the object module of your main program with the object module of the subroutine and the MACRO library (MLIB).

5. Run the program for a T.A. and turn in a listing.

Problem 10

Write a subroutine that will merge two already sorted arrays into one array, with all elements of the final array properly sorted. Since both input arrays are already sorted, all that has to be done is to start from the beginning of each array, pick the smaller, and put it in the output. Now the pointer to the array that had the selected element must be advanced, and again we compare elements from the two arrays and put the smaller element in the output array. We continue until one input array is empty. We then transfer the rest of the other input array to the output and stop.

This subroutine will be called by:

```
JSR    R5,MRGE
.WORD N1          ;ADDRESS OF SIZE OF ARRAY 1
.WORD ARRAY1      ;ADDRESS OF FIRST INPUT ARRAY
.WORD N2          ;ADDRESS OF SIZE OF ARRAY2
.WORD ARRAY2      ;ADDRESS OF SECOND INPUT ARRAY
.WORD N3          ;ADDRESS OF SIZE OF OUTPUT ARRAY
                  ;MAX VALUE PASSED TO SUBROUTINE
                  ;ACTUAL VALUE (N1 + N2) RETURNED
.WORD ARRAY3      ;ADDRESS OF OUTPUT ARRAY
```

1. Assemble this subroutine and obtain a listing.

2. Write a main program that will

    a. Read in N1, ARRAY1, N2, ARRAY2 (use .RNUM).

    b. Sort ARRAY1, ARRAY2.

    c. Print the sorted ARRAYs using .PNUM.

    d. Use MRGE to merge ARRAY1, ARRAY2 into ARRAY3.

    e. Print the merged array.

    f. Be sure to use .PTEXT properly to prompt input and title output.

3. Assemble the main program and task build it with the subroutine.

4. Demonstrate the program's operation.

Problem 11

A useful algorithm for computing the greatest common divisor is defined recursively as follows:

```
GCD(x,y) :=
    if (x>y) then GCD (x,y);
    else
    if REM(y,x)=0 then x;
    else GCD(REM(y,x),x);
    endif;
endif;
(REM(y,x) is the remainder formed when y/x is computed.)
```

Write a recursive subroutine to compute the GCD of any two numbers, X and Y, and a main program to receive values for X and Y, and then call GCD. Use the stack for X and Y and return the result in R0.

You will need to use three system MACROs: .RNUM, .PNUM, and used with three arguments NUM, DEM, and RSLT. .REM computes the remainder of NUM/DEM and stores the result in RSLT. Do not use a stack reference or R0 for any of .REM's arguments.

The main program will use .RNUM to read in the values of X and Y from the keyboard, then call GCD. X and Y will be passed to GCD by putting them on the stack before calling it.

1. Assemble the subroutine GCD and the main program separately and use .GLOBL to declare the entry label.
2. Use task builder to link the two parts together.
3. Downline load and execute your program. Use these values for X and Y: 45. and 45., 97. and 12., and 32765. and 293. (all numbers are decimal).
4. Get execution verified and turn in listing.

Problem 12

Write the following macros, doing all I/O directly without interrupts.

READ R where R is a register or label into which a single character read from the keyboard will be placed.

WRITE R where R is a register of label containing a character that will be sent to the terminal.

1. Write, assemble, and test a program that uses the above macros to do the following:
   a. Read the character.
   b. Echo that character (all control characters (1 through 37) should be echoed as ↑ <letter>. For example, 004, or EOT, should be ↑ D.
   c. Halt after receipt and proper echoing of 004.
2. Do not use .EXIT or .PTEXT.
3. Execute your program for a T.A. and turn in a listing.

Problem 13

1. Write a program that
   a. Enables the receiver interrupt and clears two memory locations CTR0, CTR1, which are used as counters. For example, 004, EOT, should be ↑ D.
   b. Adds one to a memory location CTR0.
   c. Whenever a carry occurs on CTR0, clear CTR0, increment CTR1, then go back to b.
2. Write an interrupt service routine which, whenever a keyboard interrupt occurs,
   a. Prints the character typed (as in Problem 12).

      b. Prints CTR1 then CTR0 using .PNUM1.

      c. Does a return from interrupt back to the main program.

  3. Assemble, task build, downline load, and execute.

  4. Receive verification and turn in listings.

Problem 14

You are to write a small terminal handler program. The program will start off by printing HELLO on the terminal. It will then wait to receive input from the keyboard. Your program should echo every character that is typed in. If the input is not a printable character (ASCII codes 0–037), then you should not echo anything.

If the input is a carriage return, then you should stop the current line of echoed characters, go to the next line, print HELLO again, and wait for more input.

If the input is a control Z, then the program should quit the line of echoed characters, go to the next line, print BYE, and then exit to the MCR (using .EXIT).

The main program should:

  1. Initialize interrupt vectors, device status registers, and a double precision counter (an unsigned integer double word).

  2. While waiting for an interrupt from the keyboard, continuously increment the counter until the interrupt occurs.

The keyboard service routine should:

  1. Accept an input and examine it.

      a. If the input is printable, echo it.

      b. If the input is control Z or CR, branch out to the appropriate location.

      c. If not a. or b. do nothing with the input.

  2. Print out the contents of the counter after the BYE is printed out. Print the high-order word first, then the low-order word, using .PNUM1.

Problem 15

  1. Write a macro MYPTX, which will do exactly the same thing as the system .PTEXT.

  2. Using your MYPTX, create a macro MYPNM which will replace the system macro .PNUM. The program written for Problem 7 could be used as a basis for this.

  3. Write a simple program to print several ASCII strings and several numbers, both + and −, to demonstrate these macros.

  4. Turn in an error-free listing and have the T.A. verify operation.

Problem 16

You must write a program that will act as a terminal handler in the LSI-11. It will take input from the terminal and pass it on to the PDP-11/34. At the same time, it will take output from the PDP-11/34 and send it to the terminal. The problem arises from the fact that the communication between the LSI-11 and the PDP-11/34 occurs four times as fast as the communication between the LSI-11 and the terminal. You should create a queue or temporary storage buffer to handle the faster data so that no data are lost.

Your program should consist of three parts: a main program and two interrupt service routines, one for the keyboard input and the other for data from the 11/34. The main program:

1. Looks to see if there are any data in the queue from the 11/34. If so, it outputs a byte using polled I/O to the terminal.
2. If there has been a control S sent to the 11/34 and if the queue is less than 1/8 full, sends a control Q to the 11/34.

The 11/34 input interrupt service routine does the following:

1. Adds the character to the queue.
2. If the queue is more than 7/8 full, sends a control S to the 11/34.

The keyboard interrupt service routine reads the input byte and immediately transmits it to the 11/34, using polled I/O techniques. Assemble, task build, load, and demonstrate the proper operation of your program.

APPENDIXES

Appendix A

Codes for the
ASCII Character Set

The codes for the ASCII character set may appear, in principle, to be straightforward; however, the beginner is often puzzled by the first 32 abbreviated alphabetic symbols, such as NUL, SOH, STX, in the ASCII table. First of all, the meaning of these special symbols is not immediately clear, and most of these symbols cannot be found on the keyboard of a computer terminal. To clarify these points, let us examine the ASCII character set carefully. Note that the ASCII character set is encoded by a 7-bit binary; in other words, there are $2^7 = 128$ possible characters that can be encoded by the 7-bit binary numbers. Of these 128 binary numbers, we need 96 to encode the numbers, upper/lower case alphabet, punctuation, and mathematical symbols. The remaining 32 we then use to encode the control keys that are not printable, which we need for user-machine communication.

It is these 32 control keys that cause a lot of confusion. This is partially due to the fact that most keyboards do not have 128 keys, so some compromise must be made. Logically, the control keys are the candidates for compromise. In general, most keyboards have explicit carriage return keys labeled RETURN, line feed keys labeled LF, and escape keys labeled ESC. However, the rest of the 32 control keys (with some exceptions) are entered by depressing two keys simultaneously. The first of the two keys is normally specifically labeled as CONTROL or CONT'L, ALT or CTL, and the second is a specific alphabetic key, as shown in Table A.1. With two keys depressed simultaneously, there is no problem of generating ASCII codes for each control key not explicitly shown on the keyboard. However, a few of the control keys require depressing three keys simultaneously, as shown in the table.

Before presenting the table, there is one more problem we have to take care of. This is, how do we ECHO the control key being entered by depressing two keys simultaneously on the CRT screen? This is normally done by displaying a circumflex symbol $\wedge$ or an upward arrow $\uparrow$ with whichever alphabetic character was depressed. However, there is a rule to determine which alphabetic character should be chosen. For example, if we wish to enter the control key EOT, then we choose the character having the ASCII code equal to the sum of 100_8 and the ASCII code of EOT. In this case, we have EOT = 004_8, and by adding 100_8 to it we have 104_8. This code happens to belong to the character D. Therefore, if we wish to enter the EOT key through the keyboard, we must depress the CONTROL key and D key simultaneously, and the CPU will receive the EOT code, 004_8. But the system software will send two consecutive ASCII characters, $\wedge$D, to echo what has been depressed at the keyboard on the CRT. For convenience, the ASCII code table is presented in two sections, Tables A.1 and A.2. The former contains the 32 control keys only. In both tables, the first column shows the mnemonic of the ASCII characters; the second, third, and fourth columns show their equivalent binary, 7-bit octal, and Hex numbers. Since the assemblers of most computer systems do recognize those ASCII characters in the first column, it appears logical to name the first column as the ASCII in mnemonic. For binary representation, however, the most significant bit is usually reserved for the parity bit.

TABLE A.1   ASCII CHARACTER SET (Part 1)

ASCII in mnemonic	Binary code				7-bit octal code	Hex code	Keyboard entrance	Remark
NUL	00	00	00	00	000	00	CONT'L/SHIFT/P	Null, tape feed.
SOH	00	00	00	01	001	01	CONT'L/A	Start of heading; also SOM, start of message.
STX	00	00	00	10	002	02	CONT'L/B	Start of text; also EOA, end of address.
ETX	00	00	00	11	003	03	CONT'L/C	End of text; also EOM, end of message.
EOT	00	00	01	00	004	04	CONT'L/D	End of transmission (End); shuts off TWX machines.
ENQ	00	00	01	01	005	05	CONT'L/E	Inquiry (Inqry); also WRU.
ACK	00	00	01	10	006	06	CONT'L/F	Acknowledge; also RU.
BEL	00	00	01	11	007	07	CONT'L/G	Ring the bell.
BS	00	00	10	00	010	08	CONT'L/H	Back space; also FEO format effector.
HT	00	00	10	01	011	09	CONT'L/I	Horizontal tab.
LF	00	00	10	10	012	0A	CONT'L/J	Line feed or line space (New line); advance paper to next line.
VT	00	00	10	11	013	0B	CONT'L/K	Vertical tab (VTAB).
FF	00	00	11	00	014	0C	CONT'L/L	Form feed to top of next page (Page).
CR	00	00	11	01	015	0D	CONT'L/M	Carriage return to beginning line.
SO	00	00	11	10	016	0E	CONT'L/N	Shift out; changes ribbon color to red.
SI	00	00	11	11	017	0F	CONT'L/O	Shift in; changes ribbon color to black.
DLE	00	01	00	00	020	10	CONT'L/P	Data line escape.
DC1	00	01	00	01	021	11	CONT'L/Q	Device control 1, turns transmitter (reader) on.
DC2	00	01	00	10	022	12	CONT'L/R	Device control 2, turns punch or auxiliary on.
DC3	00	01	00	11	023	13	CONT'L/S	Device control 3, turns transmitter (reader) off.
DC4	00	01	01	00	024	14	CONT'L/T	Device control 4, turns punch or auxiliary off.
NAK	00	01	01	01	025	15	CONT'L/U	Negative acknowledge; also ERR, error
SYN	00	01	01	10	026	16	CONT'L/V	Synchronous file (SYNC).
ETB	00	01	01	11	027	17	CONT'L/W	End of transmission block; also LEM, logical end of medium.
CAN	00	01	10	00	030	18	CONT'L/X	Cancel (Cancl).
EM	00	01	10	01	031	19	CONT'L/Y	End of medium.
SUB	00	01	10	10	032	1A	CONT'L/Z	Substitute.
ESC	00	01	10	11	033	1B	CONT'L/SHIFT/K	Escape.
FS	00	01	11	00	034	1C	CONT'L/SHIFT/L	File separator.
GS	00	01	11	01	035	1D	CONT'L/SHIFT/M	Group separator.
RS	00	01	11	10	036	1E	CONT'L/SHIFT/N	Record separator.
US	00	01	11	11	037	1F	CONT'L/SHIFT/O	Unit separator.

TABLE A.2 ASCII CHARACTER SET (Part 2)

ASCII in mnemonic	Binary code				7-bit octal code	Hex code	Remark
SPACE	00	10	00	00	040	20	
!	00	10	00	01	041	21	
``	00	10	00	10	042	22	
#	00	10	00	11	043	23	
$	00	10	01	00	044	24	
%	00	10	01	01	045	25	
&	00	10	01	10	046	26	
'	00	10	01	11	047	27	Apostrophe
(	00	10	10	00	050	28	
)	00	10	10	01	051	29	
*	00	10	10	10	052	2A	
+	00	10	10	11	053	2B	
,	00	10	11	00	054	2C	
−	00	10	11	01	055	2D	Hyphen
.	00	10	11	10	056	2E	
/	00	10	11	11	057	2F	
φ	00	11	00	00	060	30	
1	00	11	00	01	061	31	
2	00	11	00	10	062	32	
3	00	11	00	11	063	33	
4	00	11	01	00	064	34	
5	00	11	01	01	065	35	
6	00	11	01	10	066	36	
7	00	11	01	11	067	37	
8	00	11	10	00	070	38	
9	00	11	10	01	071	39	
:	00	11	10	10	072	3A	
;	00	11	10	11	073	3B	
<	00	11	11	00	074	3C	
=	00	11	11	01	075	3D	
>	00	11	11	10	076	3E	
?	00	11	11	11	077	3F	
@	01	00	00	00	100	40	
A	01	00	00	01	101	41	
B	01	00	00	10	102	42	
C	01	00	00	11	103	43	
D	01	00	01	00	104	44	
E	01	00	01	01	105	45	
F	01	00	01	10	106	46	
G	01	00	01	11	107	47	
H	01	00	10	00	110	48	
I	01	00	10	01	111	49	
J	01	00	10	10	112	4A	
K	01	00	10	11	113	4B	
L	01	00	11	00	114	4C	
M	01	00	11	01	115	4D	
N	01	00	11	10	116	4E	

O	01	00	11	11	117	4F	
P	01	01	00	00	120	50	
Q	01	01	00	01	121	51	
R	01	01	00	10	122	52	
S	01	01	00	11	123	53	
T	01	01	01	00	124	54	
U	01	01	01	01	125	55	
V	01	01	01	10	126	56	
W	01	01	01	11	127	57	
X	01	01	10	00	130	58	
Y	01	01	10	01	131	59	
Z	01	01	10	11	132	5A	
[	01	01	10	11	133	5B	
	01	01	11	00	134	5C	
]	01	01	11	01	135	5D	
∧ or ↑	01	01	11	10	136	5E	
− or ←	01	01	11	11	137	5F	Underline
`	01	10	00	00	140	60	Accent grave
a	01	10	00	01	141	61	
b	01	10	00	10	142	62	
c	01	10	00	11	143	63	
d	01	10	01	00	144	64	
e	01	10	01	01	145	65	
f	01	10	01	10	146	66	
g	01	10	01	11	147	67	
h	01	10	10	00	150	68	
i	01	10	10	01	151	69	
j	01	10	10	10	152	6A	
k	01	10	10	11	153	6B	
l	01	10	11	00	154	6C	
m	01	10	11	01	155	6D	
n	01	10	11	10	156	6E	
o	01	10	11	11	157	6F	
p	01	11	00	00	160	70	
q	01	11	00	01	161	71	
r	01	11	00	10	162	72	
s	01	11	00	11	163	73	
t	01	11	01	00	164	74	
u	01	11	01	01	165	75	
v	01	11	01	10	166	76	
w	01	11	01	11	167	77	
x	01	11	10	00	170	78	
y	01	11	10	01	171	79	
z	01	11	10	10	172	7A	
{	01	11	10	11	173	7B	
|	01	11	11	00	174	7C	
}	01	11	11	01	175	7D	Alt mode
~	01	11	11	10	176	7E	
DEL	01	11	11	11	177	7F	Delete, rub out

PDP-11 Mnemonic Instruction Index and Instruction Set

Page

A
ADC(B) 299
ADD 304
ASL(B) 295
ASR(B) 294

B
BCC 312
BCS 313
BEQ 310
BGE 314
BGT 315
BHI 316
BHIS 317
BIC(B) 306
BIS(B) 307
BIT(B) 305
BLT 314
BLE 315
BLO 317
BLOS 316
BMI 311
BNE 310
BPL 311
BPT 326
BR 309

Page

BVC 312
BVS 312

C
CLR(B) 290
CMP(B) 303
COM(B) 291

D
DEC(B) 292
DIV .... *

E
EMT 324

F
FADD .... *
FDIV .... *
FMUL .... *
FSUB .... *

H
HALT 330

I
INC(B) 291
IOT 326

J
JMP 318
JSR 319

*Not available for LSI-11

M

MARK 322
MFPS 301
MOV(B) 302
MTPS 301
MUL .... *

N

NEG(B) 292
NOP ....

R

RESET 331
ROL(B) 296
ROR(B) 295
RTI 327
RTS 321
RTT 327

S

SBC(B) 299
SOB 323
SUB 304
SWAB 297
SXT 300

T

TRAP 325
TST(B) 293

W

WAIT 330

X

XOR 308

PDP-11 INSTRUCTION SET

B.1   INTRODUCTION

The specification for each instruction includes the mnemonic, octal code, binary code, a diagram showing the format of the instruction, a symbolic notation describing its execution and the effect on the condition codes, a description, special comments, and examples.

MNEMONIC: This is indicated at the top corner of each page. When the word instruction has a byte equivalent, the byte mnemonic is also shown.

INSTRUCTION FORMAT: A diagram accompanying each instruction shows the octal op code, the binary op code, and bit assignments. (Note that in byte instructions the most significant bit (bit 15) is always a 1.)

SYMBOLS:

    ( ) = contents of

    SS or src = source address

    DD or dst = destination address

    loc = location

    ← = becomes

    ↑ = "is popped from stack"

    ↓ = "is pushed onto stack"

    ∧ = boolean AND

    v = boolean OR

    ⩝ = exclusive OR

    ~ = boolean not

    Reg or R = register

    B = Byte

$$\blacksquare = \begin{cases} 0 \text{ for word} \\ 1 \text{ for byte} \end{cases}$$

    , = concatenated

B.2 INSTRUCTION FORMATS

The following formats include all instructions used in the LSI-11. Refer to individual instructions for more detailed information.

1. Single Operand Group (CLR, CLRB, COM, COMB, INC, INCB, DEC, DECB, NEG, NEGB, ADC, ADCB, SBC, SBCB, TST, TSTB, ROR, RORB, ROL, ROLB, ASR, ASRB, ASL, ASLB, JMP, SWAB, MFPS, MTPS, SXT, XOR)

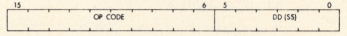

2. Double Operand Group (BIT, BITB, BIC, BICB, BIS, BISB, ADD, SUB, MOV, MOVB, CMP, CMPB)

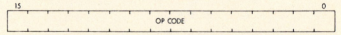

3. Program Control Group
   a. Branch (all branch instructions)

   b. Jump To Subroutine (JSR)

   c. Subroutine Return (RTS)

   d. Traps (break point, IOT, EMT, TRAP, BPT)

   e. Mark (MARK)

   f. Subtract I and branch (if = 0)(SOB)

4. Operate Group (HALT, WAIT, RTI, RESET, RTT, NOP)

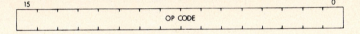

5. Condition Code Operators (all condition code instructions)

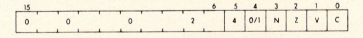

6. Fixed and Floating Point Arithmetic (optional EIS/FIS) (FADD, FSUB, FMUL, FDIV, MUL, DIV, ASH, ASHC)

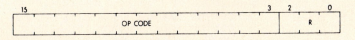

Byte Instructions

The LSI-11 includes a full complement of instructions that manipulate byte operands. Since all LSI-11 addressing is byte-oriented, byte manipulation addressing is straightforward. Byte instructions with autoincrement or autodecrement direct addressing cause the specified register to be modified by one to point to the next byte of data. Byte operations in register mode access the low-order byte of the specified register. These provisions enable the LSI-11 to perform as either a word or byte processor. The numbering scheme for word and byte addresses in memory is:

HIGH BYTE ADDRESS			WORD OR BYTE ADDRESS
002001	BYTE 1	BYTE 0	002000
002003	BYTE 3	BYTE 2	002002

The most significant bit (Bit 15) of the instruction word is set to indicate a byte instruction.

Example:

Symbolic	Octal	
CLR	0050DD	Clear Word
CLRB	1050DD	Clear Byte

B.3 LIST OF INSTRUCTIONS

The LSI-11 instruction set is shown in the following sequence.

SINGLE OPERAND

Mnemonic	Instruction	Op Code
General		
CLR(B)	clear dst	■050DD
COM(B)	complement dst	■051DD
INC(B)	increment dst	■052DD
DEC(B)	decrement dst	■053DD
NEG(B)	negate dst	■054DD
TST(B)	test dst	■057DD
Shift & Rotate		
ASR(B)	arithmetic shift right	■062DD
ASL(B)	arithmetic shift left	■063DD
ROR(B)	rotate right	■060DD
ROL(B)	rotate left	■061DD
SWAB	swap bytes	0003DD
Multiple Precision		
ADC(B)	add carry	■055DD
SBC(B)	subtract carry	■056DD
SXT	sign extend	0067DD
PS WORD OPERATORS		
MFPS	move byte from PS	1067DD
MTPS	move byte to PS	1064SS

DOUBLE OPERAND

Mnemonic	Instruction	Op Code
General		
MOV(B)	move source to destination	■1SSDD
CMP(B)	compare src to dst	■2SSDD
ADD	add src to dst	06SSDD
SUB	subtract src from dst	16SSDD
Logical		
BIT(B)	bit test	■3SSDD
BIC(B)	bit clear	■4SSDD
BIS(B)	bit set	■5SSDD
XOR	exclusive or	074RDD

PROGRAM CONTROL

Mnemonic	Instruction	Op Code or Base Code

Branch

BR	branch (unconditional)	000400
BNE	branch if not equal (to zero)	001000
BEQ	branch if equal (to zero)	001400
BPL	branch if plus	100000
BMI	branch if minus	100400
BVC	branch if overflow is clear	102000
BVS	branch if overflow is set	102400
BCC	branch if carry is clear	103000
BCS	branch if carry is set	103400

Signed Conditional Branch

BGE	branch is greater than or equal (to zero)	002000
BLT	branch if less than (zero)	002400
BGT	branch if greater than (zero)	003000
BLE	branch if less than or equal (to zero)	003400

Unsigned Conditional Branch

BHI	branch if higher	101000
BLOS	branch if lower or same	101400
BHIS	branch if higher or same	103000
BLO	branch if lower	103400

Jump & Subroutine

JMP	jump	0001DD
JSR	jump to subroutine	004RDD
RTS	return from subroutine	00020R
MARK	mark	006400
SOB	subtract one and branch (if $\neq$ 0)	077R00

Trap & Interrupt

EMT	emulator trap	104000—104377
TRAP	trap	104400—104777
BPT	breakpoint trap	000003
IOT	input/output trap	000004
RTI	return from interrupt	000002
RTT	return from interrupt	000006

MISCELLANEOUS

HALT	halt	000000
WAIT	wait for interrupt	000001
RESET	reset external bus	000005

RESERVED INSTRUCTIONS

		00021R
		00022

CONDITION CODE OPERATORS

CLC	clear C	....	000241
CLV	clear V	....	000242
CLZ	clear Z	....	000244
CLN	clear N	....	000250
CCC	clear all CC bits	....	000257
SEC	set C	....	000261
SEV	set V	....	000262
SEZ	set Z	....	000264
SEN	set N	....	000270
SCC	set all CC bits	....	000277
NOP	no operation	....	00240

B.4 SINGLE OPERAND INSTRUCTIONS

General

CLR
CLRB

clear destination   ■050DD

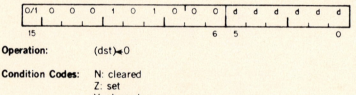

Operation:	(dst)◄0		
Condition Codes:	N: cleared		
	Z: set		
	V: cleared		
	C: cleared		
Description:	Word: Contents of specified destination are replaced with ze-roes.		
	Byte: Same		
Example:		CLR R1	

Before	After
(R1) = 177777	(R1) = 000000
N Z V C	N Z V C
1 1 1 1	0 1 0 0

NOTE

CLR and CLRB perform a DATIO bus cycle as the last bus cycle during the instruction execution. The DATI portion of the DATIO cycle is a "don't care" condition, but the addressed memory or device must be capable of responding to the DATI cycle to avoid a bus timeout error.

COM
COMB

complement dst

■051DD

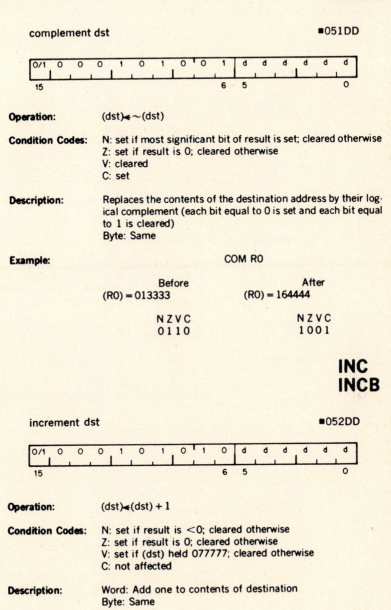

| 0/1 | 0 | 0 | 0 | 1 | 0 | 1 | 0 | 0 | 1 | d | d | d | d | d | d |

15   6 5   0

Operation: (dst)◄ ~(dst)

Condition Codes: N: set if most significant bit of result is set; cleared otherwise
Z: set if result is 0; cleared otherwise
V: cleared
C: set

Description: Replaces the contents of the destination address by their logical complement (each bit equal to 0 is set and each bit equal
to 1 is cleared)
Byte: Same

Example: COM R0

	Before		After
(R0) = 013333		(R0) = 164444	

N Z V C   N Z V C
0 1 1 0   1 0 0 1

INC
INCB

increment dst

■052DD

| 0/1 | 0 | 0 | 0 | 1 | 0 | 1 | 0 | 1 | 0 | d | d | d | d | d | d |

15   6 5   0

Operation: (dst)◄(dst) + 1

Condition Codes: N: set if result is <0; cleared otherwise
Z: set if result is 0; cleared otherwise
V: set if (dst) held 077777; cleared otherwise
C: not affected

Description: Word: Add one to contents of destination
Byte: Same

Example: INC R2

                                    Before   After
                               (R2) = 000333   (R2) = 000334

                                  N Z V C   N Z V C
                                  0 0 0 0   0 0 0 0

DEC
DECB

decrement dst   ■053DD

0/1	0	0	0	1	0	1	0	1	1	d	d	d	d	d	d
15									6	5					0

Operation: (dst)←(dst)−1

Condition Codes: N: set if result is <0; cleared otherwise
                        Z: set if result is 0; cleared otherwise
                        V: set if (dst) was 100000; cleared otherwise
                        C: not affected

Description: Word: Subtract 1 from the contents of the destination
                        Byte: Same

Example: DEC R5

                                    Before   After
                               (R5) = 000001   (R5) = 000000

                                  N Z V C   N Z V C
                                  1 0 0 0   0 1 0 0

NEG
NEGB

negate dst   ■054DD

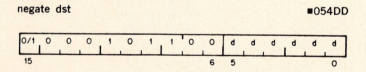

0/1	0	0	0	1	0	1	1	0	0	d	d	d	d	d	d
15									6	5					0

Operation: (dst) ← –(dst)

Condition Codes: N: set if the result is <0; cleared otherwise
Z: set if result is 0; cleared otherwise
V: set if the result is 100000; cleared otherwise
C: cleared if the result is 0; set otherwise

Description: Word: Replaces the contents of the destination address by its
two's complement. Note that 100000 is replaced by itself ·(in
two's complement notation the most negative number has
no positive counterpart).
Byte: Same

Example: NEG R0

Before	After
(R0) = 000010	(R0) = 177770
N Z V C	N Z V C
0 0 0 0	1 0 0 1

TST
TSTB

test dst   ■057DD

0/1	0	0	0	1	0	1	1	1	1	d	d	d	d	d	d
15								6	5						0

Operation: (dst) ← (dst)

Condition Codes: N: set if the result is <0; cleared otherwise
Z: set if result is 0; cleared otherwise
V: cleared
C: cleared

Description: Word: Sets the condition codes N and Z according to
the contents of the destination address, contents of
dst remains unmodified
Byte: Same

Example: TST R1

Before	After
(R1) = 012340	(R1) = 012340
N Z V C	N Z V C
0 0 1 1	0 0 0 0

Shifts

Scaling data by factors of two is accomplished by the shift instructions:

ASR · Arithmetic shift right

ASL · Arithmetic shift left

The sign bit (bit 15) of the operand is reproduced in shifts to the right. The low order bit is filled with 0 in shifts to the left. Bits shifted out of the C bit, as shown in the following examples, are lost.

Rotates

The rotate instructions operate on the destination word and the C bit as though they formed a 17-bit "circular buffer." These instructions facilitate sequential bit testing and detailed bit manipulation.

ASR
ASRB

arithmetic shift right   ■062DD

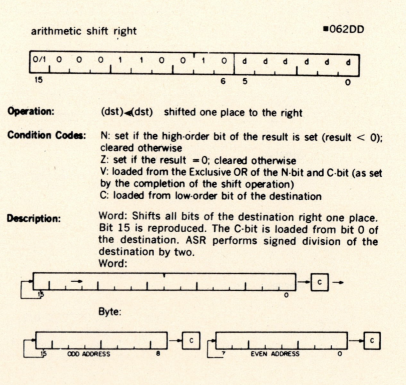

Operation:	(dst)◄(dst) shifted one place to the right
Condition Codes:	N: set if the high-order bit of the result is set (result < 0); cleared otherwise
	Z: set if the result = 0; cleared otherwise
	V: loaded from the Exclusive OR of the N-bit and C-bit (as set by the completion of the shift operation)
	C: loaded from low-order bit of the destination
Description:	Word: Shifts all bits of the destination right one place. Bit 15 is reproduced. The C-bit is loaded from bit 0 of the destination. ASR performs signed division of the destination by two.

ASL
ASLB

arithmetic shift left ■063DD

Operation: (dst)◄(dst) shifted one place to the left

Condition Codes: N: set if high-order bit of the result is set (result < 0); cleared otherwise
Z: set if the result = 0; cleared otherwise
V: loaded with the exclusive OR of the N-bit and C-bit (as set by the completion of the shift operation)
C: loaded with the high-order bit of the destination

Description: Word: Shifts all bits of the destination left one place. Bit 0 is loaded with an 0. The C-bit of the status word is loaded from the most significant bit of the destination. ASL performs a signed multiplication of the destination by 2 with overflow indication.
Word:

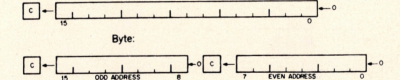

Byte:

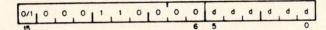

ROR
RORB

rotate right ■060DD

Operation: (dst) ← (dst)
rotate right one place

Condition Codes: N: set if the high-order bit of the result is set (result < 0); cleared otherwise
Z: set if all bits of result = 0; cleared otherwise
V: loaded with the Exclusive OR of the N-bit and C-bit (as set by the completion of the rotate operation)
C: loaded with the low-order bit of the destination

Description: Rotates all bits of the destination right one place. Bit 0 is loaded into the C-bit and the previous contents of the C-bit are loaded into bit 15 of the destination.
Byte: Same

Example:

Word:

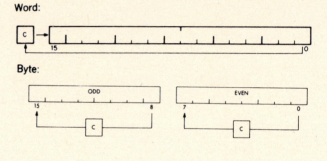

Byte:

ROL
ROLB

rotate left   ■061DD

0/1	0	0	0	1	1	0	0	0	1	d	d	d	d	d	d
15									6	5					0

Operation: (dst) ← (dst)
rotate left one place

Condition Codes: N: set if the high-order bit of the result word is set (result < 0): cleared otherwise
Z: set if all bits of the result word = 0; cleared otherwise
V: loaded with the Exclusive OR of the N-bit and C-bit (as set by the completion of the rotate operation)
C: loaded with the high-order bit of the destination

Description: Word: Rotate all bits of the destination left one place. Bit 15 is loaded into the C-bit of the status word and the previous contents of the C-bit are loaded into Bit 0 of the destination.
Byte: Same

Example:

Word:

Bytes:

SWAB

swap bytes   0003DD

0	0	0	0	0	0	0	0	1	1	d	d	d	d	d	d

15   6 5   0

Operation: Byte 1/Byte 0 ◄ Byte 0/Byte 1

Condition Codes: N: set if high-order bit of low-order byte (bit 7) of result is set;
                      cleared otherwise
                      Z: set if low-order byte of result = 0; cleared otherwise
                      V: cleared
                      C: cleared

Description: Exchanges high-order byte and low-order byte of the destina-
                      tion word (destination must be a word address).

Example: SWAB R1

	Before		After
(R1) = 077777		(R1) = 177577	

N Z V C	N Z V C
1 1 1 1	0 0 0 0

Multiple Precision

It is sometimes necessary to do arithmetic on operands considered as multiple words or bytes. The LSI-11 makes special provision for such operations with the instructions ADC (Add Carry) and SBC (Subtract Carry) and their byte equivalents.

For example two 16-bit words may be combined into a 32-bit double precision word and added or subtracted as shown below:

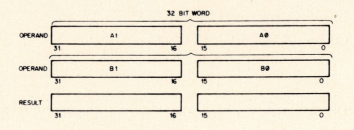

Example:

The addition of –1 and –1 could be performed as follows:

$$-1 = 37777777777$$

$$(R1) = 177777 \quad (R2) = 177777 \quad (R3) = 177777 \quad (R4) = 177777$$

```
ADD   R1,R2
ADC   R3
ADD   R4,R3
```

1. After (R1) and (R2) are added, 1 is loaded into the C bit

2. ADC instruction adds C bit to (R3); (R3) = 0

3. (R3) and (R4) are added

4. Result is 37777777776 or –2

ADC
ADCB

add carry   ■055DD

0/1	0	0	0	1	0	1	1	0	1	d	d	d	d	d	d

15   6 5   0

Operation: (dst) ← (dst) + (C bit)

Condition Codes: N: set if result <0; cleared otherwise
                      Z: set if result = 0; cleared otherwise
                      V: set if (dst) was 077777 and (C) was 1; cleared otherwise
                      C: set if (dst) was 177777 and (C) was 1; cleared otherwise

Description: Adds the contents of the C-bit into the destination. This per-
                     mits the carry from the addition of the low-order words to be
                     carried into the high-order result.
                     Byte: Same

Example: Double precision addition may be done with the following in-
                     struction sequence:
                     ADD   A0,B0   ; add low-order parts
                     ADC   B1   ; add carry into high-order
                     ADD   A1,B1   ; add high order parts

SBC
SBCB

subtract carry   ■056DD

0/1	0	0	0	1	0	1	1	1	0	d	d	d	d	d	d

15   6 5   0

Operation: (dst)←(dst)–(C)

Condition Codes: N: set if result <0; cleared otherwise
                      Z: set if result 0; cleared otherwise
                      V: set if (dst) was 100000; cleared otherwise
                      C: set if (dst) was 0 and C was 1; cleared otherwise

Description: Word: Subtracts the contents of the C-bit from the destination. This permits the carry from the subtraction of two low-
order words to be subtracted from the high order part of the
result.
Byte: Same

Example: Double precision subtraction is done by:

SUB   A0,B0
SBC   B1
SUB   A1,B1

SXT

sign extend   0067DD

```
| 0  0  0  0  1  1  0  1  1  1 | d  d  d  d  d  d |
  15                        6  5              0
```

Operation: (dst) ◄   0 if N-bit is clear
(dst) ◄ - 1 N-bit is set

Condition Codes: N: unaffected
Z: set if N-bit clear
V: cleared
C: unaffected

Description: If the condition code bit N is set then a –1 is placed in the
destination operand: if N bit is clear, then a 0 is placed in the
destination operand. This instruction is particularly useful in
multiple precision arithmetic because it permits the sign to
be extended through multiple words.

Example: SXT **A**

Before	After
(**A**) = 012345	(**A**) = 177777
N Z V C	N Z V C
1 0 0 0	1 0 0 0

B.5 PS WORD OPERATORS

MFPS

Move byte From Processor Status word   1067DD

```
| 1   0   0   0   1   1   0   1 | 1   1   d   d   d   d   d   d |
```

Operation: (dst) ← PSW
                      dst lower 8 bits

**Condition Code
Bits:**   N = set if PSW bit 7 = 1; cleared otherwise
                      Z = set if PS <0:7> = 0; cleared otherwise
                      V = cleared
                      C = not affected

Description: The 8 bit contents of the PS are moved to the effec-
                      tive destination. If destination is mode 0, PS bit 7 is
                      sign extended through upper byte of the register. The
                      destination operand address is treated as a byte ad-
                      dress.

Example: MFPS R0

        before   after

     R0 [0]   R0 [000014]
     PS [000014]   PS [000000]

MTPS

Move byte To Processor Status word   1064SS

```
| 1   0   0   0   1   1   0   1 | 0   0   s   s   s   s   s   s |
```

Operation: PSW ← (SRC)

Condition Codes: Set accoring to effective SRC operand bits 0-3

Description: The 8 bits of the effective operand replaces the cur-
                      rent contents of the PSW. The source operand address
                      is treated as a byte address.
                      Note that the T bit (PSW bit 4) cannot be set with this
                      instruction. The SRC operand remains unchanged.
                      This instruction can be used to change the priority bit
                      (PSW bit 7) in the PSW

ADD

add src to dst   06SSDD

0	1	1	0	s	s	s	s	s	s	d	d	d	d	d	d
15			12	11					6	5					0

Operation: (dst) ← (src) + (dst)

Condition Codes: N: set if result <0; cleared otherwise
Z: set if result = 0; cleared otherwise
V: set if there was arithmetic overflow as a result of
the operation; that is both operands were of the same
sign and the result was of the opposite sign; cleared
otherwise
C: set if there was a carry from the most significant bit
of the result; cleared otherwise

Description: Adds the source operand to the destination operand
and stores the result at the destination address. The
original contents of the destination are lost. The contents of the source are not affected. Two's complement addition is performed.
Note: There is no equivalent byte mode.

Examples: Add to register: ADD   20,RO

Add to memory: ADD   R1,XXX

Add register to register: ADD   R1,R2

Add memory to memory: ADD@ # 17750,XXX

XXX is a programmer-defined mnemonic for a memory
location.

SUB

subtract src from dst   16SSDD

1	1	1	0	s	s	s	s	s	s	d	d	d	d	d	d
15			12	11					6	5					0

Operation: (dst) ← (dst) − (src)

Condition Codes: N: set if result <0; cleared otherwise
Z: set if result = 0; cleared otherwise
V: set if there was arithmetic overflow as a result of the operation, that is if operands were of opposite signs and the sign
of the source was the same as the sign of the result; cleared
otherwise
C: cleared if there was a carry from the most significant bit of
the result; set otherwise

Description: Subtracts the source operand from the destination operand
and leaves the result at the destination address. The orignial
contents of the destination are lost. The contents of the
source are not affected. In double-precision arithmetic the C-
bit, when set, indicates a "borrow"

Example: SUB R1,R2

	Before		After
(R1) =	011111	(R1) =	011111
(R2) =	012345	(R2) =	001234

	N Z V C		N Z V C
	1 1 1 1		0 0 0 0

Logical
These instructions have the same format as the double operand arithmetic group.
They permit operations on data at the bit level.

BIT
BITB

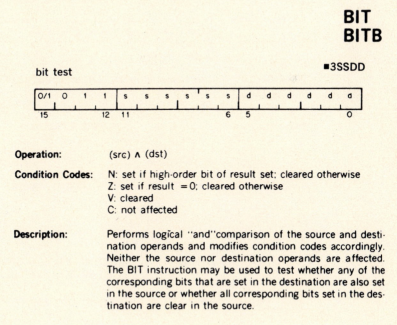

bit test   ■3SSDD

Operation: (src) ∧ (dst)

Condition Codes: N: set if high-order bit of result set; cleared otherwise
Z: set if result = 0; cleared otherwise
V: cleared
C: not affected

Description: Performs logical "and" comparison of the source and destination operands and modifies condition codes accordingly.
Neither the source nor destination operands are affected.
The BIT instruction may be used to test whether any of the
corresponding bits that are set in the destination are also set
in the source or whether all corresponding bits set in the destination are clear in the source.

Example: BIT   ≠ 30.R3   test bits 3 and 4 of R3 to see
                                                if both are off

R3 = 0 000 000 000 011 000

Before   After
NZVC   NZVC
1111   0001

BIC
BICB

bit clear   ■4SSDD

0/1	1	0	0	s	s	s	s	s	s	d	d	d	d	d	d
15		12	11						6	5					0

Operation: $(dst) \leftarrow \sim (src) \wedge (dst)$

Condition Codes: N: set if high order bit of result set; cleared otherwise
                        Z: set if result = 0; cleared otherwise
                        V: cleared
                        C: not affected

Description: Clears each bit in the destination that corresponds to a set
                       bit in the source. The original contents of the destination are
                       lost. The contents of the source are unaffected.

Example: BIC R3,R4

                        Before   After
            (R3) = 001234   (R3) = 001234

            (R4) = 001111   (R4) = 000101

                     N Z V C   N Z V C
                     1 1 1 1   0 0 0 1

Before: (R3)=0 000 001 010 011 100
                      (R4)=0 000 001 001 001 001

After: (R4)=0 000 000 001 000 001

BIS
BISB

bit set   ■5SSDD

```
| 0/1 | 1 | 0 | 1 | s | s | s | s | s | s | d | d | d | d | d | d |
  15          12  11                    6   5                      0
```

Operation: (dst)◄(src) v (dst)

Condition Codes: N: set if high-order bit of result set, cleared otherwise
                       Z: set if result = 0; cleared otherwise
                       V: cleared
                       C: not affected

Description: Performs "Inclusive OR" operation between the source and
                       destination operands and leaves the result at the destination
                       address; that is, corresponding bits set in the source are set
                       in the destination. The contents of the destination are lost.

Example: BIS R0,R1

              Before   After
(R0) = 001234   (R0) = 001234
(R1) = 001111   (R1) = 001335

         N Z V C   N Z V C
         0 0 0 0   0 0 0 0

Before: (R0)=0 000 001 010 011 100
                       (R1)=0 000 001 001 001 001

After: (R1)=0 000 001 011 011 101

XOR

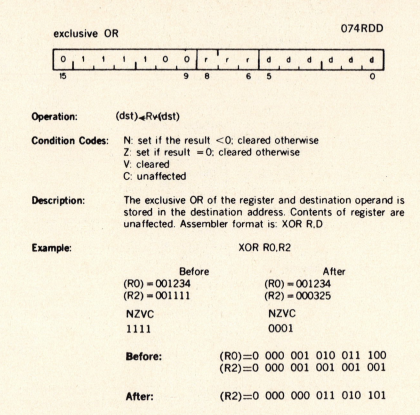

exclusive OR   074RDD

Operation: (dst)←Rv(dst)

Condition Codes: N: set if the result <0; cleared otherwise
                     Z: set if result = 0; cleared otherwise
                     V: cleared
                     C: unaffected

Description: The exclusive OR of the register and destination operand is
                     stored in the destination address. Contents of register are
                     unaffected. Assembler format is: XOR R,D

Example: XOR R0,R2

                     Before   After
          (R0) = 001234   (R0) = 001234
          (R2) = 001111   (R2) = 000325

          NZVC   NZVC
          1111   0001

          Before: (R0)=0 000 001 010 011 100
                          (R2)=0 000 001 001 001 001

          After: (R2)=0 000 000 011 010 101

B.7 PROGRAM CONTROL INSTRUCTIONS

Branches

These instructions cause a branch to a location defined by the sum of
the offset (multiplied by 2) and the current contents of the Program
Counter if:

   a) the branch instruction is unconditional

   b) it is conditional and the conditions are met after testing the condition codes (NZVC)

The offset is the number of words from the current contents of the PC
forward or backward. Note that the current contents of the PC point to
the word following the branch instruction.

Although the offset expresses a byte address the PC is expressed in
words. The offset is automatically multiplied by two and sign extended to
express words before it is added to the PC. Bit 7 is the sign of the offset.

If it is set, the offset is negative and the branch is done in the backward direction. Similarly if it is not set, the offset is positive and the branch is done in the forward direction.

The 8-bit offset allows branching in the backward direction by 200_8 words (400 bytes) from the current PC, and in the forward direction by 177_8 words (376 bytes) from the current PC.

The PDP-11 assembler handles address arithmetic for the user and computes and assembles the proper offset field for branch instructions in the form:

$$Bxx \quad loc$$

Where "Bxx" is the branch instruction and "loc" is the address to which the branch is to be made. The assembler gives an error indication in the instruction if the permissible branch range is exceeded. Branch instructions have no effect on condition codes. Conditional branch instructions where the branch condition is not met, are treated as NO OP's.

BR

branch (unconditional)   000400 Plus offset

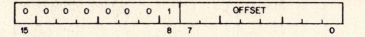

							OFFSET			
0	0	0	0	0	0	0	1				
15						8	7				0

Operation: PC ← PC + (2 x offset)

Condition Codes: Unaffected

Description: Provides a way of transferring program control within a range of -128_{10} to $+127_{10}$ words with a one word instruction.

New PC address = updated PC + (2 X offset)

Updated PC = address of branch instruction + 2

Example: With the Branch instruction at location 500, the following offsets apply.

New PC Address	Offset Code	Offset (decimal)
474	375	−3
476	376	−2
500	377	−1
502	000	0
504	001	+1
506	002	+2

BNE

branch if not equal (to zero)   001000 Plus offset

0	0	0	0	0	0	1	0	OFFSET
15						8	7	0

Operation: $PC \leftarrow PC + (2 \times \text{offset})$ if $Z = 0$

Condition Codes: Unaffected

Description: Tests the state of the Z-bit and causes a branch if the Z-bit is clear. BNE is the complementary operation to BEQ. It is used to test inequality following a CMP, to test that some bits set in the destination were also in the source, following a BIT operation, and generally, to test that the result of the previous operation was not zero.

Example:

| CMP | A,B | ; compare A and B |
| BNE | C | ; branch if they are not equal |

will branch to C if $A \neq B$

and the sequence

| ADD | A,B | ; add A to B |
| BNE | C | ; Branch if the result is not equal to 0 |

will branch to C if $A + B \neq 0$

BEQ

branch if equal (to zero)   001400 Plus offset

0	0	0	0	0	0	1	1	OFFSET
15						8	7	0

Operation: $PC \leftarrow PC + (2 \times \text{offset})$ if $Z = 1$

Condition Codes: Unaffected

Description: Tests the state of the Z-bit and causes a branch if Z is set. As an example, it is used to test equality following a CMP operation, to test that no bits set in the destination were also set in the source following a BIT operation, and generally, to test that the result of the previous operation was zero.

Example:

| CMP | A,B | ; compare A and B |
| BEQ | C | ; branch if they are equal |

will branch to C if A = B $(A - B = 0)$
and the sequence

| ADD | A,B | ; add A to B |
| BEQ | C | ; branch if the result = 0 |

will branch to C if A + B = 0.

BPL

branch if plus   100000 Plus offset

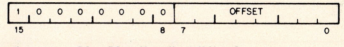

Operation: PC ← PC + (2 x offset) if N = 0

Condition Codes: Unaffected

Description: Tests the state of the N-bit and causes a branch if N is clear, (positive result). BPL is the complementary operation of BMI.

BMI

branch if minus   100400 Plus offset

1	0	0	0	0	0	0	1	OFFSET
15						8	7	0

Operation: PC ← PC + (2 x offset) if N = 1

Condition Codes: Unaffected

Description: Tests the state of the N-bit and causes a branch if N is set. It is used to test the sign (most significant bit) of the result of the previous operation), branching if negative. BMI is the complementary function of BPL.

BVC

branch if overflow is clear   102000 Plus offset

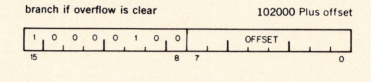

Operation:	PC ← PC + (2 x offset) if V = 0
Condition Codes:	Unaffected
Description:	Tests the state of the V-bit and causes a branch if the V bit is clear. BVC is complementary operation to BVS.

BVS

branch if overflow is set   102400 Plus offset

Operation:	PC ← PC + (2 x offset) if V = 1
Condition Codes:	Unaffected
Description:	Tests the state of V-bit (overflow) and causes a branch if the V bit is set. BVS is used to detect arithmetic overflow in the previous operation.

BCC

branch if carry is clear   103000 Plus offset

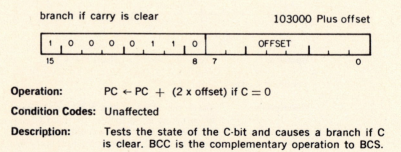

Operation:	PC ← PC + (2 x offset) if C = 0
Condition Codes:	Unaffected
Description:	Tests the state of the C-bit and causes a branch if C is clear. BCC is the complementary operation to BCS.

BCS

branch if carry is set   103400 Plus offset

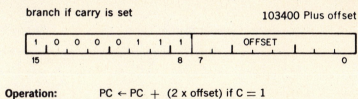

1	0	0	0	0	1	1	1	OFFSET

15   8 7   0

Operation: $PC \leftarrow PC + (2 \times \text{offset})$ if $C = 1$

Condition Codes: Unaffected

Description: Tests the state of the C-bit and causes a branch if C is set. It is used to test for a carry in the result of a previous operation.

Signed Conditional Branches

Particular combinations of the condition code bits are tested with the signed conditional branches. These instructions are used to test the results of instructions in which the operands were considered as signed (two's complement) values.

Note that the sense of signed comparisons differs from that of unsigned comparisons in that in signed 16-bit, two's complement arithmetic the sequence of values is as follows:

largest	077777
	077776
positive	.
	.
	.
	000001
	000000
	177777
	177776
	.
negative	.
	.
	100001
smallest	100000

whereas in unsigned 16-bit arithmetic the sequence is considered to be

highest	177777
	.
	.
	.
	.
	.
	000002
	000001
lowest	000000

BGE

branch if greater than or equal   002000 Plus offset
  (to zero)

0	0	0	0	0	1	0	0	OFFSET			
15							8	7			0

Operation: PC ◄ PC + (2 x offset) if N ∀ V = 0

Condition Codes: Unaffected

Description: Causes a branch if N and V are either both clear or both set.
                      BGE is the complementary operation to BLT. Thus BGE will
                      always cause a branch when it follows an operation that
                      caused addition of two positive numbers. BGE will also cause
                      a branch on a zero result.

BLT

branch if less than (zero)   002400 Plus offset

0	0	0	0	0	1	0	1	OFFSET			
15							8	7			0

Operation: PC ◄ PC + (2 x offset) if N ∀ V = 1

Condition Codes: Unaffected

Description: Causes a branch if the "Exclusive Or" of the N and V bits are
                      1. Thus BLT will always branch following an operation that
                      added two negative numbers, even if overflow occurred.
                      In particular, BLT will always cause a branch if it follows a
                      CMP instruction operating on a negative source and a posi-
                      tive destination (even if overflow occurred). Further, BLT will
                      never cause a branch when it follows a CMP instruction oper-
                      ating on a positive source and negative destination. BLT will
                      not cause a branch if the result of the previous operation was
                      zero (without overflow).

BGT

branch if greater than (zero)   003000 Plus offset

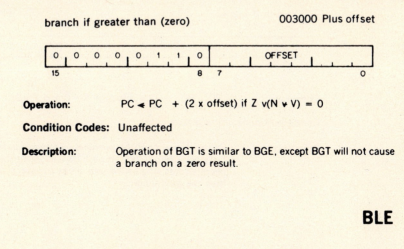

0	0	0	0	0	1	1	0	OFFSET
15							8	7 0

Operation: PC ← PC + (2 x offset) if Z v(N ∀ V) = 0

Condition Codes: Unaffected

Description: Operation of BGT is similar to BGE, except BGT will not cause a branch on a zero result.

BLE

branch if less than or equal (to zero)   003400 Plus offset

0	0	0	0	0	1	1	1	OFFSET
15							8	7 0

Operation: PC ← PC + (2 x offset) if Z v(N ∀ V) = 1

Condition Codes: Unaffected

Description: Operation is similar to BLT but in addition will cause a branch if the result of the previous operation was zero.

Unsigned Conditional Branches
The Unsigned Conditional Branches provide a means for testing the result of comparison operations in which the operands are considered as unsigned values.

BHI

branch if higher   101000 Plus offset

1	0	0	0	0	0	1	0	OFFSET
15						8	7	0

Operation: PC ◄ PC + (2 x offset) if C = 0 and Z = 0

Condition Codes: Unaffected

Description: Causes a branch if the previous operation caused neither a
carry nor a zero result. This will happen in comparison (CMP)
operations as long as the source has a higher unsigned value
than the destination.

BLOS

branch if lower or same   101400 Plus offset

1	0	0	0	0	0	1	1	OFFSET
15						8	7	0

Operation: PC ◄ PC + (2 x offset) if C v Z = 1

Condition Codes: Unaffected

Description: Causes a branch if the previous operation caused either a
carry or a zero result. BLOS is the complementary operation
to BHI. The branch will occur in comparison operations as
long as the source is equal to, or has a lower unsigned value
than the destination.

BHIS

branch if higher or same   103000 Plus offset

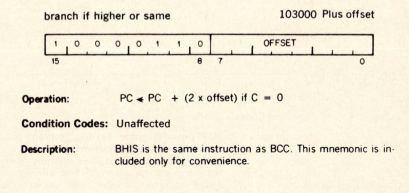

Operation: PC ← PC + (2 x offset) if C = 0

Condition Codes: Unaffected

Description: BHIS is the same instruction as BCC. This mnemonic is included only for convenience.

BLO

branch if lower   103400 Plus offset

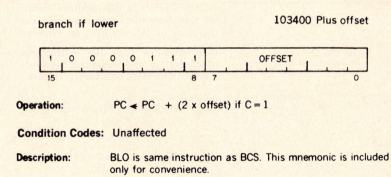

Operation: PC ← PC + (2 x offset) if C = 1

Condition Codes: Unaffected

Description: BLO is same instruction as BCS. This mnemonic is included
only for convenience.

JSR PC, dst is a special case of the PDP-11 subroutine call suitable for subroutine calls that transmit parameters through the general registers. The SP and the PC are the only registers that may be modified by this call.

Another special case of the JSR instruction is JSR PC, @(SP)+ which exchanges the top element of the processor stack and the contents of the program counter. Use of this instruction allows two routines to swap program control and resume operation when recalled where they left off. Such routines are called "co-routines."

Return from a subroutine is done by the RTS instruction. RTS reg loads the contents of reg into the PC and pops the top element of the processor stack into the specified register.

Example: JSR R5, SBR

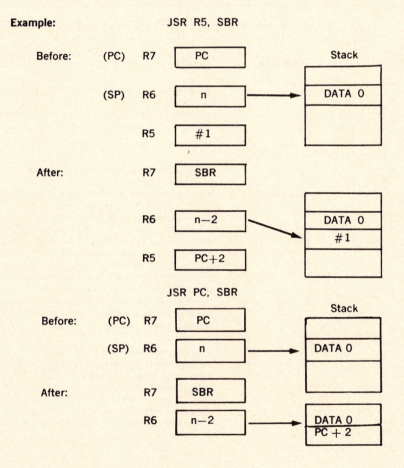

RTS

return from subroutine   00020R

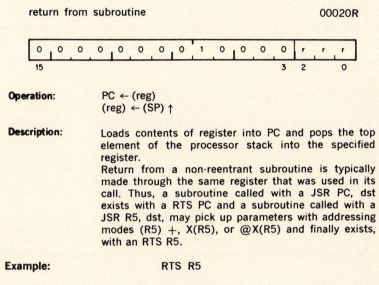

0	0	0	0	0	0	0	0	1	0	0	0	0	r	r	r

15   3   2   0

Operation: PC ← (reg)
                    (reg) ← (SP) ↑

Description: Loads contents of register into PC and pops the top
                    element of the processor stack into the specified
                    register.
                    Return from a non-reentrant subroutine is typically
                    made through the same register that was used in its
                    call. Thus, a subroutine called with a JSR PC, dst
                    exists with a RTS PC and a subroutine called with a
                    JSR R5, dst, may pick up parameters with addressing
                    modes (R5) +, X(R5), or @X(R5) and finally exists,
                    with an RTS R5.

Example: RTS R5

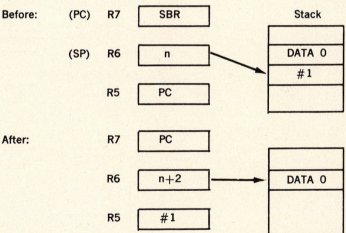

Before: (PC)   R7   [SBR]   Stack

           (SP)   R6   [n] ⟶   [DATA 0]
                                         [#1]

                  R5   [PC]

After: R7   [PC]

                  R6   [n+2] ⟶   [DATA 0]

                  R5   [#1]

MARK

mark   0064NN

0	0	0	0	1	1	0	1	0	0	n	n	n	n	n	n
15								8	7 6	5					0

Operation: SP◄ updated PC + 2 + 2n   n = number of parameters
PC ◄ R5
R5 ◄ (SP) ▲

Condition Codes: unaffected

Description: Used as part of the standard PDP-11 subroutine return convention. MARK facilitates the stack clean up procedures involved in subroutine exit. Assembler format is: MARK N

Example:

MOV	R5,–(SP)	;place old R5 on stack
MOV	P1,–(SP)	;place N parameters
MOV	P2,–(SP)	;on the stack to be
		;used there by the
		;subroutine
MOV	PN,–(SP)	
MOV	#MARKN,–(SP)	;places the instruction
		;MARK N on the stack
MOV	SP ,R5	;set up address at MARK N instruction
JSR	PC,SUB	;jump to subroutine

At this point the stack is as follows:

OLD R5
P1
PN
MARK N
OLD PC

And the program is at the address SUB which is the beginning of the subroutine.

SUB: ;execution of the subroutine itself

    RTS R5   ;the return begins: this

causes the contents of R5 to be placed in the PC which then results in the execution of the instruction MARK N. The contents of old PC are placed in R5

MARK N causes: (1) the stack pointer to be adjusted to point to the old R5 value; (2) the value now in R5 (the old PC) to be placed in the PC; and (3) contents of the old R5 to be popped into R5 thus completing the return from subroutine.

SOB

subtract one and branch (if ≠ 0)   077RNN

0	1	1	1	1	1	1	r	r	r	OFFSET
15							9	8	6	5 0

Operation: (R) ← (R) − 1; if this result ≠ 0 then PC ← PC −(2 x offset) if (R) = 0; PC ← PC

Condition Codes: unaffected

Description: The register is decremented. If it is not equal to 0, twice the offset is subtracted from the PC (now pointing to the following word). The offset is interpreted as a sixbit positive number. This instruction provides a fast, efficient method of loop control. Assembler syntax is:

        SOB   R,A

where A is the address to which transfer is to be made if the decremented R is not equal to 0. Note that the SOB instruction can not be used to transfer control in the forward direction.

Traps

Trap instructions provide for calls to emulators, I/O monitors, debugging packages, and user-defined interpreters. A trap is effectively an interrupt generated by software. When a trap occurs the contents of the current Program Counter (PC) and processor Status Word (PS) are pushed onto the processor stack and replaced by the contents of a two-word trap vector containing a new PC and new PS. The return sequence from a trap involves executing an RTI or RTT instruction which restores the old PC and old PS by popping them from the stack. Trap instruction vectors are located at permanently assigned fixed addresses.

EMT

emulator trap   104000—104377

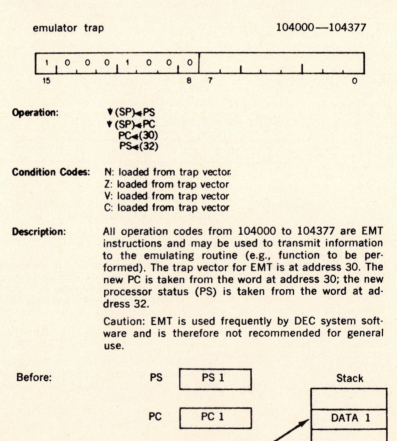

Operation:	▼(SP)◄PS
	▼(SP)◄PC
	PC◄(30)
	PS◄(32)

Condition Codes:	N: loaded from trap vector.
	Z: loaded from trap vector
	V: loaded from trap vector
	C: loaded from trap vector

Description:

All operation codes from 104000 to 104377 are EMT instructions and may be used to transmit information to the emulating routine (e.g., function to be performed). The trap vector for EMT is at address 30. The new PC is taken from the word at address 30; the new processor status (PS) is taken from the word at address 32.

Caution: EMT is used frequently by DEC system software and is therefore not recommended for general use.

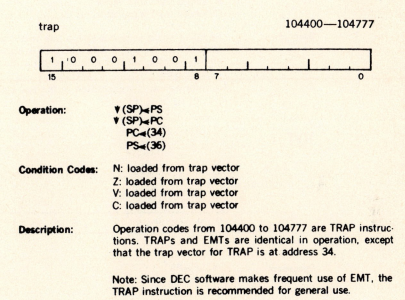

TRAP

trap   104400—104777

Operation: ▼ (SP)◄PS
                ▼ (SP)◄PC
                PC◄(34)
                PS◄(36)

Condition Codes: N: loaded from trap vector
                  Z: loaded from trap vector
                  V: loaded from trap vector
                  C: loaded from trap vector

Description: Operation codes from 104400 to 104777 are TRAP instruc-
                 tions. TRAPs and EMTs are identical in operation, except
                 that the trap vector for TRAP is at address 34.

                 Note: Since DEC software makes frequent use of EMT, the
                 TRAP instruction is recommended for general use.

BPT

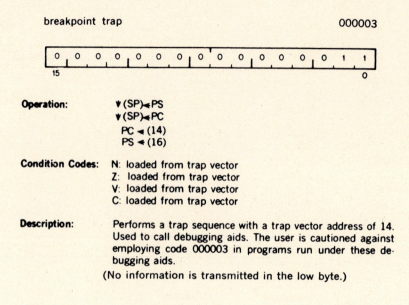

breakpoint trap   000003

Operation: ▼(SP)◄PS
                      ▼(SP)◄PC
                      PC ◄ (14)
                      PS ◄ (16)

Condition Codes: N: loaded from trap vector
                      Z: loaded from trap vector
                      V: loaded from trap vector
                      C: loaded from trap vector

Description: Performs a trap sequence with a trap vector address of 14.
                      Used to call debugging aids. The user is cautioned against
                      employing code 000003 in programs run under these de-
                      bugging aids.

                      (No information is transmitted in the low byte.)

IOT

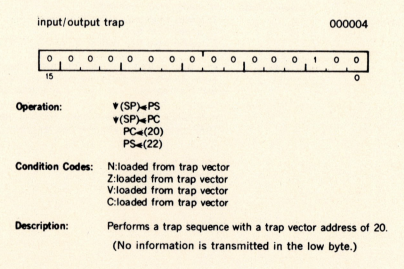

input/output trap   000004

Operation: ▼(SP)◄PS
                      ▼(SP)◄PC
                      PC◄(20)
                      PS◄(22)

Condition Codes: N:loaded from trap vector
                      Z:loaded from trap vector
                      V:loaded from trap vector
                      C:loaded from trap vector

Description: Performs a trap sequence with a trap vector address of 20.

                      (No information is transmitted in the low byte.)

RTI

return from interrupt   000002

```
| 0 0 0 0 0 0 0 0 0 0 0 0 0 0 1 0 |
  15                                              0
```

Operation: PC←(SP)↑
                     PS←(SP)↑

Condition Codes: N: loaded from processor stack
                     Z: loaded from processor stack
                     V: loaded from processor stack
                     C: loaded from processor stack

Description: Used to exit from an interrupt or TRAP service routine.
                     The PC and PS are restored (popped) from the pro-
                     cessor stack. If a trace trap is pending, the first in-
                     struction after RTI will not be executed prior to the
                     next T traps.

RTT

return from interrupt   000006

```
| 0 0 0 0 0 0 0 0 0 0 0 0 0 1 1 0 |
  15                                              0
```

Operation: PC←(SP)↑
                     PS←(SP)↑

Condition Codes: N: loaded from processor stack
                     Z: loaded from processor stack
                     V: loaded from processor stack
                     C: loaded from processor stack

Description: Operation is the same as RTI except that it inhibits a
                     trace trap while RTI permits trace trap. If new PS has
                     T bit set, trap will occur after execution of first in-
                     struction after RTT.

Reserved Instruction Traps—These are caused by attempts to execute instruction codes reserved for future processor expansion (reserved instructions) or instructions with illegal addressing modes (illegal instructions). Order codes not corresponding to any of the instructions described are considered to be reserved instructions. JMP and JSR with register mode destinations are illegal instructions, and trap to vector address 4. Reserved instructions trap to vector address 10.

Bus Error Traps—Bus Error Traps are time-out errors; attempts to reference addresses on the bus that have made no response within a certain length of time. In general, these are caused by attempts to reference non-existent memory, and attempts to reference non-existent peripheral devices. Bus error traps cause processor traps through the trap vector address 4.

Trace Trap – Trace Trap is enabled by bit 4 of the PS and causes processor traps at the end of instruction execution. The instruction that is executed after the instruction that set the T-bit will proceed to completion and then trap through the trap vector at address 14. Note that the trace trap is a system debugging aid and is transparent to the general programmer.

NOTE
Bit 4 of the PS can only be set indirectly by executing a RTI or RTT instruction with the desired PS on the stack.

The following are special cases of the T-bit and are detailed in subsequent paragraphs.

1. The traced instruction cleared the T-bit.
2. The traced instruction set the T-bit.
3. The traced instruction caused an instruction trap.
4. The traced instruction caused a bus error trap.
5. The processor was interrupted between the time the T-bit was set and the fetching of the instruction that was to be traced.
6. The traced instruction was a WAIT.
7. The traced instruction was a HALT.
8. The traced instruction was a Return from Interrupt.

NOTE
The traced instruction is the instruction after the one that set the T-bit.

An instruction that cleared the T bit—Upon fetching the traced Instruction, an internal flag, the trace flag, was set. The trap will still occur at the end of execution of this instruction. The status word on the stack, however, will have a clear T-bit.

An instruction that set the T-bit—Since the T-bit was already set, setting it again has no effect. The trap will occur.

An instruction that caused an Instruction Trap—The instruction trap is performed and the entire routine for the service trap is executed. If the service routine exists with an RTI or in any other way restores the stacked status word, the T-bit is set again, the instruction following the traced instruction is executed and, unless it is one of the special cases noted previously, a trace trap occurs.

An instruction that caused a Bus Error Trap—This is treated as an Instruction Trap. The only difference is that the error service is not as likely to exit with an RTI, so that the trace trap may not occur.

Note that interrupts may be acknowledged immediately after the loading of the new PC and PS at the trap vector location. To lock out all interrupts, the PS at the trap vector should set Bit 7.

A WAIT—T bit trap is not honored during a wait.

A HALT—The processor halts. The PC points to the next instruction to be executed. The trap will occur immediately following execution resumption.

A Return from Interrupt—The return from interrupt instruction either clears or sets the T-bit. If the T-bit was set and RTT is the traced instruction, the trap is delayed until completion of the next instruction.

Power Failure Trap—Occurs when AC power fail signal is received while processor is in run mode. Trap vector for power failure is location 24 and 26. Trap will occur if an RTI instruction is executed in power fail service routine.

Trap Priorities—In case of internal and external multiple processor trap conditions, occurring simultaneously, the following order of priorities is observed (from high to low):

    Bus Error Trap
    Memory Refresh
    Instruction Traps
    Trace Trap
    Power Fail Trap
    Halt Line
    Event Line Interrupt
    Device (Bus) Interrupt Request

If a bus error is caused by the trap process handling instruction traps, trace traps, or a previous bus error, the processor is halted. This is called a double bus error.

B.8 MISCELLANEOUS

HALT

halt   000000

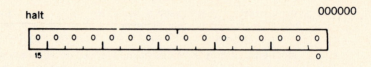

Condition Codes: not affected

Description: Causes the processor to leave RUN mode. The PC
                        points to the next instruction to be executed. The
                        processor goes into the HALT mode. The contents of
                        the PC are displayed on the console terminal and the
                        console mode of operation is enabled.

WAIT

wait for interrupt   000001

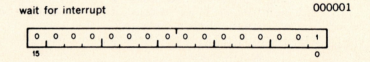

Condition Codes: not affected

Description: Provides a way for the processor to relinquish use of
                      the bus while it waits for an external interrupt request.
                      Having been given a WAIT command, the processor
                      will not compete for bus use by fetching instructions
                      or operands from memory. This permits higher trans-
                      fer rates between a device and memory, since no proc-
                      essor-induced latencies will be encountered by inter-
                      rupt requests from devices. In WAIT, as in all instruc-
                      tions, the PC points to the next instruction following
                      the WAIT instruction. Thus when an interrupt causes
                      the PC and PS to be pushed onto the processor stack,
                      the address of the next instruction following the WAIT
                      is saved. The exit from the interrupt routine (i.e. ex-
                      ecution of an RTI instruction) will cause resumption of
                      the interrupted process at the instruction following the
                      WAIT.

RESET

reset external bus   000005

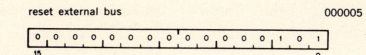

| 0 | 0 | 0 | 0 | 0 | 0 | 0 | 0 | 0 | 0 | 0 | 0 | 0 | 1 | 0 | 1 |
15   0

Condition Codes: not affected

Description: Sends INIT on the BUS for 10 μsec. All devices on the BUS are reset to their state at power-up. The processor remains in an idle state for 90 μsec following issuance of INIT.

B.9 RESERVED INSTRUCTIONS

(NO ASSIGNED MNEMONIC)

00021R

15			12	11				6	5			0
0	0	0	0	0	0	0	0	1	0	0	0	1	R	R	R

Operation: (R) ← gets contents of 5 internal 16 bit registers R ← R + 12 at end of inst.

Condition Codes: Unaffected

Description: Contents of register R (low order 3 bits of inst.) is used as a pointer. The contents of the internal hidden temporary registers are consecutively written into memory and the contents or R are incremented by 2 until the five 16 bit registers have been written. (R) ←   (R) + 12$_s$. Primarily used as a maintenance aid in diagnostic routines. The interpretation of the five words in memory is as follows:

Memory Location	Microlevel Register Symbol	Function
(R)	RBA	Bus Address Register. It contains the last non-instruction fetch bus address for destination modes, 3, 5, 6, and 7.
(R)+2	RSRC	Source Operand Register. It contains the last source operand of a double operand instruction. The high byte may not be correct if it was source mode 0.

(R)+4	RDST	Destination Operand Register. It contains the last destination operand fetched by the processor.
(R)+6	RPSW	**PS and Scratch Register. The top 4 bits are PS bits 4 through 7. The remaining bit interpretation is a function of the last instruction and may not be that useful for all cases.**
(R)+10	RIR	Instruction Register. It contains the present, not past, instruction being executed, and will always be 36R where R is the register in the format. The 360 is a result of firmware instruction decoding and is caused by 150 being added to the opcode (21R+150=36R).

(NO ASSIGNED MNEMONIC)   00022N

15				12	11					6	5					0
0	0	0	0	0	0	0	0	1	0	0	1	0	0	0	0

Operation: Causes Micro Instruction Control Transfer to Microlocation 3000

Condition Codes: Unaffected

Description: This instruction can be used to transfer Microcontrol to Microcode address 3000 in the Microprocessor. If Microaddress 3000 does not exist this opcode will cause a reserved instruction trap through memory location 10.

This is a reserved DEC instruction.

B.10 CONDITION CODE OPERATORS

CLN   SEN
CLZ   SEZ
CLV   SEV
CLC   SEC
CCC   SCC

condition code operators   0002XX

0	0	0	0	0	0	0	0	0	1	0	1	0/1	N	Z	V	C
15											5	4	3	2	1	0

Description: Set and clear condition code bits. Selectable combinations of these bits may be cleared or set together. Condition code bits corresponding to bits in the condition code operator (Bits 0-3) are modified according to the sense of bit 4, the set/clear bit of the operator. i.e. set the bit specified by bit 0, 1, 2 or 3, if bit 4 is a 1. Clear corresponding bits if bit 4 = 0.

Mnemonic Operation		OP Code
CLC	Clear C	000241
CLV	Clear V	000242
CLZ	Clear Z	000244
CLN	Clear N	000250
SEC	Set C	000261
SEV	Set V	000262
SEZ	Set Z	000264
SEN	Set N	000270
SCC	Set all CC's	000277
CCC	Clear all CC's	000257
	Clear V and C	000243
NOP	No Operation	000240

Combinations of the above set or clear operations may be ORed together to form combined instructions.

PDP-11 Instruction Timing

C.1 LSI-11 INSTRUCTION EXECUTION TIME

The execution time for an instruction depends on the instruction itself, the modes of addressing used, and the type of memory referenced. In most cases the instruction execution time is the sum of a Basic Time, a Source Address (SRC) Time, and a Destination Address (DST) Time.

INSTR TIME = Basic Time + SRC Time + DST Time

(BASIC Time = Fetch Time + Decode Time + Execute Time)

Some of the instructions require only some of these times. All timing information is in microseconds, unless otherwise noted. Times are typical; process timing can vary ±20 percent. A 350ns microcycle is assumed.

C.2 SOURCE AND DESTINATION TIME

MODE	SRC TIME (Word)	SRC TIME (Byte)	DST TIME (Word)	DST TIME (Byte)
0	0	0	0	0
1	1.40 μs	1.05 μs	2.10 μs	1.75 μs
2	1.40	1.05	2.10	1.75
3	3.50	3.15	4.20	4.20
4	2.10	1.75	2.80	2.45
5	4.20	3.85	4.90	4.90
6	4.20	3.85	4.90	4.55
7	6.30	5.95	6.65	7.00

NOTE FOR MODE 2 and MODE 4 if R6 or R7 used with Byte operation, add 0.35 μs to SRC time and 0.70 μs to DST time.

C.3 BASIC TIME

DOPS (Double Operand)	DM0	DM1-7
MOV	3.50 μs	2.45 μs
ADD,XOR,SUB,BIC,BIS	3.50	4.20
CMP,BIT	3.50	3.15
MOVB	3.85	3.85
BICB,BISB	3.85	3.85
CMP,BITB	3.15	2.80

NOTE

DM0 = Destination Mode 0
DM1-7 = Destination Modes 1 through 7

SOPS (Single Operand)	DM0	DM1-7
CLR	3.85 μs	4.20 μs
INC,ADC,DEC,SBC	4.20	4.90
COM,NLG	4.20	4.55
ROL,ASL	3.85	4.55
TST	4.20	3.85
ROR	5.25	5.95
ASR	5.60	6.30
CLRB,COMB,NEGB	3.85	4.20
ROLB,ASLB	3.85	4.20
INCB,DECB,SBCB,ADC	3.85	4.55
TSTB	3.85	3.50
RORB	4.20	4.90
ASRB	4.55	5.95
SWAB	4.20	3.85
SXT	5.95	6.65
MFPS (1067DD)	4.90	6.65
MTPS (1064SS)	7.00	7.00 *

* For MTPS use Byte DST time not SRC time.
* Add 0.35 μs to instr. time if Bit 7 of effective OPR $= 1$

JMP/JSR MODE	DST TIME
1	0.70 μs
2	1.40
3	1.75
4	1.40
5	2.45
6	2.45
7	4.20

INSTRUCTION	BASIC TIMES	
JMP	3.50 μs	
JSR (PC $=$ LINK)	5.25	
JSR (PC $\neq$ LINK)	8.40	
ALL BRANCHES	3.50	(CONDITION MET OR NOT MET)
SOB (BRANCH)	4.90	
SOB (NO BRANCH)	4.20	
SET CC	3.50	
CLEAR CC	3.50	
NOP	3.50	
RTS	5.25	
MARK	11.55	
RTI	8.75 *	
RTT	8.75 * $+$	

INSTRUCTION	BASIC TIMES
TRAP,EMT	16.80 * μs
IOT,RPT	18.55 *
WAIT	6.30
HALT	5.60
RESET	5.95 + 10.0 μs for INIT + 90.0 μs
MAINT INST. (00021R)	20.30
RSRVD INST. (00022N)	5.95 (TO GET TO μADDRESS 3000)

* If NEW PS HAS BIT 4 or BIT 7 SET ADD 0.35 μs FOR EACH
+ IF NEW PS HAS BIT 4 (T BIT) SET ADD 2.10 μs

C.4 EXTENDED ARITHMETIC (KEV11) INSTRUCTION TIMES

EIS Instruction Times

MODE	SRC TIME
0	0.35 μs
1	2.10
2	2.80
3	3.15
4	2.80
5	3.85
6	3.85
7	5.60

INSTRUCTION	BASIC TIME	
MUL	24.0 to 37.0 μs	If both numbers less than 256 in absolute value 16 bit multiply
	64.0 μs Worst Case	
DIV	78.0 μs Worst Case	
ASH (RIGHT)	10.1 + 1.75 per shift	
ASH (LEFT)	10.8 + 2.45 per shift	
ASHC (RIGHT)	10.1 + 2.80 per shift	
ASHC (LEFT)	10.1 + 3.15 per shift	

FIS Instruction Times (us)
INST. TIME = BASIC TIME + SHIFT TIME FOR BINARY POINTS + SHIFT
            TIME FOR NORMALIZATION

INSTRUCTION	BASIC TIME
FADD	42.1 μs
FSUB	42.4

EXPONENT DIFFERENCE	ALIGN BINARY POINTS
0– 7	2.45 μs per shift
8–15	3.50 + 2.45 per shift over 8
16–23	7.00 + 2.45 per shift over 16

EXPONENT DIFFERENCE	NORMALIZATION
0– 7	2.1 μs per shift
8–15	2.1 + 2.1 per shift over 8
16–23	4.2 + 2.1 per shift over 16

INSTRUCTION BASIC TIME (μs)	
FMUL	74.2 to 80.9 μs if either argument has only 7 bits of precision, i.e., the second word of the 32 bit argument is 0.
	121.1 μs worst case (i.e., arguments have more than 7 bits of precision).
FDIV	151 μs typical
	232 μs worst case

C.5 DMA (DIRECT MEMORY ACCESS) LATENCY

DMA latency, which is the time from request (BDMRL) to bus mastership for the first DMA device, is 6.45 μs, maximum. This time is the longest processor DATIO cycle which occurs for an ASR instruction with destination modes of 1 through 7. DMA requests are honored during memory refresh by the processor.

C.6 INTERRUPT LATENCY (ALL TIMES IN MICROSECONDS)

a. If processor is performing memory refresh (regardless whether KEV11 is present):

Time from interrupt request (BIRQ L) to acknowledgement (BIAK L)	118 μs max
Time from acknowledgement (BIAK L) to fetch of first service routine instruction	+ 16.5 μs max
Total time from request to first service routine instruction	134.5 μs max

b. If processor is not performing memory refresh (and KEV11 not present):

Time from interrupt request (BIRQ L) to acknowledgement (BIAK L) (Longest instruction is IOT)	18.55 μs max
Time from acknowledgement (BIAK L) to fetch of first service routine instruction	+ 16.5 μs max
Total time from request to first service routine instruction	35.05 μs max

c. If processor is not performing memory refresh
and KEV11 option is present:

Time from interrupt request (BIRQ L) to acknowledgement (BIAK L)	27.6 μs max
Time from acknowledgement (BIAK L) to fetch of first service routine instruction	$+16.5$ μs max
Total time from request to first service routine instruction	44.1 μs max

NOTE

During all KEV11 instructions (EIS and FIS), device and event interrupt requests are periodically
scanned. If present, the instruction is aborted
and all processor state information is backed up
to the beginning of the instruction. After the interrupt is processed, the KEV11 instruction is
re-executed from the beginning. Caution should
be observed with the frequency of event interrupts; if the frequency is too high, the KEV11
instruction will never complete. It is suggested
a maximum frequency of 3.3 kHz be used on the
event input if the KEV11 option is present. Without the KEV11, the maximum frequency should
not exceed 20 kHz. Both times allow approximately 50 μs for the interrupt service routine.

PDP-11
Numerical OP Code List

OP code			Mnemonic	OP code			Mnemonic	OP code			Mnemonic
00	00	00	HALT	00	02	64	SEZ	00	67	DD	SXT
00	00	01	WAIT	00	02	70	SEN	00	70	00	
00	00	02	RTI	00	02	77	SCC	.			↑
00	00	03	BPT	00	03	DD	SWAB	.			unused
00	00	04	IOT	00	04	XXX	BR	.			↓
00	00	05	RESET	00	10	XXX	BNE	00	77	00	
00	00	06	RTT	00	14	XXX	BEQ	01	SS	DD	MOV
00	00	07	————	00	20	XXX	BGE	02	SS	DD	CMP
.			↑	00	24	XXX	BLT	03	SS	DD	BIT
.			unused	00	30	XXX	BGT	04	SS	DD	BIC
.			↓	00	34	XXX	BLE	05	SS	DD	BIC
00	00	77	————	00	4R	DD	JSR	06	SS	DD	BIS
00	01	DD	JMP	00	50	DD	CLR	07	0R	SS	ADD
00	02	0R	RTS	00	51	DD	COM	07	1R	SS	MUL
00	02	10	————	00	52	DD	INC	07	2R	SS	ASH
.			↑	00	53	DD	DEC	07	3R	SS	ASHC
.			unused	00	54	DD	NEG	07	4R	DD	XOR
.			↓	00	55	DD	ADC	07	50	0R	FADD
00	02	27	————	00	56	DD	SBC	07	50	1R	FSUB
00	02	3N	SPL	00	57	DD	TST	07	50	2R	FMUL
00	02	40	NOP	00	60	DD	ROR	07	50	3R	FDIV
00	02	41	CLC	00	61	DD	ROL	07	50	40	
00	02	42	CLV	00	62	DD	ASR	.			↑
00	02	44	CLZ	00	63	DD	ASL	.			unused
00	02	50	CLN	00	64	NN	MARK	.			↓
00	02	57	CCC	00	65	SS	MFPI	07	67	77	————
00	02	61	SEC	00	66	DD	MTPI	07	7R	NN	SOB
00	02	62	SEV					10	00	XXX	BPL

OP code			Mnemonic	OP code			Mnemonic	OP code			Mnemonic
10	04	XXX	BMI	10	51	DD	COMB	10	65	SS	MFPD
10	10	XXX	BHI	10	52	DD	INCB	10	66	DD	MTPD
				10	53	DD	DECB	10	67	00	_____
10	14	XXX	BLOS								
10	20	XXX	BVC								↑
10	24	XXX	BVS	10	54	DD	NEGB				unused
10	30	XXX	BCC,BHIS	10	55	DD	ADCB				↓
10	34	XXX	BCS,BLO	10	56	DD	SBCB	10	77	77	_____
10	40	00	_____	10	57	DD	TSTB	11	SS	DD	MOVB
	.		↑					12	SS	DD	CMPB
	.		EMT	10	60	DD	RORB	13	SS	DD	BITB
	.		↓	10	61	DD	ROLB	14	SS	DD	BICB
10	43	77	_____	10	62	DD	ASRB				
10	44	00	_____	10	63	DD	ASLB	15	SS	DD	BISB
	.		↑					16	SS	DD	SUB
	.		TRAP	10	64	00	_____	17	00	00	_____
	.		↓		.		↑		.		↑
10	47	77	_____		.		unused		.		floating point
					.		↓		.		↓
10	50	DD	CLRB	10	64	77	_____	17	77	77	_____

Program Development and System Software: The RSX-11M Operating System

In this appendix we describe the procedure for user program development and the role of the system software in the process. Here we present the utilization of the RSX-11M operating system in the development of a user program. This is to clarify the necessity of an operating system for any computing system and to show how the RSX-11M operating system functions for the PDP-11.

command	ODT
EDI	program debugging
file	program link
load	RSX-11M
MAC	TKB
MCR	

When we introduced the concept of system software, we pointed out the analogy between an operating system software and the management system of a restaurant. What follows will be the description of a specific operating system for the PDP-11—namely, the RSX-11M. There are a number of operating systems for the PDP-11. The RSX-11M is a multiple-users realtime disk operating system. It is a very powerful one, but it is impossible to study the details of it here. Instead, we will introduce its structure from an elementary user point of view so that you can learn to use the essential system software modules to develop and execute application programs. Remember that we could view a specific system software module of an operating system as a staff of a restaurant management system, or a tool from a toolbox in our workshop or garage. The essential thing for you to do is to become familiar with them. Specifically, for each module we must know its name as well as its function; how to summon it from the disk when we need its service; how to communicate with it; and how to send it away when we no longer need it. Before we learn the characteristics or personality of each, let us see how we can communicate with all these modules.

E.1 COMMUNICATION BETWEEN USER AND RSX-11M

Commands

Command is a means for the user or programmer to indicate what he or she wants the "staff" to do. To achieve this, the master (programmer) has to know what language and format the servant (system program) understands. Since the general input/output (I/O) device of a computing system is a CRT terminal, the natural thing to do is to type in commands through the keyboard. Of course, a specific command would have its unique spelling and function defined by the system designer, and can be found in the user's manual. Let us use the general term COMMAND for convenience. Then the format for issuing a command is

COMMAND ⟨CR⟩

Here the symbol ⟨CR⟩ denotes that the user must depress the carriage return key of the keyboard at the end of the command. This is necessary, because the module (staff) has to know when to begin interpreting and executing the command. As soon as the module "sees" the ASCII code of the carriage return, it starts to execute the command if it understands. Obviously, in many cases, a command is just like a mnemonic instruction. It would require the "master" to provide some "operand" along with the command so that the "staff" would know what to work on. For example, if we want the system software, say, assembler, to convert the source program (program in mnemonics) ODD-NUMBER-SEARCH into its object program (program in binary machine code), then in the command we would have to tell the assembler which program to convert. Conventionally, a specific program is called a **file,** with a unique identification format.

Files

The concept of file used to identify a specific program, be it a system or an application program, is a very important one in any operating system. It is somewhat like the social security number attached to an employee in a corporation. But an employee's file would be identified not only by its social security number, but also age, sex, full name, and so on. Similarly, in the RSX-11M, a file is formally defined as follows:

dev:[g,m]filename.type;n

where   dev:$\underline{\Delta}$ Name of the disk drive where the file currently resides.
        [g,m] $\underline{\Delta}$ User's or programmer's I.D. number; g is a group number, m, a member

number of the group. Three-digit numbers such as [220,051] imply 220th group and 051st member.

filename Δ Specific name of the file assigned by the programmer with 0–9 characters— i.e., ODDNUM.

.filetype Δ 0 ~ 3 characters assigned by the user. Although the user can assign any character for it, there are some standard forms which have special meaning, and the user should avoid using these unless he or she really means the same type as conventionally defined. They are defined as follows:

.MAC = macro assembler source file
.OBJ = macro assembler output object file
.LST = macro assembler listing file
.TSK = task builder output file
.STB = symbol table information

;n Δ *n*th version of the same file

Note: Δ symbolizes "defined as."

For the ODD-NUMBER-SEARCH source program in Chapter 3, we can specify it as follows:

DK0:[100,101]BIGODD.MAC;1

Here, we mean that the first version of the source program, named BIGODD, resides on the disk which is currently in the disk drive DK0, and it belongs to member 101 of the group 100. However, the specifications allow default values; for example, if DK0 is not specified, the system would default it with drive #0 of the system disk. If the terminal has been logged in by [100,101], then that would be the default value for the user's I.D. as long as he or she has not logged off.

E.2 MAJOR ELEMENTS OF THE RSX-11M

In this section, we introduce the major software elements or modules of the RSX-11M, which are essential to program development and execution. Although we are dealing with a specific operating system here and the name of each module may be unique, its functions can be compared with those in other operating systems. Therefore, you should not encounter difficulty when you have to use different operating systems in the future. That is, all operating systems should consist of modules providing similar services, although the specific name of each module can be quite different from one operating system to another. Let us now look at the key modules of the RSX-11M.

Monitor Console Routine (MCR)

MCR is the first module or software routine that a programmer will "meet" at the CRT terminal. Its function is to interpret the user's commands typed at the keyboard and to respond accordingly. The user at the keyboard can summon any module through MCR. First, of course, the user has to make sure that MCR is "on duty." When the MCR is active, it will show the symbol ">" on the CRT screen, which is known as the **prompt** of the MCR. Now, the user can communicate with MCR by inputting information through the keyboard and receiving responses through the CRT. To minimize the confusion, we will adopt the convention of underlining all the CRT responses so that the reader can separate the input message from the output responses. For example, if the user wants to know what programs he or she developed before are on the currently active disk, the following steps can be followed:

```
1) >                ;CRT SHOWS THE MCR PROMPT
2) DIR ⟨CR⟩         ;THE USER TYPES THE COMMAND, DIR,
                    ;WHICH STANDS FOR DIRECTORY, AND
                    ;TERMINATES THE INPUT LINE OR COMMAND
                    ;BY DEPRESSING THE CARRIAGE-RETURN KEY.
                    ;THE CRT WILL THEN SHOW A LIST OF THE
                    ;FILES RESIDING ON THE DISK
```

There are a number of commands the user can use to communicate with MCR. You should read the user's manual for the machine to find out the details.

Text Editor (EDI)

EDI is a module that serves two functions. (1) Command mode: In this mode, it basically compensates for the clumsiness of human beings. That is, during program preparation, the user may make silly mistakes in typing. The user may issue commands to EDI to erase, delete, or change the text, and so on. (2) Input mode: In this mode, EDI will store whatever the user has typed through the keyboard line-by-line into the main memory. For example:

```
> EDI ⟨CR⟩                ;MCR PROMPT ON CRT, USER SUMMONS
                          ;OR INVOKES TEXT EDITOR MODULE (EDI)
                          ;BY TYPING EDI ⟨CR⟩
EDI >                     ;CRT SHOW THE PROMPT OF EDI
EDI > ADD.MAC⟨CR⟩         ;THE USER TYPED THE NAME OF THE FILE,
                          ;ADD.MAC INDICATING THAT HE/SHE WANTS
                          ;TO EDIT THE FILE BY THIS NAME
```

Note that ADD.MAC is simply a dummy name picked arbitrarily for our example. Here, we have two possible responses:

1. The file ADD.MAC; is found, and the EDI will load the file into main memory for the user to make modifications, and respond as follows:

```
N LINES READ IN
PAGE 1
*                         ;THIS IS THE EDI PROMPT WHEN IT
                          ;IS IN COMMAND MODE
```

2. If the file does not exist, EDI responds as follows:

```
CREATING NEW FILE
INPUT                     ;THIS INFORMS THE USER EDI IS
                          ;IN INPUT MODE
```

There are a number of commands the user can utilize to communicate with EDI. The user should consult with the lab or user's manual for details. For example, the user can change the EDI from command mode by typing ''I⟨CR⟩'' and return to command mode from input mode by depressing the RETURN key. When the user no longer needs EDI, he or she can type one of the following three commands:

```
EXIT ⟨CR⟩
ED ⟨CR⟩
↑Z ⟨CR⟩                   ;THE SYMBOL, ↑Z, MEANS THAT THE
                          ;CONTROL-KEY AND Z-KEY ARE DEPRESSED
                          ;AT THE SAME TIME AND THEN DEPRESS
                          ;RETURN
```

As a result, EDI will disappear and MCR is evoked again by showing its prompt, ''>'', on the CRT. Figure E.1 depicts the operation of EDI. The input and output file specifications are the

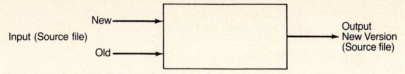

Figure E.1 Text editor operation.

same except that the version number of the output file is always the input version number plus 1 whenever EDI is evoked and then dismissed, regardless of whether any modification is made or not.

Assembler (MAC)

After a source file is edited, the next step will be to translate the source file into a binary machine-coded object file. This is done by the module MAC. In fact, the assembler does more than just generate the object file. As shown in Figure E.2, MAC accepts the source file and yields two output files, ⟨xxx.OBJ⟩, ⟨xxx.LST⟩. The brackets are used merely for ease of reading. They imply that the contents enclosed within the brackets form a unique group to represent a specific thing, or file. The bracket should not be typed on the keyboard.

Again, the assembler can be evoked through MCR.

EXAMPLE 1 _____

>MAC ⟨CR⟩   ;ASSEMBLER IS EVOKED THROUGH
                                                   ;MCR-COMMAND
MAC > ADD.OBJ,ADD.LST = ADD.MAC ⟨CR⟩

The user specifies the input file by the name ADD.MAC (it should be a source file) and wants the assembler to generate two output files. One is the object file to be named ADD.OBJ, and the other is the list file to be named ADD.LST. In response to this command, MAC will produce the corresponding object file and store it on the disk for later use. Meanwhile it will generate a list file which is also to be stored on the disk. If desired, it can be printed on the printer for the user to keep for future reference. The list file shows the object code and source code of the file side-by-side so that the user can examine both files, object and source, at the same time. In addition, the list file also shows: (1) symbolic address table, (2) status of the memory, and (3) the programming error if applicable, such as misspelled instructions, duplicated symbolic addresses, and so on, but not the logical errors of the program.

In many cases, we do not wish to have hard copy produced on the printer. Then we use the following format:

MAC > ADD.OBJ,TI: = ADD.MAC ⟨CR⟩

As a result, the list file will be shown on the CRT. Most systems will accept a one-step command with a default format, as follows:

>MAC ADD,ADD = ADD ⟨CR⟩

This command will yield the same result as the former two steps.

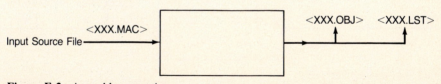

Figure E.2 Assembler operation.

EXAMPLE 2 _____

>MAC   ADD = ADD ⟨CR⟩

would yield only the object file.

EXAMPLE 3 _____

>MAC   ,ADD = ADD ⟨CR⟩

would yield only the list file.   ■ ■

Task Builder (TKB)

After an object file is produced by the assembler, we should be ready to load it into the main memory for the next action. However, in practice, life is not always so simple. For example, in many cases we would like to link or merge several object files together to do a certain task. This module is exactly for this purpose, so it is sometimes known as the linker. In the RSX-11M, this module accepts one or more object files as the input and yields three types of output files: <xxx.TSK>, <xxx.MAP>, and <xxx.STB>, as shown in Figure E.3, where <xxx.TSK> is the merged executable or loadable program ready to be loaded into main memory for execution. It is also known as memory image file. <xxx.MAP> is the memory allocation map, and <xxx.STB> is the statistics of the task builder.

EXAMPLE _____

>TKB   ADD.TSK, ADD.MAP, ADD.STB=ADD.OBJ <CR>

will yield the three output files. If we are only interested in the TSK and only wish to use the default format, we may use

>TKB   ADD=ADD <CR>

to produce the ADD.TSK file.   ■ ■

Load and Execute (LGO)

After the xxx.TKS file is generated, it again is stored on the disk by its specific name. To execute the program, it has to be loaded from the disk into the main memory, starting at a specific location in the memory. In some systems, the specific location can be 1000_8 or 1172_8 or any values determined by the installation requirements. However, it is the load and execute module's responsibility to load

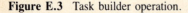

Figure E.3 Task builder operation.

the TKS-file into the proper location and start execution. Again, this module has to be evoked through the MCR and then executed, as follows.

EXAMPLE 1 ───

```
>LGO <CR>
LGO> ADD.TSK <CR>
```

or simply,

```
LGO> ADD <CR>
```

EXAMPLE 2 ───

In some cases, the user would like to break the LGO (load and go) process into two steps. Then the following steps can be taken:

```
> GET <CR>            ;EVOKE GER-MODULE
GET> ADD <CR>         ;ORDER GET-MODULE TO LOAD ADD-FILE
[LOADED]              ;THE MODULE INFORMS THE USER THAT
                      ;THE PROGRAM HAS BEEN LOADED
↑Z                    ;DEPRESS CONTROL-KEY AND Z-KEY TO
                      ;DISMISS GET AND SUMMON MCR
> BREAK               ;DEPRESS BREAK-KEY TO ENTER ODT
                      ;(OCTAL-DEBUGGING-TECHNIQUE)
@                     ;PROMPT OF ODT-MODULE
```

At this point, the user can manually execute the program starting at a specific location. For example, if we wish to execute the program beginning at location 1172, then we can do the following:

```
@ 1172G <CR>
```

Here, G is a GO command to the ODT module, which will be described briefly later in this section.

                                                                ■■

Peripheral Interchange Program (PIP)

This module can be used to transfer or manipulate the program on the file level. It can copy, delete, purge, or print files and do many other tasks for the user's convenience. It is evoked through MCR. The general format is shown below.

```
> PIP <file Specification>/xx <CR>
```

where the /xx, known as SWITCH, is a space for specifying some optional tasks that PIP can perform. Here is an example.

```
> PIP <file specification>/DE <CR>   ;DELETE THE SPECIFIED
                                     ;FILE FROM THE DISK
> PIP <file specification>/PU <CR>   ;"PURGE" OR DELETE ALL
                                     ;OF THE FILE EXCEPT THE LATEST
                                     ;VERSION
> PIP /LI <CR>                       ;LIST THE DIRECTORY OF ALL FILES
                                     ;THIS USER CREATED
> PIP <file specification> = <file specification> <CR>
                                     ;COPY THE INPUT FILE TO PRODUCE AN
                                     ;OUTPUT-FILE WHICH IS IDENTICAL IN
                                     ;CONTENTS TO THE INPUT-FILE
```

Octal Debugging Technique (ODT)

ODT, sometimes known as the on-line debugging technique, is the module that allows the user to do the last-minute "patching" for his or her program. We can use it to examine or change the contents of any registers in the CPU and any words or bytes in the main memory at any specific location. The examination and change of the contents, however, is on the octal representation level. It also allows the user to do single-step execution—that is, to hand execute the program. For example, assume that a TKS-type file has been loaded by the GET module, and the ODT prompt, @, is shown on the CRT after the BREAK key is depressed. Then,

> @ 1172/00 00 00

indicates that the number 1172 was typed. By depressing the slash key, it will cause the ODT to "open" the memory at location 1172 and display its contents. Here, the contents happen to be all zeros. If we want to change the contents to 01 23 45, we can do the following:

> @ 1172/00 00 00 012345 <CR>
> @

At this point, the octal code, 012345, has been stored at 1172. We can verify it by opening the memory located at 1172 again, as follows:

> @ 1172/012345.

Similarly, we can examine and change the contents of any registers in the CPU. For instance,

> @ R1/034750

shows that R1 has been "open" and that its contents happen to be 034750.

Relationship Among the Modules of the RSX-11M

In the preceding section, we highlighted the major elements or modules of the RSX-11M operating system. The emphases were on the "what" and "why" rather than on the detailed "how." You should read the lab or user's manual to familiarize yourself with the details of these powerful and useful tools for program development. As a beginner, however, you might be fascinated and occasionally confused by all these tools (modules). Figure E.4 shows the relationships among the modules described. It should provide you with a global picture of the operating system and serve as a reminder of how to evoke (summon) and dismiss each module.

E.3 APPLICATION PROGRAM DEVELOPMENT IN THE RSX-11M ENVIRONMENT

Procedure for Program Development

Figure E.5 shows a general procedure for program development. Note that we place a block named logical error check after the block of the program flowchart. This is an important step, because the system program would never be able to catch any logical errors in the algorithm of the program. After we have checked the logic of the program, we can begin to prepare the first draft of our assembly language source program. In what follows, we will describe the steps needed to use the EDI, MAC, TKB, and LGO, or GET and GO, modules. You may want to consult Figure E.4 for getting in and out of the modules.

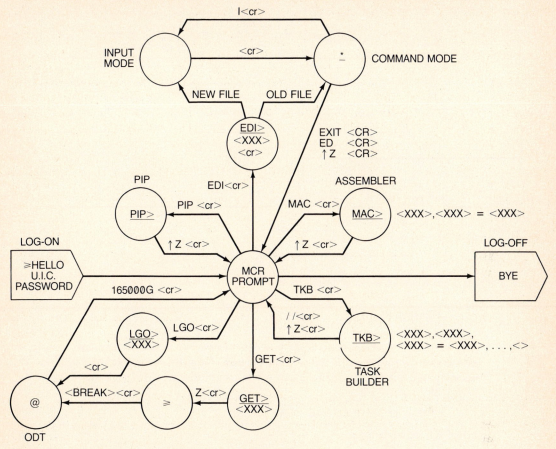

Figure E.4 Relationship among the modules of RSX-11M.

As an example, let us use the PICK-ODD-NUMBER example shown in Chapter 3 as a vehicle to illustrate the procedure. Assume that we are happy with the program shown as a first draft source program on paper. We will then enter the program through EDI with the file specification, and follow the steps described below.

Log on the System Here, we follow the "log-on" procedure, which may vary from one system to another. Typically, we might interactively type in text as follows:

```
> HELLO <CR>
U.I.C.                  ;TYPE USER IDENTIFICATION NUMBER
PASSWORD                ;TYPE USER SECRET CODE
>
```

Text Editing Here, we will evoke EDI and proceed by the following steps:

```
> EDI BIGODD.MAC <CR>
```

Of course, EDI would not be able to find this file, and thus would respond

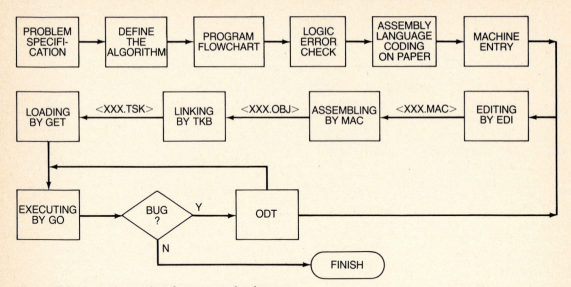

Figure E.5 General procedure for program development.

CREATING NEW FILE
INPUT

This implies that the computer is ready to accept whatever we type at the terminal. Now let us assume that we have typed in the prepared program. Normally, we would go straight into the assembly step. But if we would like to have a hard copy of what we have typed, we may evoke PIP to help us:

> PIP   LP:=BIGODD.MAC <CR>

Figure E.6 shows the result.

```
        ;THE BIG ODD NUMBER SORT
        :
        :
START:  MOV     N1,R1           ;(N1) → R1
        MOV     N2,R2           ;(N2) → R2
        MOV     #1,R0           ;R0 IS THE LSB EXAMINATION MASK
EXAM1:  BIT     R0,R1           ;EXAMINE LSB OF N1
        BNE     ODD2            ;IF N1 IS ODD, CHECK N2
EXAM2:  BIT     R0,R2           ;EXAMINE LSB OF N2
        BNE     STON2
        BR      QUIT
ODD2:   BIT     R0,R2
        BNE     COMPR           ;BOTH N1 N2 ARE ODD, SO COMPARE
STON1:  MOV     R1,ODDBIG
        BR      QUIT
COMPR:  CMF     R1,R2
        BGE     STON1
STON2:  MOV     R2,ODDBIG
QUIT:   HALT
ODDBIG: .BLKW 1
N1:     .WORD 145
N2:     .WORD 111
        .END    START
```

Figure E.6 Example for generating a hard copy of BIGODD using PIP.

```
 1                                    ;THE BIG ODD NUMBER SORT
 2                                    ;
 3                                    ;
 4 000000 016701 000050    START:  MOV   N1,R1        ;(N1) → R1
 5 000004 016702 000046            MOV   N2,R2        ;(N2) → R2
 6 000010 012700 000001            MOV   #1,R0        ;R0 IS THE LSB EXAMINATION MASK
 7 000014 030001          EXAM1:   BIT   R0,R1        ;EXAMINE LSB OF N1
 8 000016 001003                   BNE   ODD2         ;IF N1 IS ODD, CHECK N2
 9 000020 030002          EXAM2:   BIT   R0,R2        ;EXAMINE LSB OF N2
10 000022 001010                   BNE   STON2
11 000024 000411                   BR    QUIT
12 000026 030002          ODD2:    BIT   R0,R2
13 000030 001003                   BNE   COMPR        ;BOTH N1 N2 ARE ODD, SO COMPARE
14 000032 010167 000014   STON1:   MOV   R1,ODDBIG
15 000036 000404                   BR    QUIT
16 000040 020102          COMPR:   CMP   R1,R2
17 000042 002373                   BGE   STON1
18 000044 010267 000002   STON2:   MOV   R2,ODDBIG
19 000050 000000          QUIT:    HALT
20 000052                 ODDBIG:  .BLKW 1
21 000054 000145          N1:      .WORD 145
22 000056 000111          N2:      .WORD 111
23        000000'                  .END  START
```

Figure E.7(a)   A list file of the program BIGODD.LST.

```
COMPR   000040R    N1     000054R    ODDBIG  000052R    QUIT   000050R
EXAM1   000014R    N2     000056R    ODD2    000026R    START  000000R
EXAM2   000020R    STON1  000032R    STON2   000044R

   ABS.  000000    000
         000060    001
ERRORS DETECTED:  0

         000060    001
   000056R    ODD2
DYNAMIC MEMORY: 3086 WORDS ( 11 PAGES)
ELAPSED TIME: 00:00:04
,BIGODD=BIGODD
```

Figure E.7(b)   A list file of the program BIGODD.LST (continued).

Assembling the Program Let us type:

> ≥ MAC BIGODD.OBJ, BIGODD.LST = BIGODD.MAC <CR>.

Here we have generated the object and list files. Figures E.7 (a) and (b) show the hard copy of the list file. Basically the list file consists of the object and source coded program, the symbol table, and the result of any source-code errors detected. Remember that the assembler can only detect source-code errors, not logical errors. Since Figure E.7 shows that no error has been detected, we can proceed.

Program Link Here we use the object file generated by the assembler as the input file to the task-builder system software to produce the memory image or executable TSK file, with the following command:

> ≥ TKB   BIGODD.TSK = BIGODD.OBJ <CR>

or simply

> $\geq$ TKB BIGODD = BIGODD <CR>

Now, the file BIGODD.TSK has been created. We proceed to the next step.

Load and Execute Once the TSK file has been produced, we can proceed to load the TSK file into the main memory and start to execute the program, as follows:

> $\geq$ LGO BIGODD <CR>

At this point, if there is no logical error in our algorithm, the program should have placed the number 145, the bigger odd number at the location, with the symbolic address = ODDBIG. In order to verify whether the program is working properly, we could examine the contents at location ODDBIG in two ways: (1) Using the display command to have the contents of ODDBIG displayed on the CRT, or (2) using ODT, the octal debugging technique, to examine the contents at ODDBIG. Here let us use ODT to examine each memory location, including the memory word at ODDBIG.

Program Debugging Figure E.7(a) reveals that the object code file starting address is 000000. However, it is the responsibility of the TKB system software to generate a memory image or executable program to be loaded into the specified memory block for execution. In other words, the program cannot be loaded into the block starting at the 000000 address, since the memory space starting with address zero to a specific address is reserved for the system software. Thus, the application program has to be loaded after that specific address, which may vary from one system to another.

Let us assume that in our system, the application program space starts at 001172. That is, the memory area between 000000 to 001170 has been reserved for the system operation, and our program will be loaded into the area starting at 001172. As a result, the values of the symbolic address labels of the program must be displaced by 1172. For example, START = 1172. Examl = 14 + 1172 = 1206, and so on. Using ODT to examine the program, we have to know the absolute or the actual address of the instruction and type it into the system through the keyboard, followed by a slash. Then the ODT will display the contents of that memory on the CRT. Figure E.8 shows the displays of the contents of our BIGODD.TSK before and after execution. Note that the address value of ODDBIG = 52 + 1172 = 1244, whose contents, found by ODT before execution, is 000000 or just "garbage," and after execution 000145, as expected. The student should compare these contents with those shown in Figure E.7(a).

Program Discipline or Documentation The program documentation area has often been neglected by the programmer. Since the programmer is usually so deeply involved with the details of program development, all he or she seems to care about is getting the program working. Once the program is working properly, the programmer moves on to do the next project, and in a short time forgets the details of the first program and cannot even recognize it. Therefore, it is vitally important to everyone that any programs or modules developed should be well documented.

The following is a simple documentation guideline for the example in Chapter 3 suggested for all programmers.

1. Title. This usually shows the key words of the program. PDP-11 has a pseudoinstruction or directive known as .TITLE that can be used. For example, .TITLE BIGODD.
2. Initial date: Jan. 13, 1983.
3. Author: W. C. Lin.
4. Revision date: Feb. 14, 1983.

ADDRESS/CONTENTS

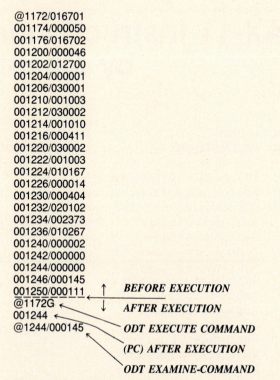

```
@1172/016701
001174/000050
001176/016702
001200/000046
001202/012700
001204/000001
001206/030001
001210/001003
001212/030002
001214/001010
001216/000411
001220/030002
001222/001003
001224/010167
001226/000014
001230/000404
001232/020102
001234/002373
001236/010267
001240/000002
001242/000000
001244/000000
001246/000145
001250/000111          ↑  BEFORE EXECUTION
@1172G                 ↓  AFTER EXECUTION
001244                    ODT EXECUTE COMMAND
@1244/000145              (PC) AFTER EXECUTION
                          ODT EXAMINE-COMMAND
```

Figure E.8 ODT examination/execution of the program BIGODD.

5. Functional description: This program module picks a bigger odd number and places it in a designated memory location.
6. Input variables: N1, N2, symbolic addresses.
7. Output variables: ODDBIG, symbolic address.
8. Commented listing program: See Figure E.6.

EXERCISES

E.1 Write a simple program in PDP-11 assembly language which will take an average of two integers stored starting at the location INTEGER and store the result at the location labeled AVERAGE. [*Hint:* The arithmetic shift right (ASR), instruction would cause a number to be divided by 2 per one shift.]

E.2 Using the program you created in Problem E.1 as a vehicle, step through the procedure depicted in Figure E.5. Pretend that you are at the computer and describe what commands you would use and what responses you would expect on the CRT. This problem should help you to clarify the necessary steps required for developing and running an application program. You may use ODT to change the two integers to verify that your program will work for any integers.

VAX-11 Instruction Index by Mnemonic

MNEMONIC LISTING

MNEMONIC	INSTRUCTION	OPCODE
ACBB	Add compare and branch byte	9D
ACBD	Add compare and branch D_floating	6F
ACBF	Add compare and branch F_floating	4F
ACBG	Add compare and branch G_floating	4FFD
ACBH	Add compare and branch H_floating	6FFD
ACBL	Add compare and branch longword	F1
ACBW	Add compare and branch word	3D
ADAWI	Add aligned word, interlocked	58
ADDB2	Add byte 2 operand	80
ADDB3	Add byte 3 operand	81
ADDD2	Add D_floating 2 operand	60
ADDD3	Add D_floating 3 operand	61
ADDF2	Add F_floating 2 operand	40
ADDF3	Add F_floating 3 operand	41
ADDG2	Add G_floating 2 operand	40FD
ADDG3	Add G_floating 3 operand	41FD
ADDH2	Add H_floating 2 operand	60FD
ADDH3	Add H_floating 3 operand	61FD
ADDL2	Add longword 2 operand	C0
ADDL3	Add longword 3 operand	C1
ADDP4	Add packed 4 operand	20
ADDP6	Add packed 6 operand	21
ADDW2	Add word 2 operand	A0
ADDW3	Add word 3 operand	A1
ADWC	Add with carry	D8
AOBLEQ	Add one and branch on less or equal	F3
AOBLSS	Add one and branch on less	F2
ASHL	Arithmetic shift longword	78
ASHP	Arithmetic shift and round packed	F8
ASHQ	Arithmetic shift quadword	79

MNEMONIC	INSTRUCTION	OPCODE
BBC	Branch on bit clear	E1
BBCC	Branch on bit clear and clear	E5
BBCCI	Branch on bit clear and clear interlocked	E7
BBCS	Branch on bit clear and set	E3
BBS	Branch on bit set	E0
BBSC	Branch on bit set and clear	E4
BBSS	Branch on bit set and set	E2
BBSSI	Branch on bit set and set, interlocked	E6
BCC	Branch on carry clear	1E
BCS	Branch on carry set	1F
BEQL	Branch on equal (signed)	13
BEQLU	Branch on equal unsigned	13
BGEQ	Branch on greater or equal	18
BGEQU	Branch on greater or equal unsigned	1E
BGTR	Branch on greater	14
BGTRU	Branch on greater unsigned	1A
BICB2	Bit clear byte 2 operand	8A
BICB3	Bit clear byte 3 operand	8B
BICL2	Bit clear longword 2 operand	CA
BICL3	Bit clear longword 3 operand	CB
BICPSW	Bit clear program status word	B9
BICW2	Bit clear word 2 operand	AA
BICW3	Bit clear word 3 operand	AB
BISB2	Bit set byte 2 operand	88
BISB3	Bit set byte 3 operand	89
BISL2	Bit set long 2 operand	C8
BISL3	Bit set long 3 operand	C9
BISPSW	Bit set program status word	B8
BISW2	Bit set word 2 operand	A8
BISW3	Bit set word 3 operand	A9
BITB	Bit test byte	93
BITL	Bit test longword	D3
BITW	Bit test word	B3
BLBC	Branch on low bit clear	E9
BLBS	Branch on low bit set	E8

Instruction Index by Mnemonic

MNEMONIC	INSTRUCTION	OPCODE
BLEQ	Branch on less or equal	15
BLEQU	Branch on less or equal unsigned	1B
BLSS	Branch on less	19
BLSSU	Branch on less unsigned	1F
BNEQ	Branch on not equal	12
BNEQU	Branch on not equal unsigned	12
BPT	Break point fault	03
BRB	Branch with byte displacement	11
BRW	Branch with word displacement	31
BSBB	Branch to subroutine with byte displacement	10
BSBW	Branch to subroutine with word displacement	30
BUGL	Bugcheck longword	FDFF
BUGW	Bugcheck word	FEFF
BVC	Branch on overflow clear	1C
BVS	Branch on overflow set	1D
CALLG	Call with general argument list	FA
CALLS	Call with stack	FB
CASEB	Case byte	8F
CASEL	Case longword	CF
CASEW	Case word	AF
CHME	Change mode to executive	BD
CHMK	Change mode to kernel	BC
CHMS	Change mode to supervisor	BE
CHMU	Change mode to user	BF
CLRB	Clear byte	94
CLRD	Clear D_floating	7C
CLRF	Clear F_floating	D4
CLRG	Clear G_floating	7C
CLRH	Clear H_floating	7CFD
CLRL	Clear longword	D4
CLRO	Clear octaword	7CFD
CLRQ	Clear quadword	7C
CLRW	Clear word	B4
CMPB	Compare byte	91
CMPC3	Compare character 3 operand	29

MNEMONIC	INSTRUCTION	OPCODE
CMPC5	Compare character 5 operand	2D
CMPD	Compare D_floating	71
CMPF	Compare F_floating	51
CMPG	Compare G_floating	51FD
CMPH	Compare H_floating	71FD
CMPL	Compare longword	D1
CMPP3	Compare packed 3 operand	35
CMPP4	Compare packed 4 operand	37
CMPV	Compare field	EC
CMPW	Compare word	B1
CMPZV	Compare zero-extended field	ED
CRC	Calculate cyclic redundancy check	0B
CVTBD	Convert byte to D_floating	6C
CVTBF	Convert byte to F_floating	4C
CVTBG	Convert byte to G_floating	4CFD
CVTBH	Convert byte to H_floating	6CFD
CVTBL	Convert byte to longword	98
CVTBW	Convert byte to word	99
CVTDB	Convert D_floating to byte	68
CVTDF	Convert D_floating to F_floating	76
CVTDH	Convert D_floating to H_floating	32FD
CVTDL	Convert D_floating to longword	6A
CVTDW	Convert D_floating to word	69
CVTFB	Convert F_floating to byte	48
CVTFD	Convert F_floating to D_floating	56
CVTFG	Convert F_floating to G_floating	99FD
CVTFH	Convert F_floating to H_floating	98FD
CVTFL	Convert F_floating to longword	4A
CVTFW	Convert F_floating to word	49
CVTGB	Convert G_floating to byte	48FD
CVTGF	Convert G_floating to F_floating	33FD
CVTGH	Convert G_floating to H_floating	56FD
CVTGL	Convert G_floating to longword	4AFD
CVTGW	Convert G_floating to word	49FD
CVTHB	Convert H_floating to byte	68FD
CVTHD	Convert H_floating to D_floating	F7FD
CVTHF	Convert H_floating to F_floating	F6FD
CVTHG	Convert H_floating to G_floating	76FD
CVTHL	Convert H_floating to longword	6AFD
CVTHW	Convert H_floating to word	69FD

MNEMONIC	INSTRUCTION	OPCODE
CVTLB	Convert longword to byte	F6
CVTLD	Convert longword to D_floating	6E
CVTLF	Convert longword to F_floating	4E
CVTLG	Convert longword to G_floating	4EFD
CVTLH	Convert longword to H_floating	6EFD
CVTLP	Convert longword to packed	F9
CVTLW	Convert longword to word	F7
CVTPL	Convert packed to longword	36
CVTTP	Convert trailing numeric to packed	26
CVTPT	Convert packed to trailing numeric	24
CVTPS	Convert packed to leading separate numeric	08
CVTRDL	Convert rounded D_floating to longword	6B
CVTRFL	Convert rounded F_floating to longword	4B
CVTRGL	Convert rounded G_floating to longword	4BFD
CVTRHL	Convert rounded H_floating to longword	6BFD
CVTSP	Convert leading separate numeric to packed	09
CVTWB	Convert word to byte	33
CVTWD	Convert word to D_floating	6D
CVTWF	Convert word to F_floating	4D
CVTWG	Convert word to G_floating	4DFD
CVTWH	Convert word to H_floating	6DFD
CVTWL	Convert word to longword	32
DECB	Decrement byte	97
DECL	Decrement longword	D7
DECW	Decrement word	B7
DIVB2	Divide byte 2 operand	86
DIVB3	Divide byte 3 operand	87
DIVD2	Divide D_floating 2 operand	66
DIVD3	Divide D_floating 3 operand	67
DIVF2	Divide F_floating 2 operand	46

MNEMONIC	INSTRUCTION	OPCODE
DIVF3	Divide F_floating 3 operand	47
DIVG2	Divide G_floating 2 operand	46FD
DIVG3	Divide G_floating 3 operand	47FD
DIVH2	Divide H_floating 2 operand	66FD
DIVH3	Divide H_floating 3 operand	67FD
DIVL2	Divide longword 2 operand	C6
DIVL3	Divide longword 3 operand	C7
DIVP	Divide packed	27
DIVW2	Divide word 2 operand	A6
DIVW3	Divide word 3 operand	A7
EDITPC	Edit packed to character	38
EDIV	Extended divide	7B
EMODD	Extended modulus D_floating	74
EMODF	Extended modulus F_floating	54
EMODG	Extended modulus G_floating	54FD
EMODH	Extended modulus H_floating	74FD
EMUL	Extended multiply	7A
EXTV	Extract field	EE
EXTZV	Extract zero-extended field	EF
FFC	Find first clear bit	EB
FFS	Find first set bit	EA
HALT	Halt	00
INCB	Increment byte	96
INCL	Increment longword	D6
INCW	Increment word	B6
INDEX	Compute index	0A
INSQHI	Insert into queue head, interlocked	5C
INSQTI	Insert into queue tail, interlocked	5D
INSQUE	Insert into queue	0E
INSV	Insert field	F0
JMP	Jump	17
JSB	Jump to subroutine	16
LDPCTX	Load process context	06
LOCC	Locate character	3A

MNEMONIC	INSTRUCTION	OPCODE
MATCHC	Match characters	39
MCOMB	Move complemented byte	92
MCOML	Move complemented long	D2
MCOMW	Move complemented word	B2
MFPR	Move from privilege register	DB
MNEGB	Move negated byte	8E
MNEGD	Move negated D_floating	72
MNEGF	Move negated F_floating	52
MNEGG	Move Negated G_floating	52FD
MNEGH	Move Negated H_floating	72FD
MNEGL	Move negated longword	CE
MNEGW	Move negated word	AE
MOVAB	Move address of byte	9E
MOVAD	Move address of D_floating	7E
MOVAF	Move address of F_floating	DE
MOVAG	Move Address of G_floating	7E
MOVAH	Move Address of H_floating	7EFD
MOVAL	Move address of longword	DE
MOVAO	Move Address of octaword	7EFD
MOVAQ	Move address of quadword	7E
MOVAW	Move address of word	3E
MOVB	Move byte	90
MOVC3	Move character 3 operand	28
MOVC5	Move character 5 operand	2C
MOVD	Move D_floating	70
MOVF	Move F_floating	50
MOVG	Move G_floating	50FD
MOVH	Move H_floating	70FD
MOVL	Move longword	D0
MOVO	Move octaword	7DFD
MOVP	Move packed	34
MOVPSL	Move processor status longword	DC
MOVQ	Move quadword	7D
MOVTC	Move translated characters	2E
MOVTUC	Move translated until character	2F
MOVW	Move word	B0
MOVZBL	Move zero-extended byte to longword	9A

MNEMONIC	INSTRUCTION	OPCODE
MOVZBW	Move zero-extended byte to word	9B
MOVZWL	Move zero-extended word to longword	3C
MTPR	Move to privilege register	DA
MULB2	Multiply byte 2 operand	84
MULB3	Multiply byte 3 operand	85
MULD2	Multiply D_floating 2 operand	64
MULD3	Multiply D_floating 3 operand	65
MULF2	Multiply F_floating 2 operand	44
MULF3	Multiply F_floating 3 operand	45
MULG2	Multiply G_floating 2 operand	44FD
MULG3	Multiply G_floating 3 operand	45FD
MULH2	Multiply H_floating 2 operand	64FD
MULH3	Multiply H_floating 3 operand	65FD
MULL2	Multiply longword 2 operand	C4
MULL3	Multiply longword 3 operand	C5
MULP	Multiply packed	25
MULW2	Multiply word 2 operand	A4
MULW3	Multiply word 3 operand	A5
NOP	No operation	01
POLYD	Evaluate polynomial D_floating	75
POLYF	Evaluate polynomial F_floating	55
POLYG	Evaluate polynomial G_floating	55FD
POLYH	Evaluate polynomial H_floating	75FD
POPR	Pop registers	BA
PROBER	Probe read access	0C
PROBEW	Probe write access	0D
PUSHAB	Push address byte	9F
PUSHAD	Push address of D_floating	7F
PUSHAF	Push address of F_floating	DF
PUSHAG	Push Address of G_floating	7F
PUSHAH	Push Address of H_floating	7FFD
PUSHAL	Push address of longword	DF
PUSHAO	Push address of octaword	7FFD
PUSHAQ	Push address of quadword	7F
PUSHAW	Push address of word	3F
PUSHL	Push longword	DD
PUSHR	Push registers	BB

MNEMONIC	INSTRUCTION	OPCODE
REI	Return from exception or interrupt	02
REMQHI	Remove from queue head, interlocked	5E
REMQTI	Remove from queue tail, interlocked	5F
REMQUE	Remove from queue	0F
RET	Return from called procedure	04
ROTL	Rotate longword	9C
RSB	Return from subroutine	05
SBWC	Subtract with carry	D9
SCANC	Scan for character	2A
SKPC	Skip character	3B
SOBGEQ	Subtract one and branch on greater or equal	F4
SOBGTR	Subtract one and branch on greater	F5
SPANC	Span characters	2B
SUBB2	Subtract byte 2 operand	82
SUBB3	Subtract byte 3 operand	83
SUBD2	Subtract D_floating 2 operand	62
SUBD3	Subtract D_floating 3 operand	63
SUBF2	Subtract F_floating 2 operand	42
SUBF3	Subtract F_floating 3 operand	43
SUBG2	Subtract G_floating 2 operand	42FD
SUBG3	Subtract G_floating 3 operand	43FD
SUBH2	Subtract H_floating 2 operand	62FD
SUBH3	Subtract H_floating 3 operand	63FD
SUBL2	Subtract longword 2 operand	C2
SUBL3	Subtract longword 3 operand	C3
SUBP4	Subtract packed 4 operand	22
SUBP6	Subtract packed 6 operand	23
SUBW2	Subtract word 2 operand	A2
SUBW3	Subtract word 3 operand	A3
SVPCTX	Save process context	07
TSTB	Test byte	95
TSTD	Test D_floating	73
TSTF	Test F_floating	53
TSTG	Test G_floating	53FD
TSTH	Test H_floating	73FD
TSTL	Test long	D5
TSTW	Test word	B5

MNEMONIC	INSTRUCTION	OPCODE
XFC	Extended function call	FC
XORB2	Exclusive OR byte 2 operand	8C
XORB3	Exclusive OR byte 3 operand	8D
XORL2	Exclusive OR longword 2 operand	CC
XORL3	Exclusive OR longword 3 operand	CD
XORW2	Exclusive OR word 2 operand	TC
XORW3	Exclusive OR word 3 operand	AD
ESCD	Reserved to DIGITAL	FD
ESCE	Reserved to DIGITAL	FE
ESCF	Reserved to DIGITAL	FF
Reserved to DIGITAL		57;59;5A;5B;77;
		00FD to 31FD;
		34FD to 3FFD;
		57FD, 58FD,
		...5FFD;
		77FD,78FD,
		...7FFD;
		80FD to 97FD;
		9AFD to F5FD;
		F8FD to FCFF.

Flowchart Symbols

American National Standards Institute
Approved 1970

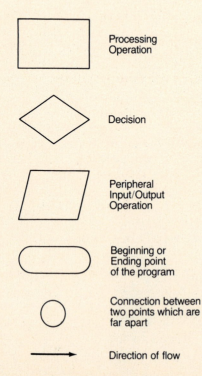

Processing
Operation

Decision

Peripheral
Input/Output
Operation

Beginning or
Ending point
of the program

Connection between
two points which are
far apart

Direction of flow

Bibliography

Digital Equipment Corporation Handbooks: *PDP-11 Software Handbook,* 1982–83. *PDP-11 Architecture Handbook,* 1983–84. *Microcomputers and Memories,* 1982. *PDP-11 Peripherals Handbook,* 1976.

Eckhouse, Richard H., Jr. *Minicomputer Systems Organization and Programming (PDP-11).* Englewood Cliffs, N.J.: Prentice-Hall, 1975.

Eckhouse, Richard H., Jr., and L. Robert Morris. *Minicomputer Systems Organization, Programming and Applications (PDP-11).* Englewood Cliffs, N.J.: Prentice-Hall, 1979.

Frank, Thomas S. *Introduction to the PDP-11 and its Assembly Language.* Englewood Cliffs, N.J.: Prentice-Hall, 1983.

Gill, Arthur. *Machine and Assembly Language Programming of the PDP-11,* 2d ed. Englewood Cliffs, N.J.: Prentice-Hall, 1983.

Hamacher, V. Carl, Zuonko G. Vranesic, and Safwat G. Zaky. *Computer Organization.* New York: McGraw-Hill, 1978.

Kapps, Charles A., and Robert L. Stafford. *Assembly Language for the PDP-11.* Prindle, Weber and Schmidt and CBI, 1981.

Lemone, Karen A., and Martin E. Kaliski. *Assembly Language Programming for the VAX-11.* Boston: Little, Brown, 1983.

Levy, Henry M., and Richard H. Eckhouse, Jr. *Computer Programming and Architecture: The Vax-11.* Bedford, Mass.: Digital Press, 1980.

Lewis, Harry R. *An Introduction to Computer Programming and Data Structures Using MACRO-11.* Reston, Va.: Reston Publishing, 1981.

MacEwen, Glenn H. *Introduction to Computer Systems Using the PDP-11 and Pascal.* New York: McGraw-Hill, 1980.

McNamara, John E. *Technical Aspects of Data Communication.* Digital Equipment Corporation, 1977.

Singer, Michael. *PDP-11 Assembler Language Programming and Machine Organization.* New York: Wiley, 1980.

Sloan, M. E. *Introduction to Minicomputers and Microcomputers.* Reading, Mass.: Addison-Wesley, 1980.

Sloan, M. E. *An Introduction: Computer Hardware and Organization,* 2d ed. Science Research Associates Inc., 1983.

Stone, Harold S., and Siewiorek. *Introduction to Organization and Data Structure: PDP-11 Edition.* New York: McGraw-Hill, 1975.

Index

@, 64
ABI. *See* Asynchronous backplane interconnect
Absolute addressing mode, 74, 257–258
A bus. *See* Address bus
AC. *See* Accumulator
Access
  protection code for, in VAX-11, 246
  serial, 164
Accumulator (AC) register, 3–5, 11
A/D/C. *See* Analog-to-digital converter
ADD instruction
  bits used in, 61
  vs. TST instruction, 97
Addition, hardware for, 41
Address. *See also* Addressing
  effective, 61
  information and operand specifier, 229
  information in machine instruction, 10
  of information in memory, 2–3
  range, of VAX-11 virtual memory, 237–239
  relocatable, 99–100
  symbolic. *See* Symbolic address
  trap vector, 212
Addressable memory element, in VAX-11, 237–238
Address bus (A bus), 9, 167
Addressing
  branch instruction, 81–89
  JMP instruction, 85–86
  SOB instruction, 84–85
  stack memory using R6, 86–89
  techniques, summary of, 89–90
Addressing mode(s)
  calculating, for PDP-11, 61–63

for general-purpose registers, 251–257
and instructions, for VAX-11, 248–260
PC register reference as, for VAX-11, 257–260
sample programs using, 90–94
summary of, 89
for VAX-11 instructions, 251–260
Address label, 250–251
Address space, of VAX-11, 229
Address translation
  block, and virtual address memory, 231–232
  buffer, in VAX-11, 236
  with virtual memory, 242–243
A-error, 85
Alarm clock simulation, 200–203
Algol, 15
AL instruction, 250
Alphabetic order, bubble sort for, 134–135
Alphanumeric character, 19
ALU. *See* Arithmetic and logic unit
American Standard Code for Information Interchange (ASCII)
  binary conversion table, 15
  character, conversion to binary string, 18
  character set, codes for, 279–282
  and CRT/keyboard terminal, 164
  explained, 14–15
Analog-to-digital converter (A/D/C)
  with DMA technique, 225–227
  as I/O device, 164–165
  and I/O programming, 176–180
AND logic operation, 51–52, 97
ANSI flowchart symbols, 364–365
AP. *See* Argument pointer
Apostrophe, with relocatable address, 100

Application program, example of, 56–59
Application software, 13
Argument, transmitting, 111–119
Argument pointer (AP), in VAX-11, 235, 262
Arithmetic and logic unit (ALU)
  function of, 2–3
  location of, in CPU, 22–23
  overflow, and interrupt, 182
Arithmetic left shift, 40
Arithmetic right shift, 40
ASCII. *See* American Standard Code for Information Interchange
.ASCII directive, 174
.ASCIZ directive, 174, 175
ASL A, 97
ASR A, 97
Assembler, 15, 53–54
Assembler (MAC), 266, 345–346
Assembling process
  and coroutine, 130
  description of, 7
  with RSX-11M, 351
Assembly language
  vs. high-level languages, 15, 22
  I/O programming with, 164
  programming, description of, 7
Asynchronous backplane interconnect (ABI), 230
Asynchronous communication, between CPU and I/O, 166
Auto decrement mode
  in PDP-11, 229
  in VAX-11, 253–254
Auto increment deferred mode, 252–253
Auto increment mode, 114, 229
Automatically created local symbols, 145–150

BAR. *See* Bus address register
Base. *See* Radix
Base Code, of branch instruction, 83
Basic language, 15
BCD. *See* Binary coded decimal
BGE POS instruction, 99
BHI POS instruction, 99
BIC src, dst instruction, 97
Binary
  to ASCII conversion table, 15
  conversion from decimal, 33
  conversion to decimal, 33–34
  to hexadecimal table, 13
  information in memory, 6
  numbers, true, vs. ASCII numbers, 11
  from octal to octal, 35–36
Binary coded decimal (BCD), 31–32
Binary machine language, 12–14
B instruction (byte), 250
BIS instruction, 51, 97
BIT instruction, 51–52, 97
Bits, number of, in byte, 223
BLKW pseudoinstruction, 54
BNE instruction, 52–53
BNE LOOP instruction, 55–56
Boot, 22
Borrowing a register, in subroutine, 114
BPT. *See* Breakpoint trap
BR. *See* Buffer register
Branch instruction(s)
  addressing, 81–89, 260
  Base Code of, 83
  conditional, 82
  explained, 81
  vs. jump instruction, 105
  limitations of, 85
  signed vs. unsigned conditional, 98–99
Breakpoint trap (BPT), 212
BSBB (branch subroutine byte), 261
BSBW (branch subroutine word), 261
Bubble sort, 134–139
Buffer, for I/O data queue, 195–200
Buffer memory, circular, 196–197
Buffer register (BR), 3–5
Bus
  adapter, in VAX-11 system, 229–230
  in computer organization, 2–3
  structure of, 9, 166–167
  in transferring control between CPU and
    DMA, 221
Bus address register (BAR), 222–223
Byte
  description of, 23
  in PDP-11 memory, 25
  VAX-11 definition for, 234
  vs. word, 27
Byte-addressable, PDP-11 as, 25

C bit, as flag, 23–24
C bus. *See* Control bus
CALLG and RET, 262–263
Calling, from disk, 164
CALLS and RET, 262–263
Carry, vs. overflow, 43
Central processing unit (CPU)
  in computer organization, 2–3
  error, trap vector address of, 212
  function of hardware in, 9

and handshaking, 166
in I/O interface programming and interrupts, 221
and MDR and MAR, 8–9
in multiprogramming, 232–234
of PDP-11, 22–24
time sharing with, in multiprogramming,
  233
in VAX-11, 234–236
Channel multiplexer, 179
Close routine, 142
CMP instruction, 51, 98
Cobol language, 15
Colon, 49
COM instruction, 98
Command(s)
  vs. instruction, 18
  for RSX-11M, 342
Comment, 250–251
Comment field, 49
Compatibility mode, of VAX-11, 229
Compiler, 15
Complement
  of complement, 40
  and negative number, 36
  of positive number, 40
Complement arithmetic, 41–48
  basic concept of, 41
  overflow in, 43–45
  subtraction by adding eights complements,
    46–47
  subtraction by adding hexadecimal com-
    plements, 47–48
  subtraction by adding ones complements,
    45–46
  subtraction by adding twos complements,
    41–43
Complement representation, 40
Computer(s)
  digital, basic structure of, 8–12
  hardware and system software, 15–16
  languages, and system software, 12–17
  organization and operation of, 2–5
Computer word, 2
Conditional branch instruction, 82
Conditional macro, 153–162
Conditions, table of, 162
Connectors, for interface boards, 165
Content in memory, 2–3
Context. *See* State information of a process
Context switching, 234, 247
Control bit, 168
Control bus (C bus), 9, 167
Controller. *See* Control unit
Control-status register (CSR), 222–223
Control unit, 2–5, 22–23
Coroutine, 110–111, 130–132
Coroutine configuration, 130
Counter, DMA equivalent of, 221
CPU. *See* Central processing unit
CRT terminal
  function of, 9
  as I/O device, 164
  message on, using ASCII directive, 173–
    174
  relationship to keyboard, 14
  and user communication, 17–18
CSR. *See* Control-status register
Cycle stealing technique, 224–225

D/A converter. *See* Digital-to-analog conversion (D/A/C)
Daisy chain technique, 217, 218
Data
  area, and subroutine, 127
  collecting bursts of, 195
  format, and I/O devices, 164
  manipulation of, 50–51, 221
  as memory contents, 7
  vs. numbers, 54
  passing, between host and subroutine,
    111–119
  paths, dashed lines for, 111
  section, at start of program, 122
  in specific exclusive area, 114–116
  transfer of. *See* Data transfer
  transmission of, 165–166
Data array, 263
Data buffer, 196–197
Data bus (D bus), 9, 167
Data pointer, 83–84, 196
Data transfer
  and DMA, 221, 226–227
  instructions for, 50
  and I/O, 165, 176–180
Data types, in VAX-11, 248–249
D bus. *See* Data bus
Debugging, 17, 57
DEC instruction, 52–53
Decimal
  conversion from binary, 33–34
  conversion from octal, 35
  conversion to binary, 33
  conversion to octal, 34
  octal and hexadecimal preferred to, 26–27
  system, meaning of, 31
Decision making, instructions for, 53–54
Deferred addressing mode. *See* Indirect ad-
  dressing mode
''Defined as,'' symbol for, 7
Destination operand. *See* Source operand
Destination-operand field, 10
Device-enable bit, 223
Digital Equipment Corporation (DEC), 49–
  50, 184, 229
Digital-to-analog conversion (D/A/C), 164–
  165, 176–180
Direct addressing mode, 63–64, 251–252
Directive. *See* Pseudoinstruction
Direct memory access (DMA), 220–227
  data transfer in, 226–227
  explained, 221
  hardware organization for, 222, 223
  request signal, 227
  technique, example of, 225–227
Disk drive, 9
Disk memory, in VAX-11, 230
Disk operating system (DOS), 17
Displacement deferred mode, 254–255
Displacement mode, 254
Divisor, greatest common, 275
DLVII-F I/O board, 184–187
DMA. *See* Direct memory access
Documentation
  for RSX-11M, 352–353
  for subroutine and host, 119–122
Done/ready bit, 223
DOS. *See* Disk operating system
Dot symbol. *See* Period symbol

Double indirect addressing
 with index mode, 71–72
 with post auto increment, 67
 with pre auto decrement, 69
Downgrading, with 8085 microprocessor,
  229
Dynamic address translation scheme, 232

EDI. *See* Text editor
Effective address, 61
8085 microprocessor system, 229
Eights complement
 for octal system, 38
 parallel with twos complement, 38–39
 subtraction by adding, 46–47
EMT. *See* Emulator trap instruction
Emulator trap instruction (EMT), 212–213,
  215
End of conversion signal (EOC), 177, 225
English language, and computer language,
  15
Entry point, of subroutine, 105
EOC. *See* End of conversion signal
Error bit, 168
Error, human, and text editor, 266–271
Error message, for overflow, 43–45
ERRORS DETECTED, 266
 EVEN directive, 174
Exception, 264
Execution
 cycle, in program execution, 54–56
 map, before and after instruction, 63
 sequence control instructions, 52–53
 single-step, 348
Executive access mode, 246
.EXIT
 instruction, 90–92
 macro instruction, 143
 system macro, 203–211
Expansion of macro, 145
Exponent, in floating-point representation,
  248–249
External interrupt. *See* Hardware interrupt

Fetch cycle, 54–55, 61
Field of the instruction, 10
Fifteens complement, in hexadecimal, 40
File management, 17
Files, in RSX-11M, 342–343
F instruction (floating point), 250
Flag, 9, 23
Floating point
 data representation, 48, 248–249
 F instruction, in VAX-11, 250
 fractions with, 48
 with VAX-11, 229, 248–249
Floppy disk, 164
Flowchart symbols, 52–53, 364–365
Format and device controls, on keyboard, 19
Fortran language, 15
FP. *See* Frame pointer
Fractions, floating point with, 48
Frame pointer (FP), 235, 262
Function bit, 168

General-purpose registers. *See* Register(s),
  general purpose
 GLOBL pseudoinstruction, 121–122
Graphic terminal, 164

HALT instruction
 in decision making, 52–53
 and .EXIT instruction, 92, 143
 vs. NOP instruction, 199–200
 and ODT mode, 99
Hand assembly, 89–90
Handshaking
 with DMA, 221
 explained, 166
 in I/O programming, 176–180
Hardware
 DMA organization of, 222–225
 in DMA process, 225–227
 functional description of, 8–9
 function, with software, 13–16
 and interrupts, 182–183, 215–218
 of PDP-11, 22–27
 process control block for context switching, 247
 software interface, for DMA, 221
Hexadecimal
 to binary table, 13
 for data representation, 26–27
 vs. decimal, 26–27
 description of, 13–14
 subtraction by adding complements of, 47–48
High-level language, 15, 22
Host program
 and exception process, 264
 explained, 182
 linking to subprogram, 106–111
 and subroutine, 104–105, 119–122

IDBR. *See* Input data buffer register
Illegal instruction
 and interrupt, 182
 and trap provision, 211
 trap vector address of, 212
Immediate mode, 72–74, 257–258
Index mode, 100, 254–257
Indicator bit, 9
Indirect addressing mode
 explained, 64–66
 with index mode, 69–71
 with post auto increment mode, 65–66
 with pre auto decrement mode, 67–68
Indirect indexed mode, 254–255
Information, as memory contents, 31, 86–89
Input data buffer register (IDBR), 223
Input/output
 in computer structure, 2–3
 data queue buffer program, 195–200
 devices, 165–166, 182
 interface board, 166–168
Input/output (I/O) programming, 163–180
 for A/D and D/A converters, 176–180
 examples of, 174–180
 interface programming and CPU, 221
 in multiprogramming, 232
 for PDP-11 system, 166–174
Input/output trap (IOT), 212
Instruction format, 49–50
Instruction link, 11
Instruction(s). *See also* Instruction set for
  PDP-11
 and addressing modes, for VAX-11, 248–
   260
 vs. command, 18
 functional classification of, for PDP-11,

50–54
 vs. memory management, 244
 statement, 250–251
 timing, 334–338
 variable length, on VAX-11, 229
 on VAX-11 vs. PDP-11, 250–251
Instruction register (IR)
 in CPU, 22–23
 memory and, 8–9
 operation of, 3–5
Instruction set for PDP-11
 addressing mode instructions, 61–94
 less obvious applications of, 94–99
 position-independent code (PIC) instructions, 100–101
 relocatable address instructions, 99–100
 simple and explicit instructions, 48–59
Integer(s)
 and complement arithmetic, 48
 data types of, in PDP-11 vs. VAX-11,
   250
 in VAX-11, 248
Interactive action, computer-user, 266–271
Interface, 165
Interpreter, 15
Interrupts(s), 181–211
 alarm clock simulation with, 200–203
 on A/D/A I/O board, 179–180
 concept of, 182
 CPU with, 221
 examples of, 190–200
 external, 182, 211–212
 hardware for, 182–183
 nesting of, 215, 217
 operation of, 182–190
 process, 183–184
 request, 182, 217
 saving and retrieving contents of, 190–
   195
 simulating stopwatch with, 203–211
 in VAX-11, 264
Interrupt acknowledge. *See* Interrupt grant
Interrupt acknowledge signal, 217
Interrupt enable bit, 223
Interrupt grant, 182
Interrupt identification number. *See* Interrupt
  vector
Interrupt priority, 23–24, 264
Interrupt resolver, 217
Interrupt service routine
 developing, 184
 for DMA operation, 224
 and hardware structure, 183
 for saving and retrieving register contents,
   190
 transferring characters with, 187–190
Interrupt system, 234
Interrupt vector
 hardware for, for DMA board, 222–
   223
 initializing, 184
 and private memory area, in multiprogramming, 233
Interrupt vector address information provider, 223
I/O. *See* Input/output
IOT (input/output trap), 212
I/O unit-select bit, 168
IR. *See* Instruction register

JMP instruction, 85–86, 104–106
JSR instruction
  explained, 106
  parameters next to, 111–114
  and RTS, 261
  and TRAP instruction, 215
JUMP. *See* JMP instruction

Kernal access mode, 246
Keyboard, 17–18, 169

Lab exercises for PDP-11, 265–278
Last-in–first-out (LIFO), 11, 89
Least significant bit (LSB), 22
LGO. *See* Load and execute
Lineprinter, 164
Linking instructions, 105, 106–111
  process. *See* Task building process
  register, PC as, 108–109
  subroutine and host, 122–125
L instruction (longword), 250
.LIST, 155
Load and execute (LGO) command example
    of, 266, 271
  linking subroutine with host, 122
  in RSX-11M, 346–347, 352
Loading, from disk, 164
Logical address space. *See* Virtual address
    space
Logic error, 99
Logic operation, 50–51
Log on procedure for RSX-11M, 349
Longword, 234, 245
LOOP program, 84–85
LSB. *See* Least significant bit

MAC (assembler), 345–346. *See also* As-
    sembler
Machine code, 49–50
Machine-dependent, 7
Machine instruction, 10–12
Macro(s), 141–162
  automatically created local symbols in,
    145–150
  for converting binary to octal, 206–208
  for displaying current time, 208
  examples of, 203–206
  explained, 142
  nested conditional, 155–161
  nesting of, 150–153
  as open routine, 142
  realtime, 152
  vs. subroutine, 142, 143
  system-defined, 90, 143–144
  time-base, 201
  user-defined, 144–162, 236
  using .ASCIZ, 208
  in VAX-11, 261
Magnetic core, 24
Magnetic disk drive, 9
Magnetic tape drive, 164
Magnetic tape transport, 9
Main memory, 24–27, 86
MAR. *See* Memory address register
Mask, 172–173
Massbus adapter, in VAX-11, 229–230
Mass-storage device, 9
.MCALL pseudoinstruction, 143
MCR.*See* Monitor console routine

MCR prompt, 266, 343
MDR. *See* Memory data register
Memory
  in computer organization, 2–3
  DMA, 221
  executable image, 122–125
  hardware of, 8–9
  last-in–first-out, 89
  main, 24–27, 86
  size of, 8
  stack. *See* Stack memory
  in VAX-11, 230
Memory address reference, 61
Memory address register (MAR)
  in CPU, 22–23
  function of, 8–9
  and main memory, 24–25
  in PDP-11, 24
Memory data register (MDR)
  in CPU, 22–23
  function of, 8–9
  and main memory, 24
Memory extension bit, 168
Memory loading process, 7
Memory location, nonexistent, and trap, 211–
    212
Memory management
  block, 244
  explained, 232
  on VAX-11, 236, 244–246
Memory map, 25, 142–143, 167
Memory reference, 61, 72–81
Memory unit, 6
Memory word. *See* Memory location
Message, 6
Micro instruction set, 236
Microprogrammable control memory, 236
Microprogramming, 236
Mixed register reference. *See* Memory refer-
    ence
Mnemonic instruction, 7, 12–13, 49. *See
    also* Machine instruction
Mnemonic operation code, 250–251
Monitor console routine (MCR), 343–344
Most significant bit (MSB), 22
MOV instruction, 50, 52–53
MSB. *See* Most significant bit
Multiplexing, 230
Multiprogramming, 229–230, 232–234, 247

Native mode, of VAX-11, 229
NB condition, 161
N bit, as flag, 23–24
Negative number, 36–40
NEG instruction, 98
Nested subroutine, 128–130
Nesting, of interrupts, 215–217
Nesting macros, 150–153
Nines complement, in decimal, 40
.NLIST, 155
NOP instruction, 99, 199–200
NO SUCH FILE, 266
n$, with macro, 147
Numbers, 36–40, 48, 54

Object program, 50
Octal
  from binary from octal, 35–36
  to binary to octal, 35–36

for data representation, 26–27
  from decimal, 34
  to decimal, 35
  vs. decimal, 26–27
  eights complement for, 38
  eliminated in PDP-11, 251
  sevens complement for, 38
Octal debugging technique (ODT)
  example of, 266
  NOP instruction in, 99
  in RSX-11M, 348
  and .WRTE instruction, 92
Octaword, VAX-11 definition for, 234
ODBR. *See* Output data buffer register
ODT. *See* Octal debugging technique
Offset value, of branch instruction, 82–83
One-address instruction, 11
One-operand instruction, 62
Ones complement, 36–39, 45–46
Op code, for VAX-11 instruction, 251
Open routine, 142
Operand(s)
  address, 12
  explained, 10
  field, in macro, 142
  number of, for PDP-11 instruction, 49
  specifier, 229, 250–251
Operating system
  explained, 16–17
  in multiprogramming, 233, 247
  and virtual memory, 231
Operation-code field, 10, 142
Optical character recognizer, 164
OR logic operation, 51, 97, 217
Output data buffer register (ODBR), 223
Overflow, in complement arithmetic, 43–45
Overhead cost, of subroutine, 142

Page, 239–241, 243
Page table, 243, 245
Page table entry (PTE), 243, 245, 246
Paper tape drive, 164
Paper tape puncher and reader, 169–171
Parallel data transfer, 165
Parameter passing
  between host and subroutine, 105
  and JSR instruction, 111–114
  in procedure vs. subroutine, 262
  in specific exclusive area, 114–116
  through stack memory, 116–119
Pascal, 15
PC register. *See* Program counter (PC) reg-
    ister
PDP-11
  bit definition in, vs. VAX-11, 234–235
  CPU in, vs. VAX-11, 234–236
  vs. 8085 microprocessor, 229
  functional description of, 22
  hardware organization of, 22–27
  indirect addressing in, vs. PTE in VAX-
    11, 245
  input/output programming for, 166–174
  instructions for, 7, 48–59
  lab exercises for, 265–278
  learning assembly language on, 229
  machine structure of, vs. VAX-11, 229–
    248
  mnemonic codes for, 283–333
  numerical OP code list, 339–340

PDP-11 (*Continued*)
  physical memory in, vs. VAX-11, 237
  programs, on VAX-11, 229
  RSX-11M operating system for, 342
  sequence of operations in, 27–28
  transition to VAX-11 from, 228–229
Period symbol, 143
Peripheral interchange program (PIP), 347
Peripherals
  connections in VAX-11, 229–230
  function of most common, 9
  and operating system, in multiprogram-
    ming, 233
  types of, 2
Physical address space, 230
Physical memory, in VAX-11, 237, 244
PIC. *See* Position-independent code
PIP. *See* Peripheral interchange program
PIP/LI command, 266
.PNUM N, 143
Pointer, 262
Polling, vs. interrupt, 182
POP. *See* PUSH/POP
Position-independent code (PIC), 100–101
Power-fail, trap vector address of, 212
Power failure, 182, 211
Precheck. *See* Handshaking
Precision, 249
Primary memory, 232. *See also* Physical
  memory; Semiconductor memory
Printers and printing
  "echoing" format and function keys, 19
  function of, 9
  message on, using ASCII directive, 173–
    174
  of teletype, 169–170
Priority condition, 215
Priority rank, of I/O, 183
Priority resolver, with interrupt nesting, 215–
  218
Privacy, in time sharing, 233
Procedure, in VAX-11, 235–236, 262
Process, 234, 247
Process control block (PCB), 247
Processor status longword (PSL), 234–235
Processor status word (PSW), 22–24, 234
Program(s). *See also* Programmers and programming; Programs, examples of
  converting to subroutine, 125–128
  debugging, in RSX-11M, 352
  development of, 104–105
  development, with RSX-11M, 348–353
  discipline. *See* Program, documentation of
  documentation of, 352–353
  execution, 54–56
  explained, 7
  host program, 104–105
  link, in RSK-11M, 351
  source program and object program, 50
Program counter (PC) register
  DMA equivalent of, 221
  function of, in VAX-11, 235–236
  and host program, 105
  as linking register, 108–109
  and memory, 8–9
  memory reference modes, 72–81
  operation of, 3–5
  in PDP-11, 24
  reference addressing mode, in VAX-11,

    257–266
  and virtual address space, 231
Programmers and programming
  assembly language, 7, 22
  input/output, 168–175
  and main memory, 24
Programs, examples of
  copying data array, 83–84
  displaying message with ASCII directive,
    173–174
  reading from paper reader, 187
  reading paper tape and echoing to printer,
    171
  security gate controller, simulation of, 176
  simple application, 56–59
  simulating alarm clock, 200–203
  simulating stopwatch, 209–211
Program sequence control instruction, 105
Pseudoinstruction, 53–54
PSL. *See* Processor status longword
PSW. *See* Processor status word
PTE. *See* Page table entry
PUSH/POP, 87–89, 108–109

Q-bus vs. Unibus, 166–167
Q instruction (quadword), 250
Quadword, VAX-11 definition for, 234
Queue buffer, 195–200

.RAD instruction, 92
Radix, 31, 32–36
.RAD macro, 148–149
Random access memory device, 164
RD. *See* Relative distance
READ, 2–3, 8–9, 86–89
READ/WRITE, 8–9, 25–26, 221
Realtime digital computing system, VAX-11
  as, 229
Recursion, 132–134
Reentrant subroutine, 127
Register(s)
  accumulator. *See* Accumulator register
  address of interrupt vector in DLV11-F,
    184
  addressing modes, 63–72
  control-status, 167, 168
  data buffer, 167–168
  description of, 3–5
  for DMA interface board, 222–223
  general purpose. *See* Register(s), general
    purpose
  input, 169, 184
  instruction. *See* Instruction register
  I/O interface board as, 167
  linking, PC as, 108–109
  output, 170, 184–187
  PC. *See* Program counter (PC) register
  R5, 106
  R1, 97
  R*n*, 106–108
  R6, 86–89
  R0, 189
  saving and retrieving contents of, for in-
    terrupt, 190–195
  stack pointer. *See* Stack pointer (SP) reg-
    ister
  status. *See* Status register
  in VAX-11, 235–236

Register(s), general purpose
  addressing modes for, in VAX-11, 251–
    257
  location, in CPU, 22–23
  in PDP-11, 24
  saving contents of, 147–148
  and stack memory, 86
Register deferred (indirect) mode, 252
Register masks procedure, 263
Register mode, in VAX-11, 251–252
Register reference, 61, 100
Relative addressing mode, 75–80
Relative deferred addressing mode, 80–81
Relative deferred mode, 257, 259–260
Relative distance (RD), 75–80, 106, 260
Relative mode, 257, 258–259
  relay, 164
  relocatable address, 99–100
Request for new data signal, 177–179
Reserved instruction, 212
RET. *See* CALLG and RET; CALLS and
  RET
Retrieving, 147–148, 190–195
.RNUM N macro instruction, 143
ROM, storing subroutines in, 127
RSB (return from subroutine), 261
RS-232-C communication link, 165
RSX-11M operating system, 17, 341–353
  application program development with,
    348–353
  automatically created local symbol for,
    146–147
  modules of, 343–348
  subroutine and host format with, 119–120
  user communication with, 342–343

SAVE macro, 147–148
SBR. *See* System base register
Secondary memory. *See* Disk memory
Section, of program, 231, 239
Semicolon, 49, 121
Semiconductor(s), 24, 230
Sequential logic network, 5
Serial access, 164
Serial data transmission, 165, 169
Sevens complement, 38–39
SET, 97
Sign bit, and overflow, 44–45
Signed representation on VAX-11, 248
Sign magnitude (S/M), 36, 41
Sixteens complement, 40
Slot, 231, 239
SLR. *See* System length register
S/M. *See* Sign magnitude
SOB instruction, 84–85
Software, 6–7, 10–12, 212. *See also* Pro-
  gram(s)
Sort program, 134
Source operand, 22
Source-operand field, 10
Source program, 50, 89–90, 209–211
SP. *See* Stack pointer
Special function keys, 19
Speech recognizer/synthesizer, 164
SPT. *See* System page table
Stack machine, 11
Stack memory
  addressing, using R6, 86–89
  area, for process, 234

description of, 11
with interrupts, 190
and nested subroutines, 128–130
PUSH with, 87
as temporary storage, 24
transmission of parameters through, 116–119
Stack pointer (SP) register
vs. FP, 262
function, in VAX-11, 235–236
in PDP-11, 24
R6 as, 86
Start to convert signal, 176
State information of a process, 234
Statement. See Comment
Status bit, 168
Status register, 9
SUB instruction, 50–51, 98
Subprogram, 100, 105–111. See also Subroutine
SUBR, 261
Subroutines(s), 104–140
basic concept of, 105
call, 105. See also JMP instruction
as close routine, 142
and coroutine, 130–132
entry point of, 105
format of, 121
and general data area, 127
high-speed tape reader with error checking, 171–173
and host, documentation for, 119–122
interrupt, and stack memory, 116
vs. macro, 142, 143
nested, 116, 128–130
procedure as, 235
reasons for using, 104–105
recursion with, 132–134
in VAX-11 vs. PDP-11, 261
written by others, documentation for, 119–122
Subtraction
by adding eights complements, 46–47
by adding hexadecimal complements, 47–48
by adding ones complements, 45–46
by adding twos complements, 41–43
and complement arithmetic, 41
Supervisor access mode, 246
Symbolic address
comparing address value of, with branch instruction, 99
example of, 57–59
and instruction format in PDP-11, 49
label, in macro, 145
Symbolic switch, 171
System base register (SBR), 245
System-defined macro, 90, 143–144

System designer, 143
System length register (SLR), 245
System page table (SPT), 245
System programmer, 143
System software
in assembly language, 15
and computer languages, 12–17
explained, 12–13
functions of, 19
as operating system, 16
RSX-11M as, 342
vs. user and hardware, 15–16

T bit. See Trace (T) bit
Tape reader, high speed, 171–173
Task, 241, 245, 247
Task builder (TKB)
example of, 266
process, 79
and relocatable address, 99–100
for RSX-11M, 346
subroutines and host program, 122–125
Teletype, programs for, 169–171
Tens complement, in decimal, 40
Terminal, 17–19, 164
Text editor (EDI), 266, 344–345, 349–351
Three-address instruction, 10
Time-multiplexing, 232, 247
TKB. See Task builder
Trace (T) bit, 23–24, 212
Translation, 242–243, 245
Transmission, data, 165–166
Trap handler, 212–214
Trap instruction, 181, 211–218
description of, 213
and EMT n instruction, 215
vs. JSR instruction, 215
mnemonic format of, 212–213
trap vector address of, 212
typical example of, 214–215
Trap vector, 211–212
TSK file, 122–125
TST instruction, 97
Two-address instruction, 10–11
Two-operand instruction, 62
Twos complement
for data representation, in VAX-11, 248
by logic procedure, 37
math derivation of, 36
for negative numbers, 36–37
operation, symbol for, 41
parallel with eights complement, 38–39
Typewriter, vs. terminal keyboard, 19

UCS. See Microprogrammable control memory
UD (PC), 107
Unconditional branch instruction, 82

Unibus adapter, 229–230
Unibus vs. Q-bus, 166–167
UNSAVE macro, 147–148
Unsigned representation, in VAX-11, 248
Updated (PC), 106
Upgrading, with VAX-11, 229
User access mode, 246
User control store (UCS). See Microprogrammable control memory
User-defined macro. See Macro, user-defined
User-machine interactive program, 148
Utility, 17

Variable-length bit field, 237
VAX Architecture Handbook (DEC), 264
VAX-11 system, 228–264
address translation in, 242–243
CPU in, 234–236
instruction index, by mnemonic, 354–363
instructions and addressing modes for, 248–260
machine structure of, 229–248
memory organization of, 237–243
microprogramming with, 236
organization of virtual memory in, 237–241
system, 229–230
transition to, from PDP-11, 229
VAX-11/750 memory space, 230
V bit, as flag, 23–24
Vector interrupt system, 183
Virtual address extension (VAX), 229
Virtual address space, 230
Virtual memory
machine process as, 234
organization of, in VAX-11, 237–241
space, principle of, 230–232
system, 230
Voice I/O, 165

WCR. See Word count register
W instruction (word), 250
Word(s)
vs. byte, 27
computer, description of, 23
with DMA, 221
VAX-11 definition for, 234
Word count register (WCR), 222, 223
.WORD pseudoinstruction, 53–54
WRITE, 2–3, 8–9, 86–89
.WRITE instruction, 90–92
.WRITE macro, 148–149
.WRITE system macro, 190–199

Z bit, as flag, 23–24
Zero-address instruction, 11–12
Zero-operand instruction, 62–63